*Understanding and Teaching
the Holocaust*

The Harvey Goldberg Series
for Understanding and Teaching History

The Harvey Goldberg Series for Understanding and Teaching History gives college and secondary history instructors a deeper understanding of the past as well as the tools to help them teach it creatively and effectively. Named for Harvey Goldberg, a professor renowned for his history teaching at Oberlin College, Ohio State University, and the University of Wisconsin from the 1960s to the 1980s, the series reflects Goldberg's commitment to helping students think critically about the past with the goal of creating a better future. For more information, please visit www.GoldbergSeries.org.

Series Editors

John Day Tully is a professor of history at Central Connecticut State University and was the founding director of the Harvey Goldberg Center for Excellence in Teaching at Ohio State University. He has coordinated many Teaching American History grants and has received the Connecticut State University System's Board of Trustees Teaching Award.

Matthew Masur is a professor of history at Saint Anselm College, where he has served as codirector of the Father Guerin Center for Teaching Excellence. He has also been a member of the Teaching Committee of the Society for Historians of American Foreign Relations.

Brad Austin is a professor of history at Salem State University. He has served as chair of the American Historical Association's Teaching Prize Committee and has worked with hundreds of secondary school teachers as the academic coordinator of many Teaching American History grants.

Advisory Board

Leslie Alexander   Associate Professor of History, University of Oregon
Kevin Boyle   William Smith Mason Professor of American History, Northwestern University
Ross Dunn   Professor Emeritus, San Diego State University
Leon Fink   UIC Distinguished Professor of History, University of Illinois at Chicago
Kimberly Ibach   Principal, Fort Washakie High School, Wyoming
Alfred W. McCoy   J.R.W. Smail Professor of History, Director, Harvey Goldberg Center for the Study of Contemporary History, University of Wisconsin–Madison
David J. Staley   Associate Professor of History, Director, Center for the Humanities in Practice, Ohio State University
Maggie Tran   Chair of Social Studies, McLean High School, Virginia
Sam Wineburg   Margaret Jacks Professor of Education and (by courtesy) of History, Director, Stanford History Education Group, Stanford University

Understanding and Teaching the Holocaust

Edited by

LAURA J. HILTON
AVINOAM PATT

The University of Wisconsin Press

The University of Wisconsin Press
728 State Street, Suite 443
Madison, Wisconsin 53706
uwpress.wisc.edu

Gray's Inn House, 127 Clerkenwell Road
London EC1R 5DB, United Kingdom
eurospanbookstore.com

Printed in the United States of America

This book may be available in a digital edition.

Library of Congress Cataloging-in-Publication Data

Names: Hilton, Laura June, 1969– editor. | Patt, Avinoam J., editor.
Title: Understanding and teaching the Holocaust / edited by Laura
    Hilton and Avinoam Patt.
Other titles: Harvey Goldberg series for understanding and teaching
    history.
Description: Madison, Wisconsin : The University of Wisconsin Press,
    [2020] | Series: The Harvey Goldberg series for understanding and
    teaching history | Includes bibliographical references and index.
Identifiers: LCCN 2019052161 | ISBN 9780299328603 (cloth)
Subjects: LCSH: Holocaust, Jewish (1939–1945)—Study and teaching.
Classification: LCC D804.33 .U53 2020 | DDC 940.53/18071—dc23
LC record available at https://lccn.loc.gov/2019052161

To my husband, Greg, and my daughter, Kate,
I love you 3,000

—LJH

In memory of Hersch and Dwora Heiliczer,
deported from Vienna on April 27, 1942

And in honor of Maya, Alex, and Micah,
who give me hope that we may yet repair
the world

—AJP

Contents

Contents

**Part Two: Sources, Methods, and Media
for Teaching the Holocaust**

Contents

Acknowledgments

We want to thank the series editors—Brad Austin, Matt Masur, and John Tully—for offering us the opportunity to edit this volume. Their support and guidance throughout this project has been outstanding. As this project progressed, it informed our own teaching and led to many productive exchanges with our authors and each other about how best to understand and teach the Holocaust. To our chapter authors, we thank you for your contribution, your patience, and your commitment to this project. To the Art Gallery of Ontario, the United States Holocaust Memorial Museum, and Yad Vashem, a sincere thank you for permission to use images in your collections for this volume. The staff and faculty editorial board at the University of Wisconsin Press (past and present) have been firm champions of this edited collection. We would like to thank especially Gwen Walker, Dennis Lloyd, Anna Muenchrath, Nathan MacBrien, Adam Mehring, Ivan Babanovski, and Jane Curran for their assistance in bringing this project to fruition. To our blind reviewers, thank you for your time, wisdom, and suggestions.

Laura thanks the scholars who taught her about the Holocaust and engaged in serious conversation about how best to teach it and why: Alan Beyerchen (The Ohio State University) and through the United States Holocaust Memorial Museum (USHMM), Henry Friedlander and Peter Hayes. In addition, the scholars brought together through the Holocaust Education Foundation (HEF) 21st Annual Summer Institute for the Study of the Holocaust and Jewish Civilization in 2016 provided insight and guidance that informed this project, especially Doris Bergen, Benjamin Frommer, Danny Greene, Dagmar Herzog, and Paul Jaskot. She appreciates her institution, Muskingum University, for its embrace of her proposal in her first year of teaching to bring a permanent course offering on the Holocaust to its curriculum. Her departmental colleagues, Karen Dunak, Keith Eberly, Alistair Hattingh, Tom McGrath, and Bil Kerrigan, offered important support and encouragement, through suite conversations and long dog-walking sessions. To her students for the past two decades, she offers a heartfelt thank you for understanding and learning right by her side: your eagerness and willingness to read, write, and speak about the Holocaust provide her with motivation and inspiration. Most importantly, the unconditional love and support of her family, Greg, Kate, and Scout, sustained her each day, even the hard ones.

Avi thanks his many mentors in the field from years of study at Emory University and New York University, as well as colleagues at the United States Holocaust Memorial Museum, the University of Hartford, and the University of Connecticut. As it is written in *Pirkei Avot* 4:1, "Ben Zoma says: Who is the wise one? He who learns from all, as it says, 'I have acquired understanding from all my teachers'" (Psalms 119:99). A special thank you to my students in lectures and seminars at the University of Connecticut, the University of Hartford, Trinity College, and Clark University for your thought-provoking and probing questions; you have helped me become a better teacher. If I have advice to offer in classroom instruction, it is thanks to you. To my colleagues at the Greenberg Center, Voices of Hope, the Holocaust Resource and Outreach Center (HERO Center), the teachers around the state of Connecticut committed to Holocaust and Genocide Education, and, above all, to the Holocaust survivors and their descendants, who continue to dedicate themselves to sharing their experiences with the next generation of students, I am indebted to you for your strength and generosity. Finally, all my love to my family, Ivy, Maya, Alex, and Micah, who always support me in this work and understand why this matters so much.

Understanding and Teaching
the Holocaust

Introduction

*The Challenges and Necessity of Teaching
the Holocaust in the Twenty-First Century*

LAURA J. HILTON AND

AVINOAM PATT

Auschwitz. Anne Frank. Warsaw. Crematoria. Elie Wiesel. Dachau. Hitler. Genocide. These places, terms, and people evoke immediate responses and recognition. People encounter them in different ways, ranging from feature films to memoirs assigned in schools, to museums and memorials, to internet discussions. Yet, popular knowledge is often superficial or lacking context, even as collective memory of World War II and the Holocaust continue to play a central role in contemporary society.[1] In other words, people hold collective memory of the Holocaust, even if their understanding of it is cursory. The Holocaust has become synonymous with horror, unspeakable atrocities, unbearable suffering, and soul-searching reckoning. Therefore, there are few topics in modern history that draw the attention, both scholarly and public, that the Holocaust does.

The systematic mass murder of six million Jews and millions of other "undesirables" (Roma/Sinti, physically and mentally handicapped, homosexuals, Slavs, and other victims) raises questions pertinent to all of humanity. Understanding the events and their impact has such a central place within our current world that learning about it is necessary on a fundamental and powerful level. The planning and implementation of the Final Solution are key topics in most classes about twentieth-century European and world history, often invoked to help students understand the present, especially in terms of civic engagement. When taught well, the subject has the potential to help students understand political power, particularly the role of the state in everyday lives. The events of the Holocaust also demonstrate the thought patterns and processes that lead to the persecution and ostracization of minority populations, as well as their devastating results.

Although it commands an enormous amount of attention, specific training to teach the Holocaust is not always readily available for all those who teach it, and teaching the Holocaust demands far more than a superficial understanding. Teachers must guide students through sensitive and often emotional subjects, mindful of grounding topics within their specific historical context, pushing beyond a shallow or incomplete explanation. In addition to providing historical grounding, educators must also understand and explain how it is represented. Indeed, the way we encounter and access the Holocaust is through representations: written primary sources (from perpetrators, witnesses, collaborators, victims), images, oral and video testimonies, memoirs, diaries, novels, poems, plays, art, film (both documentary and feature), monuments and memorials.[2] It is a subject that requires careful guidance for educators whether they have a day, a week, a month, or a full year to teach the topic.

This book offers readers the content knowledge and the instructional strategies educators need to teach this vital history accurately, effectively, and thoughtfully. Part One provides an overview of current scholarship on key topics of the Holocaust, and Part Two contains focused explanations of how to teach multiple types of representations of the Holocaust and how these understandings have developed over the past several decades. Chapters in each section combine content knowledge with pedagogical advice for educators, seeking to bridge the gap between the sheer volume of information available and best practices in terms of teaching it. While there has been a proliferation of excellent opportunities for teachers to go to teacher training workshops (e.g., such as those offered by the US Holocaust Memorial Museum [USHMM], the Holocaust Educational Foundation [HEF], the Anti-Defamation League [ADL], Facing History and Ourselves [FHAO], and others), the large number of educators teaching this topic far exceeds the capacity for on-site training. And although there are many websites devoted to content information with suggestions for sources, it is uncommon to find ones that directly address how to teach the information or that provide specific examples from the rich and varied representations of the Holocaust that exist.

Understanding and Teaching the Holocaust bridges this gap between interest in and preparation for teaching, specifically assisting educators at universities and in secondary education who are not content experts or who lack Holocaust-specific pedagogical training. The vital necessity for effective teacher training has been pertinent to the teaching of the Holocaust ever since survivor and historian Henry Friedlander highlighted this need in the late 1970s.[3] This volume can serve as both a starting point for educators new to teaching this topic and a professional development tool for experienced educators to continue to learn and improve their teaching. Its focus is on helping teachers at multiple levels integrate the teaching of the Holocaust into their classes and curricula. In this respect, it answers Thomas Fallace's call to continue to build a bridge between scholars who specialize in researching and teaching the Holocaust and those who teach the topic in a variety of classrooms.[4] Its chapters, written by seasoned teachers from a wide variety of institutions (universities, high schools, and museums) who possess considerable experience and training, push educators to consider how to explain this subject matter in order to engage the student in critical thinking through a diverse set of strategies, resources, and primary source material. It encourages teachers to employ multiple paths and strategies to engage with this difficult history, especially to guide students through reflection on what they are learning. Instead of feeling overwhelmed by the enormity of the topic, educators who read this volume will learn how to understand and teach the Holocaust in multiple contexts and courses with specific suggestions for how to incorporate key sources in the classroom. This volume also provides an excellent starting point for faculty across disciplines who lack specific training in the subject and its pedagogy but wish to develop a course or a portion of one dedicated to the Holocaust.

While there were a few early trailblazers, only a small number of universities and colleges in the United States had courses focused on the study of the Holocaust by the 1970s.[5] In 1978, the confluence of the NBC miniseries entitled *Holocaust: The Story of the Family Weiss*, the controversy surrounding the proposed Nazi march in Skokie, Illinois, and President Carter's establishment of the President's Commission on the Holocaust increased the public's awareness of the scale and horrors of the Holocaust. An increase in courses offered at the collegiate level has occurred, with estimates ranging between 140 and 700 colleges and universities offering them by the late 1980s and an explosion in course creation between 1985 and 1989.[6] This upward trend has continued in subsequent decades. Although no definitive statistics exist that count every course in each discipline taught on the Holocaust in American universities and colleges, the Holocaust Education Foundation's recent survey of course catalogs indicates that more than 75 percent of American college and universities surveyed offer at least one course on the Holocaust. Course offerings on the Holocaust at the collegiate level exist in a wide variety of departments, most notably in history and English, but also in interdisciplinary programs such as Jewish studies, gender studies, and German studies. In addition, multiple universities have centers established to study the Holocaust and other genocides, and students can now earn focused degrees at the BA, MA, and PhD levels.

The prevalence of teaching the Holocaust at the high school level in the United States follows a similar pattern. Public high school curricula rarely addressed it with great specificity until the 1970s, although some of the earliest US educators to teach the Holocaust did so in Jewish schools.[7] However, since the 1980s and 1990s, considerable political and educational attention has focused on this topic, especially given the opening of the United States Holocaust Memorial Museum and the release of *Schindler's List*, both of which occurred in 1993. In the mid-1990s, as a product of dedicated efforts by Holocaust survivors and their descendants and politicians to encourage students to recognize the links between an educated citizenry and the importance of combating racism and bigotry, several states mandated Holocaust education, including New York, New Jersey, Florida, and California.[8] In recent years, a noticeable rise in hate speech, antisemitism, racism, and xenophobia has provided renewed momentum to legislative efforts, bringing the number of states requiring some form of Holocaust and genocide education to eleven, as of 2019.[9] Even so, state boards of education rarely provide the additional resources necessary to gain specialized instruction on the topic. Also, it has become more common in the past two decades for high school teachers to offer a term-length specialized course on the Holocaust. This volume provides guidance for this specific target audience as well, helping educators think about how to teach it respectfully and thoroughly.

There are a number of important volumes that focus on the Holocaust and teaching. For those who are team-teaching a course, Howard

B. Tinberg and Ronald Weisberger provide sage advice for how to make such a course truly interdisciplinary, but their work focuses on only a few subtopics: bystanders, witnesses, trauma, and faith.[10] *Teaching about the Holocaust* is a collection by second-generation Holocaust scholars, drawn from a variety of disciplines, that provides a fascinating reflection on the development of the field over the past two to three decades, while offering less in the way of concrete advice on how and why to teach specific topics.[11] *Shedding Light on the Darkness* is an edited collection centered on Holocaust pedagogy specifically for Germanicists teaching at the collegiate level.[12] *Teaching the Holocaust* approaches the topic from morally grounded pedagogy; it argues that learning about the Holocaust helps students morally and spiritually, in addition to engaging them in critical thinking. Each chapter provides a brief summary of the topic and concludes with numerous teaching ideas, many of which are more suited to pre-college education.[13] The edited volume *Teaching the Representation of the Holocaust* is an essential tome for best practices in Holocaust pedagogy, especially for teaching different types of representations and provides focused chapters on many key poems, memoirs, diaries, works of fiction, and documentary films.[14] *Holocaust Representations in History* uses a case study approach to teach educators how to contextualize and explain key representations of the Holocaust. By laying these out in roughly chronological order, it also provides a historiography of how representations emerged into postmemory and cautions how they can (and have been) misused or oversimplified.[15] This book, *Understanding and Teaching the Holocaust,* fills an important gap among these works, combining cutting-edge scholarship on critical aspects of Holocaust history while also providing educators with specific ways to integrate multiple methodologies and source material into a wide variety of classrooms.

We live in an age where seemingly everything is available at the touch of one's fingertips and when far too little vetting of information and sources has become the norm. Therefore, when educators teach the Holocaust, it is imperative that their instruction is rooted in the incredibly deep and broad scholarly literature that has emerged in recent decades. The numerous existing sources, both primary and secondary, speak to the high level of interest in the topic. Yet at the same time, their abundance makes it difficult for those without detailed training and with limited time to immerse themselves in the scholarship and to identify which of the available sources will work well within their classrooms and complement each other. This volume provides current and scholarly overviews of main topics, incorporating effective strategies to impart this information to different audiences. It also recommends a wide variety of accessible sources including introductions to major collections and specific teaching strategies for using them appropriately, through which students can learn more deeply about and reflect upon this genocide.[16]

This introduction encourages educators to think through five foundational elements when designing their courses: the wide range of experiences that collectively represent the Holocaust; the narrative arc of one's course or unit; context for teaching the Holocaust; balancing the emotional labor of learning about this topic with critical analysis; and clearly establishing and sharing their purpose in teaching the subject.[17] First, a crucial aspect of this volume is to ensure that educators and students alike understand the full landscape of persecution and wartime experiences, from concentration camps to ghettos, labor camps, extermination camps, and death marches, as well as life in hiding, resistance, seeking refuge, and life in the aftermath. It deliberately incorporates the stories of a very geographically diverse Jewish population that stretched from the crowded urban streets of Paris, Vienna, and Berlin to the countrysides of Romania, Poland, and Ukraine. In addition, it integrates varied linguistic, spiritual, gendered, and political experiences in order to move students away from essentializing one experience, in particular Auschwitz, as their sole understanding of the Holocaust. While Auschwitz is sometimes used as a shorthand for the entire Holocaust, the complexity of the topic should not be reduced to an oversimplified and one-dimensional explanation. Across the chapters, authors provide a wide range of stories and experiences, with which educators can engage students and encourage critical thinking and long-term reflection. By utilizing this thickly layered approach, educators can present effectively both the demographic and geographic scope of the Holocaust as well as its profound impact on its contemporaries and the generations that followed.

Second, educators must decide how to frame their discussions of the Holocaust within their units or courses. Where will the explanation begin? What are the implications of beginning with the roots of religious tensions between Jews and Christians or with the surge of antisemitism in the nineteenth century, with the coming of World War I or with the rise of the National Socialist German Workers' Party (NSDAP)?

Where will the unit or course end? Will it end with the liberation of the extermination and concentration camps and the end of World War II, with the struggles of Jewish Displaced Persons through the late 1940s and the establishment of the state of Israel, or with the ways in which the world has remembered and memorialized these experiences? For those educators teaching a unit on the Holocaust, as opposed to a course, how many class periods can be dedicated to the topic? Given these time constraints, upon which topics and sources will educators focus and why? Each one of these choices shapes a specific historical narrative, one that will lead educators to emphasize or de-emphasize certain elements of the story and will have an impact on the sources that they provide to their students to deepen their knowledge. In addition, educators should take time to explain the frame to students, so they can engage critically with the material and understand its context more fully.[18]

Third, especially for those who teach it as part of a larger unit or course on genocide, ethnic cleansing, or human rights, how will the Holocaust be situated? Will it be the foundational example against which other genocides are posited? Or will it be one example out of many? Three related questions ask teachers to consider whether the Holocaust was unique, whether it is exclusively a Jewish event, and how it fits (or does not) within the growing field of genocide studies. Entrenched in this discussion is the very term used to define the event.[19] Most commonly, educators in the United States refer to the *Holocaust* as such, with its connotations of being a burnt offering to God, drawing on the sacrifices made in the ancient Temple in Jerusalem. However, others choose to call it by its Hebrew name, *The Shoah*, meaning desolation, calamity, or destruction. In readings, students will also encounter the term *The Final Solution*, a Nazi euphemism. All of these decisions about language and titles must be purposeful and informed and, therefore, mindful of the framework that they create.

Fourth, in addition to all of these scholarly conundrums, educators who teach the Holocaust must tackle the emotional and psychological difficulties of this topic. As Tinberg and Weisberger explain, the Holocaust "engages students in a visceral way, evoking intensely strong emotions,"[20] so educators need to find ways to help students practice empathy but still engage in critical thinking. It is important to engage openly and honestly with students, letting them know that the subject is difficult for educators as well, while also resisting the temptation to posit it as beyond human comprehension.[21] Leonard Grob encourages educators who teach this topic to be co-learners and to listen intently to students.[22] It is important to provide classroom space and assignments that allow students to express their emotions, but at the same time, teachers need to set clear expectations of critical reflection from their students.

Teachers have to review sources, especially visual and oral history sources, and ponder the potential impact that these may have and the age-appropriate nature of the source. What is the appropriate balance between encouraging comprehension and running the risk of numbing students when images and information become overwhelming? There is great educational value in using an image to encourage students to understand a particular experience and to confront historical reality. However, educators should weigh the benefits and drawbacks of watching forty-five minutes of black and white US Army Signal Corps footage of the liberation of concentration camps in Germany versus one segment of seven or eight minutes. When showing images of emaciated prisoners to convey the level of deprivation and suffering that they endured, teachers should provide context for each image and think about how many images the students should view. In assigning written sources, educators should consider whether students may experience desensitization to the hunger and deprivations suffered if they read two full years of diary entries from one person within the Łódź ghetto or whether this approach assists them in grappling with the horrors within the ghetto on a very personal level. For some students or classes, having students read diary entries from several different Jewish authors across different ghettos, since experience varied, may enable them to better grasp the multilayered experiences of life within ghettos.

Finally, educators should reflect on their objective in offering a course or unit on the Holocaust. For those at the collegiate level, how does it fit within your department or program offerings and the general education curriculum? For those teaching at the junior high or high school level, how does this fit within the larger course and does it meet a set of state standards? While there are a host of reasons educators at all different levels teach this topic, being cognizant of these while designing the course or unit is crucially important. Some make use of it to teach tolerance, empathy, and appreciation of diversity, while others utilize examples of resistance against the Third Reich and its collaborators to inspire action, provoke discussion, and provide hope. Samuel

Totten, Paul Bartop, and Steven Leonard Jacobs provide a list of objectives, which include honoring the lives lost, bearing witness, shaping how students understand the world in which they live, combatting racism, developing civil courage, and providing moral education. Other scholars take issue with utilizing the Holocaust and its representations for other purposes, especially in pre-college education.[23] Being mindful of why it is being taught and the framework used to deliver the information helps educators establish transparency and, hopefully, helps them avoid simplistic and misguided attempts to draw parallels. Lastly, educators must be alert to the industry of Holocaust denial, readily available in a variety of forms especially online, some of it couched in pseudo-scholarly formats.

Our volume has two parts, each with a distinct focus. Yet, each chapter has the same central goal: the integration of content with pedagogical suggestions. To this end, each author is a teacher-scholar, both immersed in the scholarship of the topic and its teaching in the classroom to a variety of students. Part One, "Teaching Specific Content," contains eleven chapters, each of which focuses on a specific topic and provides concrete methods for teaching it.[24] Jonathan Elukin provides an overview of the problematic nature of the term *antisemitism* and the long history of antipathy toward Jews.[25] Mark E. Spicka explores the complicated question of how Nazism rose to power. His chapter explains the worldview of Hitler and the ideology of the Nazi Party and places these within the broader context of economic, political, and cultural conditions following the conclusion of World War I and during the Weimar Republic. The chapter by Russel Lemmons and Laura J. Hilton explains the Nazis' use of legislation as one of the primary tools used by the state to marginalize and exclude persecuted populations including Jews and other targeted groups (homosexuals, the handicapped, and the Roma and Sinti) and situates Jewish persecution within the larger Nazi worldview. Ilana F. Offenberger details the many responses by Jews initially in Germany to the ascendance of the NSDAP and then weaves in many personal stories of Jews within the newly annexed Austria in 1938 and 1939, especially in terms of how they responded to the Anschluss and Kristallnacht.

The next five chapters deal with the wartime years, 1939 to 1945. First, Waitman Wade Beorn presents an integrative view of the Holocaust and its connections to World War II. Too often, these topics are covered separately in scholarship and teaching, while in reality they were inextricably connected in the Nazi mind and in the reality on the ground. The chapter highlights ways in which the Holocaust can be integrated into courses that are more general or World War II courses and vice versa. Geoffrey P. Megargee provides an innovative explanation of the full scope and complexity of the Nazi camp universe that helps educators understand and teach the concentration, labor, and extermination camps' central position in Nazi society and government, in a concise format, while also situating the persecution of Jews within the larger Nazi worldview. Martin Dean addresses the place of the ghettos within Nazi persecution and economic exploitation and explains how they connected to the development of extermination camps. Moving beyond the traditional paradigm of perpetrator, victim, and bystander, the next two chapters grapple with the complexity of life in Nazi-occupied Europe. Steven P. Remy delves into the intertwined issues of who collaborated with the Nazis or was complicit in their persecution of Jews during the Holocaust, using three case studies to probe the larger questions embedded in this topic: Poland, France, and the Arab world. Laura J. Hilton explains the continuum of Jewish and non-Jewish rescue and resistance to the Nazi persecution of Jews across Europe.

The final two chapters in Part One deal with the aftermath of the Holocaust. Avinoam Patt describes the immediate needs of Jewish survivors in the postwar period and highlights aspects of the Jewish Displaced Person experience, including searching for family, taking stock of the devastation of the war, beginning the process of documenting the destruction of the recent past, and working to build a future for themselves in unknown new homelands. The final chapter in Part One, authored by Gabriel N. Finder, discusses how teachers and students might explore the pursuit of justice after World War II and the Holocaust. His chapter also examines legal responses from 1945 onward to Nazi atrocities in general and the Nazi genocide of Europe's Jews in particular through the lens of pivotal postwar and post-Holocaust trials.

Part Two, "Sources, Methods, and Media for Teaching the Holocaust," consists of nine chapters that capture the extensive array of representations that educators can use to teach the Holocaust. In each of these chapters, the authors are mindful of the ways in which understandings of the Holocaust have been mediated through representations, in multiple forms: literature, photography, testimony, film, museums, memorials, and more. The initial three chapters deal with written sources;

each one delves into the importance of teaching texts in context—who wrote it, where, and when. Amy Simon assesses the benefits of teaching with Holocaust diaries, discussing the particular factual and emotional knowledge students can gain through an understanding of these sources, as well as the challenges these sources can pose. Jennifer Goss provides an overview of the history of Holocaust survivor memoirs with a particular emphasis on their use in American classrooms and examines strategies to engage students in using memoirs to study the Holocaust both in full and excerpted form. Victoria Aarons guides educators through a careful examination of the uses of literature, by a wide variety of authors, in the teaching of the Holocaust. The next three chapters deal with video, aural, and visual sources, each of which presents different aspects of Holocaust representations. Alan Marcus provides key considerations and recommendations about how to use film, particularly nondocumentary film, effectively in the classroom and which films work best at different educational levels. Engaging students effectively with survivor testimonies is the focus of Margarete Myers Feinstein's chapter, which teaches how to ground the narratives within a full context and to teach students how to consider how the narratives are shaped, by both interviewer and interviewee, as well as time and postmemory. Valerie Hébert provides a thought-provoking discussion of how images have shaped public and scholarly understanding of the Holocaust and how to use them to examine issues of representation, experience, persecution, collaboration, and liberation.

The next two chapters in Part Two explore how people encounter and process public history and memorialization of the Holocaust. Daniel Greene, curator of the *Americans and the Holocaust* special exhibit at USHMM, walks educators through how to best immerse students in a Holocaust museum experience, including how to interact with information and exhibits and how to prepare them for the experience. Stuart Abrams examines the ways in which societies (the United States, Europe, and Israel) have memorialized Jewish experiences during the Holocaust, including specific examples of monuments, memorials, and experiential learning. Part Two closes with a reflection by a veteran educator, Robert Hadley, a long-time Holocaust educator who now trains high school teachers through the SHOAH Foundation. This reflection draws upon the legacy of Harvey Goldberg (the namesake of the University of Wisconsin Press series that includes this volume) to work toward a better future collectively by encouraging students to examine the past critically and thoroughly and to understand how the Holocaust fits amid other genocides.

By providing scholarly explanations of key events, places, and beliefs and a wide variety of sources and how to use them, this volume provides educators with both context and pedagogical techniques. It recognizes that many educators will not have a full semester or term to engage with the topic, so it provides multiple avenues to enter and engage with the Holocaust across many different types of courses (history, literature, film, visual representation, memory). While it is not intended to be an exhaustive or sole means of understanding the Holocaust and how to teach it, the careful pairing of historical scholarship with sound and classroom-tested pedagogical practices make it unique among the resources available to educators at multiple levels of teaching.

In addition, the timing of this volume, more than seven decades after the end of World War II, amid the passing of the last generation of eyewitnesses to the devastation of that war, is critical. For better or worse, the Holocaust has become "a touchstone of public and intellectual discourse,"[26] even as antisemitic incidents, Holocaust denial, and politicized debates on the memory of the Holocaust continue to rise. As we finalized our book proposal in August 2017, Nazis were literally marching in Charlottesville, Virginia, chanting, "Jews will not replace us." As we engaged with the first drafts of chapters, the *New York Times* released a report in April 2018 that 41 percent of Americans and just over two-thirds of people ages nineteen to thirty-five do not know what Auschwitz was, although 93 percent think that students in school should learn about the Holocaust.[27] And as we read through second drafts of chapters in October 2018, a gunman entered the Tree of Life synagogue in Pittsburgh, murdering eleven, injuring seven, and desecrating a house of worship, the deadliest attack on a Jewish community in United States history. As we made final edits in December 2019, three Jews lost their lives in a gun attack on a kosher grocery store in Jersey City, New Jersey, and a machete-wielding assailant wounded five Jews at a Hanukkah celebration at a rabbi's house in Monsey, New York. The Holocaust must be taught and taught well. It is our intent that this volume support those who have this as their goal.

NOTES

1. Marianne Hirsch and Irene Kacandes, *Teaching the Representation of the Holocaust* (New York: MLA, 2004), 14.

2. Daniel Magilow and Lisa Silverman, eds., *Holocaust Representations in History* (London: Bloomsbury, 2015), 1.

3. Henry Friedlander, "Toward a Methodology of Teaching about the Holocaust," *Teachers College Record* 80, no. 3 (1979): 519–542, Historical Abstracts, EBSCOhost (accessed April 10, 2017).

4. Thomas Fallace, *The Emergence of Holocaust Education in American Schools* (New York: Palgrave Macmillan, 2008), 7–8.

5. One of the first courses was offered at Brandeis in the mid-1960s.

6. Stephen R. Haynes, "Holocaust Education at American Colleges and Universities: A Report on the Current Situation," *Holocaust and Genocide Studies* 12, no. 2 (1998): 282–307.

7. Fallace, *Emergence of Holocaust Education*, argues that "the affective revolution" in education coupled with grassroots efforts by public school teachers predated the surge of larger public interest in the late 1970s. Rona Sheramy, "'Resistance and War': The Holocaust in American Jewish Education, 1945–1960," *American Jewish History* 91, no. 2 (June 2003): 287–313, explains that these earlier treatments of the Holocaust in Jewish schools focused on stories of heroism and resistance rather than emphasizing Jewish victimization.

8. Fallace, *Emergence of Holocaust Education*, 104–5.

9. The eleven states that mandate the teaching of the Holocaust in public schools are California, Connecticut, Florida, Illinois, Kentucky, Michigan, New Jersey, New York, Oregon, Pennsylvania, and Rhode Island.

10. Howard B. Tinberg and Ronald Weisberger, *Teaching, Learning, and the Holocaust: An Integrative Approach* (Bloomington: Indiana University Press, 2014).

11. Samuel Totten, Paul Bartop, and Steven Leonard Jacobs, eds., *Teaching about the Holocaust: Essays by College and University Teachers* (Westport, CT: Praeger, 2004).

12. Nancy Ann Lauckner and Miriam Jokiniemi, eds., *Shedding Light on the Darkness: A Guide to Teaching the Holocaust* (New York: Berghahn Books, 2000).

13. Simone Schweber and Debbie Findling, *Teaching the Holocaust* (Los Angeles: Torah Aura Productions, 2007).

14. Hirsch and Kacandes, *Teaching the Representation*.

15. Magilow and Silverman, *Holocaust Representations in History*.

16. Many educators who teach this topic use reflective journals as one type of assignment to help students work through the material in a less formal written work. For examples of how to structure reflection journals, see Tinberg and Weisberger, *Teaching, Learning, and the Holocaust*, 117–118; Stephen Haynes, "Reflection on a Decade of Teaching the Holocaust," in Totten, Bartop, and Jacobs, *Teaching about the Holocaust*, 105–121, 107–108; Hirsch and Kacandes, introduction to *Teaching the Representation*, 20–22.

17. Educators should also review the recommendations of the US Holocaust Memorial Museum for teaching about the Holocaust: https://www.ushmm .org/educators/teaching-about-the-holocaust/general-teaching-guidelines.

18. Tinberg and Weisberger, *Teaching, Learning, and the Holocaust*, 28–29.

19. For a thorough review of the many terms used for the Holocaust, see Schweber and Findling, *Teaching the Holocaust*, 23–30.

20. Tinberg and Weisberger, *Teaching, Learning, and the Holocaust*, 2.

21. David Patterson states, "What the Nazis did was not unimaginable. On the contrary, they did everything imaginable, since they had no limiting principle to curb their actions." See Patterson, "Seeking the Fire in the Ashes: A Journey into the Holocaust," in Totten, Bartop, and Jacobs, *Teaching about the Holocaust*, 139–151, 149. As Peter Hayes suggests, describing the Holocaust as incomprehensible precludes the possibility of actually learning from it. See Hayes, *How Was It Possible?* (Lincoln: University of Nebraska Press, 2015), xiii.

22. Leonard Grob, "Reflections of a Holocaust Scholar/Philosopher," in Totten, Bartop, and Jacobs, *Teaching about the Holocaust*, 81–93, 84.

23. Totten, Bartop, and Jacobs, introduction to *Teaching about the Holocaust*, xi.

24. Our volume cannot cover the vast scope of scholarship on this topic. For additional topics, see Peter Hayes and John Roth, eds., *The Oxford Handbook of Holocaust Studies* (Oxford: Oxford University Press, 2010).

25. This volume uses antisemitism instead of anti-Semitism, as the latter implies that Semitism exists. See Peter Hayes, *Why? Explaining the Holocaust* (New York: Norton, 2017), 3–5.

26. Hayes and Roth, *Oxford Handbook of Holocaust Studies*, 2.

27. Maggie Astor, "Holocaust Is Fading from Memory, Survey Finds," *New York Times*, April 12, 2018, https://www.nytimes.com/2018/04/12/us/holocaust-education.html (accessed April 20, 2018).

PART ONE

Teaching
Specific Content

Antisemitism

Understanding Its Meaning, Context, and History When Teaching the Holocaust

JONATHAN ELUKIN

W hy did the Germans and their European collaborators slaughter millions of Jews in what has
become known as the Holocaust? Scholars have identified a range of
factors motivating the Nazis and their helpers including the influence
of traditional anti-Jewish Christian theology that portrayed the Jews as
killers of Christ, murderers of Christian children, or moneylenders; a
conflation in Nazi ideology of the Jews and the terrifying Bolsheviks;
revenge for the putative Jewish betrayal of Germany in World War I;
fear of the world conspiracy of Jewish financial power; and a sense of
Aryan racial superiority with its accompanying dread of Jewish infec-
tion and impurity. This last notion of a distinctive Aryan racial superiority to the Near Eastern Semitic peoples was the culmination of racial
thinking that became popular in nineteenth-century Europe. Europeans
applied the pseudo-science of a physicalized racial identity to different
national and ethnic populations, largely to separate Christian Europeans
from nonwhite colonial peoples.

The particular racial animosity that was directed towards the Jews,
who were often seen as interlopers in a Christian European society, came
to be known as *antisemitism*. The term itself has its origins in nineteenth-
century Austrian political discourse when various right-wing parties,
adapting the contemporary pseudo-scientific language of racial categories of Aryans and Semites, tried to stop the extension of civil rights

to the increasingly visible and economically mobile communities of Jews in Central European societies.[1] *Antisemitische* was the term these groups used to describe their opposition to granting the rights and privileges of citizenship to Jews. The term was soon popularized by the German activist and journalist Wilhelm Marr. Ironically, contemporary Jewish political writers also took up the expression to capture what they felt to be a burgeoning hatred of Jews in Europe. They observed contemporary pogroms in Russia and feared similar violence might be germinating in Europe's more liberal societies. Once all these rhetorical, political, and physical forms of contemporary violence against Jews became classified as *antisemitism*, it was easy to characterize persecution of Jews in the past as manifestations of the same antisemitic ideology.

The Holocaust demonstrated with unsurpassed urgency that historians, religious thinkers, political leaders, and other social critics had to acknowledge the power of antisemitism, an ideology that seemed to have had such a catastrophic impact on European society. The idea of a resilient, timeless, and powerful antisemitism at least seemed to offer to postwar scholars in Europe and America the promise of understanding and explaining the Holocaust. The destruction of European Jewry could be explained in terms that made sense historically. Accepting the historical reality and power of antisemitism also served the needs of religious and secular (gentile) scholars as they tried to understand the unique horror of the destruction of European Jewry. For those who were attached to Christianity, the idea of racial antisemitism could mitigate Christianity's responsibility for the Holocaust. The preoccupation with antisemitism made sense as well in the larger context of thinking about other so-called racial minorities. The larger idea of racism as a catchall way to explain discrimination had been gaining traction as a means to identify discrimination against racial minorities in Europe and North America. Indeed, as *racism* came to dominate academic and human rights discourse in the twentieth century, it became natural to see antisemitism as a subset of this larger ideology. It is almost impossible now to try to understand the Holocaust without reference to the idea of antisemitism; so, too, educators must think deeply about how to incorporate it into their classrooms.

Unfortunately, antisemitism is an idea that is profoundly anachronistic; it is unbounded by time or context. It is the anachronistic nature of the idea of antisemitism that makes invoking it in the study of the Holocaust so deeply problematic. The term has come to be used to describe anti-Jewish feeling throughout history. By doing so, scholars or others invoking the term make it appear that the hatred of Jews manifested by Germans and their European allies was identical to that or somehow fundamentally related to that of earlier generations of Christians throughout European history. Another problem with the term *antisemitism* is that it reinforces the idea of a linear and teleological connection (drawing a straight line from early Christianity or even nineteenth-century Germany to Hitler) from the earliest hatred of Jews to the genocidal efforts of the Nazis. This ignores both the historical specificity of post–World War I Germany and factors that not only distinguished Nazi antisemitism but also that led to the Final Solution. Doing so flattens our understanding of the Holocaust and distorts the actual premodern history of Jewish-Christian relations. The nature of Christian attitudes toward Jews in the ancient, medieval, and early modern world is far more diverse and dynamic than a one-dimensional history of animosity toward Jews.

Both scholarly and popular accounts have tended, since the nineteenth century, to assume the existence of a deep-rooted Christian animus toward Jews—one that had its origins at the birth of Christianity (or even before in the classical world). According to this narrative, Christianity's relentless animosity toward Jews flowers during the Middle Ages and thus provides a foundation for modern attacks on Jews. Many academic and popular authors believe that some form of that same hatred survives in the modern world.[2] Unfortunately, the fluid and idiosyncratic nature of medieval Christianity, as well as changing relationships among Christians and Jews, is often lost in most of these conventional portraits of unchanging persecution and violence.

There are a variety of reasons why this monochromatic vision of Christian animosity toward Jews during the Middle Ages has been so resilient. One factor is a persistent misconception about medieval European society itself. Despite the best efforts of medieval historians, the Middle Ages cannot escape the shadow first cast over it by Renaissance intellectuals. Ever since Petrarch and his Renaissance followers in the fourteenth and fifteenth centuries created the "Middle Ages" as a means of self-promotion to set off their own "modern" identity inspired by classical antiquity, Western culture has undermined the importance of medieval Europe. Renaissance, Reformation, and Enlightenment thinkers derided the Middle Ages as a crucible of superstition, fanaticism, primitivism, and prejudice.[3] Except for the enthusiasm of nineteenth-century Romantics, Victorians, and their cultural heirs, most people who think about the Middle Ages consider the world of medieval Europe to have contributed little to modern society. At best, the Middle Ages provides a pastoral refuge from the challenges of modernity and a playground for romantic notions of chivalry and honor. The assumption is that Antiquity discovered rational thought and democracy, and the Renaissance and Enlightenment forged individualism and secularization. The persecution of Jews easily fits into this larger picture of medieval society's supposed predilection for superstition and intolerance.

Antisemitism as an explanatory ideology for the Holocaust has attracted Jews as well. For Jews after the Holocaust, antisemitism was a "clean" answer that reinforced the traditional sense among religious Jews of unrelenting persecution in *galut*, that is, exile, a belief that had its theological origins in the earliest days of Israel's expulsion from the Holy Land. Cultivating belief in a resilient antisemitism worked as well to preserve and strengthen Jewish identity in the postwar world. The openness of American society, in particular, was a threat to Jewish communal solidarity and continuity. Acknowledging the reality, and seeming timelessness, of antisemitism helped maintain a sense of Jewish identity and group loyalty. Even in an increasingly pluralistic society, Jews could see themselves as always vulnerable. An external enemy, even one that was increasingly abstract in an American context, could help reinforce group loyalty and continuity. The Holocaust also gave the Jewish community in the United States a viable status as victims to compete with African Americans and other American minorities in what was becoming a pluralistic American world that celebrated communal suffering.

Recognizing the anachronistic quality of antisemitism does not mean making the case to see the past as free from violence or antagonism toward Jews. The ideologies that contributed to anti-Jewish hatred among Nazis and their allies certainly drew some of their energy from historical attitudes toward Jews and Judaism.[4] By returning to the historical reality of Christian-Jewish relations, we can see how thinking in terms of antisemitism obscures a more historically accurate picture of the dynamic relationship among Christians and Jews. Recently scholars have become more sensitive to the potential for anachronism in their use of the term *antisemitism* to describe earlier manifestations of hatred or animosity toward Jews. They have largely embraced the term *anti-Judaism* to identify a premodern Christian hatred of Jews for their rejection of Jesus and Christianity as opposed to a modern attitude based on the pseudo-scientific ideas of racial thinking that emphasized the biological inferiority of Jews. In many ways, however, the term *anti-Judaism* has simply replaced *antisemitism* without resolving any of the fundamental problems in trying to capture a totalizing view of antagonism toward Jews. Anti-Judaism has many of the same flaws and problems that bedevil antisemitism.

Given what we know of the way gentiles and Jews interacted in late antique and medieval societies, it becomes difficult to imagine an all-encompassing ideology of anti-Judaism as a real factor that influenced the way Greeks or Romans thought about or treated Jews. Did any group of non-Jews before the advent of Christianity imagine themselves to have systematic negative attitudes toward Judaism that motivated violence against Jews or deeply felt animosity toward them? As Martin Goodman and Erich Gruen have recently demonstrated, most Greeks and Romans had only the vaguest notions of what Judaism was, and what they knew of it, they mostly found laughable or bizarre.[5] The comments of Tacitus and others about the absurdity of circumcision, avoidance of pork, and other Jewish habits make it unlikely that their casual disparagement of Judaism could lead to an intense hatred of Jews. The infamous attack on Jews in the Egyptian city of Alexandria in 38 CE is perhaps the only example of popular violence against Jews in the ancient world. Was this the result of a pervasive "Judeophobia" (another new term that has not achieved real traction in recent scholarship), as Peter Schäfer has argued, or a product of local rivalries and frustrations particular to the Alexandrian context?[6] Even if local Alexandrians had cultivated a particularly virulent distaste for Jews, it did not spread to other places, and Judaism qua Judaism was never the target. The Roman victories over Jewish rebellions had very little to do with the content of Judaism or the nature of Jews themselves. It was about enforcing Roman authority and exploiting a military victory for internal Roman political needs. The recurring military conflicts with Jews might have cultivated suspicion toward Jews if such animus toward Jews was widespread, but even after the Jewish revolts, Jewish communities thrived throughout the Roman world of Late Antiquity. Whatever animosity had developed toward Jews, it did not become a pervasive ideology directed against Jews. And, certainly, it had very little to do with sustained opposition to Judaism itself. The Jews were largely tolerated in antiquity because they were an ancient people, and as long as they obeyed the civil laws of their cities and did not disrupt public religion, it is difficult to see any pervasive anti-Jewish thought or feeling. The Roman suppression of the Jews and the destruction of the Temple in 70 CE was a military and political decision prompted by internal Roman politics and Jewish resistance to Roman rule. It was not the result of a Roman policy of genocide or racial hatred of the Jews.

Scholars have generally adopted the convention of writing about the anti-Judaism expressed in some parts of the New Testament or early Christian polemical writings against Jews as opposed to early antisemitism.[7] These polemical texts or sermons focused on how the Jews rejected Jesus as the Messiah or how they supposedly betrayed God's prophets, or how they misunderstood the nature of divine law or history. In fact, it is almost impossible to find early Christian language about Jews that dwells upon the physical or "racial" identity of Jews. For those Jews who embraced Jesus, they did not see themselves in opposition to Judaism but rather as participating in its fulfillment. Gentiles of the early Christian communities at first likely shared that enthusiasm for Judaism, albeit with a messianic focus on Jesus. For the earliest Christians, many wished to continue the observances of Jewish law, with the added element of belief in Jesus as the messiah. They could not really express an anti-Judaism without undermining their own claims to be the true Israelites. Once people identifying as Christians began to withdraw or were harried out of local Jewish communities, there was an increased alienation from what Jews did or believed. But even for Paul, who first articulated this approach, it was not so much a sense of the danger of Judaism but rather its irrelevance after Jesus that shaped his thinking. Indeed, the observance of the law, in one generous reading of Paul, was restricted to Jews but not in itself demonized. To be sure, the New Testament, which reflected at least in part some of the attitudes of various early Christian communities, contained language criticizing the Jews for rejecting Jesus and indicting various Jewish elites for stage-managing the crucifixion. To what extent were these ideas internalized by individual Christians? But such uncertainty reminds us that we do not have a clear view of what the range of early Christians thought about Judaism. It is easy to assume a neat divide between the opposing religious communities, but it has become increasingly clear that communities of early Christians and Jews interacted more intimately and in nuanced ways that remind us to look beyond the rhetoric of community leaders. Early Christians who felt most threatened by the popularity of Late Antique Jewish communities seemed more concerned with the failings of early Christians than with the nature of Judaism itself. The clear divide between early Christians and Jews may have come much later under pressure of Christian imperial authority.[8]

It was under the pressure of a Christianized Roman Empire that rabbinic Judaism coalesced. At that time, as well as in post–Constantine Christianity, the anti-Jewish rhetoric of imperial laws is often bound up with animosity toward pagans and heretics. The persecutorial language of the laws seems less specifically focused on Judaism per se, than on identifying any opposition to Christian orthodoxy. Interestingly, when Augustine set out his famous manifesto about the need to preserve the Jews as witnesses to the authenticity and antiquity of Christianity, he was not concerned about Judaism per se.[9] The specific nature of the religion of the Jews was unimportant. What mattered was the survival of the Jews as a people. Indeed, Judaism had not undermined the essential role Jews had to play in Augustine's theology; they were thought to preserve the Hebrew Scriptures, which were the core of both Judaism and Christianity. Whatever distortions the rabbis had imposed on Jewish beliefs or rituals, they had not undermined the value of the Jews as witnesses to Christian truth. Given the complicated history of early relations between Jews and Christians, then, it hardly seems viable to categorize the dynamic as one of anti-Judaism let alone antisemitism.

Neither anti-Judaism nor antisemitism can be usefully deployed in the classroom to understand the complicated relationships among Jews and Christians in the European Middle Ages. We find the same complexity and interconnectedness between Jews and Christians in medieval Europe.[10] By trying to classify all negative Christian attitudes toward Jews under one rubric, we seriously distort the complicated and fluid nature of Christian thinking about Jews in medieval and premodern Europe. The existence of Jewish communities (or at least small groups of Jews) in many locations in the medieval world is powerful evidence that most medieval Christians tolerated the presence of Jews in their towns. Most of these Jewish communities thrived and allowed for the development of the rich culture of medieval Ashkenaz. Jews accommodated themselves to the tension between a quasi-tolerance and idiosyncratic violence. There is a fundamental disconnect in using a totalizing word such as *anti-Judaism* or *antisemitism* to describe the feelings of Christians who lived and worked with Jews for generations.

Even some of the violence directed against Jews might be difficult to categorize solely under a rubric of anti-Judaism or antisemitism. To be sure, some of the fantasies of child murder associated with the blood libel accusations asserted that the Jews killed Christian children as part of ritual preparations for Passover. In that sense, what Christians saw as a perverted kind of Judaism could be held responsible, although the animus was usually directed at putatively evil Jews. At the same time, some Christians recognized that Jewish religious law made these accusations ludicrous. But the Jews were accused of many other things that could not be ascribed to a specific religious commandment. How are accusations during the years of the plague in 1348–1349, in which some Christians imagined Jews to have spread the plague by poisoning wells, related to the nature of Judaism or any of its ritual commandments? The violence in Spain in 1392 and the later expulsion seem to have more to do with a post-Crusade nationalism or even proto-racial ideas of purity of lineage (or class warfare in urban settings) than with animosity toward Judaism itself. Increasing concerns that *conversos* were being drawn back to Judaism triggered the expulsion. In this case, again, it seems as if the culprits were thought to be Jewish friends and family rather than a vaguer sense of the power of the religion's hold on former Jews. In the disputations between Christians and Jews, it was Jewish blindness or corruption that was thought to be at the core of the rabbis' refusal to understand the "true" meaning of scripture.

Perhaps there is an even more fundamental issue to be addressed in trying to understand and teach the utility of the terms *anti-Judaism* or *antisemitism*, and that is the nature of Christianity itself. Why do we assume that there was one consistent Christian identity that produced the same attitudes toward Jews?[11] Where do we find this stable, authentic, and monochromatic Christianity? We have already seen the differences among leading Christian thinkers. Surely religious culture and identity varied enormously across space and time in medieval and early modern Europe. The expulsions of Jews from cities and towns in late medieval and early modern Germany was idiosyncratic. And the Jews who were expelled found refuge in the Christian land of Poland-Lithuania. It is thus unreasonable to imagine that popular attitudes toward Jews and Judaism would have remained stable as well. The definition of medieval and early modern Christianity itself presents the first challenge. Do we mean the official theology of the church? The attitudes and ideologies of the clergy? The opinions and behaviors of the laity? However we define Christianity, we can be sure that it was very different in the ninth century than it would be in the twelfth or even later in the fifteenth century.

With the advent of the Reformation, trying to identify a common Christian ideology becomes infinitely more difficult. Moreover, Christian identities also varied widely according to time and place. No doubt people living in a cosmopolitan city in Spain thought about Christianity and behaved as Christians in ways very different from peasants in a village in France or Germany. How can we then make any constructive generalizations about "Christian" attitudes toward Jews? The anti-Jewish attitudes that manifested themselves in Christian Europe came from a wide variety of Christian cultures and identities.

The Manichean quality of *anti-Judaism* or *antisemitism* ultimately obscures the much more complicated entanglement of Christianity and Judaism that transcended simple persecution and animus. A great deal of Christian thinking about Judaism was not "anti" in any one-dimensional sense. Christians appropriated aspects of Judaism and Jewish history in order to advance their own particular theological or political agendas. For example, Christians throughout late antiquity and the Middle Ages accused their theological or political enemies of Judaizing, that is, indicting them for displaying putative Jewish characteristics as a way to defame them. What often looked like anti-Jewish expressions were dramas about internal Christian issues that relied upon Jewish actors. Many of the tales of Jews stealing or stabbing the Eucharist, for example, ended with them converting when they saw a vision of a child in the Eucharist or when they witnessed a bleeding Host. The Jews thus became unwilling actors in a drama driven by contemporary Christian needs to reinforce belief in the real presence of God in the Eucharist.[12] Even the portraits of Jews in crucifixion scenes with distorted features and clothing did not originally express prejudice toward Jews as individual human beings in the Middle Ages. They were actually symbols used in an internal Christian dialogue about the nature of Jesus's physical body. Christian artists used the distorted features of the Jews to make them stand out in the depictions of the crucifixion. These Jews were meant to represent contemporary Christians who seemed reluctant to embrace Jesus's physicality. They, like the

27

Jews, mocked the crucified Christ.[13] In a similar vein, Christians may have used the Jews as an outlet for their own anxieties about the financial and legal nature of Christian culture. Christians could displace that anxiety by condemning Jews as usurers and Judaism as legalistic. Even some actual physical attacks on Jews had double meanings or an underlying meaning. Often when different elements in a town or kingdom persecuted the Jews, it was a way to strike at local powers, such as a king or local lord, who stood behind the Jews. Think, for example, of the attacks on English Jews as ways for indebted knights to strike at the kings who ultimately held the Christian debts owed to the Jews.

In the early modern period, the capacity of Christianity to use Judaism as a vehicle for internal Christian disputes increased greatly, particularly in the context of the struggles between Catholics and Protestants. For example, even Protestant books that seemed like they anticipated Enlightenment toleration toward the Jews actually used the Jews to convey coded messages attacking Catholics.[14] Jews and Jewish history were taken up by Christians as a way to explore their own religious ideas. In the English histories of Jews derived from Josephus in the eighteenth and nineteenth centuries, for example, the survival of the Jews became a way of asserting the miraculous intervention of God in history for Protestants who were reluctant to embrace the more extravagant miracles of the Catholic tradition.[15] These efforts at rereading Jewish history were a kind of violent appropriation. However, they complicate a one-dimensional understanding of animosity toward Jews. The phenomenon of *philosemitism*, which could be defined as the marked interest in or appreciation of Judaism and Jews, also makes it difficult to see Christianity and Judaism as always in a state of conflict. Christian scholars in the Renaissance, for example, searched in Jewish sources for coded references to Christian revelation. Gender was a particularly interesting point of intersection. Shakespeare, Sir Walter Scott, George Eliot, and a host of lesser writers and artists highlighted the beauty and piety of Jewish women.[16]

At the close of this all too brief exploration of the idea of antisemitism and the Holocaust, we should also ask: what impact does the Holocaust have on contemporary expressions of what we think of as antisemitism? In one sense, the Holocaust has invested antisemitism, or rather the ideas and images traditionally associated with antisemitism, with an enormous amount of energy. The terrifying scale of the Holocaust acts like a beacon to those who embrace antisemitic ideology. The

Holocaust appears to be a "victory" for the ideology associated with antisemitism. It was a world historical event that could be repeated if the language and imagery demonizing the Jews is preserved and disseminated. It should not be surprising then that the so-called alt-right has embraced many of the traditional tropes of antisemitism and Nazi imagery. We have only to recall the rhetoric of neo-Nazi demonstrators in the Charlottesville, Virginia, riot of August 2017 that Christians will "not be replaced" by Jews, or the accusation that the Jewish financier and philanthropist George Soros is the source of nefarious conspiracies, to see the power of these ideas. The Holocaust confers world-changing power on this ideology and on its largely marginalized and disenfranchised believers.

The malign or at least disruptive influence of the Holocaust extends also to how we understand contemporary manifestations of so-called antisemitism. The Holocaust can overwhelm distinctions and evolutions in contemporary expressions of anti-Jewish thought and rhetoric. For example, we may not take seriously enough an antisemitic expression if it does not rise to the bar of what we associate with the Holocaust. Or, on the other hand, the Holocaust may have created such a sense of paranoia or anxiety that we overreact to these expressions or actions. Or we may simply misunderstand the context and origins of what appears to be antisemitic rhetoric that had been traditionally associated with the Holocaust. For example, the negative attitudes toward Jews in many Muslim communities, particularly in France, seem to be focused on fears of Jews controlling the French government, which echoes, of course, traditional antisemitic tropes of Jewish financial influence. However, what is missing from these contemporary Muslim attitudes is anything resembling a controlling idea of the racial inferiority of the Jews. Muslim antisemitism, if we can call it that, also derives its energy from animosity toward Israel, which seems to be the result of anxiety about the traditional reversal of the historical position of the Jews in Islam. In any case, too closely associating the Holocaust with contemporary antisemitism (or what we identify as anti-Jewish attitudes) might obscure our ability to identify new developments or pathways in these anti-Jewish ideologies.

The specific context of Muslim antisemitism or that exhibited by the so-called alt-right may be drawing upon some ideas from the traditional repertoire of antisemites, but the ideas of these groups are likely generated by different ideological goals or social contexts than those associated with the thinking that led to the Holocaust. Another instance is the use by some elements of the political left, both in Europe and in the United States, of antisemitic tropes and imagery directed against Israel. This so-called anti-Zionism is built clearly on an intellectual infrastructure that draws its energy and inspiration from the received ideas of antisemitism. Like the antisemitism of the alt-right and some Muslims, that of the political left is produced in a very different context from the ideas that precipitated the Holocaust. That does not mean, of course, that we should ignore or belittle these developments. They deserve scrutiny and denunciation, but it is important to make sure we are not conflating very different kinds of anti-Jewish sentiment.

One theological principle of Christianity that has been at the core of its anti-Jewish thinking even before the development of racial antisemitism is *supercessionism*: the replacement of Judaism by Christianity. The old, carnal, particular, legalistic religion of the Israelites was determined by God to be supplanted by the new universal religion of love and spirituality embodied in Christ. In the same way that Christians shunted Judaism aside or tried to claim its core values and history, various groups are now trying to appropriate the Holocaust from its particularly Jewish context. The Holocaust is being universalized, that is, being treated as a tragedy for all humanity (which in a way it is, of course) and not specifically or exclusively for the Jews. This approach denies the uniqueness of the Jewish experience. Indeed, this "theologizing" of the Holocaust goes further by implicitly arguing that when the Jews suffered, all humanity suffered. That approach makes the Jews writ large into Christ figures who suffered for all humanity. The Jews become actors in a larger Christianized drama, in the same way that the Israelites became actors in the story of the victory of Christianity. Any systematic study of the relationship between antisemitism and the Holocaust must take these new developments into account. Universalizing the Holocaust, both its experience and its memory, may be a new form of a very old anti-Jewish effort. It is one that has none of the traditional images of antisemitism that we associate with the Holocaust, but it may in the end have the most enduring effect on how the Holocaust is remembered.

NOTES

1. Steven Beller, *Antisemitism: A Very Short Introduction* (Oxford: Oxford University Press, 2015).

2. Robert Wistrich, *A Lethal Obsession: Antisemitism from Antiquity to the Global Jihad* (New York: Random House, 2010). See the recent roundtable in the *American Historical Review* 123, no. 4 (October 2018): 1122–1245.

3. Marcus Bull, *Thinking Medieval: An Introduction to the Study of the Middle Ages* (New York: Palgrave Macmillan, 2005).

4. See the volume edited by Jonathan Adams and Cordelia Hess, eds., *The Medieval Roots of Antisemitism: Continuities and Discontinuities from the Middle Ages to the Present Day* (New York: Routledge, 2018).

5. Martin Goodman, *Rome and Jerusalem: The Clash of Ancient Civilizations* (New York: Vintage, 2008); and Erich Gruen, *Diaspora: Jews amidst Greeks and Romans* (Cambridge, MA: Harvard University Press, 2002).

6. Peter Schäfer, *Judeophobia: Attitudes towards the Jews in the Ancient World* (Cambridge, MA: Harvard University Press, 1998).

7. Jonathan M. Elukin, "Anti-Judaism," in Sol Goldberg, ed., *Key Terms in the Study of Anti-Semitism* (forthcoming).

8. Seth Schwartz, *Imperialism and Jewish Society: 200 B.C.E to 640 C.E.* (Princeton: Princeton University Press, 2004).

9. Paula Fredriksen, *Augustine and the Jews: A Christian Defense of Jews and Judaism* (New Haven: Yale University Press, 2010).

10. Jonathan Elukin, *Living Together, Living Apart: Rethinking Jewish-Christian Relations in the Middle Ages* (Princeton: Princeton University Press, 2007); and David Malkiel, *Reconstructing Ashkenaz: The Human Face of Franco-German Jewry, 1000–1250* (Stanford: Stanford University Press, 2008).

11. Jonathan M. Elukin, "Christianity and Judaism, Christians and Jews," in R. N. Swanson, ed., *Routledge History of Medieval Christianity 1050–1500* (New York: Routledge, 2015), 239–250.

12. Miri Rubin, *Gentile Tales: The Narrative Assault on Late Medieval Jews* (Philadelphia: University of Pennsylvania Press, 2004).

13. Sara Lipton, *Dark Mirror: The Medieval Origins of Anti-Jewish Iconography* (New York: Metropolitan Books, 2014).

14. Jonathan M. Elukin, "Jacques Basnage and the *History of the Jews*: Polemic and Allegory in the Republic of Letters," *Journal of the History of Ideas* 53, no 4 (1992): 603–631.

15. Jonathan Elukin, "Post-Biblical Jewish History through Christian Eyes: Josephus and the Miracle of Jewish History in English Protestantism," in David J. Wertheim, ed., *The Jew as Legitimation: Jewish-Gentile Relations beyond Antisemitism and Philosemitism* (New York: Palgrave Macmillan, 2017).

16. On philosemitism, see the essays in Wertheim, *Jew as Legitimation*; and in Jonathan Karp and Adam Sutcliffe, eds., *Philosemitism in History* (Cambridge: Cambridge University Press, 2011). And on the Jewess, see for example, Jonathan Hess, *Deborah and Her Sisters: How One Nineteenth-Century Melodrama and a Host of Celebrated Actresses Put Judaism on the World Stage* (Philadelphia: University of Pennsylvania Press, 2017).

The Rise of Nazism

MARK E. SPICKA

The question of why by January 1933 Adolf Hitler and the Nazi Party were able to rise to power from relative obscurity is crucial to understanding the origins and perpetration of the Holocaust. Although many Holocaust educators understandably focus their attention on the period of 1933 to 1945, an examination of Nazi electoral success and the demise of the Weimar Republic reveals how the Holocaust was part of a larger process whose outcomes were not preordained. The period of 1918 to 1933 illustrates quite distinctly how a racist, extremist political movement came to power, destroying a democracy, and how social and political cohesion within Germany frayed into "insiders" and "outsiders," setting the stage for the creation of the racial state of the Third Reich.

To be sure, teaching the complexities of the various factors contributing to Hitler and the Nazis' ascendency within the context of teaching the Holocaust is fraught with difficult decisions. Within clear constraints of time and focus of the class as a whole, educators must decide how to balance and make sense of long-term and contextual factors such as antisemitism in German society, the defeat in World War I, political instability of the Weimar Republic, the impact of hyperinflation and the Great Depression, and more immediate factors such as the personality and leadership of Hitler himself and the dynamism of the Nazi Party. Furthermore, teachers must confront the assumptions and preconceptions that many students bring to class regarding Hitler and the Nazis, which oftentimes are the product of the popular media and documentaries on Nazism. A common conception is that Hitler and the Nazis simply took advantage of the conditions of defeat in World War I and the terms of the Treaty of Versailles, compounded by economic depression in the early 1930s, making the triumph of the Nazi political movement appear almost inevitable. Furthermore, the uncritical use of Nazi propaganda itself in documentaries helps cultivate the incorrect impression that somehow the German public was brainwashed or passively followed the charismatic leadership of Hitler. A related common misconception among students is that all of the Germans were rabid antisemites who recognized and applauded a future goal of the elimination of Jews from German life, if not outright extermination.

These depictions of the German electorate obscure crucial dynamics explaining Nazi electoral success and also hinder drawing out some of the larger implications of the rise of the Nazis for us today. The simplest but ultimately unsatisfying answer to why the Nazis came to power is that a plurality of Germans decided to vote for them. The question then is why this happened. Undoubtedly, the political, economic, and social conditions of postwar Germany created a toxic environment of resentment and disappointment. However, a key point for students to understand is that rarely do voters act purely in negation or reaction against something, but that any successful political party must speak effectively to the aspirations and desires of the electorate.

Pedagogical Challenges and Questions

In the context of a class on the Holocaust, the challenge for the teacher is how to approach the interplay of various factors and contexts that are most important to explain why the German people put into power a regime that sought to tear down the democratic system in which it operated. Clearly, the conclusion of World War I and terms of the peace are a critical, but not a complete, explanation for the rise of Hitler. It is important for students to know that Germany might have taken a different political path following the war, such as reverting to a military dictatorship or embracing Communism. Political movements on both the left and right sought to overturn the Weimar Republic and revise the Treaty of Versailles, so these factors by themselves did not ensure Nazi electoral success. Instead, educators should focus on what made the Nazis stand out from other parties and why were they able to exploit the conditions of the Weimar Republic to their own advantage.

With this in mind, students should understand how Nazi ideology operated in the context of defeat and political instability in the postwar years.[1] When beginning to look at the Weimar period, it is constructive to ask students how German citizens might have thought about the war, what kind of sacrifices and contributions they would have made, and how they might have responded to defeat. During World War I, the German imperial government consistently pushed the prospect that victory was at hand. As a result, the abdication of Kaiser Wilhelm II and sudden defeat in November 1918 came as a shock to many Germans. Military and conservative elements almost immediately cultivated the "stab in the back" legend that denied the fact that German soldiers were defeated on the battlefield. Instead, they placed blame for defeat on what they described as "Jewish" socialist uprisings at the end of the war. Thereafter, right-wing circles attacked the legitimacy of the Weimar Republic by referring to the republican politicians who signed the armistice and established the new democracy as "November Criminals." It is also worthwhile to discuss the impact the Bolshevik Revolution in Russia would have had on Germany at this time and consider which members of society would have felt particularly threatened by Communism and why.[2]

A review of the key conditions of the Treaty of Versailles, particularly the loss of territory, reparations, limitations of the military, and acceptance of "war guilt," helps students assess how the forced acceptance of the treaty would have hindered citizen confidence in the newly formed democratic Weimar Republic. To contextualize the terms of the treaty, point out to students that while Germans perceived the conditions as harsh, they were less punitive than what the Germans demanded from the Russians in the Treaty of Brest-Litovsk in March 1918. Furthermore, the Germans actually paid relatively little of the reparations as stipulated by the treaty. The rise of the Nazis did not directly follow the Treaty of Versailles, but the treaty created an environment of bitterness and humiliation that the Nazis exploited. To follow up, students may consider why citizen confidence in a democratic system is vital for its strength and stability. This topic is a good opportunity to push students to reflect on what really constitutes a functioning democracy. That is, not only does a viable democracy require access to the vote and a set of laws, but also active participation by its citizens, functioning civil institutions and norms, and protection of civil liberties. Although born under chaotic conditions, the Weimar Republic was built upon longer-standing democratic traditions within German society and should not be seen as a preordained failure before the arrival of the Nazis.

Once the class has a solid understanding of the immediate postwar years, students are prepared to examine the development of the Nazi Party itself. A review of Hitler's early life is important, particularly how he soaked up the antisemitic ideas of pre-World War I Vienna. After serving and being wounded during the war, Hitler attended his first meeting of the German Workers' Party in Munich in September 1919 and quickly rose to prominence in the small party. The party, renaming itself the National Socialist German Workers' Party (NSDAP) in February 1920, was one of many extreme, nationalist, racist political parties forming in postwar Germany. From this perspective, the role of Hitler as an outstanding organizer and orator was crucial in attracting supporters.

In general, early Nazi supporters tended to be younger men, oftentimes veterans, who felt disillusioned with the Weimar Republic and the social and economic conditions of the postwar period. In order to understand Adolf Hitler's worldview, students may examine an excerpt of *Mein Kampf* or one of his early speeches. This helps students see the rabid antisemitism that was central to Hitler's ideology and the Nazi movement overall, even if it was sometimes downplayed as a tactic in some election campaigns in the late 1920s and early 1930s as the Nazis sought to become a "respectable" party.[3] The Nazis paired antisemitism with a populist message that promised a regeneration of German power and nation, renewal of Germany's influence on the international stage, including destroying the hated Treaty of Versailles, and protection of the common citizen's interests against corrupt Weimar politicians. Furthermore, oftentimes Hitler expressed this antisemitism in terms of anti-Communism, such as his ranting about the threat of "Judeo-Bolshevism" and the need for the German creation of *Lebensraum* (living space) in the East. It is useful for students to examine Hitler's views in terms of historical antisemitism (see Jonathan Elukin's chapter in this volume), plotting out the continuities and differences. This is also an opportunity to introduce some of the contours of the intentionalist versus functionalist debate among historians, which helps students assess the range of explanations of the origins of the Holocaust. The intentionalist view focuses on the role of Hitler himself and Nazi ideology while stressing that Hitler envisioned the elimination of the Jews already in the 1920s. The functionalist view contends that the structure and conditions of the Third Reich contributed to a continual radicalization of Nazi policy toward Jews, ultimately resulting in genocide.[4]

Despite the political and economic turmoil of the early Weimar period, the Nazis remained a fringe political party through the 1920s. After the failed Beer Hall Putsch of November 1923 and the sentencing of Hitler to prison for treason, the Nazi movement languished. Upon his release from prison in December 1924, Hitler pursued power within the Weimar system rather than through a coup and worked to reorganize and strengthen the party. The Nazi Party garnered relatively small electoral returns until the Great Depression hit Germany in 1930. In the last Reichstag election before the Great Depression in May 1928, the Nazi Party earned only 2.6 percent of the vote, jumping to 18.2 percent of the vote in September 1930 with the onset of the economic crisis, and reaching 37.3 percent in July 1932, the party's highest result in a free election. This raises the important question: To what extent did economic catastrophe push voters into the Nazi camp versus the Nazis attracting voters to the party? The classic view of historians is that the fear of both economic dislocation caused by the Great Depression and Communism drove members of the middle class to support the Nazis.[5] A chart laying out the electoral results of the Reichstag during the Weimar Republic is useful for students to see this shift and shows the rapid increase of the Nazi vote, along with the rise of the Communist alternative on the far left (see also the classroom exercise described below). In contrast, some historians contend that German voters were already searching for an alternative before the Great Depression hit. Middle class loyalties toward traditional bourgeois parties had already eroded by the mid-1920s, thereby making it more difficult for the construction of parliamentary coalitions. Hitler and the Nazi Party were in the position to pick up their support as they searched for an alternative. In the late 1920s, the Nazi Party did much to construct a vibrant organization at the local level to connect with voters and were adept at fine-tuning their message to local inclinations.[6]

Finally, an important point to convey in class is that once conservative interests had convinced President Paul von Hindenburg in backroom deals to name Hitler as chancellor in January 1933, he and the Nazis had by no means a monopoly of power in Germany, as there were only two other Nazi cabinet members other than Hitler himself. Over the course of the first half of 1933, Hitler dismantled the Weimar Republic and established himself as dictator. My class discusses how violence on the streets between Nazis and the Communists and the Reichstag fire in February 1933 played into the Nazi hand of cracking down on political opponents and eliminating civil liberties, ultimately leading to the passing of the Enabling Act in March 1933, which essentially gave Hitler dictatorial powers. In this way, the establishment of the Nazi State reflects the severing of social bonds and erosion of political space to resist the state, developments that would intensely radicalize during the Third Reich. Already by early 1933, Germans were accommodating themselves to policies of racism and violence.

A Sample Classroom Exercise

A key component in the Nazi electoral success was the party's ability to attract voters across class, religious, regional, and cultural lines, even if its base support tended to be from members of the middle class. A classroom activity using primary sources that explores Nazism from the perspective of the German voter is an effective way to explain the myriad reasons why the Nazis appealed to disparate electoral groups that previously aligned themselves with other political movements. Undoubtedly, the writings and speeches of Hitler and the propaganda that the party churned out are crucial to understanding Nazi ideology and image. However, assessing individual Germans' reactions to the Nazi movement helps students understand more deeply the ways in which voters perceived these messages, particularly in the context of the larger political and economic forces sweeping across Germany during the Weimar Republic. The Nazis had significant appeal as a protest party, rejecting the whole Weimar political, economic, and social system—a point many scholars have underscored.[7] But Nazi electoral success should not only be understood as a reaction against the Weimar Republic, but also as the electorate responding positively to the Nazi message calling for a *Volksgemeinschaft*, or national community, within Germany. A complex combination of factors motivated the electorate, and Hitler and the Nazis were a force different from anything seen before in German electoral politics.

As a prelude to this activity, explain to students the sharp ideological divisions that characterized Weimar politics and were strongly associated with the social and religious backgrounds of voters. On the left, the Communists and Social Democrats, which were made up mostly of members of the working class, believed in outright seizure of the means of production or some form of redistribution of the fruits of the capitalist system. Toward the middle of the political spectrum, the Catholic

Center Party, whose supporters crossed social classes, was united by the party's defense of Catholic interests in a country that was about two-thirds Protestant. Liberal and national political parties in the political center generally garnered their support from the middle class. The conservative political parties of the right had the support of the old aristocracy and economic elite and sought a return to the world prior to the Weimar Republic. The Nazis occupied the far right and hated the Weimar democracy but did not want to reestablish a prewar political and social system. The political center generally supported the Weimar system, from the Social Democrats to the middle-class parties, while the extremes at either end of the political spectrum sought its destruction. It is important for students to understand the wide divergence of ideological views within this party system that made it difficult for certain political parties to work together and how each political party tended to speak only to its political base. In discussion, students might consider how such a situation could contribute to political instability, particularly in the context of a parliamentary system in which no single party gained a majority and that relied on the creation of a coalition of political parties in order to govern.

The basis of the document analysis and discussion among students are personal testimonies of Nazi supporters who joined the party before 1933. They are drawn from research conducted in the summer of 1933 by Theodor Abel, a sociologist from Columbia University. He led a prize contest in which he asked early Nazi supporters to write a short essay on the circumstances that led them to National Socialism, a project that the Nazi regime, quite surprisingly, allowed to go forward. In the contest, Abel received more than seven hundred responses. These autobiographies became the basis of his book, *Why Hitler Came into Power*, published in 1938.[8] For this exercise, I have drawn from some of the personal testimonies collected by Abel and later published in an edited work.[9] Abel's original book provides a wealth of excerpts of personal testimonies that could be effectively used in the classroom.

The testimonies reflect a variety of social and political backgrounds, which contributes to discussion of the Nazis' wide appeal, but most heavily represent the lower middle class and are almost entirely from males. One should use caution in the sample that Abel has assembled and guide students in detecting some inherent biases in the testimonies, particularly since the interviews were conducted after the Nazis had come to power, and the interviewees tended to be party activists.

Furthermore, since the testimonies are predominately from men, the sample misses the fact that by 1930 the Nazi Party more intensely targeted women in its electioneering, softening its open misogyny by offering protection of the "natural" female sphere of the household and motherhood from the economic and political maelstrom of the Weimar system. Although the data are incomplete, by the July 1932 Reichstag election, the Nazi Party made significant gains with women, who made up the majority of the electorate, and garnered more votes from women than men in many voting districts.[10] The four testimonies I have used in the classroom include a man from the Free Corps (a paramilitary group that fought against the far-left after the war), an unemployed bank clerk, a disillusioned socialist, and a schoolteacher. Explain to students that each of the four individuals would have supported different political parties prior to the Nazis, ask them which parties were most likely and why, and delve into how each of the individuals had a unique reason for their attraction to the party, although often overlapping with other responses.

In conjunction with the testimonies, provide students with the Program of the German Workers' Party from February 1920. Hitler and a few other party leaders wrote this document, and it continued to be the party platform after the party became the NSDAP. The document lays out the Nazis' nationalistic, imperialistic, and antisemitic views while also condemning the Weimar Republic, Treaty of Versailles, and capitalistic profiteering. In the classroom activity, divide the class into groups and ask each group to examine one of the testimonies and to identify some specific issues that attracted this particular individual to Nazism. Students should also comment on how their individual's specific social background would influence that person's views toward the Weimar Republic and the Nazis. Furthermore, they are to refer to the Nazi program and identify specific points in the platform that would appeal to their individual, particularly in light of the individual's social background. After approximately ten or fifteen minutes, each group reports back to the class on what they found.

As students report their findings to the class, I write some of each group's comments on the board. As discussion progresses, it becomes clear that although each personal testimony is unique, an overall pattern quickly begins to emerge. The sentiments expressed in the testimonies include anti-Marxist attitudes, a desire to continue comradeship from World War I, and a deep disappointment in the failures of the Weimar government to protect the social and national interests of the people. The individuals also point to different aspects of the Nazi movement that attracted them. The testimonies uniformly see the Nazis as strengthening the communal spirit, often at the exclusion of Jews and members of the far-left, and approve of the melding of ideas of nationalism and social reform, which are issues also underscored in the party platform.

In class discussion, ask students to consider to what extent the conditions of the Weimar Republic influenced the political views held in the personal testimonies. Students comment that all of the testimonies reflect how defeat, the conditions of the Treaty of Versailles, and economic turmoil had impacted each individual personally, all the while also expressing a sense of grievance and resentment. Significantly, the personal testimonies show how each person searched for what he saw as a political solution to Germany's perceived ills with other political movements, be it socialist, national, or conservative parties, or the paramilitary *Stahlhelm* organization, before arriving at his support of the Nazis. In these testimonies, all of the other political parties as compared to the Nazis seemed to pursue politics as usual within what was seen as a corrupt system. A key aspect that students begin to realize is that the Nazi appeal was not merely negation but held out an aspirational or positive appeal to the voters. Clearly, hatred of the Treaty of Versailles or bitterness over what was seen as a corrupt Weimar Republic churned up quite a bit of resentment in the voters, but they all saw Hitler and the Nazi Party as redemptive for Germany. In fact, oftentimes the testimonies described Hitler and Nazi movement in quasi-religious language. Furthermore, there were elements of Nazism that appealed to the different social classes. The former socialist could support the Nazi movement's attention to protecting the living standards for all Germans and promotion of various social programs, while the former member of the Free Corps could embrace the renewal of the national community.

Another important aspect for students to see in the testimonies is that each of the personal testimonies expressed antisemitism or racism and the desire to restore the strength of the German *Volk*, although some to a greater extent than others. However, it is significant that oftentimes the interviewees expressed antisemitism through other resentments. The hyperinflation was the result of Jewish bankers, the socialist movement expressed "Jewish materialism," or Slavic peoples were flooding the eastern borders. Specific elements of the Nazi program

Germans holding propaganda posters, July 1932. (Bundesarchiv, Bild 102-03497A; https://commons.wikimedia.org/wiki/File:Bundesarchiv_Bild_102-03497A,_Berlin,_Propaganda_zur_Reichstagswahl.jpg)

statement reflect this aspect of racism—such as the statement that "None but those of German blood, whatever their creed, may be members of the nation. No Jew, therefore may be a member of the nation." The program goes on to demand that any foreigner who arrived in Germany after 1914 should be compelled to leave, and that the press should be purged of all foreign elements.[11] Students observe that the Nazis were already defining what constituted a "true" German versus those who were racially or politically suspect. In other words, even before coming to power, the Nazi message was already dividing German society. As a way to build upon the idea of Hitler and the Nazis responding to the desires and aspirations of a variety of German voters, it is effective to display PowerPoint slides of various Nazi electoral campaign posters between 1930 and 1933 when Nazi electoral support rapidly expanded.[12] At this point, many of the posters focused on economic issues, such as proclaiming "Work and Bread" and showing an arm with a swastika armband handing tools to outstretched hands or "Hitler—Our Last Hope!" displaying a forlorn group of presumably out-of-work men and women. In our class discussion, students analyze the symbols and visual image of the posters and speculate to whom the posters might appeal in the midst of economic crisis.

To pull things together, ask the students why they think the Nazis were able to come to power in light of the testimonies and propaganda. It is here that students can weigh the larger context of the problems of the Weimar period versus consideration of the specific aspects of the Nazi platform and image. Students very quickly pick up on the idea that these people from different social backgrounds saw something attractive in the Nazi Party and sensed that they were different from other political parties. Clearly, by the 1930s the Nazi Party had become a *Volkspartei*, or catchall people's party. It had its base of middle-class voters, but it had made inroads also with the working class and some upper-class voters. I try to make it clear to students that much of the Nazi propaganda spewed out antisemitism, and that it was a message that appealed to a significant part of the electorate, but it also was something a voter might ignore if attracted to other elements of the Nazi platform and image. The Nazi political strength was not that its message was necessarily logical, but it coherently expressed the party's values, allowing voters to ascribe their own views upon it and ignore particular aspects of the party platform. Posters stressing economic issues are a good resource to highlight the flexibility of the Nazi message to take advantage of the particular political and economic environment. The tendency among students is to create a binary of the motivation of voters based on antisemitism or economic factors. A useful outcome of examining personal testimonies is that it helps students see that single issues do not necessarily motivate voters, but oftentimes they approach issues through the lens of other interests and inclinations. Individuals might identify with a political party for particular reasons and then often will modify their views on other issues to match the party's position. As one historian has argued, many German voters were "drawn to anti-Semitism because they were drawn to Nazism, not the other way around."[13]

Teaching Resources

There are numerous primary source collections that cover Nazism and the Holocaust. The following list includes books that provide substantial materials from pre-1933.

Crew, David F., ed. *Hitler and the Nazis: A History in Documents*. Oxford: Oxford University Press, 2005.

Hill, Jeff, ed. *The Holocaust*. Detroit, MI: Omnigraphics, 2006.

Noakes, Jeremy, and Geoffrey Pridham, eds. *Nazism, 1919–1945*, vol. 1, *The Rise to Power, 1919–1934: A Documentary Reader*. Exeter: University of Exeter Press, 1998.

Rabinbach, Anson, and Gilman, Sander L., eds. *The Third Reich Sourcebook*. Weimar and Now: German Cultural Criticism. Translated by Lilian M. Friedberg. Berkeley: University of California Press, 2013.

Sax, Benjamin C., and Dieter Kuntz, eds. *Inside Hitler's Germany: A Documentary History of Life in the Third Reich*. Lexington, MA: DC Heath, 1992.

Stackelberg, Roderick, and Sally A. Winkle, eds. *The Nazi Germany Sourcebook: An Anthology of Texts*. London: Routledge, 2002.

Notes

1. For a thorough overview of how scholars have posited Nazi ideology, its uses, and its impact, see Geoff Eley, "How Do We Explain the Rise of Nazism? Theory and Historiography," in Shelley Baranowski, Armin Nolzen, and Claus-Christian Szejnmann, eds., *A Companion to Nazi Germany* (Hoboken: John Wiley & Sons, 2018), 17–32, especially 23–25.

2. One key source for primary sources on these and other German history topics is housed at the German Historical Institute: http://germanhistorydocs .ghi-dc.org/Index.cfm?language=english.

3. An excellent biography of Hitler during his rise to power is Ian Kershaw, *Hitler, 1889–1936: Hubris* (New York: W. W. Norton, 2000).

4. For more on this debate see Ian Kershaw, *The Nazi Dictatorship: Problems and Perspectives of Interpretation* (London: Hodder Arnold, 2000).

5. See William Sheridan Allen, *The Nazi Seizure of Power: The Experience of a Single Town, 1922–1945* (Brattleboro, VT: Echo Point Books, 2014).

6. See Thomas Childers, *The Nazi Voter: The Social Foundations of Fascism in Germany, 1919–1933* (Chapel Hill: University of North Carolina Press, 1983); and Peter Fritzsche, *Germans into Nazis* (Cambridge, MA: Harvard University Press, 1998).

7. See Richard J. Evans, *The Coming of the Third Reich* (New York: Penguin Books, 2003), 262–265.

8. Theodore Abel, *Why Hitler Came into Power* (Cambridge, MA: Harvard University Press, 1986).

9. Henry Cord Meyer, ed., *The Long Generation: Germany from Empire to Ruin, 1913–1945* (New York: Walker, 1973), 118–128.

10. Julia Sneeringer, *Winning Women's Votes: Propaganda and Politics in Weimar Germany* (Chapel Hill: University of North Carolina Press, 2002), 219–246; and Childers, *The Nazi Voter*, 260. Female voting patterns differed significantly between Catholic and Protestant areas, and there are major gaps in the data, so an overall voting breakdown by gender is not possible.

11. "The Party Program," in Benjamin C. Sax and Dieter Kuntz, eds., *Inside Hitler's Germany: A Documentary History of Life in the Third Reich* (Lexington, MA: DC Heath, 1992), 72–75.

12. These posters are available from the Nazi and East German Propaganda website and at a United States Holocaust Memorial Museum special exhibit on Nazi propaganda accessible at https://www.ushmm.org/propaganda/. See also the collection of propaganda posters housed by Calvin College: http://research.calvin.edu/german-propaganda-archive/index.htm.

13. Allen, *Nazi Seizure of Power*, 84.

Legislation as a Path to Persecution

RUSSEL LEMMONS AND
LAURA J. HILTON

Prior to the Nazi seizure of power, most Germans prided themselves on living in a *Rechtstaat*, a country governed by laws administered in an unbiased fashion and applied by a well-trained, independent judiciary. The German concept of law emphasized its rationality as well as the role that it played in maintaining order in a society. In this positivist legal philosophy, the law must provide the firm basis for all of the state's policies, and it must be followed to the letter. Indeed, within a Rechtstaat, lawlessness meant chaos; the rule of law, however, was a precondition for any civilized society. Hence, most Germans believed that authorities should apply the law equally, and a person's position in society should have no effect upon his or her treatment by either the police or the courts. Although, in practice, the German legal system often fell short of this ideal, citizens of Imperial Germany and the Weimar Republic, like those of other Western countries, could reasonably rely upon the effectiveness of the rule of law.[1]

The National Socialist conception of law, however, was strikingly different. In the eyes of Adolf Hitler and other leaders of the Third Reich, the legal system served an important purpose that went far beyond merely maintaining order. In keeping with the racialist ideology of National Socialism, law should serve the *Volk*, the biologically defined majority of German citizens who qualified as "Aryan." In other words, the Nazi approach to the law asserted the right of the Volk to use the police and judicial powers of the state to protect the German people from the perceived threat of heinous intentions and actions of biologically (and politically) defined enemies—especially the Jews. For Hitler and other leaders of the Third Reich, racial considerations must be embedded in the making, administration, and enforcement of the law. As a result, the concept of equality before the law was antithetical to National Socialist jurisprudence. Rather, for the Nazis, the law must serve the interest of the Volk in its struggle with the enemies of Germany, and any legislation that contributed to this effort was justified.[2] One of the earliest laws passed under Hitler's chancellorship, The Enabling Act, passed on March 24, 1933, exemplified this. Following in the wake of the Reichstag Fire and the banning of the Communist Party, democratically elected members of the Reichstag voted to give the chancellor the power to rule by decree. Passed by a vote of 444 to 94, this law, officially called the Law for the Removal of the Distress of People and the Reich, presented Hitler with the ability to issue laws without the Reichstag's input or approval.[3] This law served as the underpinning for *Gleichschaltung* (coordination of society), whereby all of Germany's major institutions were Nazified. The confluence of these philosophies of law—the positivist approach endorsed by the proponents of the Rechtstaat and the racialist view championed by Nazi ideologues—created the circumstances in which the leaders of the Third Reich introduced legislation designed to isolate the perceived racial enemies (Jews, mentally and physically handicapped, homosexuals, and Roma and Sinti) of the German people.

Introducing students to how the NSDAP used legislation and manipulated the existing political structure highlights several intertwined themes. First, the Nazis targeted several groups of people, each of whom already faced societal prejudice, persecuted them in similar ways, and used analogous language such as *criminal, dangerous, subversive, immoral, unnatural,* and *unhealthy* to describe them. Second, growing party and state bureaucracies, especially between 1933 and 1939, built social approval for ostracizing these groups by positing it as necessary in order to protect the *Volksgemeinschaft* (people's community). Third, the Nazis' use of legislation strengthened this process of exclusion by providing legitimacy in the eyes of many Germans. Indeed, the innocuous titles of many of these laws drew upon Germans' respect for the law. Lastly, an analysis of this process of exclusion through legislation allows educators to teach how a society accepts discrimination when it is bolstered through a well-publicized and publicly approved process and when the process to introduce it is gradual and incremental. In other words, the regime used the institutions of liberalism in an effort to undermine the liberal order, and many of its citizens participated willingly in this process.

Legislation Aimed at Jews within Germany

Antisemitic legislation went well beyond the intention of separating the Jews from the Aryan population. As Nazi antisemitic policy radicalized, so did the goals of anti-Jewish legislation. The result was a series of hundreds of laws—such as those forbidding Jews to use public parks, drive a car, or own a pet—intended to dehumanize them. The most infamous of these laws, the September 1941 decree requiring German Jews to wear a yellow Star of David, was the product of an often ad hoc process designed both to dehumanize and isolate the Jewish population.[4] In short, the legal restrictions upon "Non-Aryans" increased as anti-Jewish policy in Germany evolved incrementally between 1933 and 1938 and then accelerated after Kristallnacht and the start of World War II. Although the Jews were among the first victims of the legal system of the Third Reich, authorities targeted other groups as well. Eventually, the government extended the goals of its legislation to incorporate other biologically defined enemies of the "Aryan" race, including the mentally and physically handicapped, homosexuals, and the so-called Gypsies—the Sinti and Roma peoples.[5] In the eyes of the Nazis, however, the Jews were the most important racial enemy.

Therefore, the initial target of National Socialist racial legislation was the Jews, whom German leaders sought to isolate, to cut off from contact with "good" Germans in the name of protecting average citizens from the "dreadful" motives of Jews with power. Given the Nazi worldview, which inflated the power that Jews held within Germany, German leaders promulgated laws based on this skewed understanding. On April 7, 1933, the interior minister, Wilhelm Frick, issued the "Law for the Restoration of the Professional Civil Service," which had the effect of forcibly retiring "Non-Aryan" (i.e., Jewish) civil servants employed by the central government. This first major piece of antisemitic legislation introduced a self-inflicted problem that the Nazis repeatedly confronted over the course of the next twelve years: how does one define Jewishness in a society that had experienced a great deal of intermarriage, as well as other forms of assimilation, over the course of the previous century? As a result, four days later, the Interior Ministry issued a decree defining as "Non-Aryan" anyone with a single Jewish grandparent, which, of course, only perpetuated the ambiguity. The April 11 decree, however, marked the first of many attempts on the part of the leadership of the Third Reich to establish a legal definition of Jewishness based upon biologically determined principles. Although sympathetic overall to the new law, Germany's president, Paul von Hindenburg, insisted upon some exemptions. Those civil servants who had served in the trenches during the Great War, or had lost a son or father in the conflict, or had served in their position since August 1, 1914, could keep their jobs, at least for the time being. As a result, nearly half of the judges legally defined as Jews, not to mention the majority of Jewish lawyers, initially fell outside the purview of this legislation. Almost 70 percent of Jewish lawyers and 47 percent of Jewish judges and state prosecutors retained their positions because of these exemptions,[6] calling into question the Nazi belief that Jews had shirked their duty in fighting in the Great War. However, the Third Reich's attempt to isolate Jews through legislation was bolstered by the national association of lawyers' exclusion of Jews from its ranks, and many Germans avoided using a Jewish attorney. Thus, this law established an important precedent. For the near future, the best that Germany's Jewish minority could hope for was the status of second-class citizenship. Indeed, the "Law for the Restoration of the Professional Civil Service" marked the extinction of the principle of equality before the law. It also served to further the Nazis' goal of Gleichschaltung, the process of exerting control over every component of society and the economy. As Nazi leaders continued to refashion the law in service to the regime's racist goals, circumstances only worsened for the Jews.[7]

Between 1933 and 1935, the Nazis enacted multiple pieces of legislation aimed at driving a wedge between Jews and "Aryans" within the Third Reich, many professional organizations drove Jews from their ranks, and local government and community organizations took action, often before such legislation became mandatory at the national level. As you explain the following examples, have students create a chart with two columns, one that describes these restrictions and then another column where the students can consider the consequences, short and long-term. The Third Reich banned Jewish physicians from practicing at hospitals and clinics run by its National Health Insurance Organization. While Jewish doctors could still see private patients, fewer Germans were likely to utilize their services, especially once later decrees forbade all insurance payments to Jewish doctors who saw Aryan patients. In late April 1933, the state passed the Law against the Overcrowding of German Schools and Universities. This placed serious restrictions on incoming Jewish students, limiting them to 1.5 percent of the total of new students and mandated that the total number of Jewish students could not exceed 5 percent of all students. In September 1933, the Third Reich forbade Jews from owning farms or engaging in agriculture for a living and limited the participation of Jews in the cultural realm. Authorities also banned Jews from belonging to the national journalists' association and from working as newspaper editors. Sports facilities and teams systematically stripped Jews of membership, at the city, regional, and state levels.[8] A statute in May 1935 forbade Jews from joining the German military. In the summer of 1935, cities across Germany banned Jews from swimming at public pools and indoor bathing facilities. Additional local initiatives restricted the ability of Jews to buy or rent property, to attend movie theater performances, to patronize libraries, and to make use of public transportation.[9]

The most important legislation to discuss directly with students in terms of Jewish isolation, racial policy, and legally ostracizing Jews are the foundational Nuremberg Laws, both promulgated in the fall of 1935.[10] The Law for the Protection of German Blood and Honor had four elements: it forbade both marriage and sexual relations between Jews and "Aryan" Germans; it stated that Jews could not fly the German flag; and Jewish households could not employ Aryan women under the age of forty-five. Teachers can encourage class discussion by providing students with the text of this legislation, asking them what its main components are, and then walking them through the repercussions and implications of these four provisions. For example, students often want to discuss what happened to "mixed marriages," including whether they ended in divorce and what happened to the children of these marriages.[11] In addition, encourage students to think about the public display of flags and the implications of Jews being forbidden from flying the German flag. With the question of employment of German women in Jewish households, ask students why forty-five was the cut-off age, and how this links to Nazi beliefs regarding race, morality, and fears concerning degeneration.

The second major component of the Nuremberg Laws was the Reich Citizenship Law, which sought to define legally and definitively who

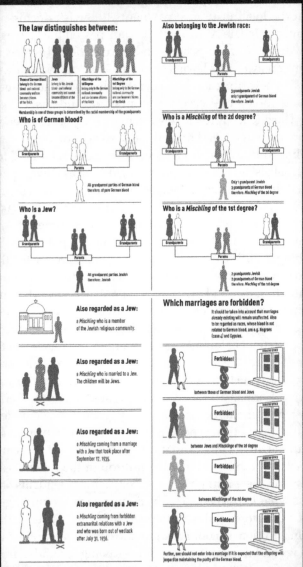

Nuremberg Racial Laws, 1935. (United States Holocaust Memorial Museum, IWitness)

was Jewish within the Third Reich, linking Jewish descent to one's grandparents. This law defined citizens as those with German or kindred blood, thereby rendering Jews subjects of the Reich, effectively stripping them of their citizenship rights and the protection of the state. See the visual explanation from the USHMM in the figure, which can help students see the full implications of this legislation. While in 1933 approximately 530,000 Germans identified themselves as Jewish, these new definitions transformed thousands of people overnight into Jews, dramatically increasing the total number as defined by this statute. It also stated that a citizen, "through his conduct, proves that he is both willing and able faithfully to serve the German people and the Reich." This last point can help students see the critical role that legislation played not only in defining who belonged to the Volksgemeinschaft but also what someone of "Aryan" heritage had to do to remain within the community's fold.

Legislation that targeted Jews economically and socially accelerated between 1936 and 1938, including the blocking of bank accounts and the registration of property, followed swiftly by the forced sales of businesses and property (Aryanization). The ability of Jews to communicate decreased, as they had to hand over their radios, telephones, and typewriters. In the latter half of 1938, the state forbade Jews to broker real estate, ended all Jewish medical practices, and stripped Jews of their ability to practice law. Jews had to hand their passports over to the state and obtain a new identification document, on which Jewish males acquired the middle name of Israel and Jewish females the middle name of Sara. At the urging of the Swiss government, new passports issued to Jews solely for emigration purposes were marked with a large red J. Students, through the close examination of the legislation and a bird's-eye view of its brutal thoroughness, can acquire a deeper understanding of how the Nazis utilized the apparatus of the state to give their antisemitic actions and beliefs legitimacy.

Legislation Targeting the Physically and Mentally Handicapped

Instructors should also introduce their students to the other categories of people whom the Nazis persecuted. The attempt to eliminate the physically and mentally handicapped was another important component of the Nazi effort to promote "racial hygiene" and provide legal underpinning to do so. It is important to set Nazi eugenics within a larger, historical framework, especially the writings of internationally known eugenicists such as Cesare Lombroso, Francis Galton, and Charles Davenport, so students understand that this effort was not an isolated movement.[12] In this case, the victims were "Aryans" who exhibited what eugenicists considered undesirable genetically determined characteristics. Consistent with the times, Nazi eugenicists' understanding of congenital disease was all-embracing, including not only such conditions as blindness, deafness, extremely low intelligence and schizophrenia, but also depression, alcoholism, and habitual criminality. According to Nazi eugenicists, the state should not permit people who exhibited such characteristics, even those of good "Aryan" stock, to pass them on to future generations. Not surprisingly, the effort to eradicate what the Nazis called "life unworthy of life," initially through the sterilization of the biologically undesirable population, was a high priority for the leaders of the Third Reich.[13]

Bolstered by the influential work of Karl Binding and Alfred Hoche entitled *Permission for the Destruction of Worthless Life, Its Extent and Form*, the Third Reich posited that the worth of its citizens should be measured by their potential contributions to the Volksgemeinschaft. The result was the "Law for the Prevention of Hereditarily Diseased Progeny," announced on July 14, 1933. Known more widely as the "Sterilization Law," this measure took effect on January 1, 1934.[14] This law had a variety of results, not the least of which was the forced sterilization of 350,000 to 400,000 people between 1934 and 1945, which was roughly 0.5 percent of the total population of the Third Reich. Nazi officials targeted people who had what they considered to be congenital diseases, including such conditions as schizophrenia, epilepsy, severe physical handicaps, and "congenital feeblemindedness." In addition, the law made it possible to compel the sterilization of those exhibiting extreme alcoholism, as well as other conditions that the regime considered "antisocial." While the law encouraged those suffering from these conditions to pursue voluntary sterilization, the vast majority did not. This was not an obstacle, however, to preventing those with hereditary disabilities from passing on their "defective" genes to future generations. Physicians, family members, administrators of health-care institutions and prisons, even—on occasion—other hospital patients, could supplant the will of the victims by appealing to "hereditary health courts," which had the power to compel the sterilization of those whom the State deemed unfit to reproduce. These courts had three members, a judge and two physicians, one of whom had to be an expert in hereditary diseases. In cases of resistance, either by the victim or his or her family, the law provided for police intervention. While some of the categories had a finite number of people to whom the Nazis could apply this law, the more flexible categories of "congenital feeblemindedness" and "severe alcoholism" allowed the Nazis great latitude in terms of whom they sterilized, including people the state labeled as "work-shy" or chronically unemployed.[15]

The Sterilization Law served as the foundation of Nazi persecution of the physically and mentally handicapped. The "Law for the Protection of the Hereditary Health of the German Nation," which went into effect in October 1935, was a natural extension of the racialist mindset behind the July 1933 measure. The terms of this new law forbade marriages if either person had a mental handicap, had one of the hereditary diseases specified in the 1933 law, or was under legal guardianship, thus limiting their ability to perpetuate their genetic deficiencies. It required submission of a Marriage Fitness Certificate in order to ensure that the hereditary health of the German Volk would not be at risk. This law, however, was difficult to enforce, and its effect was undoubtedly limited.[16]

The regime's plans for the elimination of "life unworthy of life," however, went well beyond efforts to reduce the chances of those with genetic "deformities" to pass on their traits to their children. Under the cover of World War II, promoters of "racial hygiene" launched the infamous T-4 program, which sought to murder the mentally and physically disabled. Indeed, the first people whom German authorities murdered using poison gas were handicapped, an effort that had absolutely no legal sanction. When officials at the Ministry of Justice pointed out that these killings were illegal, Nazi officials began to discuss the prospect of introducing a euthanasia law. This would have made the murders, ex post facto, legal and would pave the way for future killings. This effort, however, was ultimately rejected because of fear of taking the program public; religious institutions, especially the Roman Catholic Church, would (and did) object strongly. The abandoning of the proposed euthanasia law, however, did not stop the mass murder of between 250,000 and 300,000 handicapped people between 1939 and 1945. In the estimation of T-4 officials, the führer's order in their possession had the effect of law and made their efforts completely legal.[17]

Legislation Targeting the Romani People

When it came to the Nazi effort to persecute yet another targeted group, the Romani people, which includes the Sinti and Roma, the regime relied largely upon laws and institutions that predated the seizure of power. As early as 1899, for example, the Bavarian government created the Central Office for Gypsy Affairs to keep a close eye on these communities, which officials in Munich considered inherently "asocial," immoral, and criminal in their purpose. By the beginning of the Great War, the law required that all Romani people living in Bavaria be registered and fingerprinted by local authorities, regardless of whether they were accused of actual criminal activity; soon most other German states followed suit.[18] In spite of the persecution they suffered at the hands of the Imperial government, the number of Romani people living in Germany continued to grow, reaching a total of approximately twenty-six thousand by the time that the Nazis came to power.

During the early years of the regime, the Sinti and Roma were relatively low on the Third Reich's list of priorities, although the police continued to view their communities with suspicion. An unknown number of them fell victim to the sterilization law as a result of their "asocial" behavior.[19] Once Heinrich Himmler became chief of the German police in June 1936, however, the situation facing Germany's Romani population deteriorated.[20] Himmler, determined to impose law and order throughout the Third Reich, saw the Sinti and Roma communities as making a disproportionate contribution to criminal and asocial behavior, especially "work shyness." Indeed, in the spring of 1936, Himmler ordered the Gestapo to begin arresting the "work shy," those without permanent jobs, interning them in concentration camps such as Buchenwald and later Sachsenhausen. Although it is uncertain how many of the approximately ten thousand men arrested under this policy over the next two years were Sinti or Roma, anecdotal evidence makes it clear that this number included the Roma and Sinti disproportionately. Himmler's determination to deal with the Romani drove his decision to move the Central Office of Gypsy Affairs to Berlin in 1938.[21] In addition, the Third Reich applied the restrictions of the Reich Citizenship Law and the Law for the Protection of German Blood and Honor (1935) to the Roma and Sinti communities.[22]

As with other victims, the outbreak of war in 1939 witnessed a dramatic intensification of the persecution of the Roma and Sinti. While scholars disagree concerning how many the Nazis murdered, clearly a majority of the approximately twenty-nine thousand Roma and Sinti living in Germany and Austria at the start of the war perished at the hands of the regime. Scholars' conclusions regarding the total number of European Romani killed vary widely, with estimates running as high as 219,000, or just under one quarter of their European population.[23]

Legislation Targeting Homosexual Men

The Third Reich also targeted homosexuals, especially gay men, lumped in with other "asocial" groups such as the Roma and Sinti and the work-shy. Dating back to 1871, the German criminal code (Paragraph 175) defined sexual relations between men as a crime, saying "An unnatural act of sexual indecency committed between persons of the male sex . . . is punishable by imprisonment; a loss of civil rights may also be imposed."[24] The Weimar Republic continued to criminalize same-sex relations, but enforcement was laxer during the 1920s. Upon coming to power, the Nazis outlawed homosexual rights organizations and targeted prominent homosexuals such as the sex researcher Magnus Hirschfeld, emphasizing gay men's unwillingness to procreate and strengthen the master race. In addition, the state emphasized the supposed cowardly and "unmanly" nature of homosexual men. The public was either indifferent to the initial violence against gay bars, clubs, and individuals or supported it.[25] During the Night of the Long Knives, the SS (police force) purged the SA (Stormtroopers), targeted in part due to the open homosexuality of its leader, Ernst Röhm. Thereafter, political philosopher Carl Schmitt legitimized Hitler's actions in an article entitled "The Führer Protects the Law," in which he argued that Hitler was the "supreme judicial authority of the German Volk," and that as such, Hitler could directly create the law.[26]

In June 1935, the Nazi-controlled Reichstag enacted changes to Paragraph 175 that specified penalties for men engaging in "an indecent sexual act" with other men, thereby broadening the scope of the law beyond intercourse itself, given that prosecutors found this difficult to prove.[27] Using these broader legal definitions, the Third Reich took aggressive actions against men suspected of being homosexual by raiding gay establishments, seizing mailing lists, and encouraging denunciations. Between 1933 and 1945, the state arrested more than one hundred thousand men, accusing them of homosexual actions. Of these, it convicted fifty thousand, between five thousand and fifteen thousand of whom it incarcerated in concentration camps. Both the Federal Republic of Germany and the German Democratic Republic did not decriminalize homosexuality until the late 1960s, which made it impossible for homosexuals to seek reparations for their persecution.

The Third Reich also persecuted Jehovah Witnesses, but this oppression was rooted in their steadfast refusal to belong to the Volksgemeinschaft, rather than the racially or biologically grounded targeting of the aforementioned groups. The Third Reich began targeting Jehovah's Witnesses in 1933 and outlawed their organization in 1935 due to their beliefs and actions, especially their refusals to be citizens of any state, except Jehovah's Kingdom, and to serve in a nation's military. Jehovah's Witnesses refused to engage in politics, including voting, performing the Nazi salute or displaying the Nazi flag, and joining the NSDAP. They did not allow their children to join the Hitler Youth. Nazi persecution increased in 1935 when many Jehovah's Witnesses refused to comply with the March decree that reintroduced conscription. Of the 20,000 to 25,000 who remained in Germany during the Third Reich, approximately half served time for political crimes, and between 2,500 and 5,000 Jehovah's Witnesses died in either prisons or concentration camps.[28] Notably, unlike the other groups in this chapter, the Jehovah's Witnesses could have chosen to renounce their faith and practices to escape persecution.

Conclusion

Careful study of the ways that the Nazis manipulated the law and the German legal system teaches students much regarding the ways that the Third Reich functioned. It shows that every component of German society was to be mobilized to promote the benefit of the "Aryan" race and to tyrannize minorities characterized as "subhuman." Indeed, as the Nazi empire expanded after 1939, German leaders extended their legal doctrines to much of the rest of Europe—with dire consequences. It also demonstrates how the Nazi state utilized German respect for the law to further its own aims. Such an approach is also useful for raising questions concerning the role that the law can play in a society that seeks to persecute parts of its population. For example: Are citizens obligated to obey unjust laws? If not, what constitutes an unjust law and how should people of conscience resist it? While German leaders manipulated the law in such a way as to persecute various groups deemed undesirable, there were limits concerning how far the Nazis were willing to go. For example, while the Nuremberg Laws stripped German Jews of their citizenship, no legislation ever made it legal to kill Jews or other victim groups, and the Holocaust was technically illegal. Yet, it happened; so what does this tell us?

Closer to home, students will likely want to compare Nazi racial and eugenic laws to those of the United States from the same period. In what ways were the Third Reich's anti-Jewish laws similar to the Jim Crow laws of the United States? In what ways were they different? Similar questions can be raised concerning eugenics laws, which were a common feature of legal systems across the Western world, including the United States, in the early twentieth century. In short, a thoughtful investigation of the legal system and legislation of the Third Reich can lead to a fruitful discussion concerning the role that these play in any society—not just in the past, but also in the present and the future.

NOTES

1. Concerning the *Rechtstaat* and its shortcomings, see Ingo Müller, *Hitler's Justice: The Courts of the Third Reich*, translated by Deborah Lucas Schneider (Cambridge, MA: Harvard University Press), 3–21.

2. Concerning the Nazi approach to law, see Michael Burleigh, *The Third Reich: A New History* (New York: Hill and Wang, 2000), 158–177.

3. For the full text of this law, see "Document 30—The Enabling Act," in Benjamin C. Sax and Dieter Kuntz, eds., *Inside Hitler's Germany: A Documentary History of Life in the Third Reich* (Lexington, MA: DC Heath, 1992), 136–137.

4. The Nazis required Jews in occupied Europe to wear the badge from the outset of the war or their occupation. On all of this, see Leni Yahil, *The Holocaust: The Fate of European Jewry*, translated by Ina Friedman and Haya Galai (Oxford: Oxford University Press, 1990), 292.

5. It is important to explain to students that the term *gypsy* is pejorative. Therefore, educators should use Roma and Sinti in discussion instead. The Sinti are those who lived in Western and Central Europe, while the Roma were geographically in Eastern and Southern Europe.

6. Saul Friedländer, *Nazi Germany and the Jews*, vol. 1 (New York: Harper Perennial, 1998), 29.

7. Richard J. Evans, *The Coming of the Third Reich* (New York: Penguin, 2004), 437.

8. Saul Friedländer, *Nazi Germany and the Jews*, 30–36.

9. Saul Friedländer, *Nazi Germany and the Jews*, 139.

10. The primary source collection by Anson Rabinbach and Sander Gilman, eds., *The Third Reich Sourcebook* (Berkeley: University of California Press, 2013), provides a thorough overview of the legislation passed between 1933 and 1939 on pages 204–208. The full texts of the two Nuremberg Laws are available on pages 209–210.

11. An excellent source for personal stories of Jews in mixed marriages and how they navigated these new challenges is chapter 3 in Marion Kaplan's *Between Dignity and Despair* (New York: Oxford University Press, 1998).

12. Henry Friedlander provides an excellent overview of the links between European and American eugenicists and the growth of this movement in chapter 1 of *The Origins of Nazi Genocide: From Euthanasia to the Final Solution* (Chapel Hill: University of North Carolina Press, 1995).

13. For a useful effort to place Nazi eugenics in a broader historical context, see Burleigh, *Third Reich*, 345–353. Concerning the links between Nazi and American eugenics, see Stefan Kühl, *The Nazi Connection: Eugenics, American Racism, and German National Socialism* (Oxford: Oxford University Press, 1994).

14. Michael Burleigh and Wolfgang Wippermann, *The Racial State: Germany, 1933–1945* (Cambridge: Cambridge University Press, 1991), 48.

15. Henry Friedlander, *Origins of Nazi Genocide*, 23–30.

16. Richard J. Evans, *The Third Reich in Power* (New York: Penguin, 2005), 520–521; and Henry Friedlander, *Origins of Nazi Genocide*, 31.

17. Michael Burleigh, *Death and Deliverance: "Euthanasia" in Germany, 1900–1945* (Cambridge: Cambridge University Press, 1994), 169–171.

18. Guenter Lewy, *The Nazi Persecution of the Gypsies* (New York: Oxford University Press, 2000), 5.

19. Evans, *Third Reich in Power*, 524–525.

20. Peter Longerich, *Heinrich Himmler*, translated by Jeremy Noakes and Lesley Sharp (Oxford: Oxford University Press, 2012), 200.

21. Lewy, *Nazi Persecution of the Gypsies*, 28–30. Following the German annexation of Austria, the Nazis also targeted a third Romani group, the Lalleri.

22. Henry Friedlander, *Origins of Nazi Genocide*, 24–25.

23. Yehuda Bauer provides a detailed analysis of these estimates in his essay "Gypsies," in Yisrael Gutman and Michael Berenbaum, eds., *Anatomy of the Auschwitz Death Camp* (Bloomington: Indiana University Press, 1994), 441–455; see also Lewy, *Nazi Persecution of the Gypsies*, 221–222.

24. Rabinbach and Gilman, *Third Reich Sourcebook*, 374.

25. Doris Bergen, *War and Genocide*, 3rd ed. (Lanham, MD: Rowman and Littlefied), 33–34, 73–74.

26. Carl Schmitt, "State, Movement, Volk: The Tripartite Division of Political Unity," in Rabinbach and Gilman, *Third Reich Sourcebook*, 63–67.

27. Rabinbach and Gilman, *Third Reich Sourcebook*, 374–375.

28. Bergen, *War and Genocide*, 34–35, 115–117. See also: https://www .ushmm.org/learn/students/learning-materials-and-resources/jehovahs-wit nesses-victims-of-the-nazi-era/jehovahs-witnesses-wartime-persecution.

Jewish Responses to Nazism in Vienna after the Anschluss

ILANA F. OFFENBERGER

The new leadership of the Weimar Republic in 1933, under the rule of Adolf Hitler, selected a religious minority within Germany, stole the right of self-determination from its members, and imposed upon them a new identity that legally defined them as inferior. This act of creating a false identity and officially marking a group of individuals as such eventually charted the course to the institutionalized murder of some 6 million human beings by the Nazis and their allies.[1] This act first targeted 525,000 (0.8 percent) of the population in Germany in 1933. Through territorial annexations and war, the Nazis then removed this basic human freedom from another 185,000 (2.8 percent) in Austria; 357,000 (2.4 percent) in Czechoslovakia; 3,325,000 (10.3 percent) in Poland; 330,000 (0.9 percent) in France; 7,800 (0.2 percent) in Denmark; 1,700 (0.02 percent) in Norway; 7,800 (0.2 percent) in Sweden; 401,000 (4.9 percent) in Hungary; 757,000 (4.2 percent) in Romania; 70,000 (0.5 percent) in Yugoslavia; 49,000 (0.75 percent) in Bulgaria; 200 (0.02 percent) in Albania; 77,000 (1 percent) in Greece; 42,500 (1 percent) of Italy; and 3,020,000 (1.8 percent) in the Soviet Union.[2] The action of robbing one's identity and imposing another, which may initially appear to be a minor hate crime, was one of the first steps toward genocide. The Holocaust did not begin in Auschwitz; it ended there. The Nazi effort to usurp the individual and collective right to self-identification marked the beginning of the process of destruction.

Austrian Nazis and local residents observe Jews forced to get on their hands and knees and scrub the pavement. (USHMM, courtesy of National Archives and Records Administration, College Park, https://en.wikipedia.org/wiki/File:Austrian_Nazis_and_observers_watching_Jews_scrub_the_pavement.jpg)

Exploring Shared Concepts of Identity

James Baldwin, the great American novelist and civil rights activist, poignantly noted, "History is not the past; it is the present. We carry our history with us. We are our history."[3] What did he mean? To begin our study of how Jews in Vienna reacted to Nazism after the Anschluss, the German annexation of Austria in 1938, it is essential to unpack what it means to be Jewish, both during the Nazi period and today. Exploring various historical definitions of Judaism and Jewish identity, from both secular and religious sources, one begins to understand how complex and multifaceted this identity is. According to *The American Heritage Dictionary*, a Jew is "1. An adherent of Judaism. 2. A member of the people descended from the ancient Hebrews and marked by adherence to Judaism."[4] Yet this dictionary description is a drastic oversimplification. There are various religious denominations of Jews: Hasidic, orthodox, conservative, and reform. There are also

Jews who do not practice the religion of Judaism but who consider themselves ethnically Jewish or to be secular Jews. Being a Jew in Nazi Germany, by contrast, was radically different. The Nazi Regime used propaganda and law to officially redefine Judaism. The Nazis' twentieth-century definition of "The Jew" was based on false scientific premises; it was completely mythological yet managed to legally classify millions of people as members of an inferior race. Nazism produced a group of people within society who were not to be trusted, but feared.

The *Facing History and Ourselves* resource book asks students to consider: "What rights are most important to us today? What would it mean to lose the right to self-identification?"[5] As students begin this lesson, they are prompted to consider these questions.[6] While students attempt to identify themselves in the present tense, they organically cultivate self-awareness, self-reflection, and empathy. Choosing our own identity may seem a fundamental freedom and basic human right in the twenty-first century, but as the primary sources in this chapter reveal, throughout history *this was seldom the case*. By introducing themselves to their classmates, students become active participants in their current community and are forced to confront a civil liberty that they may take for granted: the ability to define and maintain their own identity. The Nazi German government denied millions of individuals this right. Through implementation of extensive anti-Jewish legislation, over a six-year span leading up to World War II, they defined, identified, marked, and targeted "The Jews," setting the stage for attempted permanent removal.

Lost Identity: Understanding Anti-Jewish Legislation in Nazi Germany

During the years 1933–1939, social death forcefully descended upon the Jews of Germany as Nazism began to take people's livelihoods away; more than five hundred thousand individual lives were abruptly and unjustly reorganized, regulated, and, simply put, changed. Following Hitler's rise to power in January 1933, the Nazi regime began to impose a series of anti-Jewish policies aimed to remove the Jewish minority from all aspects of German society and push them to seek life anew outside of the borders of their homeland.[7] In the ensuing years, these policies multiplied in both size and scope. By September 1935, the German government employed new official legislation to precisely define who was a Jew and then distinguish what one could and could not do (as the chapter in this volume by Russel Lemmons and Laura J. Hilton explains). The regime expected both the Jewish community and Aryans alike to adhere to these policies. The segregation of Jews from the rest of the community was of the highest priority to the Nazi Regime and was part of their plan to "protect German blood."

What could Jews do in Nazi Germany? They could remain, temporarily. However, beginning in 1933 they could not securely be a part of German society. They could not work for Germany; they could not own land or property in Germany; they could not openly practice their religious customs in Germany; they could not introduce ideas to or express ideas in Germany via written word, spoken word, or art, and they could not learn or develop new ideas in Germany. Thus, they had no future in Germany as members of this inferior race. Due to the so-called racial definition of the Nazis, they also could not choose to convert or not be a Jew; Nazism told them who they were and imposed regulations upon them from that point forward.

Beginning in 1933, almost all government employees whom the Nazis defined as non-Aryans were dismissed from their posts. For doctors, lawyers, teachers, professors, engineers, and clerks, the right to practice such professions came to an end with the intention that they never resurface. People were not only dismissed from current positions but also barred from entering new professions, signifying the Nazi intent to stop the Jewish "infiltration" of the German professions forever. Reinhard Heydrich, head of the SD (Intelligence branch of the SS), forcefully noted that Germany was a place where the older generation of Jews could die off, but where the younger Jews had no future. Just as the Nazi regime barred Jews from all public positions, private ownership of Jewish businesses would also come to an end.[8] Jewish businesses were briefly boycotted in April 1933 as an attempt to dismiss them from their work, and shortly thereafter the right to ownership of both land and property was taken away from all designated Jews.

If one could not practice his or her profession in the public sphere nor through privately owned businesses, one most certainly did not have the right to think freely and express ideas deemed unacceptable. Ideas formulated by those of Jewish descent were illegal. Jewish artwork, manuscripts, theater pieces, and musical scores were privately and publicly denounced as degenerate and prohibited. The German

Reich banned Jews from all art professions; they could not work for the radio or the theaters or produce or sell their own artwork. Indeed, Jewish ideas were seen as so dangerous that not only were the ideas themselves forbidden to be produced and or reproduced, but the idea makers needed to be imprisoned and or banished from the state. Moreover, the ideas, wherever they surfaced, needed to be extinguished. Book-burning spectacles illuminated the skies to the delight of large crowds filled with mesmerized young men and women willing to die for the Nazi cause. Still, the key groups involved with the book burnings stretched far beyond adolescent onlookers or teenage members of the Hitler Youth; adults, including members of the SA, University Chapters of the NSDAP, and the Nazi German Students' Association, led the bonfires while celebrating the elimination of "degenerate" publications from the Reich. Throughout Germany in May 1933, the printed words of Bertolt Brecht, Karl Marx, Heinrich Mann, Ernst Hemingway, Arthur Schnitzler, Franz Werfel, Stefan Zweig, Helen Keller, and countless others turned to ash.[9]

During 1933–1934, the Nazis passed some sixty-one anti-Jewish measures designed to segregate German Jews from German Aryans in order to protect "Aryan blood." These laws successfully stripped Jews of their identity and their livelihoods. Yet in September 1935, the Third Reich passed another three laws to further enforce this separation between Jews and non-Jews and to ultimately help ensure the complete destruction of German Jewry. These laws, infamously known as the Nuremberg Laws, invaded people's personal lives at yet an even deeper level than one's profession or education—the laws applied to one's personal identity, most intimate relationships, and even one's family. Suddenly, grandchildren of Jews, great-grandchildren of Jews, and even Christian decedents of Jews—who didn't know they were "Jews"—were defined as Jewish. The Nuremberg Laws defined Jews according to blood lines and introduced a new identity for those with "mixed" blood; these individuals would be called *Mischlinge*.[10] The laws tore Jews and non-Jews apart, ending friendships, preventing new friendships, outlawing binding contacts such as marriage, and terminating marriages already in place. The laws also took away German citizenship from Jews, which made life inside the Reich an impossibility, leaving them literally homeless . . . stateless . . . without a country of residence to call their own.

Responding to Lost Identity: Jewish Reactions
to Life under Nazism

How did the Jews of Germany react and respond to the
horrific years of 1933–1939 under the Nazi Regime and the ensuing
social death that engulfed their lives? When identifying, analyzing, and
attempting to understand "Jewish" responses to Nazism, one confronts
an enormous task: laying bare the responses of some hundreds of thousands of *individuals* who experienced an onslaught of terror—beginning
with the removal of their basic identity—each in their own unique way.
It is important to explore the responses of Jews to Nazism by researching them as individuals and identifying their actions, thoughts, and
words without generalizing and without perpetuating the myth that
they were one group of people with the same thoughts, beliefs, values,
and motives.

A thorough investigation of primary source material such as memoirs, diaries, testimonies, and letters (personal and bureaucratic) reveals
that Jewish responses to Nazism vary according to many factors—age,
sex, class, occupation, assets, family, education, connections, residence,
neighbors, and exact place and date within the Greater German Reich
during 1933–1938.[11] Decisions depended upon options available, and
the options varied according to all these factors and more. With this
understanding set, we can narrow our scope to a specific time and place
and begin to scrutinize individual reactions. While Marion A. Kaplan,
Jürgen Matthäus, and Mark Roseman provided educators with excellent scholarship on how Jews within Germany reacted to Nazi persecution,[12] the swift imposition of Nazi rule over Austria following the
Anschluss provides students with an important case study. Jews had to
grapple with the incredible speed and disorientation of the loss of individual and collective rights in a manner that would foreshadow the
experiences of Jews throughout Europe in the years to come. Austria's
Jewish minority totaled approximately 2 percent, more than double that
of Germany, most of whom lived in the capital of Vienna. Some 10 percent of the city's population identified themselves as members of the
Jewish community, and during the first months of the Nazi occupation—
March–November of 1938—they were forcefully and rapidly subjected
to the previous five years of anti-Jewish legislation developed and implemented in Germany proper.

Nazi Vienna 1938: Anschluss

When Germany occupied neighboring Austria in the spring of 1938, Nazi law immediately reclassified two hundred thousand persons as Jewish. Following the Nazi takeover of this country, infamously known as the *Anschluss*, these people were instantly stripped of their citizenship, isolated, expropriated, persecuted, demonized, segregated, terrorized, harassed, humiliated, marked, and left defenseless—without basic human and civil rights. Fear and trepidation set in shortly after the Austrian leader, Chancellor Schuschnigg, gave his radio farewell on the Friday afternoon of March 11, 1938.[13] Religious Jews gathered with family and prepared for the Sabbath, while non-observant Jews went about their typical weekend activities. At home, at work, or even away on vacation, Austrian Jews heard or got word of the chancellor's speech very quickly, and with this notice, their daily lives instantly changed.[14] Whether or not they understood it at the time, they were living through an extreme turning point: Nazism had taken over Austria. They were no longer free to choose their identity and be individuals. They were now a target for destruction as German Jews had been for the previous five years. "They pursue us like wild animals" (*Man hetzt uns wie die wilden Tiere*), one elderly female explained to a member of the United States consulate while describing the experiences she and her family endured after Anschluss.[15] The Nazis imposed the Nuremberg Laws right away, and public demonstrations of unrestrained violence against Jews followed at the hands of their fellow Austrians. The consequences of legalized Nazism in Austria surprised many; it unveiled a new and unanticipated level of hatred harbored by ordinary citizens, changing the social norms of a previously coexistent population. Austrian citizens unleashed such a rush of brutality against Jews that it came as a surprise to many witnesses, including members of foreign delegations. Contemporary reports including newspapers, letters, and US State Department records document the strange and barbaric acts that the Nazis and their new Austrian citizens required Jews to perform in the streets, locales, and even some of the city's most popular recreational venues. Examining these in the classroom helps students move beyond statistics and legal changes and to witness the deeply personal impact of the changes wrought by these events.

Example 1

A common way for the Nazis to dehumanize and persecute Jews directly following the March takeover was by forcing them to perform various types of forced labor. These assignments were spontaneous and applied to men and woman equally. The persecutions occurred all around the capital city at different times of the day. Members of the SA and Hitler Youth selected Jews from their homes or from the streets and assigned them to hideous cleaning details: scrubbing the sidewalks or streets, or washing the floors and toilets of the Nazi barracks. To make the work more humiliating, male victims might have their heads shaved and a black swastika painted thereon, while female victims might be told to wear their finest holiday attire before getting on their hands and knees. These forced labor details occurred in public areas to the joy of a jeering and entertained crowd.[16]

Example 2

A member of the US consulate in Vienna in 1938 noted how Jews were publicly disgraced in cafés and restaurants throughout the city. In one particular café on Favoritenstrasse, the eyewitness explained how the curtains of the establishment were all drawn back so a gathering crowd outside could watch the "show": Jews forced to clean the restaurant. He made note that the men in charge of this crime were a young group of Nazis, who entered the popular café and demanded that all the Jews inside move furniture, pile up the chairs, wash the floors, and clean the silver. But this was not sufficient for them. While cleaning the café, the victims were ordered to jump over the tables and chairs, do knee-bending exercises, and chant insulting and humiliating words.[17]

Example 3

In a third example, another consular witness described a much larger spectacle: several hundred uniformed Nazis invaded the most famous of Vienna's parks, the Prater Park, drove the Jews to the entrance square, and forced them—approximately seven hundred people of all ages and both sexes—to gather together and perform physically and spiritually degrading exercises. For one of these exercises, the victim was forced to lift one leg and extend it forward. Then, the Nazis would pass by and seize the extended foot, throwing the victim backward off balance onto the cobblestones. Many wound up in the hospital to be treated for head injuries.[18] The entire spectacle reminded the witness of "beaters driving rabbits through a cornfield."

In addition to these few eyewitness examples of public violence and humiliation, after the Anschluss, Austrian Jews lost their professions immediately. Hitler Youth and members of the SA helped to designate and defame Jewish-owned shops while prohibiting Aryan customers from shopping there. The NS-Vermögensverkehrstelle (Nazi Assets Transfer Agency) organized the official registration, confiscation, and transfer of all Jewish-owned businesses into Aryan hands. Important Jewish institutions such as the Israelitische Kultusgemeinde Wien (Jewish Community of Vienna) were temporarily shut down and reopened only under Nazi supervision. Influential Jewish men were selected from all over the city—in various spots at various times—taken to the police station for questioning, arrested, and deported to Dachau. They were not summoned in advance or given any time to make preparation for their departure; rather, they were apprehended by officers in plain clothing and tricked to believe they had nothing to fear. The new regime also warned all Austrian non-Jews against associating with Jews, whether it be their neighbors, friends, or loved ones. A woman who disobeyed this order and purchased an item from a Jewish store was paraded down the street wearing a sign that read: "I am an Aryan pig who buys from Jews!"[19] Through this public act of shaming, the Nazis intended to transcend the humiliation from one Aryan woman onto a multitude of onlookers, instill fear into that local population, and ensure the total segregation of Jews and Aryans.

The overtly sadistic environment that Nazism created in Vienna in 1938 is suggestive of how the roots of mass murder can flourish in such an atmosphere of demonization. The perpetrators and bystanders were free to treat Jews as they wished, and the victims—stripped of all aid and denied protection from the police—were defenseless against their attacks. Anti-Jewish legislation made it practically unbearable for Jews to carry on with their daily lives. Some victims of Nazism faced a temporary bout of denial, while others sought to remain calm, cooperate, and exit the country as carefully and quickly as possible. Still others fell to deep despair and panic and took their own lives. Primary documents such as testimonies, memoirs, and letters let the victims speak for themselves about how they felt when Nazism invaded their daily lives.

Response I: Denial

Perhaps one of the most common questions educators face when explaining Jewish reactions to the Nazi persecution is "why didn't they just leave?" While there is no simple answer to why and how an individual managed to flee, there are a number of factors to consider that may have either enabled or prohibited one's escape. First-hand accounts reveal that many individuals did not understand or believe the reality of the Nazi threat—before and after Anschluss; they were in complete denial. While some persons received warnings to leave Austria before the Nazi invasion, few were capable of uprooting their lives based on a morbid prophecy of impending doom. To be precise, during the years 1934–1938, only 1,739 of a total 191,458 Jews chose to emigrate from Austria.[20] A sense of disbelief applied equally to men and women; to children, adults, and the elderly.

Elderly Veterans

Jewish veterans of World War I, men who had offered their lives to serve their country, felt dually protected by their citizenship. Their spouses and children shared this sense of security. For example, when relatives phoned Karl Langer and warned him to leave Austria, he said, "'Why? I haven't done anything. I was an officer! I have medals!'" His daughter Marion recalled him as "very optimistic, thinking: 'It will pass.'"[21] Another veteran, Hugo Spitzer, told his daughter, "Don't be silly. Austria will never come under Hitler. No Austrian will ever be a Nazi!'"[22] Max Weiss recalled that his parents were *not* panicking about the situation, "primarily because Father and Grandfather had been in the Austrian army."[23] Curt Klein-Bernard shared a similar memory of his father, Bela, who served four years of the war on the Russian front: "Father was hopeful, always said it couldn't get any worse."[24] Alix Kowler nee Grabkowicz recalled how her father Dr. Joseph Grabkowicz was "an officer in the Austro-Hungarian Army . . . and a very devoted Austrian." She remembered with remorse how he didn't take the threat of Anschluss seriously enough."[25]

Adults

Did these men not know what was happening to Jews in neighboring Germany? Or were they just unable to accept that something so tragic was true? According to Valerie Abrahams, an Austrian Jew in her early twenties: "We knew what was going on there [in Germany], but we were dumbfounded. We said that could never happen in Austria! All those proud Austrians! Oh Austria, the country of love and music and fun. That could not happen to Austria!"[26] Twenty-four-year-old Raoul Klugmann concurred: "We expected it, but you always hoped . . . You don't like to divorce everything and just leave."[27] Twenty-four-year-old Erika Spitzer was even warned by gentile friends, on multiple occasions, "Get out of Austria!" They advised her to leave the country and to transfer her father's money to Switzerland immediately.[28] But she did not take action. Thus, this deep sense of disbelief was not exclusive to the older generation of war veterans; it extended to women and men who were just at the beginning of their careers and building their families. Thirty-one-year-old Alois Gottfried explained the dilemma clearly. He recalled: "The atmosphere in Vienna was gray leading up to the Anschluss. We knew Hitler wanted Austria, it was on the menu a long time before, but—the young people didn't pay attention, just like we didn't pay attention during World War I. We just went on with our lives. . . . we didn't believe it. Intellectually you knew it was wrong, but since you thought you belonged to this country, this is your home—you couldn't realize it." Alois received personal warnings to leave Austria, and he considered the threat of Nazism, but could not move himself to leave the country in which he was born until it became a matter of life or death. His younger brother Walter, who had fled to Palestine, wrote to him in early 1938 and begged him to get out of Austria; he was hesitant. Ultimately, he did not listen. Sixty years later, he reflected sadly upon his decision to stay calm despite the warnings. "We waited and waited . . . and it did happen . . . and our world broke down."[29]

Children

The sense of denial permeated yet another level and seeped into the lives of some young children. Karl Grunwald, who was ten years old at the time of Anschluss, recalled many years later: "In the enlightened world of 1938, nobody ever dreamt that such a thing would happen—it was unthinkable." Reflecting on his youth as a Jewish boy living in Vienna after Anschluss, he recalled learning about the persecution of Jews under the Russian Czars and about the pogroms in Eastern Europe in the late nineteenth century, and how he was taught that those barbaric times had passed! He reflected some fifty years later: "Nobody thought that something like this could ever happen. Even if you told them at the beginning—nobody would have believed it."[30]

Younger children, like George Wellwarth, experienced a subconscious form of denial, not understanding the significance of Anschluss at all. Instead, they found themselves swept up in the giant pageantry. "It all seemed very exciting to me," George Wellwarth recalled, six years old at the time of the takeover. George lived in the ninth district, very close to the city center where the vast majority of Nazi demonstrations took place. His Gentile nanny took him outside to view the crowd on March 12, 1938, and the image was engraved in his mind. Decades later George reflected: "The event that remains so vivid was, of course, the euphemistically named Anschluss. Naturally I had no idea what it meant at the time and was thrilled by the seemingly endless pageantry of the marchers strutting uniformly as if the little lead soldiers in my toy box at home had come to life . . . and the endless hysterical cheering as if the whole world as I knew it had become populated exclusively with people who had their mouths stuck open in a rectus of ecstasy and their right arms paralyzed at a 45-degree angle."[31]

Countless examples surface, of both men and women, young and old, who were stunned by the reality of the Nazi takeover and found themselves initially trapped in a state of denial. Using testimonies available online, through the University of Southern California, Visual History Archive, The Fortunoff Video Archive at Yale, and other reputable repositories, students can take an in-depth look at the personal histories of these individuals. They can also search through various databases that hold the names and last addresses of the thousands of individuals from Vienna who did not manage to escape from the Nazi Reich.[32] In doing so they can better assess the weight of the decisions that people were forced to make under duress in March of 1938. This is also an ample opportunity to recommend that students journal and cultivate self-reflection on difficult choices present in their current lives.

Response 2: Escape and Cooperation

Escape and cooperation surface as common ways Jews responded to life under Nazism. For those individuals caught in a state of denial, who sought to remain calm in the face of the Nazi threat, individual turning points or moments of great disaster (such as the November Pogrom of 1938 or the outbreak of World War II in September 1939) would prompt them to change their initial response and desperately seek flight. Each Jew targeted by the Nazi regime ultimately learned that their chosen identity had been seized: their only chance for survival was to escape immediately or to conform to and comply with any and all enemy demands required for emigration. For Martha Donath, the turning point came on the eve of the Anschluss, Friday night, March 11, 1938. A twenty-seven-year-old woman from an assimilated, middle-class, non-observant Jewish family, she and her husband had never spoken of leaving Austria, but all of that changed overnight. The impending Nazi invasion was the end of their settled life; they immediately began preparations to escape.[33] Charles Stein, also understood on the evening of Friday, March 11, that life as he knew it had come to an abrupt end. As a twenty-two-year-old medical student at the University of Vienna, he suddenly feared that the Gestapo might come looking for him, and he sought temporary safety on the streets—alone, out of sight, and on the run. After avoiding his home for many nights, he immediately sought help escaping the country.[34] Ilse Schueller Mintz, a thirty-year-old mother of two, had the same response to Anschluss as Martha and Charles, and she began to take action immediately. She began packing her bags as soon as she heard the chancellor's resignation speech on Friday, March 11. "We are no longer Austrians. Hitler has taken Austria," she told her children. Just two days later, on Sunday, March 13, at ten o'clock at night, Ilse, with a few members of her extended family, boarded a train to Switzerland. She left everything behind except for a few suitcases. At the train station, she said a quick goodbye to those family members who could not come along, and she never saw them again. She was one of many who chose to leave everything behind for the chance to start again and be free.

How difficult was it for Jews to leave Nazi Vienna and other cities within the Greater German Reich? What was the process like? Students often question, "If the Nazis wanted to expel the Jews from the Reich, why would they make it so difficult?" Once again the answer is not clear, but dependent upon numerous factors. The process of obtaining, signing, and filing all the papers required to emigrate was overwhelming. To emigrate legally one required most if not all of the following documents: quota numbers, affidavits, travel visas, exit visas, transit visas, security deposits, train tickets, ship tickets, medical examinations, tax clearance certificates, and emigration questionnaires. Likewise, one had to find a country that was willing to accept the Jewish refugee and apply for entrance to that country.[35] This involved waiting in terrible queues for days on end and subjecting oneself to the wrath of the Nazi mobs. Together with the help of the Jewish Community of Vienna (Israelitsche Kultusgemeinde Wien) and Foreign Aid Committees overseas (such as the American Jewish Joint Distribution Committee), enough money was eventually raised and exchanged for wealthy and poor Jews alike to exit Austria and obtain entrance to other countries around the world. Ultimately, the Nazis would set up an agency called the *Zentralstelle* (Central Office for Jewish Emigration) under the auspices of Adolf Eichmann to speed up the emigration process and ensure its efficiency. The model system was such a success in Vienna that two more were created in Berlin and Prague to further aid the process.

Efraim Hasten, a wealthy businessman in the timber industry, a husband, and father of three, faced a similar dilemma as Ilse Mintz and took a similar action. Immediately following the Anschluss, he began planning his family's escape from the country, although they did not flee until two months later. One night he came home, shut the blinds, and declared to his family: "Pack one bag, we are leaving tonight!" When his wife Betty resisted the idea, Efraim showed his determination by threatening to take the children and go without her. Later that evening the family fled south to Italy. Efraim did not have all the authorized papers for his family to exit Austria, nor did he have permanent entry visas to Italy; rather he had temporary travel visas to Palestine that proved sufficient for transit stay in Italy only. He took a serious risk of being turned back at the border with his entire family and facing imprisonment and great danger; it was the risk he chose to take. Fortuitous circumstance allowed Ephraim and his family to slip through the cracks.[36] He was one of more than 115,000 Jews who managed to flee Vienna between May 1938 and December 1939. Miraculously, over two-thirds of the total Jewish population of Austria emigrated during these first eighteen months of Nazi occupation and entered over fifty countries around the world.[37]

Response 3: Desperation/Panic/Suicide

Suicide looms large as an alternate response to life under Nazism. The act of taking one's own life by choice demonstrates to students the ferocity of the situation Jews faced, and the immense feelings of helplessness that many found simply too heavy to bear. On April 6, 1938, less than a month after the German annexation of Austria, the United States consulate in Vienna received and forwarded to the White House a letter from an anonymous victim. The consulate in Vienna translated this letter and sent it to the State Department in Washington with a number of other eyewitness reports on the situation. The report, entitled: "S.O.S. Appeal to the World" described one victim's reaction to life under Nazism in Vienna, Germany, now a city of the Greater German Reich:

> It is revolting and beneath human dignity what the S.S. people are doing with the Jews in Vienna. . . . Defenseless women have been fetched every day . . . compelled to wash the streets . . . even if it is pouring rain. The women have wounds on their hands and many have fallen ill.
>
> Jewish men have been maltreated by these gangs for several weeks . . . they must perform the most . . . dirty work ten hours a day, without getting anything to eat. If one of them faints . . . he is beaten until he gets up again . . . the exhausted and starved men were then stood against a wall and shots were fired just over their heads. . . . These people come home half crazy, physically and mentally broken and ruined for their whole life. And this happens day after day. But not only young men are fetched, even sixty to seventy year old Jews (men of high education and culture). . . . Many older Jews have suffered apoplectic strokes as a result of overexcitement. . . . Hundred[s] and thousands of suicides occur which are not published in the papers.
>
> I could fill many pages, but I have not the strength. Sleeplessness and excitement have ruined my nerves. You will certainly understand that I cannot give you my name, but I swear to you that everything I write is true. When one of these tormented people complains to the police . . . the people merely shrug their shoulders and say . . . "we

cannot do anything." Please help us. The only help which we can expect is from abroad. Give ear to the cry for help of the hundreds of thousands of honest Jews whose only fault is that they are Jews.

[Signed] One of the unhappy people who went through it personally.[38]

The atmosphere in the spring of 1938 as described by the anonymous victim above was enough to drive an unprecedented number of Viennese Jews at an abnormally fast pace to end their lives by suicide.[39] An American journal described the situation in Vienna as "the most sickening spectacle of Nazi barbarity in one of the most highly civilized cities in the world," and prodded, "Is it any wonder that prominent men and women—including skilled doctors and writers—have killed themselves rather than endure this senseless persecution?"[40] While the new Nazi regime forbade newspapers to publish accounts of suicides, at least five hundred documented suicides occurred within the first two months of the Nazi terror.[41] Some individuals reacted with dire despair to their new circumstances and chose to end their lives before matters became any worse. Among them was Herr Bergmann, a proprietor of a large furniture store in the Praterstrasse, which had been plundered and taken over. He chose suicide not only for himself, but also for his wife, son, daughter-in-law, and grandchild.[42] In another documented case, the family was still living in its own home, still had adequate financial means, and nobody had been arrested; still the atmosphere so worked upon the father that he killed himself, his wife, and child.[43] Why suicide in the spring of 1938? According to the American consul and others in his delegation, "There has been a campaign of indignity inflicted upon the Jews,"[44] "ruthless, spirit-breaking gangster tactics calculated to bring them to terms or to commit suicide."[45] Long before the implementation of the Final Solution, prior to the establishment of the ghetto system and the deportations, at a time when emigration from the Reich was still a possibility, the desperation was so extreme that some individuals viewed death by suicide as their only possible fate.

Conclusions

For all Jews within Greater Germany in November 1938, Kristallnacht (the Night of Broken Glass) would surface as a final warning sign of the Nazis' intentions to rid its country of the Jews. On the evening of November 9-10, under the orders of high-ranking Nazi Party officials, Joseph Goebbels and Reinhard Heydrich, members of the SA and Hitler Youth unleashed a mass frenzy of destruction in cities and towns throughout Germany, Austria, and the Sudetenland. That night, as 267 Jewish prayer houses went up in flames, and more than seven thousand Jewish-owned businesses were destroyed, the general public became acutely aware that the Nazis intended to permanently extinguish all signs of Jewish life. Following the public display of un-restricted vandalism and unrestrained violence, the SS and Gestapo arrested more than thirty thousand Jewish men for deportation to Dachau, Buchenwald, or Sachsenhausen. Meanwhile, the German gov-ernment imposed a one billion RM fine on the remaining Jews to pay for the damage of the pogrom that they were unbelievably held respon-sible for and seized all insurance payments. Now, all persons designated as Jews—regardless of self-identification and individuality—were will-ing to do anything and sacrifice anything for the chance of survival. This major turning point invoked a new degree of panic and increased desperation to escape. Adults were willing to immigrate to any country that would accept them and fled around the world. The parents of ten thousand Jewish children were even willing to separate their families and send their children to England in an emergency rescue effort known as the Kindertransport.[46] Whoever remained in Europe after September 1939 and the start of the world war would be subject to the Nazis' future plans of ghettoization, deportation, and ultimately annihilation.

To help students grasp an accurate understanding of Jewish re-sponses to Nazism in Germany during the years 1933–1938, it is essen-tial that classes begin by investigating the experiences of individuals, in different locations, at specific points after Hitler's rise to power and to carefully scrutinize their various trajectories. Then too, we can return to these individuals the basic human freedom that was taken from them: their identity. By making connections to our own identity through this study, and examining our own actions or inactions to hatred in the twenty-first century, we can also highlight the importance of choosing to participate before it's too late.

NOTES

1. For more on the figure of 6 million, see Father Patrick Desbois, *The Holo-caust by Bullets* (New York: St. Martin's Griffin, 2009). For more figures, see Raul

Hilberg, *The Destruction of the European Jews* (New Haven: Yale University Press, 2003).

2. See resource book, *Echoes and Reflections*, produced through a partnership of ADL, USC Shoah Foundation, Yad Vashem. Available online: https://echoesandreflections.org/unit-2-antisemitism.

3. For more on James Baldwin, see James Baldwin Project, http://www.jamesbaldwinproject.org/; Poetry Foundation: James Baldwin, https://www.poetryfoundation.org/poets/james-baldwin.

4. *American Heritage Dictionary*, 4th ed. (2001), 458.

5. See Margot Stern Strom, *Facing History and Ourselves: Resource Book* (Brookline, MA: Facing History and Ourselves National Foundation, 2017) 202. Also available online: https://www.facinghistory.org/for-educators/educator -resources/publications.

6. See also George Ella Lyon's poem "Where I'm From." Available online: http://www.georgeellalyon.com/where.html.

7. For more on anti-Jewish Laws, see Abraham J. Edelheit and Hershel Edelheit, "Legislation, Anti-Jewish," in *History of the Holocaust: A Handbook and Dictionary* (Boulder, CO: Westview Press, 1994), 299-331.

8. For more on Aryanization in Austria, see Tina Walzer and Stephan Templ, *Unser Wien—"Arisierung" auf österreichisch* (Berlin: Aufbau Verlag, 2001). For Germany, see Frank Bajohr, *"Aryanization" in Hamburg: The Economic Exclusion of Jews and the Confiscation of Their Property in Nazi Germany* (New York: Berghahn, 2002).

9. For more on the burning of books in Germany 1933, see "Book Burning," United States Holocaust Memorial Museum, https://encyclopedia.ushmm.org/content/en/article/book-burning.

10. For a thorough study of the impact of the Nuremberg Laws in Austria, see Evan Burr Bukey, *Jews and Intermarriage in Austria* (Cambridge: Cambridge University Press, 2015).

11. The Greater German Reich refers to the territory originally allotted to Germany in the Treaty of Versailles plus the land they then annexed (e.g., Austria in March of 1938).

12. Marion A. Kaplan, *Between Dignity and Despair: Jewish Life in Nazi Germany* (New York: Oxford University Press, 1998); and Jürgen Matthäus and Mark Roseman, *Jewish Responses to Persecution*, vol. 1, *1933-1938* (Lanham, MD: AltaMira Press, 2010).

13. Additional descriptions of the immediate post-Anschluss period can be found in Gerhard Botz and Karl R Stadler, *Wien, Vom "anschluss" Zum Krieg: Nationalsozialistische Machtübernahme U. Polit.-soziale Umgestaltung Am Beispiel D. Stadt Wien 1938/39* (Wien: Jugend & Volk, 1978). For an analysis of heightened antisemitism during this period, see Bruce Pauley, *From Prejudice to Persecution: A History of Austrian Anti-Semitism* (Chapel Hill: University of North

Carolina Press, 1992). For general descriptions, see Herbert Rozenkranz, "The Anschluss and the Tragedy of Austrian Jewry, 1938–1945," in Josef Frankel, ed., *The Jews of Austria: Essays on Their Life, History and Destruction* (London: Valentine Mitchell,1967.

14. "I can assure you that the events of March 13, '38 have changed my life forever." Letter from Alix G. Kowler to the author, August 1, 2003.

15. See NARA, US-State Dept. Records, RG 59/M1209/Reel 7, 863.4016/172, "Seizure of Jewish Property and Persecution of Jews in Austria," in dispatch No. 166, "Action Taken against Jews in Austria," Vienna, March 25, 1938, Gardner Richardson, commercial attaché, 2.

16. This is confirmed by the US consular reports and oral testimonies. Gardner Richardson, US commercial attaché and US Treasury representative Hugo Wallenfels both report suicide after Anschluss. See NARA, US-State Dept. Records, RG 59/M1209/Reel 7, 863.4016/174, Dispatch No. 202, "Situation of Jews in Austria," Vienna, April 15, 1938, 1. Also see A. Trude, "Interview by Survivors of the Shoah Visual History Foundation," West Los Angeles, January 10, 1996, Interview Code 10786, Tapes 1–3.

17. NARA, US-State Dept. Records, RG 59/M1209/Reel 7, 863.4016/177. See Enclosure No. 4 to dispatch No. 217, "Statement by Treasury Representative Wallenfells," Vienna, May 4, 1938, 1.

18. NARA, US-State Dept. Records, RG 59/M1209/Reel 7, 863.4016/177. See Report No. 217, "Intensified Persecution of the Jews in Austria," Vienna, May 4, 1938, 3.

19. *New York Times*, March 14, 1938, p. 8.

20. These figures are derived from charts and graphs printed in the following report drawn up by the Jewish Community of Vienna in 1940. See USHMM microfilm #294, CAHJP- A/W 126, *Report of the Vienna Jewish Community: A Description of the Activity of the Israelistische Kultusgemeinde Wien in the Period from May 2nd 1938–December 31st 1939*, pp.10, 18.

21. Marion Alflen, Interview Code 42176, Tapes 1–4, *Visual History Archive*, USC Shoah Foundation, 1998. Available online: vhaonline.usc.edu.

22. Erika Betts, Interview Code 20825, Tapes 1–6, *Visual History Archive*, USC Shoah Foundation, 1996.

23. Max Weiss, Interview Code 12544, Tapes 1–4, *Visual History Archive*, USC Shoah Foundation, 1996.

24. Curt Klein, Interview Code 00382, Tapes 1–6, *Visual History Archive*, USC Shoah Foundation, 1994.

25. Alix Kowler, Interview Code 34544, Tapes 1–5, *Visual History Archive*, USC Shoah Foundation, 1997.

26. Valerie Abrahams, Interview Code 08291, Tapes 1–4, *Visual History Archive*, USC Shoah Foundation, 1995.

27. Raoul Klugman, Interview Code 14413, Tapes 1–3, *Visual History Archive*, USC Shoah Foundation, 1996.

28. The Spitzer family had circles of friends in Vienna that included well-known actors and actresses; the Von Trapp Family Singers were the first people to warn them to leave Austria. The Spitzers waited too long. After Anschluss, German law marked Elsa as a Jew and Erika as a Mischlinge child. Hugo converted to Judaism to keep the family together. Erika was twenty-five when she fled to England in 1939, after incarceration at Dachau. The Nazis deported Hugo and his wife to the extermination site Minsk, Maly Trostinecs in 1942. For more see Erika Betts, Interview Code 20825, Tapes 1–6, *Visual History Archive*, USC Shoah Foundation, 1996.

29. Alois Gottfried, Interview Code 12444, Tapes 1–2, *Visual History Archive*, USC Shoah Foundation, 1996.

30. Karl Grunwald, Interview Code 27992, Tapes 1–8, *Visual History Archive*, USC Shoah Foundation, 1997.

31. See George E. Wellwarth, *Leben mit oesterreichischer Literatur: Begegnung mit aus Oesterreich stammenden amerikanishen Germanisten 1938/1988: Elf Erinnerungen* (Wien: Dokumentationsstelle fuer neue oesterreichische Literatur, 1990), 43–52. Note: this text was originally composed in English and translated into German by Gabrielle Pisarz for this 1990 collection.

32. See the following websites: *Documentation Center of the Austrian Resistance*, www.doew.at; and *A Letter to the Stars*: Archive and Online Database, www.lettertothestars.at.

33. Martha Donath, Interview Code 34975, Tapes 1–4, *Visual History Archive*, USC Shoah Foundation, 1997.

34. Charles Stein, private interview conducted by Ilana Offenberger, Washington, DC, May 2005.

35. See the examples provided by the *Americans and the Holocaust* web resources on USHMM: https://exhibitions.ushmm.org/americans-and-the-holocaust/what-did-refugees-need-to-obtain-a-us-visa-in-the-1930s.

36. Jacques Hasten, private interview conducted by Ilana Offenberger, Newton, MA, May 2004. Also see "Why Newton Man Fled Austria," *Boston Herald*, February 17, 2000, 35.

37. For more on the emigration of Austrian Jewry to points around the globe, see Ilana Offenberger, "Rescue and Destruction: Daily Life during a Mass Exodus," in *The Jews of Nazi Vienna, 1938–1945: Rescue and Destruction* (London: Palgrave Macmillan, 2017).

38. NARA, US-State Dept. Records, RG 59/M1209/Reel 7, 863.4016/174. See Enclosure No. 1 to dispatch No. 202, "Translation of Anonymous Letter Received by the Consulate General," Vienna, April 6, 1938, 1–2.

39. NARA, US-State Dept. Records, RG 59/M1209/Reel 7, 863.4016/177,

Dispatch No. 217, "Intensified Persecution of the Jews in Austria," Vienna, May 4, 1938, John C. Wiley, American General Consul, 14.

40. "The Week: Hitler v. Freud," *The New Republic*, March 30, 1938, 205.

41. This number is the author's estimation. Rosenkranz claimed that there were 311 Jewish deaths in March and 367 in April 1938, and that the majority of these deaths were by suicide, but not all. See Herbert Rosenkranz, *Verfolgung und Selbstbehauptung: Die Juden in Österreich, 1938–1945* (Wien, Munich: Herold, 1978), 485. Jonny Moser puts forward a lower figure of 482 persons. See Jonny Moser, *Demographie der jüdischen Bevölkerung Österreichs, 1938–1945* (Vienna: DÖW, 1999), 22.

42. NARA, US-State Dept. Records, RG 59/M1209/Reel 7, 863.4016/177, Dispatch No. 217, "Intensified Persecution of the Jews in Austria," Vienna, May 4, 1938, John C. Wiley, American General Consul, 2.

43. NARA, US-State Dept. Records, RG 59/M1209/Reel 7, 863.4016/172, "Seizure of Jewish Property and Persecution of Jews in Austria," in dispatch No. 166, "Action Taken against Jews in Austria," Vienna, March 25, 1938, Gardner Richardson, commercial attaché, 2.

44. See NARA, US-State Dept. Records, RG 59/M1209/Reel 7, 863.4016/172, Dispatch No. 166, "Action Taken against Jews in Austria," Vienna, March 25, 1938, John C. Wiley, American General Consul, 2.

45. NARA, US-State Dept. Records, RG 59/M1209/Reel 7, 863.4016/177. See Enclosure No. 4 to dispatch No. 217, "Statement by Treasury Representative Wallenfells," Vienna, May 4, 1938, 1.

46. For an exceptional film on the Kindertransport see *Into the Arms of Strangers: Stories of the Kindertransport* (Warner Bros., 2000).

Understanding the Holocaust in the Context of World War II

WAITMAN WADE BEORN

Regarding the conduct of troops towards the Bolshevistic system, vague ideas are still prevalent in many cases. The most essential aim of war against the Jewish Bolshevistic system is a complete destruction of their means of power and the elimination of Asiatic influence from the European culture. In this connection the troops are facing tasks that exceed the one-sided routine of soldiering. The soldier in the Eastern territories is not merely a fighter according to the rules of the art of war but also a bearer of ruthless national ideology and the avenger of bestialities which have been inflicted upon German and racially related nations.

Therefore, the soldier must have full understanding for the necessity of a severe but just revenge on sub-human Jewry.

> ORDERS FOR CONDUCT IN THE EAST,
> FIELD MARSHAL WALTER VON REICHENAU,
> OCTOBER 10, 1941

For a very long time, the history of the Holocaust remained absent from most secondary or university education. If taught, the crimes of the Nazis appeared as part of the history of the Third Reich. As Holocaust studies gained prominence in the 1970s, the field focused primarily on the Nazi persecution and murder of the Jews. However, it seemed that, for both scholars and educators, the Holocaust and World War II were detached from each other, to be written and taught about separately. World War II was a subject preoccupied with military history, which eventually incorporated issues of economy, the home front, and broader trends in the writing of social history. Work on the Holocaust primarily concerned itself with Nazi anti-Jewish policy. Little, if any, dialogue occurred between these two subjects. Only recently have scholars begun to recognize that the war, that is, Nazi military planning and outcomes, was inseparable from the Holocaust and the larger Nazi genocidal project.[1] Indeed, one of the best synthetic books on the Holocaust is entitled *War and Genocide: A Concise History of the Holocaust.* Author Doris L. Bergen begins by explicitly "situating [the Holocaust] in the context of the Second World War." She goes on to unequivocally state, "Without the war, the Holocaust would not—and could not—have happened."[2]

This, then, is our starting point for this chapter. How do we understand and teach the Holocaust in the context of the war itself? By exploring the entanglements between the war and the Nazi genocidal project, we can see a myriad of points where we can teach the Holocaust and the war *together*, rather than as separate events taking place concurrently. The demands of the war effort, the behavior of the military, and the larger course of the war itself critically impacted the course of the Holocaust. Constraints of time and space preclude an exhaustive presentation; however, this chapter provides an overview introducing the reader to the inseparability of the Holocaust and the war. For educators, this discussion highlights connections and provides examples of areas of overlap that can be introduced in the classroom.

Ideologies of War and Genocide

Field Marshal Reichenau's order at the beginning of this chapter provides a striking introduction to these connections.[3] It explicitly links antisemitism, anti-Jewish policy, and the prosecution of the war itself. Nazi ideology and its accompanying theory of warfighting are fitting places to start our discussion. We must first recognize the Eastern Front as *the* most important military space of World War II *and* the most important space for the Holocaust. The overwhelming majority of both Jewish and non-Jewish victims of the Nazis lived in the East. Almost seven million Jews lived in Eastern Europe compared to six hundred thousand in the West.[4] Put another way, more Jews lived in the Warsaw ghetto than in all of France.

For the Nazis (and many Germans before them), the East also held a special significance. They viewed it ahistorically as lost land previously settled by Germans, to be reclaimed by the Third Reich. Further, it was the source of their *Lebensraum* (living space) enabling Germany to be self-sufficient and to dominate the European continent. As such, this area held incredible spiritual but also strategic military significance with its vast agricultural and mineral resources. Hitler wrote in *Mein Kampf*, "We are ceasing the perpetual German movement toward Southern and Western Europe and leveling our gaze at the land in the East."[5] The Nazis also viewed Eastern Europe through a racist, imperialistic lens resulting in utterly ruthless treatment of Jews and non-Jews.

The single-minded Nazi fixation on the East led to an intentional characterization of the war there as a "war of annihilation." The war against the Soviet Union would be without rules, without peace treaties, and without surrenders. It was a zero-sum clash of ideology, race, and culture from which only one society would emerge victorious; the other would be utterly and irrevocably destroyed.[6] In concrete terms, this resulted in explicitly genocidal plans by the Nazis to starve thirty to forty million people in the East to feed the German home front, the German military (the *Wehrmacht*), and the remnant Slavic populations of Eastern Europe earmarked for slavery. These plans, commonly referred to as the Hunger Plan, prescribed the transfer of food from Eastern Europe first to the military, then to Germany, and finally to any remaining workers in productive regions of the Soviet Union. Civilians in cities and "non-productive" regions were to be left to starve. Already, we can see a plan to leverage genocide to support military objectives.

Nazi imperialism combined with another important ideology: Judeo-Bolshevism. In this antisemitic construct, the Jews controlled Communism (and the Soviet state), which was hated and feared by many Germans as well as military officers and servicemen. As Reichenau's statement (and many others) suggested, the war against the Soviet Union was also a war against Jews. Three infamous official orders were issued by the German Army high command prior to the invasion of the Soviet Union in 1941. These "Criminal Orders" ordered the immediate execution of all Red Army political officers upon capture and another limited the prosecution of soldiers for actions deemed criminal elsewhere. The third explicitly stated that "Bolshevism is the mortal enemy of the German people," and that "this war demands ruthless and aggressive action against Bolshevik agitators, snipers, saboteurs, and Jews and tireless elimination of any active or passive resistance."[7] These orders explicitly defined Jews as military targets to be eliminated simply based on their ethnicity. The German military added a third component to this antisemitic thinking, conflating all Jews with partisans (armed guerillas) and further stressing violent actions by the military against Jews.[8] As a result, the war in the East became literally a war on Jews, not just in the context of the Holocaust but in a military sense as well. For students, this may be a new perspective from which to view a war that many may feel they understand.

Racist worldviews, antisemitic ideologies, and an annihilationist perspective on warfare formed part of the foundation for both the Holocaust and the Nazi genocidal project. Recognizing this allows us to address the oft-asked question: Why did the Nazis expend energy and resources on the Holocaust when they were also fighting an increasingly desperate military campaign? The implication is that the Holocaust detracted from the more important war effort. However, for the Nazis, the Holocaust was *part* of that military campaign, not a separate event that was drawing resources away from some more important endeavor. This is the key point for students to understand. After all, in the ideal planned colonies in the East, there could be no Jews. The SS certainly viewed the struggle to annihilate European Jewry as their role in the military conquest of Europe. Indeed, Himmler's SS received official sanction and responsibility for the murder of European Jews via a memorandum from Göring to Heydrich in July 1941. The military arm of the SS (the *Waffen-SS*) and the Wehrmacht both became complicit in assisting the SS in this task.

The Military as Enabler of the Holocaust

German generals after the war created and perpetuated the myth of the "Clean Wehrmacht" where the German Army had remained apolitical and had simply fought a courageous and honorable conventional war against the Soviet hordes, with any "excesses" being the fault of the SS. Many students may have consumed this propagandized view as well in their own popular readings. This sanitized history led many to overlook the participation of the Wehrmacht in the Holocaust. Despite this attempt to obscure the truth, it is clear that the Wehrmacht was deeply complicit in the Holocaust, and its leadership generally approved of Hitler's anti-Jewish policy. Indeed, many generals took bribes in return for their support.[9] One of the most effective ways to reconnect the war and the Holocaust is through the behavior of the military, so often the focus of purely military histories. Rather than simply fighting a conventional war, the Wehrmacht played a pivotal role in enabling, supporting, and, ultimately, carrying out both the Holocaust and the larger Nazi genocidal project.[10]

Beginning during the Polish campaign in 1939 and peaking during Operation Barbarossa, the relationship between the SS killing squads (*Einsatzgruppen*) and the regular army was disturbingly close. By the time of the invasion of the Soviet Union in June 1941, the Wehrmacht had entered into a closely negotiated arrangement with the SS whereby they agreed to support the Einsatzgruppen in terms of logistics and transportation while recognizing that they would receive their operational orders from the Reich Security Main Office (RSHA), led by Himmler and Heydrich. A March 13, 1941, memorandum from the Military High Command (OKW) notified the Wehrmacht that the *Reichsführer-SS* (Himmler) would be "entrusted, on behalf of the Führer, with special tasks" in the East. Moreover, the military was ordered to provide close "collaboration to support the *Reichskommissar* in his political tasks."[11] The military's experience in Poland in 1939–1940 left no doubt in their minds that these "tasks" would involve the systematic mass murder of civilians. Indeed, at least one general complained about these killings carried out by the Einsatzgruppen. General Johannes Blaskowitz reported that "deviant personalities" were committing "pathological" violence. His career was swiftly ended.

As academic scholarship and public history projects such as the 1995 *Wehrmacht Exhibition* have demonstrated, the Wehrmacht not only facilitated the Nazi genocidal project but also actively participated. It witnessed these mass murders firsthand. It provided security for roundups, guarded execution sites, and on occasion dug the graves. This participation began with a particularly military task: the collection and treatment of prisoners of war. Knowing that it would capture immense numbers of Red Army soldiers (see discussion of POW camps in Geoffrey P. Megargee's chapter in this volume), the German Army specifically planned to let the majority of them die. It intentionally deprived hundreds of thousands of prisoners, deemed racially inferior, of food, medical treatment, and shelter . . . with predictable results. One army officer noted how "these cursed *Untermenschen* [subhumans] have been observed eating grass, flowers and raw potatoes. Once they can't find anything edible in the camp they turn to cannibalism."[12] Beyond this particular atrocity, the German military actively assisted in identifying Jewish prisoners and turning them over to the Einsatzgruppen for execution (or killing them themselves). At least half a million POWs were shot by the army and the Einsatzgruppen.[13] All told, 3.3 million Soviet POWs died in German custody; of those, 2 million had already died in the first eight months of the war against the Soviet Union.[14] The death toll of Soviet POWs was eight times the number of American casualties in the entire war.

In addition, the Wehrmacht directly murdered Jews in much the same fashion as the Einsatzgruppen in many documented instances. In Belarus, an army unit participated in the murder of ten thousand Jews in the town of Slonim.[15] Also in Belarus, Waffen-SS military formations led the way in the murder of Jewish women and children. In Serbia, the Wehrmacht carried out brutal reprisal operations, murdering thousands of innocent Jewish civilians.[16] The German Army instigated and assisted in the massive Babi Yar massacre of thirty-three thousand Jews in Kiev. General Kurt Eberhard suggested to Einsatzgruppen leaders that the Jews there be murdered as "retaliation" for bombs left behind by retreating Red Army soldiers.[17] Throughout the occupied Soviet Union, army units combined anti-partisan units with "Jew Hunts" in a particularly clear connection between the war and the Holocaust. Indeed, at least one army division had an agreement with the SS to murder Jews in the countryside, freeing the SS to focus on cities. In the guise of hunting much more elusive guerillas, the Wehrmacht would instead murder Jews, often reporting them as partisans. During some of these large anti-partisan military operations, the Wehrmacht went so far as to use Jewish civilians as human minesweepers, jokingly referring to them as a piece of equipment: "Minesweeper-42s." They also explicitly admitted that these individuals were Jews and celebrated that these people had been killed by mines rather than German soldiers.[18]

Beyond killings, the military involved itself in Nazi anti-Jewish policy of all kinds. In newly conquered areas, the Wehrmacht itself set up ghettos, instituted curfews, and mandated forced labor, all before

Wehrmacht Signal Company killing in Serbia. (USHMM Photo Archives #18122)

civilian Nazi administrators could arrive. The military stole Jewish property for its own use. One of the most egregious examples of this was the series of "Fur Aktions" that took place across Eastern Europe. Jews were forced to surrender fur clothing (but also ski jackets and any other warm clothing) to supply the Wehrmacht with the cold weather gear it desperately lacked for winter combat. In addition, the control exercised by Wehrmacht troops over Jewish prisoners allowed for sexual violence of all kinds, from rape to forced sex work in brothels.[19] At the individual and unit levels, the hyper-masculinity and bonds of "comradeship" in military units proved critical as factors enabling complicity in all aspects of the Holocaust, particularly in killing operations.

As mentioned, the army took full advantage of Jewish slave labor at the local level from janitors to auto mechanics. However, at a national and strategic level, the Nazi military industrial complex relied in part on both Jewish and non-Jewish slave labor in the armaments industry. The Siemens company alone exploited 45,000 foreign forced laborers, 4,600 prisoners of war, and 15,200 concentration camp prisoners, which constituted 34 percent of its entire workforce.[20] At Volkswagen's main facility, 60 percent of the work force was forced and slave labor.[21] One of the most notorious examples was the Dora-Mittelbau camp, where the *Luftwaffe* produced the V-2 rocket. Dora-Mittelbau was a subcamp of Buchenwald, and the majority of its prisoners labored in the creation of underground tunnels for protected factories. Thousands died here and in other camps, carving these tunnels out of stone, practically by hand.[22] At the Nordhausen complex, six thousand prisoners died in the first seven months of operation, mainly from the brutal construction conditions.[23] Thus, at all levels of war, from the murder of individuals on the ground to the use of concentration camp slave labor in military production, the war was inextricably connected with Nazi racial and genocidal policy. And, as a result, the military and the industries that supported it knowingly collaborated.

The Impact of the War on the Holocaust at the Macro Level

Incorporating the course of the war in teaching about the origins of the Final Solution (the physical extermination of the Jews of Europe) ties the Holocaust and World War II together for students in important ways. Military outcomes and events at the strategic and international level had critical impacts on the course of the Nazi genocidal project. Three prominent examples of this influence are the evolution of policy toward the Final Solution, the changing complicity of Hitler's allies, and the experience of Jews at the end of the war. Each of these subjects again links the conventional war against enemy combatants with the Nazi war against its racial enemies.

The decision for the Final Solution evolved over time; it was not a preconceived plan present in 1933. Instead, the Nazis explored a variety of different options in an attempt to remove Jews from Europe. All but the Final Solution were so-called territorial solutions—attempts to deport Jews. These plans anticipated large death tolls, but were not designed to murder all Jews. Those responsible took this planning very seriously. The success or failure of these plans was, however, greatly impacted by the course of the war itself. The Madagascar Plan is a good example. After the defeat of France in May 1940, Nazi Germany controlled the continent of Europe (and, at least notionally, all French possessions). One of these was the island of Madagascar off the east coast of Africa. Franz Rademacher, head of the Jewish department of the

Foreign Office, worked closely with Adolf Eichmann, the deportation expert in the Jewish Affairs section of the Reich Security Main Office (RSHA). This plan was serious: one scholar has written that "both Rademacher and Eichmann tackled the [Madagascar] plan in full earnest."[24] Indeed, even the idea of this plan brought a halt to the evacuation of Jews to occupied Poland.[25] Yet, just as a military victory had made the Madagascar plan a possibility, the course of the war soon made it impossible. When the Germans lost the Battle of Britain and were unable to control the seas, any transport of Jews by ship to Madagascar became impossible.

The next territorial solution was much less clear but anticipated a deportation of European Jews into eastern Russia, beyond the Ural Mountains. Again, the fortunes of war made this impossible as the Wehrmacht found itself in bitter combat with the Red Army far west of the Urals. Thus, at least partially as a result of the military situation, Nazi planners found themselves moving ever closer to a physical solution: the murder of European Jews. It seems that initially Hitler planned to deal with his self-imposed "Jewish Question" once Germany was victorious in the war, but he then changed his mind in favor of solving it during the war. Scholars have debated precisely when this change occurred. Some argue it took place later (end of 1941 into 1942) when a quick victory in the East seemed less and less likely in the near term. Others convincingly argue for a decision made earlier in late summer or early fall 1941, in the "euphoria of victory," when the Wehrmacht was sweeping across the East, and all indications pointed to an imminent collapse of the Soviet Union. Regardless of which interpretation one finds more credible, both are directly related to the course of the war itself. With the military situation having stymied forced emigration, the Nazis turned to a plan for mass murder. The first test victims for the poisonous gas Zyklon-B at Auschwitz were Soviet POWs in September 1941.

An even stronger argument for the importance of the war in the context of the Holocaust can be made by examining with students the behaviors of Hitler's main independent allies in the East: Bulgaria, Hungary, and Romania. Each nation was led by an authoritarian regime that was only too happy to carry out its own anti-Jewish policy, including the mass murder of Jews or handing them over to the Nazis for extermination. Romania and Hungary in particular also provided substantial numbers of troops and amounts of vital resources to the

Third Reich. However, in 1942 Romania ended deportation of Jews to Bełżec extermination center and by 1944 allowed them to emigrate to Palestine. Hungary's leader, Admiral Miklós Horthy, told Hitler in 1943, "I had done everything I could against the Jews within the limits of decency, but I can hardly murder them or do away with them in some other way."[26] While Hungary had participated in the deportation and murder of many of its Jews, it was only after the March 1944 German military occupation that the mass deportation of more than four hundred thousand of its Jews to Auschwitz began. In Bulgaria, King Boris III refused to allow Bulgarian Jews to be deported when it became clear that Germany would lose the war, though it willingly gave up newly acquired Jews in Thrace and Macedonia.[27]

What caused these changes in direction from Hitler's allies? One of the most important factors was the course of World War II. After the catastrophic defeat at Stalingrad, it became increasingly clear that Nazi Germany would not triumph. This caused Hitler's allies to begin reconsidering their alliance as well as their complicity in the Holocaust. Romania and Hungary had both suffered heavy military losses fighting alongside Hitler in the East; for example, in January 1943, the Second Hungarian Army was practically annihilated by the Soviets, losing 50 percent of its men.[28] The Allied Powers exerted both diplomatic and military pressure as well. Roosevelt demanded a "cessation of all anti-Jewish measures" in Hungary and highlighted the demand with a heavy air raid on Budapest.[29] Even Hitler's staunchest ally, Italy, dragged its feet in complying with Nazi anti-Jewish policy; the Holocaust only hit Italy with full force after the German military takeover in 1943. Thus, the outcome of the war had a very real impact on the lives and survival of Jews in these countries. The failure of the Germans made their allies less cooperative and fearful of Allied retribution (and also resulted in the Soviet conquest of these countries, ending the Nazi threat to Jews there decisively).

While the impact of the war on Hitler's allies may be seen as more positive, the effects of German military failures could also be disastrous. One of the ways in which this manifested itself was in the series of death marches that took place in Eastern Europe in 1944–1945. As the Red Army crashed through German lines, the Nazis began to order evacuations of remaining concentration camps in Eastern Europe, theoretically to maintain control of prisoners as a slave labor force and to prevent them from giving evidence of Nazi war crimes. These death marches took place in winter from places such as Auschwitz but also within Greater Germany as the Allies closed in. For example, the SS forcibly marched almost sixty thousand starved and exhausted prisoners from the Auschwitz camp system; more than fifteen thousand would die. Elsewhere in the East, the SS and police murdered survivors of camps and ghettos to prevent them falling into the hands of the Allies. These three examples show us how the larger elements of the ebb and flow of German military success directly impacted the lives and deaths of Holocaust victims.

Echoes: The Impact of the War on Memory and Scholarship

It may not seem immediately obvious that highlighting the military outcomes that led to the final disposition of Europe at the end of World War II had very real and important repercussions on how we remember, study, and *teach* the Holocaust, repercussions that continue to be felt today. The simple fact that the Soviet Union ended up occupying almost all the ground on which the Final Solution took place and also the former home of the majority of its victims was decisive in a number of ways.

One positive outcome was the establishment of the Soviet Extraordinary State Commission, which began documenting Nazi crimes, including those related to the Holocaust, as early as 1944. These reports, while not without issues, are still valuable sources. Unfortunately, until the fall of the Soviet Union, most of these records remained inaccessible to almost all Holocaust scholars. In addition, the postwar Cold War environment meant that the West was not particularly interested in Soviet suffering, even in the context of the Holocaust; the story of the experience of many Holocaust victims, therefore, remained only incompletely told. On the other hand, the Soviet Union, which was increasingly experiencing a resurgence in antisemitism, followed a "don't divide the dead" policy. This meant that the specific suffering of Jews during the Holocaust was subsumed into a larger narrative of Nazi crimes against "peace-loving Soviet citizens." The Holocaust as historical event was, therefore, minimized and hardly studied in the USSR.

In addition, the different endings of the war in the East and West had significant impacts on the "coming to terms with the past" associated with the Holocaust. In Germany, the Western Allies forced society to confront the Holocaust directly and admit its own guilt, however imperfect the process. This also applied to a lesser extent to other Western European nations that collaborated with the Nazis. Although this process is still ongoing and certainly fraught, in Eastern Europe, where the bulk of the Holocaust took place, it is almost nonexistent. The Soviet occupation of this region greatly influenced current memory struggles. Though some collaborators *were* punished by the Soviets, the majority were not, and areas under Soviet control were not subjected to the painful process of recognizing their own antisemitism and role in the Holocaust. The Soviets did not wish to highlight that their "peace-loving Soviet citizens" had collaborated with the Nazis, as such an admission would shatter the carefully cultivated image of cohesion in the USSR. The repercussions of this policy can still be seen today in the antisemitism in Eastern Europe and treatment of the Holocaust there. In particular, the incomplete coming to terms with the past can be seen in recent Polish legislation attempting to criminalize any implication that Poles collaborated with the Nazis or were complicit in victimizing Jews.

This chapter highlights the many ways in which the Holocaust and World War II must be viewed and taught in conversation with each other, not as independent events. From direct participation in the Holocaust and the Nazi genocidal project by the military itself to the impact of war and its aftermath on a national and continental scale, both the course and nature of the Holocaust cannot be disarticulated from more conventional military histories. When teaching about either the war or the Holocaust, it is important to step outside these artificial boundaries and identify the myriad points of intersection between these two topics. Put another way, the Holocaust must be taught as part of World War II, and World War II must be taught as critical to the unfolding of the Holocaust. This has a particularly contemporary relevance in that almost every genocide in history has taken place in the context of a war. By not combining these two events, we risk perpetuating the misleading idea that we can fully understand the Holocaust when it is separated from the military cataclysm in which it occurred.

NOTES

1. I define the term *Nazi genocidal project* as a much larger Nazi genocide whereas the term *Holocaust* is largely the murder of Jews by the regime.

2. Doris L. Bergen, *War and Genocide: A Concise History of the Holocaust* (Lanham, MD: Rowman & Littlefield, 2009), vii.

3. The chapter-opening epigraph can be found in Anson Rabinbach and Sander L. Gilman, eds., *The Third Reich Sourcebook* (Berkeley: University of California Press, 2013), number 361.

4. Waitman Wade Beorn, *The Holocaust in Eastern Europe: At the Epicenter of the Final Solution* (London: Bloomsbury Academic Press, 2018), 13.

5. Helmut Hieber, "Der Generalplan Ost," *Vierteljahrshefte für Zeitgeschichte* 6, no. 3 (1958): 281.

6. Compare this approach to that in Western Europe, where racial affinities were closer and colonial ambitions nonexistent.

7. "Richtlinien für das Verhalten der Truppe in Russland, 29 May 1941," Bundesarchiv. Militärarchiv (hereafter BA-MA): RH 26–252–91, 33.

8. For more, see Waitman Wade Beorn, "A Calculus of Complicity: The Wehrmacht, the Anti-Partisan War, and the Final Solution in White Russia, 1941–42," *Central European History* 44, no. 2 (2011).

9. See Norman J. W. Goda, "Black Marks: Hitler's Bribery of His Senior Officers during World War II," *Journal of Modern History* 72, no. 2 (2000).

10. Unless otherwise specified, the term *Wehrmacht* denotes the German Army.

11. "Document 447-PS: Top-Secret Directive by the High Command of the Wehrmacht (Keitel), March 13, 1941, on Special Matters in Connection with Directive No. 21, Case Barbarossa," in *Trials of the Major War Criminals before the International Military Tribunal: Documents and Other Material In Evidence, 405-PS to 1063(d)-PS*, vol. 26 (Nuremberg: US Government Printing Office, 1947), 54–55.

12. Thomas Earl Porter, "Hitler's Forgotten Genocides: The Fate of Soviet POWs," *Elon Law Review* 5, no. 2 (2013): 363.

13. Timothy Snyder, *Bloodlands: Europe between Hitler and Stalin* (New York: Basic Books, 2012), 184.

14. Alex J. Kay, "The Purpose of the Russian Campaign Is the Decimation of the Slavic Population by Thirty Million: The Radicalization of German Food Policy in Early 1941," in Alex J. Kay, Jeff Rutherford, and David Stahel, eds., *Nazi Policy on the Eastern Front, 1941: Total War, Genocide, and Radicalization* (Rochester, NY: University of Rochester Press, 2012), 196.

15. Waitman Wade Beorn, *Marching into Darkness: The Wehrmacht and the Holocaust in Belarus* (Cambridge, MA: Harvard University Press, 2014), 146. See also Waitman Wade Beorn, "Negotiating Murder: A Panzer Signal Company and the Destruction of the Jews of Peregruznoe, 1942," *Holocaust and Genocide Studies* 23, no. 2 (2009).

16. See Christopher R. Browning, "Wehrmacht Reprisal Policy and the

Murder of the Male Jews in Serbia," in *Fateful Months: Essays on the Emergence of the Final Solution* (New York: Holmes & Meier, 1991).

17. Geoffrey P. Megargee, *War of Annihilation: Combat and Genocide on the Eastern Front, 1941* (Lanham, MD: Rowman & Littlefield, 2006), 95.

18. "Befehl Nr. 1 für Unternehmen 'Dreieck,' 11 September 1942," BA-MA: RH 23–25; "Gefechtsbericht über Unternehmen 'Dreieck' und 'Viereck' vom 17.9–2.10.1942, 19 October 1942," BA-MA: RH 23–25.

19. For more on this, see Waitman Wade Beorn, "Bodily Conquest: Sexual Violence in the Nazi East," in Alex J. Kay and David Stahel, eds., *Mass Violence in Nazi-Occupied Europe* (Bloomington: Indiana University Press, 2018).

20. Bärbel Schindler-Saefkow, "Siemens & Halske Im Frauenkonzentrationslager Ravensbrück," *UTOPIEkreativ* 115/116 (2000): 513.

21. Bernhard Rieger, *The People's Car: A Global History of the Volkswagen Beetle* (Cambridge, MA: Harvard University Press, 2013), 82.

22. J. Adam Tooze, *The Wages of Destruction: The Making and Breaking of the Nazi Economy* (London: Allen Lane, 2006), 623.

23. John Cornwell, *Hitler's Scientists: Science, War, and the Devil's Pact* (New York: Penguin, 2003), 346.

24. Christopher R. Browning and Jürgen Matthäus, *The Origins of the Final Solution: The Evolution of Nazi Jewish Policy, September 1939–March 1942* (Lincoln: University of Nebraska Press, 2004), 195.

25. Browning and Matthäus, *Origins of the Final Solution*, 163.

26. Attila Pok, "German-Hungarian Relations, 1941–1945," in Jonathan R. Adelman, ed., *Hitler and His Allies in World War II* (New York: Routledge, 2007), 159.

27. For more on Bulgaria, please see Frederick B. Chary, *The Bulgarian Jews and the Final Solution, 1940–1944* (Pittsburgh: University of Pittsburgh Press, 1972).

28. Pok, "German-Hungarian Relations, 1941–1945," 159.

29. Randolph L. Braham, *The Politics of Genocide the Holocaust in Hungary* (condensed ed.) (Detroit: Wayne State University Press, 2000), 161.

Tools of the State

The Universe of Nazi Camps

GEOFFREY P. MEGARGEE

Auschwitz. That one word brings forth associations. Images of Dachau, Buchenwald, and Bergen-Belsen usually follow. The camps are among the first things to come to mind when people think of Nazi Germany. At the same time, most people do not know how central they really were to the Nazi state, how common and dominating. The camps existed in seemingly incredible numbers: more than forty-four thousand of them between 1933 and 1945, of over two dozen types.[1] They were the tools that tied together and advanced all the Nazis' fundamental, overlapping goals for Germany: protecting the "Aryan" race; promoting the *Volksgemeinschaft* ("people's community"); conquering *Lebensraum* (living space); and defeating Germany's enemies, internal and external. The camps were the practical embodiment and instrument of Nazism.

Even brief descriptions of all the different types of camps, their victims, and the conditions within them would more than fill this chapter, without helping students grasp the system's workings and importance. Instead, educators are better off examining the camps' more specific, often interrelated purposes—detention, punishment, labor, racial policy, and fighting a "total war"—and how those purposes served the Nazi regime's broader objectives.[2] This approach will allow students to develop some understanding of the complexities involved, complexities that helped define the Nazi regime. It will allow them to see beyond the oversimplifications and abstractions that dominate most people's ideas about the Holocaust. Students need to know about more than Auschwitz.[3]

As you describe the camp universe, students may not see the connection to the Holocaust immediately. That apparent disconnection is unavoidable—and you can use it to your advantage. It goes, again, to the complexities inherent in the history. Your students will come to understand that there were connections between the Holocaust and each of Nazism's fundamental goals, and with the camp system's subordinate and supporting purposes. The Nazis' victims were not all Jews, and most camps did not hold Jews, but everything was linked. The persecution and murder of the Jews, in which the camps were crucial, was also part and parcel of Nazism's wider nationalistic, expansionistic, racist, genocidal project.

Detention, which involves control over people's space and time, was the most basic rationale for every kind of camp. Explain that the means of control could vary, from the fences and guard towers that form our standard image of a camp, to so-called open ghettos, where there might be a crude barrier or even just placards that threatened death to anyone caught outside the boundaries. The underlying idea remained the same, though, in all cases. Whatever the inmates' particular circumstances, they remained confined against their will and subject to the whims of whoever ran the camp: the state, an agency, a private company, and often the other prisoners.

Fundamental though it was, however, detention was never a camp's sole purpose. It made all the other purposes possible. For example, the camps for interned Western civilians, so-called enemy aliens, involved little more than detention. The prisoners were not being persecuted or forced to work; they really just had to stay put. There *was* a larger purpose, though: these camps, which all warring nations used, controlled individuals who might present a security risk.

In every other instance, detention overlapped with other major purposes. The ghettos in German-occupied Eastern Europe, for instance, were primarily holding facilities, but with some important distinctions. The Germans created them as an ad hoc measure, a way of controlling the Jewish population until a "final solution" became clear, and a means of extorting wealth in the meantime; there were no other purposes, at first. Soon, however, other objectives crept into the equation. Some authorities—especially the military, the *Wehrmacht*—wanted to put the Jews to work, so, in the ghettos themselves and in nearby "forced labor camps for Jews" (*Zwangsarbeitslager für Juden*), the Germans extracted what labor they could.[4] Other authorities, especially the

SS, wanted to see the Jews die off. They withheld food and medicine, and so the ghettos took on a genocidal purpose.

Prisoners of war (POWs) might seem like targets for simple detention, since they came into German captivity purely as a side effect of the war itself. Certainly, detention and control were important functions. The Wehrmacht had a sophisticated system (at least in principle) for processing and holding POWs. The system included mobile collection points immediately behind the front; transit camps—also mobile—farther to the rear; separate, permanent camps for officers and enlisted men (Oflags and Stalags) scattered throughout Germany and occupied Poland; and specialized camps for wounded or sick prisoners or those being exchanged. When this system worked as it was supposed to, and in accordance with international agreements to which the Germans were parties, prisoners of war fared relatively well.

As they did with the Jews in the ghettos, however, the Germans soon decided to exploit the POWs' labor. By 1944, few POWs actually lived in the Stalags. Instead, they were spread out among tens of thousands of so-called subcamps (*Nebenlager* or *Aussenlager*) or work details (*Arbeitskommandos*), which the Wehrmacht established at work sites. Moreover, for some POWs, especially Soviet soldiers, their captors' ideas about race, nationality, and politics dictated a harsher fate. The camps that held these men were places of sorting and murder: all Jews, Communists, and some men who simply looked "Asiatic" were systematically shot or sent to concentration camps and killed there. Soviet soldiers were the victims in the first tests of gas chambers at Auschwitz. The remainder were marched hundreds of miles, starved, abused, confined without shelter or medical care, and forced to work. The Germans considered them *Untermenschen* (subhumans) and so did not believe that they deserved or needed decent treatment. The death rates among the different prisoner groups reflected the different realities: 2 to 3 percent of American and British POWs died in German captivity, versus 58 percent or more of Soviet troops. All told, roughly 3.3 million Red Army prisoners died while in Wehrmacht custody.

The next major theme is labor: students should understand that this was not a secondary but a primary purpose. More than thirty-five thousand camps for foreign (non-Jewish) forced laborers existed solely to provide labor for the German war economy. They served every conceivable economic sector, from agriculture, manufacturing, and mining to retail, transportation, and even social services. Thousands of individual

97

firms had their own camps, including well-known names such as IG Farben-Bayer and Mercedes. Where the demand for labor was decentralized, as in a farming town, the labor authorities often set up so-called *Gemeinschaftslager* ("community camps") from which the workers would depart in small numbers every day, and to which they would return at night. Other kinds of sites added their prisoners' work to the mix, as well: POW camps, ghettos, and separate "forced labor camps for Jews," mentioned previously, plus concentration camps, Wehrmacht labor camps, and several smaller categories.

Forced labor fulfilled three overlapping goals for the Germans. First, of course, there was an economic benefit involved, which tied into the war. The millions of forced laborers in Germany—who constituted over 20 percent of the German labor force by autumn 1944—were helping to offset a huge labor shortage. They were filling in for the millions of men who had gone off to fight and were producing much of the weaponry, equipment, and munitions that those men needed, as well as fulfilling other roles, including building the camps themselves. The German war economy would have been significantly less productive, if not for its forced and prisoner labor.

Second, the Nazis also considered labor a tool for reform. The slogan *Arbeit Macht Frei* ("work will set you free") that appeared on the camp gates at Auschwitz and elsewhere was mostly a bit of cruel irony, but it also reflected the Nazi belief that hard labor could foster rehabilitation, by breaking the prisoners' will and making them compliant. This was the reality for some concentration camp prisoners, but even more for the inmates of "work education camps" (*Arbeitserziehungslager*) and "youth protection camps" (*Jugendschutzlager*). Both those latter kinds of camps aimed particularly to instill discipline and diligence through hard work. They targeted workers whom the authorities considered lazy, slipshod, or resistant, on the one hand, or juvenile delinquents (broadly defined), on the other.

More frequently, in some facilities, labor served a third, overlapping goal, as a means of punishment and control. Such was clearly the case in the "early camps" (the historians' term), where the Nazis confined their political enemies, mostly Communists and Socialists, from 1933 to 1935.[5] Along with more direct methods of punishment, prisoners often had to perform hard physical labor. The work itself was often meaningless: dig a hole and fill it in, for example. The only goal was to exhaust the prisoners, sometimes to the point of death. That model persisted, to a degree, in other types of facilities: the concentration camps, Wehrmacht penal facilities, "youth protection camps," and "work education camps," among others.[6] By 1937, however, the SS, which ran the concentration camps, was beginning to see the possibilities for more economically profitable labor. The advent of the war and the dawning realization that it would not end quickly made productive work an important goal in most kinds of camps. Still, punishment remained central, and within the SS concentration camp administration, for example, there was disagreement over whether punishment or labor should be paramount. The pace of work and the conditions within the camps became matters for debate between the sides, with considerations of race thrown into the mix. As far as the Jews were concerned, from 1941 on, the SS never wavered from its exterminationist end goal; no amount of economic benefit was going to do more than delay the Jews' fate.[7] On average, other concentration camp prisoners fared better, because they occupied higher positions on the Germans' scale of racial worth, and because the work was necessary, after all. That fact did not guarantee a prisoner's life, but it did usually indicate a recognition, on the camp administration's part, that some minimal level of care was necessary to obtain meaningful amounts of labor. It also gave opportunities to any prisoners with valuable skills, such as chemists or carpenters. Even a Jew stood a slightly better chance of survival if he or she had some talent that the Germans valued.

The next major purpose, punishment, was central to many parts of the camp universe. It was an additional tool for reform. It helped control the prisoners. It also helped deter those people outside the system who might be inclined to misbehave. Detention was one kind of punishment, of course: losing one's freedom is a burden in itself. Beyond that, students need to grasp that every aspect of camp life could constitute a punishment, to some degree. The quantity and quality of food, housing, and clothing, the nature and pace of work, even the duration of roll calls were all subject to manipulation, all ways to make the prisoners' lives more or less miserable. To those relatively ordinary measures, the camp authorities could and did add various kinds of physical abuse, whippings, torture, and even execution. Much of it occurred without cause or justification. Officially, the Germans regulated the type and severity of punishment, but harsh though it was, there was still leeway for a great deal of gratuitous cruelty, especially in the concentration camps, police camps, and prisons.

A section of the Bergen-Belsen concentration camp. (USHMM Photo Archives #74106)

Nazism was a hierarchical ideology that defined many categories of enemies—political, social, national, and racial—as deserving of punishment. They included the Jews, whom the Nazis considered an existential threat, a parasitic people outside of and below the normal racial classification system. They were treated more severely than almost anyone else, simply because of their racial status. Then there were the so-called career criminals, the homosexuals, Roma and Sinti, the chronically unemployed, drunks, Jehovah's Witnesses, Wehrmacht soldiers who "diminished the fighting strength" of the army, and anyone who appeared hostile to the regime, within Germany or in the occupied territories. These people, in addition to political enemies, populated the SS early concentration camps, whose primary purpose was punitive from the start, in March 1933. They occupied cells in Gestapo prisons. They filled Wehrmacht and police penal camps. Many of them were subject to "protective custody" (*Schutzhaft*), with which the authorities did not aim to protect the prisoner, but rather to protect society *from* the prisoner. This practice, which also went by the name *preventive custody*, eventually placed hundreds of thousands of people in the camps for indefinite sentences.[8] Such prisoners were also often victims of other policies that grew out of racial theory, such as medical experimentation that was painful, often fatal, and always involuntary: just another way in which the Third Reich made supposedly inferior peoples serve the interests of the "Aryan" Volksgemeinschaft.

Students should always remain aware that racial theory was central to Nazi thinking, and so it affected every kind of camp. We have already seen how different groups of POWs fared. The same pattern held true for ordinary forced laborers: those from Western European nations received much better care than the millions of Slavs whom the Germans rounded up and sent to the Reich. The distinction was especially obvious in the "care" that pregnant eastern workers received. The labor authorities sent them to special "care facilities for foreign children" (Ausländerkinderpflegestätten), where most of them were either forced to undergo abortions or had their newborns taken away; then the mothers returned to work. The Germans usually killed the children, whom they considered of low racial value. There were more than one hundred such facilities, which were usually associated with German hospitals.

Other kinds of sites served racial goals even more directly, as part of their core missions, once World War II began. There were the "Germanization" facilities, where Polish, Czech, and Russian children—some of them taken from orphanages, some simply kidnapped off the street— were evaluated for their potential racial worth. If the children qualified as "Aryans," German couples would adopt and raise them. There were the "euthanasia" centers. These places had nothing to do with euthanasia as most people understand it today: the victims, Germans with disabilities in the care of German medical personnel, had no choice in the matter. At first, they were gassed, using chemically produced carbon monoxide; later they were killed using lethal injections or starvation. In total, the program murdered between 250,000 and 300,000 people. They died because the medical authorities considered them "life unworthy of living" or "useless mouths" who were using up valuable resources. The effort to husband resources, especially food, is a connected theme: the Nazis did not want their enemies to use up anything that racially pure, genetically healthy Germans might need, especially during the war years; hence another reason for starvation or near-starvation rations in so many camps and ghettos.

In the "euthanasia" centers, the Nazis eliminated people whom they claimed were burdens on the Volksgemeinschaft.[9] Explain to students that the centers also gave the Nazis experience with gassing technology. In 1941, they began applying that technology to carry out the so-called Final Solution of the Jewish Question, in the gas vans and gas chambers of the killing centers, or extermination camps (*Vernichtungslager*). There were five of them: Auschwitz (including Birkenau), Chelmno, Sobibor, Belzec, and Treblinka.[10] These were the ultimate expression of Nazi racial theory, sites that, even more than the concentration camps, placed the Nazi regime most firmly apart from any other in history. They were facilities dedicated to the mass slaughter of people whom the Nazis believed to be racial enemies. Those camps killed about 2.7 million men, women, and children, almost all of them Jews.

Auschwitz remains the best known of the camps, in part because of its horrific nature, and in part because, ironically, more people survived it than any other extermination camp. The selections on the ramp, with which so many people are familiar, separated those who were capable of work from those who were not. Members of the former group were used within the enormous forced labor complex that surrounded the main camp or were sent on to other concentration camps, and some prisoners survived long enough to be liberated. Those incapable of work went straight to the gas chambers—as was the immediate fate of nearly all arrivals at the other four extermination centers. At Auschwitz, all the purposes for which camps existed—detention, labor, punishment, racial ordering, and military necessity—operated together in one place. Moreover, because the Germans did not manage to destroy much of the camp before the Red Army got there, evidence of the crimes still existed, which was not the case at the other extermination centers.

As the previous chapter by Waitman Wade Beorn explains, World War II's connection to the Holocaust has not received appropriate emphasis in classes on either subject. Students and the wider public often ask: Why did the Germans expend so much effort to kill the Jews, when they had a war to fight? Why tie up so many human and material resources in an enormous camp system? The short answer is that these were not diversions. First, to whatever limited and imperfect degree, most of the camps and ghettos contributed to the war effort, through production of food, arms, or other important goods. More fundamentally, however, destroying the Jews was a Nazi war aim, not a diversion or a distraction. It was a reason for the war and a part of the war. So, too, was the persecution that other victim groups suffered: the aim was to weed out those who weakened the Volksgemeinschaft and so threatened to undermine the total war that Germans believed they were fighting. The myth of the "stab in the back" that supposedly ended the Great War fed into that line of thought: under no circumstances could Jews, leftists, foreigners, or malingerers threaten the war effort again.

Students should understand that the German war was also very much about acquiring living space, Lebensraum. Hitler had long maintained that Germany needed Lebensraum in order to survive, so its acquisition became part and parcel of the larger Nazi project. Living space meant self-sufficiency over the long term, as well as the resources needed to fight the war in the shorter term. To that end, the Germans set up camps to assist in reordering the population map of Eastern Europe. Foremost among these were the *Polenlager*, the Poles' camps, most of them in Silesia, which Germany annexed after the Polish campaign. Between 1942 and 1945, a branch of the SS moved Poles out of their homes and off their land into these camps, so that ethnic Germans (*Volksdeutsche*) from outside the Reich proper could move in (ironically, many of the Volksdeutsche also stayed in camps when Polish lands could not be freed up quickly enough). The Polenlager existed longer than the Germans anticipated, because there seemed to be no place to send their inmates while the Soviet Union remained unconquered. In the meantime, the Poles in the camps suffered from the usual mix of inadequate food, poor housing, and nearly nonexistent medical care, while being forced to work; the death rate was high. If the Nazis did not have their immediate extermination in mind, they certainly did not shy away from enslavement under brutal and often fatal conditions.

Teachers will want to emphasize that the concept of *military necessity* was another important element feeding the camp system, especially for the Wehrmacht. In the USSR, the Wehrmacht threw hundreds of thousands of people, usually men of military age but also including others, into POW compounds or separate internment camps as the front moved forward in 1941. Those civilians were then subject to screening, much as the POWs were, to eliminate the Jews and the Communists. Later on, during the occupation, the Wehrmacht sent waves of civilians back to Germany, often as part of so-called anti-partisan campaigns; the idea was to deprive the partisans of civilian supporters and provide labor for war production. That process, too, required constellations of camps. Finally, as the Wehrmacht began its long retreat from the USSR, it held hundreds of thousands of civilians in camps and used them to dig defenses. This left the Germans with masses of people who were incapable of work, especially the elderly, the sick, and women with young children. At best, the Germans often deprived these people of food. In one particularly egregious case, in March 1944, the army herded more than forty thousand such civilians, including around seven thousand typhus patients, into three enclosures (*camps* is too generous a term) in a marshy forest on the front line near Ozarichi, Belorussia. The Germans then surrounded the camps with mines and pulled back, leaving the freezing, starving civilians there to hinder the Red Army's advance. More than nine thousand people died.

Educators should address how sexual relations was another area in which the army combined concern for its own with callous disregard for others. Many people have heard of the so-called comfort women whom the Japanese forced into sexual slavery, but very few know that the Germans did exactly the same thing. In an effort to control venereal disease, and in the firm belief that men needed a sexual outlet, the Wehrmacht took control of existing brothels or set up their own, where the whole process could be strictly supervised. There were several such places in every city where the Germans had troops. In Poland, women who committed offenses against the occupiers could be sent to work in brothels as punishment. Others were simply rounded up off the streets, forced by circumstances into "volunteering," or sent from concentration camps. Most of the victims never spoke of their experiences. Brothels also existed outside the Wehrmacht, in some of the larger concentration and forced labor camps, mostly for the benefit of privileged prisoners.

We have concentrated here on what we could call *persecutorial* camps, but we should note, if only briefly, that the camp universe did not end there. There was something fundamental about the idea of a camp, something that Nazis, and Germans more generally, found as an attractive means for dealing with all sorts of challenges in the early to mid-twentieth century. Naturally, there were training camps for the military, but that was just the start. There were about five thousand so-called *Kinderlandverschickungslager*, camps to get children out of cities and away from bombing raids. There were camps for Germans who worked on the Autobahn; at the height of the Great Depression, men were happy to get work, even if they had to live in barracks. The Nazi

Party sent boys to camps to toughen them up, instill national pride, and prepare them for military life. There was virtually no communal task that the Germans did not try to solve with camps, and virtually no institution that did not organize its own constellation of them.[11] If the Nazis included a healthy dose of indoctrination in the daily fare, they believed that was all to the benefit of the Volksgemeinschaft.

Teaching students about this vast and various camp universe, and the camps' roles within Nazi Germany, also teaches them about ordinary Germans' knowledge of that universe. They may not have known, indeed could not have known, about the system's full extent, or all the details of what went on within the camps. The existence of the camps, however, was undeniable. Early on, the regime had made sure that people knew about them, through radio and newspaper stories. Heinrich Himmler issued a press release in March 1933, announcing the opening of the SS concentration camp at Dachau.[12] The early camps for political prisoners, which evolved into the concentration camps, were meant to terrify and deter: they could hardly do so if their existence was a secret. Once the war began, the system expanded rapidly. Anyone who was willing to pay attention knew that prisoners were being abused and killed. The camps themselves were everywhere: by the hundreds in large cities, dozens in every sizeable town, and scattered around nearly every rural community. Even word of the extermination centers got around; by March 1942, for example, the Jewish diarist Victor Klemperer had heard of Auschwitz as "the most dreadful concentration camp . . . death within a few days."[13] Klemperer was writing from within Germany, a mere six months after the first gassing experiments at the camp, so information was obviously spreading quickly. Those most secret of camps were really a badly kept secret, and the others were no secret at all. A German had to engage in willful self-deception on a monumental scale to deny knowledge of their existence and their purposes.

The Nazis aspired to control every aspect of Germans' lives, purportedly for their own good. At the same time, anyone who was not a member of the Volksgemeinschaft was a target. Racial enemies, political enemies, social outcasts, military opponents: all faced detention, indoctrination, abuse, and even death. This was war on many levels, total war, in support of which the Germans forced millions to sacrifice their freedom and their lives. The camps were the tools the Nazis used in that effort. They were the means by which Germany supplied its armies, rebuilt its infrastructure, and grew its food. They kept soldiers and civilians from resisting the goals that the state set for them. They corralled, controlled, and eliminated the weak, the sick, the unproductive, the suspect, the hostile, the criminal, and those whom the state deemed racially inferior. All of this aimed to improve life for the Volksgemeinschaft, the so-called people's community, to allow it to conquer the land it needed to prosper and to benefit from the work of people it considered less worthy. In the end, of course, the camps achieved none of those things and in fact became the most visible reason why much of the world banded together to eliminate the Nazi state.

NOTES

1. As calculated to date by the team behind the *United States Holocaust Memorial Museum Encyclopedia of Camps and Ghettos, 1933–1945*. It is a conservative figure. It does not include, for example, tens of thousands of POW subcamps, which were too numerous and too poorly documented to include individually. The count also excludes camps below a minimum size or that existed for less than a minimum period, and it only includes camps that were persecutorial.

2. For simplicity's sake, this chapter sometimes uses the term *camp* broadly to cover all the different facilities the Germans ran, including, for example, prisons and ghettos. It is not a perfect solution, but the alternative is too cumbersome.

3. Unfortunately, chronology suffers in this approach. There was a burst of camp creation from 1933 to 1935, a short retrenchment, a slow buildup to the start of the war, and then a rapid expansion, accelerating as the war went on. The numbers and types of prisoners also changed over time. Some other worthwhile analytical themes, such as gender, must also be addressed elsewhere.

4. There were about 1,150 ghettos and roughly 1,900 forced labor camps for Jews. For an overview of the ghettos, see Christopher R. Browning, introduction to Geoffrey P. Megargee, ed., *The United States Holocaust Memorial Museum Encyclopedia of Camps and Ghettos, 1933–1945*, vol. 2, *Ghettos in German-Occupied Eastern Europe*, ed. Martin Dean (Bloomington: Indiana University Press, 2012), xxvii–xxxix.

5. *Early camps* is the historians' term for them; their contemporary designations varied. There were about 110 early camps, which eventually held tens of thousands of prisoners. See Joseph Robert White, "Introduction to the Early Camps," in Geoffrey P. Megargee, ed., *The United States Holocaust Memorial Museum Encyclopedia of Camps and Ghettos*, vol. 1, *Early Camps, Youth Camps, and Concentration Camps and Subcamps under the SS-Business Administration Main Office (WVHA)* (Bloomington: Indiana University Press, 2009), 3–16.

6. At the system's peak, there were twenty-three main concentration camps and about nine hundred subcamps. Additional information is available in volume 1 of the *Encyclopedia of Camps and Ghettos*. See also Nikolaus Wachsmann, *KL: A History of the Nazi Concentration Camps* (New York: Farrar, Straus and Giroux, 2015). The other camp categories named here will be covered in forthcoming volumes of the *Encyclopedia*.

7. On this issue, see Michael Thad Allen, *The Business of Genocide: The SS, Slave Labor, and the Concentration Camps* (Chapel Hill: University of North Carolina Press, 2002). On the wider phenomenon of forced labor, see Adam Tooze, *The Wages of Destruction: The Making and Breaking of the Nazi Economy* (London: Penguin Books, 2006), esp. chap. 16; and Ulrich Herbert, *Hitler's Foreign Workers: Enforced Foreign Labor in Germany under the Third Reich* (Cambridge: Cambridge University Press, 1997).

8. *Heinrich Himmler*, by Peter Longerich (New York: Oxford Univ. Press, 2012), contains much useful material on the Nazi police state.

9. For more on the "euthanasia" program and its connection to the Holocaust, see Gabriel Finder's chapter in this volume; Henry Friedlander, *The Origins of Nazi Genocide: From Euthanasia to the Final Solution* (Chapel Hill: University of North Carolina Press, 1995); and Michael Burleigh, *Death and Deliverance: "Euthanasia" in Germany c. 1900–1945* (Cambridge: Cambridge University Press, 1994).

10. USHMM defines *killing centers* as places whose primary and immediate purpose was to murder. Some would add Majdanek to the list, but even though thousands of Jews died there, it does not quite meet the strict standard for inclusion. This is not meant to minimize the deaths that took place there or in other "death camps" and killing sites, but simply to highlight the uniquely horrible role that the extermination camps played.

11. The camp was a powerful concept in many states at the time. Camps existed for purposes that ranged from benign (Boy Scouts, Civilian Conservation Corps) to malignant (US camps for Japanese Americans, the Soviet Union's prison camps). Arguably, however, no other system was as pervasive as the Germans', and certainly none approached the Nazis' genocidal intent. For one comparison, see Kiran Klaus Patel, *Soldiers of Labor: Labor Service in Nazi Germany and New Deal America, 1933–1945* (Cambridge: Cambridge University Press, 2005).

12. See "Himmler Sets Up Dachau," http://www.camps.bbk.ac.uk/documents/003-himmler-sets-up-dachau.html.

13. Victor Klemperer, *I Will Bear Witness, 1942–1945: A Diary of the Nazi Years* (New York: Modern Library, 2001), 28. See also Nicholas Stargardt, *The German War: A Nation under Arms, 1939–1945* (New York: Basic Books, 2015).

The Decentralized System of Nazi Ghettos in Eastern Europe

MARTIN DEAN

The establishment of ghettos formed the core of Nazi anti-Jewish policy in Eastern Europe, in preparation for the Final Solution. It paved the way for the deportations to the extermination centers and the local mass shootings by concentrating the Jews and progressively weakening their ability to respond. Yet an analysis of what happened on the ground reveals that ghettoization varied enormously from one German-occupied region to another, and that most key decisions were taken at the local level. As Christopher Browning has noted, the process of creating ghettos stretched over many months, "as there was no centrally ordered, uniform policy of ghettoization."[1] There was also no central institution running the ghettos, as was the case with the concentration camps, and for this reason, until recently, nobody even knew how many ghettos there were.

This chapter examines some of the ways that our view of the ghettos has been changed by more detailed local research and how we can better understand and teach the subject, given the increased source basis now available. Previously most historians focused on the larger and more enduring ghettos, such as those in Łódź, Warsaw, Vilna, Kraków, and Minsk. Now we are aware that there were more than 1,140 ghettos run by the Germans in Eastern Europe, as well as hundreds more under Romanian and Hungarian authority. Most of these ghettos were much smaller than the prominent ones and comparatively

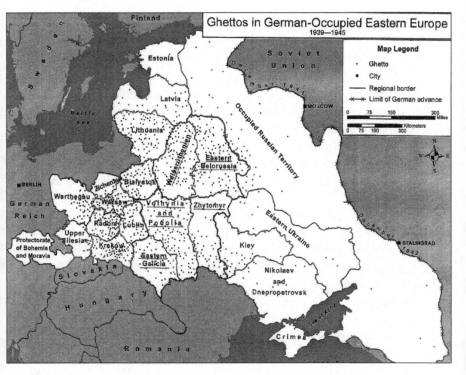

Ghettos in German-Occupied Eastern Europe, 1939–1945. (*The USHMM Encyclopedia of Camps and Ghettos, 1933–1945*, vol. 2, lii)

short-lived, existing for periods ranging from a few weeks to two years at most. In order to better grasp the functions of the ghettos and how the inmates perceived them, the diversity of experiences in these smaller ghettos needs to be incorporated into how we study and teach the Holocaust.

Ghettoization Policy

Why did the German authorities decide to establish ghettos in Eastern Europe? In internal correspondence, the German civil administration and the SS gave a variety of reasons, such as fearing the spread of disease, freeing up housing space, or controlling black-market activity, as well as isolating Jews on both ideological and security grounds. The initial rationale given by Reinhard Heydrich, head of the *Sicherheitsdienst* (SD), was "to facilitate a better possibility of control and later expulsion" of the Jews.[2] However, military priorities delayed the initial push for ghettoization in occupied Poland in 1939, and developments in the war postponed the deportation of the Jews from Poland.

The intertwined processes of isolation and exclusion began in the fall of 1939. The Germans established the first ghetto in Piotrków-Trybunalski (Distrikt Radom), ordering the Jews to move into an old and impoverished part of town, by October 31, 1939. Signs bearing the word *Ghetto* above a skull and crossbones marked the ghetto's borders, but no fence enclosed it. The Piotrków ghetto was only sealed much later, in April 1942.[3] Other ghettos soon followed in Distrikt Krakau and the Warthegau, most notably the Łódź ghetto established in spring 1940. On November 23, 1939, Hans Frank, appointed by Hitler to run the General Government (comprised of the bulk of German-occupied Poland), ordered that all Jews over the age of ten had to wear a white armband bearing a blue six-pointed star. In those parts of Poland annexed directly to Germany, the badge consisted of a yellow star worn on the front of their clothing. These distinctive markings served to further isolate and thereby "ghettoize" the Jewish population.

The process of actual ghetto establishment, however, remained sporadic and varied considerably from region to region. In Distrikt Warschau, the first ghettos were established in the *Kreise* (administrative areas) to the west of Warsaw in the late spring and summer of 1940. Then a large wave of ghettoization accompanied the establishment of the Warsaw ghetto in October and November. By the end of 1940, the Germans had established six open (or unfenced) ghettos in Kreis Grojec, in Błędów, Tarczyn, Mogielnica, Góra Kalwaria, and Warka, as well as in the Kreis center, Grójec.[4] The ghettos established to the west and south of Warsaw were short-lived as the Germans then transferred more than fifty thousand Jews from these smaller ghettos into the Warsaw ghetto by April 1941. In January 1941, the *Kreishauptmann* (senior German official) in Grójec ordered that all the Jews be concentrated in the six named ghettos and that any Jew caught outside of a ghetto after January 27, 1941, would face the death penalty.[5] This is the first example of such a shooting order for Jews who left ghettos illegally, predating a similar order for the entire General Government, dated November 1941, by some nine months.

High walls enclosed the major ghettos in Warsaw and Łódź. In Warsaw, the Jewish community had to pay for construction of the ghetto

Young Jewish men conduct a business transaction over the Warsaw Ghetto wall, undated. (USHMM Photo Archives #05923, courtesy of Jerzy Tomaszewski)

wall, and Jewish forced laborers built it. It was three meters high and eighteen kilometers (eleven miles) long. Some of the most iconic images are of smugglers scaling these high walls, conveying in a directly visible manner the sense of isolation imposed by the ghettos and the obstacles imprisoned Jewish inhabitants needed to overcome in order to survive. As a result, these images have dominated our understanding of what ghetto life was like and how we teach it, yet students should also know that hundreds of smaller ghettos remained unfenced or open, while many others were considerably more porous, simply enclosed in barbed wire. This facilitated vital economic contacts with the surrounding population, despite official German prohibitions. Yet it was the severe German regulations and the actions of the police, even more than the physical barriers, that enforced ghettoization upon the Jews.

Enduring Debates about Jewish Councils

Predating the creation of ghettos in many towns and cities was the establishment of a Jewish Council and the conscription of Jews to perform forced labor. Reinhard Heydrich had issued a general instruction to form Jewish Councils (*Judenräte*) in the fall of 1939, which German authorities applied locally. In some places, the Jews initially welcomed the participation of the Jewish Councils in labor conscription, as this put a stop to the random seizure of Jews off the streets by German patrols. However, the Jewish Councils soon became the main instrument of control applied by the Germans in the ghettos. They were responsible for implementing the various German orders, such as wearing the Star of David; and punishments for any disobedience were draconian. They also had to collect valuables for the German authorities. The Jewish Councils were assisted by a Jewish police force in implementing these tasks; in some places, Jewish policemen were armed with clubs, and other Jews resented them for enforcing German demands. There has always been much debate about the behavior of Jewish Councils and the Jewish police, which of course varied considerably from one ghetto to another.[6] When assessing their conduct, it is important to bear in mind that they also faced an almost constant threat of death themselves, and very few of their members survived.

In the small towns of Volhynia, for example, the German authorities established Jewish Councils from July 1941, before most ghettos were established. In some places, Jews organized committees themselves to meet the demands of the situation. In others, Jews were selected with input from German-appointed local mayors. The vast majority of Jews appointed to these positions of authority were men. Jewish leaders from the Polish period, including rabbis, teachers, and community activists, were among those appointed, together with some refugees from central Poland, especially lawyers. Although these groups were a minority among the councils' members, they played a leading role. In Volhynia, the Jewish Councils comprised twelve people in larger towns, but fewer elsewhere; sometimes just the head and the secretary were active. Members of Jewish Councils were punished for the community's failure to obey Nazi edicts, and a number were killed and replaced in the first months of occupation.

Descriptions from the time reveal the constant tensions between the Jewish Councils and the Jewish population. In the ghetto of Łokacze, the German *Gebietskommissar* (district commissioner) demanded a poll tax in January 1942. The Judenrat and Jewish police with fifteen Jewish muscle men broke into homes shouting: "Give us the money!" They confiscated all valuables and also some food. Everyone was very angry, but the Judenrat insisted that the money had to be turned over.[7] In Rokytne, the Judenrat imposed a religious interdiction (*cherem*) on those who did not pay their share; and in Volodymyrets, the Jewish Council received assistance from a Catholic priest to meet a large contribution.

Many Jewish Councils did their best to spread the burdens and distribute meager rations fairly. Yet labor assignments fell mainly on the poor, as in many ghettos the wealthier could buy exemptions. This enabled the councils to pay meager wages to those who worked and create a financial reserve for bribes and to meet the expected financial contributions or special taxes. Some accused the Jewish Councils of corruption and especially resented the use of force by the Jewish police. Ultimately, the behavior of Jewish leadership relied much on the individual qualities of local leaders. The strategy of bribing local officials proved ineffective in the long term as ultimately the German drive to eliminate the ghettos came from Berlin and the regional centers of German power.

Case Study: The Ghetto in Drzewica

To help students understand the complexities and conditions of ghetto life, teachers might want to focus on one representative example. Conditions in the smaller ghettos in Distrikt Radom, in the heart of the General Government, can be illustrated by the well-documented case of Drzewica. In March 1941, there were more than two thousand Jews in Drzewica, including eight hundred refugees and deportees, who had arrived from towns to the north being emptied of Jews, including Tomaszów Mazowiecki, Skierniewiece, and Płock. The Płock Jews living in Drzewica were in the worst situation; due to lack of housing, most were crammed together in the synagogue on bunk beds with straw mattresses.[8] The ghetto in Drzewica was not set up until the fall of 1941. First, in August, the Jewish Self-Help Committee reported expenses "in connection with the ghetto's establishment." Then, on October 29, 1941, the German-sponsored newspaper *Gazeta Żydowska* reported changes implemented with the "recent" establishment of the ghetto. The Jewish Council in Drzewica consisted of seven people, and there were nine members of the Jewish police. There were significant struggles between members of the Jewish Social Self-Help Committee (JSS) and Judenrat members whom they accused of corruption. Such conflicts are not uncommon in the reports of local JSS branches to their headquarters in Kraków.

From the summer of 1941, German gendarmes (rural policemen) based in the town of Nowe Miasto supervised the Jews in Drzewica. Although the ghetto was never fenced and guarded only by the Jewish police, its residents were forbidden to leave after December 1941. Not even members of Jewish institutions received the Germans' permission to leave the ghetto. Occasionally, the Nowe Miasto Gendarmerie would enter the ghetto unexpectedly and shoot people randomly. Sometimes the Germans accepted bribes for releasing those who had been caught outside the ghetto. Nevertheless, the Jews still traveled into the countryside to obtain food out of necessity. Despite the overcrowding, the Germans regularly reduced the ghetto's borders. Lajbke Kuczyński, who "strayed three meters to the toilet" into an area the Germans had excluded from the ghetto, was shot and wounded. Smuggled back into the ghetto by Polish friends, Kuczyński later died of his wounds.[9]

Death rates due to disease increased as the ghetto inhabitants became more crowded. By February 1942, more than sixty-three people had died of disease in the Drzewica ghetto. One source reported three or four deaths per day. The refugees from Płock, living in the worst conditions, were hardest hit. A Polish doctor and an elderly Jewish hospital attendant treated the sick. After a partisan unit attacked the Judenrat office in July of 1942, stealing money and cutting its telephone line, the Gestapo shot the members of the Judenrat and handed authority to the Jewish police, who had assisted the Gestapo with their investigation. At this time, a number of ghetto inmates were sent to work in the Skarżysko-Kamienna forced labor camp.[10]

On October 23, 1942, the German Gendarmerie marched all the Jews from the Drzewica ghetto to nearby Opoczno, including around five hundred Jews brought in the previous night from Klwów. They shot those who could not keep up along the way. From Opoczno, they then deported the remaining Drzewica Jews to the Treblinka extermination camp by train a few days later. Around fifty Jews worked in a remnant ghetto clearing out Jewish property in Drzewica, before being sent to the official remnant ghetto in Ujazd by December 1942. These remnant ghettos were also used to lure Jews out of hiding, so they could be killed.[11]

This overview of ghettoization in Distrikt Radom, using the example of Drzewica, confirms that Jews were often transferred or fled from one ghetto to another, such as the six thousand Jews from the Płock ghetto who were deported into various ghettos in Distrikt Radom in early 1941. The mass deportations in October 1942 also included a series of transfers from smaller to larger ghettos, to facilitate the transports by rail to killing centers. During the deportation operations, many Jews who were too old or sick to travel were not put on trains but were murdered locally. Documenting each of the ghettos individually helps us understand how the deportations in the General Government were organized and how they were connected to the establishment of extermination centers, as they were unleashed by the Security Police in a series of regional waves in the second half of 1942, emptying ghetto after ghetto until only small groups of workers remained.

Ghettos, Forced Labor Camps, and Concentration Camps

Revealing and mapping the full extent of German ghettoization has uncovered the close links between the networks of ghettos and forced labor camps for Jews. In many regions, able-bodied Jews were selected, often with the participation of the Jewish Councils, to be sent away to forced labor camps soon after the establishment of ghettos, leaving behind a population composed mainly of the elderly and women with children, who had little prospect of resisting German measures aimed at their destruction.

For example, from the fall of 1940, thousands of able-bodied Jews from the ghettos of the Warthegau were sent to a network of around 230 forced labor camps for Jews, established mainly in the vicinity of the towns of Poznań (Posen) and Inowrocław (Hohensalza). Some were also sent to road construction camps within the pre-1939 German borders, in the provinces of Brandenburg and Danzig-Westpreussen. Although conditions were very harsh in many of the camps, a few of these Jews survived, as they thereby avoided the main deportations from the Warthegau ghettos to the Chełmno extermination camp between December 1941 and August 1942. Even during the ghetto liquidation Aktions in the Warthegau, in the first half of 1942, a few Jews were selected and sent to the Łódź ghetto, which remained a site of forced labor and production until August 1944.

Similar patterns can be seen in most other regions, as the Germans established hundreds of forced labor camps for Jews to support infrastructure projects such as road and rail construction, irrigation, and bridge building. Others engaged in war-related production, such as textiles or aircraft parts, or agriculture, peat digging, quarrying, and forestry. These camps were run by a variety of German agencies, including local authorities, the *Organisation Todt* (a civil and military engineering organization named after its founder Fritz Todt), and private companies, as well as the SS. Most of these projects were not long-term, resulting in Jews being transferred frequently from one camp to another, such that some survivors passed through seven or eight camps, or more. From short survivor biographies preserved in the archives of the International Tracing Service (ITS), it is now possible to see the close links between specific ghettos and forced labor camps and how many forced labor camps ultimately fed into the camp system in 1943 and 1944. This also explains the presence of thousands of Jews in German concentration camps at the end of the war (see Avinoam Patt's chapter in this volume). Yet for most of the few Jewish survivors in occupied Eastern Europe, the first place of incarceration was a ghetto, before either starting an odyssey through various camps, or going into hiding on the "Aryan" side.

Ghettoization in Occupied Soviet Territory:
The Example of Russia

From July 1941, the Germans established around fifty ghettos on the occupied territory of the Russian Federation, which held some twenty-two thousand Jews. Most of these ghettos were located along the western fringe of Russian territory (in the former Vitebsk and Chernigov gubernias). This area had been within the Pale of Settlement up to 1917, which restricted Jews from settling further east under tsarist rule. The German Army occupied the western part of the Smolensk *oblast'* (region) in July 1941. In this region, the Germans established twenty ghettos, most within weeks of their arrival. In the western part of the Briansk oblast' (in 1939 part of Orel' oblast'), which the Germans occupied in August 1941, they established another twelve ghettos (including larger ghettos of around one thousand people or more in Klintsy, Starodub, Pochep, and Novozybkov), most in the fall of 1941. Another small cluster of ghettos existed to the north of Smolensk toward Leningrad (now St. Petersburg).

Other than for Smolensk, the process of ghettoization is documented for only a few locations, including Rudnia. Here the *Ortskommandantur* (military commandant) ordered all the Jews into a ghetto in August 1941, threatening to shoot those who did not comply. The Russian local police (*Ordnungsdienst*, or OD) used force to intimidate the Jews and confiscated property as Jews moved into the ghetto, including all livestock. Located on one street, the ghetto consisted of twenty half-destroyed houses fenced off with barbed wire and guarded by German soldiers and the OD. They assembled around twelve hundred Jews, including some refugees, on the market square and herded them into the ghetto. Initially, the Jews could still come and go freely, and some received food from non-Jewish neighbors.[12]

A variety of different types of buildings were used as ghetto sites. The typical small wooden houses common in the region were used in a number of towns. In Karachev and Krasnyi, the ghetto consisted only of an open-air holding camp with no shelter, similar to many camps for Soviet POWs. In other ghettos, such as Nevel' and Starodub, due to insufficient housing, some Jews had to sleep in dugouts or barns. In Opochka and Pochep, former barracks were used; in Zlynka, a Machine Tractor Station (MTS) became a ghetto, and in Mglin, they converted a prison into a ghetto. In several smaller ghettos (e.g., Dmitriev-L'govskii and Loknia), all the Jews were forced into a single house. The Jewish populations of these ghettos sometimes increased, due to the forced arrival of Jews from surrounding villages; this is documented, for example, in Klimovo and Monastyrshchina. The population of most ghettos was composed primarily of women, children, and the elderly, with only a few males of working age. The large ghetto in Smolensk was one of the last to be liquidated by Einsatzgruppe B in this region in July 1942. In Smolensk, a forced labor camp for Jews brought in from western Poland outlasted the ghetto and existed into 1943, but ultimately very few of these Jews survived due to the harsh conditions.[13]

Ghetto Determination and Sources

In Distrikt Lublin, the pattern of ghettoization was further complicated by successive waves of deportations and resettlements, which brought in Jews from the Polish territories incorporated into the Reich, from within the General Government, particularly from the city of Kraków, and also from Germany, Austria, the Protectorate of Bohemia and Moravia, and even Slovakia. Many of these deportees were housed together in temporary accommodations that resembled ghettos in many respects. However, close examination of the sources, especially contemporary reports of the German authorities and the Jewish Social Self-Help Committee (JSS), revealed that only a few of the destinations of these resettlements were viewed at the time as ghettos. In some places, the aim was rather to disperse the Jews, not concentrate them, and it was not uncommon for mixed patterns of residency to persist with no concentration of the native Jews within a demarcated area.

The decisive evidence of whether a ghetto existed or not was frequently found in answers to a questionnaire distributed to many local branches by the central office of the JSS in Kraków in the spring of 1942. These forms included the question, "Was there a separate Jewish residential district (*dzielnica żydowska*) in the town?" Rarely used by historians previously, these questionnaires provide contemporary evidence from the Jewish communities themselves, answering yes or no, and in some cases giving more details. The JSS reports and questionnaires provided valuable insights into conditions in the smaller ghettos, as some included population figures for locals and refugees, information about Jews performing forced labor, and details about the distribution of social welfare. Using these sources, as well as postwar testimonies from *yizkor* (memorial) books, survivor testimonies, and also a variety of postwar official investigations, scholars have determined where ghettos existed and where they were absent.[14]

A wide variety of sources are now available for reconstructing what Jews experienced in the smaller ghettos. Among the most important sources are the yizkor books, memorial books commemorating the lives and histories of Jewish communities destroyed in the Holocaust, mainly in Yiddish and Hebrew, but now increasingly also available in English translation.[15] Then there are also Soviet, Polish, and German postwar investigations, including trial records, contemporary German documentation, and also survivor testimonies in a variety of forms. The largest collection of survivor testimonies was gathered by the Shoah Foundation during the 1990s; it has been carefully indexed for references to ghettos and includes testimonies from many smaller, little-known ghettos. Another very useful collection, also due to its size and careful indexing, is composed of testimonies by the Jewish Historical Institute in Warsaw (AŻIH), which are mostly in Polish or Yiddish. Additional key resources available more recently include the thousands of interviews conducted with local inhabitants by the French charitable organization Yahad-in-Unum, increasingly available directly on the web. The use of photographs from smaller ghettos is also a very important teaching tool. Where available, these can show the porous nature of the ghetto boundaries, which permitted direct interactions with the local population, and the primitive nature of the housing conditions. For example, the Brody yizkor corroborates what we see in the photograph:

> In locations marked as the entrances to the ghetto, the authorities stuck poles and posted on them in large letters signs in Polish and Ukrainian: "Stop! This is the Ghetto Boundary!" From the Christian side of the sign, it warned that entering the ghetto was punishable by death. The warning on the Jewish side stated that leaving the ghetto was punishable by death. Despite the warnings, many people left and entered the ghetto daily.[16]

A group of Jewish women at the entrance to the Brody ghetto, 1942. (USHMM Photo Archives #23380, courtesy of Eugenia Hochberg Lanceter)

Ghettoization and Jewish Responses in Volhynia-Podolia

In September 1941, Reichskommissar of Ukraine Erich Koch ordered the establishment of ghettos in towns with a notable Jewish population, but not in places with fewer than two hundred Jews. The German administration established more than 130 ghettos in Volhynia-Podolia (south-southwest of Minsk) between August 1941 and summer 1942, in successive waves. In many cases, the Germans ordered Jews from the surrounding area brought into the ghetto as it was set up. In the town of Bar, the *Rayonchef* (county head) put up posters in mid-December, informing the Jews they had five days to move into one of three ghetto areas in Bar or to a separate ghetto in Yaltushkiv. After a first wave of ghettoization in fall 1941, a second wave took place in the spring, with ghettos established in places including Kamien-Koszyrski, Kowel, and Olyka. Finally, the Germans established improvised ghettos in Maniewicze and Powórsk just prior to mass shootings there in early September.

Ghettoization was a very traumatic event. Sudden relocation meant the loss of property, identity, and self-esteem. Jews driven into ghettos from the villages suffered especially as they lost local contacts and received the worst living quarters. Overcrowding was severe, ranging from eight to fifteen people per room. In smaller ghettos, Jews could still obtain food through barter. It was smuggled into the ghetto by those who worked outside, or by children sneaking under the ghetto fence. Jews were subjected to forced labor, with some sent out to nearby labor camps. However, beginning in late 1941, the Germans sent hundreds of Volhynian Jews to work on construction at camps in Vinnytsya and Kyiv. Almost none of these Jews survived.

The Łokacze ghetto was initially open, but the Jews had to construct a wooden fence in early 1942. Its completion was accompanied by severe penalties for leaving the ghetto. When a Jew was shot on March 16 for leaving it illegally, black-market food prices instantly soared.[17] Sometimes the Germans permitted separate areas for Jewish craftsmen alongside the ghetto, so that non-Jews could visit them for trade purposes. The craftsmen received higher rations and could demand "gifts" from local peasants in return for their work. This provided a vital source of extra supplies that could be traded within the ghetto.

The fate of the Jews in ghettos was tied to the path of the war, the German need for labor, and the desire to eliminate Jews who could not work. In some places, the Jewish population was separated into two or more ghettos, usually divided between those able to work and the others. This was in preparation for initial *Aktions* conducted in May 1942, in which those deemed unfit were killed. Such Aktions occurred in Dubno, Kołki, and Werba. By summer 1942, many Jews recognized that their fate was sealed. Jews considered escaping to the partisans but were reluctant to abandon family members. Many Jews constructed bunkers and other hiding places, mostly inside the ghettos. Others sought to hide with acquaintances outside. In late August 1942, Reichskommissar Koch informed his subordinates that all remaining Jews would be killed in the next few weeks. In September and October 1942, almost all remaining ghettos in Volhynia and Podolia were destroyed; skilled workers temporarily spared were killed shortly afterward. The German police, assisted by the local police, shot the Jews close to their hometowns in pits. This meant that the local population had few illusions about their fate. In Serniki, the Jews heard rumors of pits being prepared nearby, and 272 people fled the ghetto just before its destruction.[18] Many of the escapees were caught and killed in the ensuing manhunts. The region's last remnant ghetto or labor camp, in

Włodzimierz-Wołyński, was destroyed by the German Security Police on December 13, 1943.

In some Volhynian and Podolian ghettos, considerable efforts were made to give a proper burial to those who died, and religious and family holidays were observed, if more modestly than before. Schooling was continued in some ghettos, but these were private initiatives. Many synagogues were destroyed or converted into storage houses, and others became residences for new arrivals. Over meals, or when Jews did gather, they spoke mostly of their hopes for a change in the fortunes of war, spinning rumors around any positive news. Even in despair, many Jews demonstrated a defiant spirit. In the Łokacze ghetto, people decided to destroy remaining property, denying it to their tormentors. In Kowel, Jews held prisoner in the synagogue after the liquidation of the ghetto wrote desperate last messages on the walls before they were shot. As the last days for some ghettos coincided with the high holidays, people gathered in remaining synagogues or prayer houses to pray. Some rabbis used these final gatherings to offer words of consolation or urge their congregations to revolt or flee.

Conclusions

German authorities in Eastern Europe established ghettos beginning late in 1939 to concentrate the Jews and isolate them from the rest of the population. The initial motives included freeing up space within the town, seizing Jewish property, isolating Jews for security and health reasons, or the desire to restrict food supplies for the Jews and exploit them for forced labor. The process of ghettoization was prolonged and sporadic, dependent mostly on local factors. As the systematic deportations to the extermination centers commenced in German-occupied Poland in 1942, a last wave of ghettoization took place to assemble and control the Jews during this final phase. Nevertheless, there remained a few places where the Germans did not establish ghettos right up to the deportations in the summer and fall of 1942.

In determining the existence of a ghetto in a town, a crucial indicator was whether the German authorities ordered the Jews to move into a designated quarter, where only Jews were permitted to reside. Since the Germans established many open ghettos not enclosed by a wall or fence, the existence of such barriers could not serve as part of the definition of a ghetto. Likewise, Jewish Councils also existed in places where no ghetto was set up, so this variable could not be used as an indicator for a ghetto. Many open ghettos were marked by signs warning of severe penalties for Jews leaving without permission. Nonetheless, the absence of a barrier or effective guards often facilitated barter with the local population and smuggling, so that Jews in such ghettos could supplement their rations more easily.

It is now known that there were more than 1,140 German-run ghettos in Eastern Europe. If we are to understand the full scope of Holocaust experiences among Jews, it is vital that we examine the conditions in these smaller ghettos, which differed in important respects from the pattern of the larger ghettos such as Warsaw or Łódź. Two additional types of ghettos that are worthy of mention are the destruction ghettos, established for the purpose of facilitating the Jews' destruction within only a few weeks, and the remnant ghettos, used to hold a rump labor force after the main liquidation Aktions. In some places, the remnant ghettos were also exploited to lure Jews out of hiding. Many of the short-lived ghettos in the occupied territories of the Soviet Union can be characterized as destruction ghettos. Of the 115 ghetto sites in occupied Lithuania, for example, many served as destruction ghettos that existed for less than three months. The failure to provide adequate food or accommodation and the rapid transition to the killing phase are distinctive characteristics of these ghettos. In Distrikt Galizien, by contrast, many of the ghettos were only remnant ghettos, created at the end of the process of concentration and destruction, for those Jews selected (often with their families) to perform specific labor tasks after the main deportations and killing operations.

Throughout the ghettoization period, from late 1939 until 1943, a consistent theme is the steady concentration of the Jews from the surrounding areas into the ghettos, to establish German control over the Jews and clear them from the countryside. Ghettoization was also accompanied almost everywhere by the exploitation of Jewish labor and the extraction of wealth through confiscation, special taxes, and extortion. Ultimately, the ghettos served also to facilitate the process of deportation and murder. In some places, Jews passed through two or three separate ghettos in rapid succession on their way to the extermination camps.

Despite German efforts to conduct the deportations and mass shootings of Jews from the ghettos in a swift and concealed manner, by the summer of 1942 many Jews knew what to expect. Local peasants would come to ask Jews for their remaining property, and escapees from de-portation trains and ghetto liquidations spread news of the intensifying massacres. Younger Jews tried to flee to the partisans or organize armed resistance in the ghettos, but for the majority of ghetto inmates (women, children, and the elderly) such ideas offered no real prospect of success. It was mainly in the smaller ghettos of occupied eastern Poland that lay close to the forests that Jews organized several ghetto revolts that en-abled hundreds of Jews to flee.[19] The last resort was to hide in concealed compartments in basements or attics, trying to evade the repeated searches conducted by the Germans and local police. Thousands of Jews escaped from the ghettos at the time of their liquidation, usually assisted by several different neighbors or even strangers who offered help. Yet every encounter ran the risk of betrayal, and this constant fear could become unbearable. The pervading attitude of much of the local population was hostility, reinforced by severe German punishments for those caught helping Jews and generous rewards for those who be-trayed them.

Some escaped Jews even accepted false German promises of an amnesty and returned to the last remnant ghettos, as they despaired of being able to survive in the forests. It is notable that from some of the first ghettos to be liquidated, such as Koło in the Warthegau in Decem-ber 1941, there were almost no survivors, as these Jews did not expect they would be sent to their deaths. In addition, the longer Jews had to survive after fleeing the ghettos, the less likely they were to be success-ful. In this respect, the oft-criticized strategy of survival through labor, pursued by many Jewish Councils in the ghettos, may have enabled a few more Jews to make it through to liberation, as it shortened the period Jews had to endure in the camps or as fugitives on the "Aryan" side.

NOTES

1. Christopher R. Browning, "Before the 'Final Solution': Nazi Ghettoiza-tion Policy in Poland (1940–1941)," in *Ghettos 1939–1945: New Research and Per-spectives on Definition, Daily Life, and Survival: Symposium Presentations* (Wash-ington, DC: Center for Advanced Holocaust Studies, United States Holocaust Memorial Museum, 2005), 4.

2. National Archives and Records Administration (NARA), College Park,

MD, Nuremberg Document 3363-PS, Express Letter from Reinhard Heydrich to Heads of All the Einsatzgruppen, September 21, 1939.

3. "Piotrków-Trybunalski," in Geoffrey P. Megargee, ed., *The United States Holocaust Memorial Museum Encyclopedia of Camps and Ghettos, 1933–1945*, vol. 2, *Ghettos in German-Occupied Eastern Europe*, ed. Martin Dean (Bloomington: Indiana University Press, 2009), 279–283.

4. Archiwum Żydowskiego Instytutu Historycznego (AŻIH; Archive of the Jewish Historical Institute), 210/680 (AJDC, Tarczyn); AŻIH, 210/266 (AJDC, Błedów), 35.

5. United States Holocaust Memorial Museum Archives (USHMM), RG-15.079M, Ring I/881 [760].

6. See Shmuel Lederman, "Hannah Arendt's Critique of the Judenräte in Context: Modern Jewish Leadership and Radical Democracy," *Holocaust and Genocide Studies* 32, no. 2 (Fall 2018): 207–223.

7. Michael Diment, *The Lone Survivor: A Diary of the Lukacze Ghetto and Svyniukhy, Ukraine*, trans. Shmuel (Diment) Yahalom (New York: Holocaust Library, 1992), 65.

8. *Gazeta Żydowska*, October 29, 1941; AŻIH, 210/322 (AJDC, Drzewica), 1, 7, 15, 18, 21; AŻIH, 211/1035 (JSS, Tomaszów Mazowiecki), 25.

9. Shoah Foundation Testimony (VHA), #33497; AŻIH, 301/3132.

10. AŻIH, 301/3132; AŻIH, 211/367, 65–66.

11. For further details concerning the ghetto in Drzewica, see Jolanta Kraemer, "Drzewica," in *United States Holocaust Memorial Museum Encyclopedia of Camps and Ghettos*, vol. 2, 218–220.

12. Gosudarstvennyi arkhiv rossiiskoi federatsii (GARF; State Archives of the Russian Federation), Moscow, 7021-44–630, 285 and 293; testimony of Taisia Lupikovaia, in I. Tsynman, *Bab'i Iary Smolenshchiny* (Smolensk, 2001), 79; and USHMM, RG-50.378*0006, testimony of Ida Moyseyevina Brion.

13. On the forced labor camp for Jews in Smolensk, see Martin Dean, "Jews Sent into the Occupied Soviet Territories for Labour Deployment, 1942–1943," in David Stahel and Alex J. Kay, eds., *Mass Violence in Nazi-Occupied Europe: New Debates and Perspectives* (Bloomington: Indiana University Press, 2018), 47–50.

14. The contemporary ghetto questionnaires can be found in AŻIH, 211 (JSS). Polish official postwar questionnaires concerning camps and ghettos can be found in USHMM, RG-15.019M (IPN, ASG). Information about a number of ghettos on occupied Soviet territory can be found in the reports of the Soviet Extraordinary State Commission (ChGK); see USHMM, RG-22.002M (GARF, 7021). Other postwar investigations into war crimes can be found, for example, at the Bundesarchiv, Aussenstelle Ludwigsburg (BA-L) and the Polish Institute for National Memory (IPN).

15. See examples of digitized Yizkor books (New York Public Library, https://digitalcollections.nypl.org/collections/yizkor-book-collection#/?tab=navigation; and Yiddish Book Center, https://www.yiddishbookcenter.org/collections/yizkor-books) and translations on JewishGen, https://www.jewishgen.org/yizkor/translations.html.

16. *An Eternal Light: Brody in Memorium* (Tel Aviv: Organization of former residents of Brody in Israel, 1994), 163–164.

17. Diment, *Lone Survivor*, 72.

18. Meylekh Bakalchuk-Felin, *Zikhroynes fun a Yidishn partisan* (Buenos Aires, 1958), 17–19.

19. "Resistance in the Smaller Ghettos of Eastern Europe," Holocaust Encyclopedia, https://encyclopedia.ushmm.org/content/en/article/resistance-in-the-smaller-ghettos-of-eastern-europe.

Teaching
about Collaboration

A Case Study Approach

STEVEN P. REMY

Teaching the history of the Holocaust is one of the most demanding challenges I have faced in twenty years of teaching modern world and European history to American college students. The scope of the Final Solution, the determination of the perpetrators, the number of victims, and the magnitude of their suffering all demand but resist rational explanation. And while the explosion of research since 1990 has greatly expanded our knowledge of the genocide, it has also complicated our efforts to teach about its origins, execution, and aftermath.

Compounding the difficulty is the fact that most of my students know little about the subject when they enter my classrooms. While they understand, correctly, that the Nazi regime was the initiator and driving force of the genocide, knowledge of collaboration is lacking. Therefore, I emphasize that the Holocaust was a German-led pan-European assault on a vulnerable minority. It could not have taken place the way it did without the complicity of hundreds of thousands of non-Jewish Europeans. While it is true that many took enormous risks to protect Jews, Europe as a whole "did badly," as the historian and Holocaust survivor István Deák put it.[1]

The Germans found collaborators everywhere. The Vichy government in France, the Slovak Republic, the Independent State of Croatia, the Government of National Salvation in Serbia, the Italian Social Republic, and the Iron Cross in Hungary were all collaborationist regimes that participated to varying degrees in the persecution, robbery, roundup, deportation, and murder of Jews. In German-controlled Europe, civil servants, policemen, and business owners formed a kind of local infrastructure of persecution. Farmers and homemakers betrayed and robbed their neighbors. Hundreds of thousands of non-Germans also served in the Wehrmacht and Waffen-SS or in various German-controlled auxiliary units. They guarded ghettos and camps and benefited from Jewish slave labor. Thousands of others perpetrated mass killings of Jews in the Baltic States, Poland, and the USSR. Local participation was so extensive in Eastern Europe that Omer Bartov has characterized the Holocaust there as "a communal genocide."[2]

I open discussions of the subject by noting that *collaboration* and *collaborator* are historically contingent terms. *Collaboration* was first used early in the war, and for many it did not carry negative connotations. The prospect of a Europe led by Germany and mobilized against communism, Jews, and liberalism was appealing to conservative nationalists everywhere. Aggrieved ethnic groups in Eastern Europe hoped that cooperation with the Nazis would produce revisions of hated post–World War I territorial settlements. But the brutal nature of German rule and the destructiveness of the war changed the meaning of collaboration, and in the postwar period, many saw Nazi collaborators as traitors. In the war's immediate aftermath, being identified as a collaborator could get one summarily executed or subjected to ritualized public degradation.

Purges and trials of suspected collaborators followed this wave of violent score settling. But these became controversial in Western Europe—too vindictive or too lenient, depending on one's point of view. In Eastern Europe, communist regimes used them to solidify their hold on power by identifying "class enemies" as collaborators. Collaboration in the Holocaust, however, was rarely addressed anywhere.[3] Postwar governments had no desire for an extended legal reckoning with those who had facilitated the Final Solution. They required the expertise and political allegiance of former collaborators. Extensive purges, trials, and the blacklisting of businessmen, technocrats, civil servants, policemen, army officers, and others would not have been conducive to rapid recovery or political stability. In any case, most Europeans were consumed with rebuilding their disrupted lives. Few wished to be reminded that resistance was relatively rare. Fewer still wanted to remember whatever roles they had played in the persecution, robbery, and murder of millions of people. Finally, there was the Cold War, which rapidly turned former enemies into allies and vice versa.

Survivors, rescuers, and historians also played a role in suppressing the memory of collaboration. Those who managed to return to their home countries frequently found that former neighbors now occupied their homes, businesses, and farms. Yet survivors often did not want to call attention to themselves as victims, particularly as the victimizers were their fellow countrymen, now brittle and defensive, with whatever guilt they might have felt assuaged by a postwar mythology of widespread resistance. The relatively few non-Jews who rescued Jews were reluctant to talk about what they had done, especially in Eastern Europe.[4] Historians, too, remained largely silent about collaboration for decades after the war's end. Some prominent European scholars had compromised pasts, and it was understandable that their students avoided pursuing the subject. A lack of access to sources was another limitation, and an especially debilitating one when it came to Eastern Europe, where the vast majority of victims were killed.[5]

Given the contingent and contested nature of the problem, therefore, defining *collaboration* and *collaborator* is difficult. While it may seem relatively easy to label a regime and its officials as collaborationist, doing so at the level of civil society is much trickier. For ordinary Europeans, what constituted acts of collaboration? Is there a meaningful distinction to be made between active and passive collaboration? Could bystanders who were fully aware of what was going on around them be considered collaborators? What about Jews who worked in some capacity with the Nazis, most notably on the "Jewish Councils"? These were composed of leaders of local Jewish communities forced by the Germans to facilitate the mobilization of slave labor and deportations to death camps. Were they collaborators or victims? Were those Zionists who worked with Nazi officials to arrange for some Jews to emigrate to Palestine collaborators or rescuers? Or are they better understood as agents of an imperial enterprise? The closer one looks at the messy reality, the more complicated the situation appears.

Rather than attempting to come up with a one-size-fits-all definition or neat categories of collaboration, I present a framework proposed by Omer Bartov, whose research on the Holocaust focuses on Eastern Europe. Bartov argues that a fluid "triangular relationship" existed between and among Jews, Germans, and non-Jews.[6] Applying the framework does present certain pedagogical challenges. Regional variations, assessing the behavior of others in hindsight, and the delicate task of disentangling the historical record from ethno-nationalist myth-making can produce frustratingly inconclusive class discussions. And wrestling with all this complexity presents a dilemma to educators pressured to produce predetermined "learning outcomes."

A series of case studies allow students to explore how the triangular relationship played out in very different contexts. They also develop an essential tool of historical analysis: systematic comparison. Moreover, emphasizing the history of collaboration and its memory forces students to reckon with the contingent nature of all historical interpretation. What follows is an overview of how I approach three cases: France, Poland, and parts of the Arab world.

France

In June 1940, the French government capitulated to Nazi Germany. Until the fall of 1942, the Germans occupied Paris, northern France, and the Atlantic coast while leaving central and southern France (the "Free Zone") under the control of the authoritarian Vichy regime. Marshal Philippe Pétain, a World War I hero and conservative nationalist, led the government. He and the new regime's officials were not simply puppets of the Germans. They used the defeat to launch a "national revolution" against liberalism and the left. In the year following the debacle of 1940, public support for collaboration with Germany and for Pétain personally was strong. Conversely, there was little support in metropolitan France or in most of France's colonies for General Charles De Gaulle and his exiled Free French government.[7]

There was no place in the "national revolution" for those the regime considered non-French, namely Jews. From 1940 to 1944, it revoked the citizenship of fifteen thousand people (six thousand were Jews) and forced refugees to work in segregated "foreign work units." Without orders from the Germans, Vichy officials moved to identify, segregate, persecute, and rob Jews, particularly foreign-born Jews. The roundups and deportations were ordered by the SS and coordinated with Vichy officials. In the end, the active complicity of the Vichy regime, a compliant French civil service and police force, and a general public attitude that ranged from callous to fear-driven indifference made the Holocaust in France possible.[8]

Mass roundups began in the spring of 1941 and continued until the liberation in August 1944. The best known took place in July 1942 in Paris when French police arrested 13,152 foreign-born Jews (mostly women and children) rendered stateless by the regime. They were held in atrocious conditions in a stadium located near the Eiffel Tower, the Velodrome d'Hiver. French police dispersed the prisoners to four internment camps constructed by Vichy and then assisted the Germans in deporting them to the death camps. By 1944, the Germans had deported 75,721 Jews from France, with 4,000 more dying in French camps or otherwise killed in France. Of 80,000 victims, 24,000 were native-born. Only around 2,500 returned. The roundups and deportations could not have been carried out without the willing participation of the French policemen who arrested 75 percent of the total arrested during the war. In comparison with similar collaborationist regimes, the historian Julian Jackson concluded, "few others . . . offered as much help as Vichy."[9]

Fifty years after VE Day, successive French leaders began publicly acknowledging the country's role in the Holocaust. These acknowledgments and the culture of memorialization that surrounded them have recently been contested in national politics. In April 2017, Marine Le Pen, the leader of the far right National Front and at that moment a serious contender for the presidency, told a reporter, "I don't think France is responsible for the [Velodrome]." She claimed French schoolchildren were being taught nothing more than the "darkest aspects of our history" and that she "want[ed] them to be proud of being French again."[10]

While no competent historian can now deny the great extent of French complicity in the Holocaust, gray zones exist that complicate our understanding of France's "dark years." Beginning in 2007, a series of memoirs, novels, and feature films dealing with the roundups and postwar memory appeared in France. They are notable for their unflinching depiction of French complicity, but also for avoiding the kind of blanket condemnations Le Pen believes are pervasive in France. I assign one of them, Tatiana de Rosnay's novel *Sarah's Key,* and show the eponymously named feature film to get students to think about the complexities of collaboration and its legacies in France, particularly as they manifested themselves among ordinary French men and women.

Set in the present, the novel recounts how Julia Jarmond, an American journalist living in Paris, uncovers the story of a Polish-born Jewish family arrested in July 1942. Jarmond discovers that the Starzynski family had lived in the apartment into which she and her French husband Bertrand and daughter were about to move. Bertrand's family had taken the apartment a month after the roundup and knew about the Starzynskis, though his parents hid the truth about their fate from him.[11]

De Rosnay intertwines the story of Julia's investigation with flashbacks to the Starzynskis' ordeal, relating the latter through the eyes of one of the children, the ten-year-old Sarah. Jarmond discovers that during the arrest, Sarah hid her four-year-old brother Michel by locking him in a cabinet, believing the arresting policeman's assurances that the family would be allowed to return in a few days. Instead, they endure the horrors of the Velodrome before being transferred to an internment camp. Desperate to save Michel, Sarah escapes—with the help of a French policeman—and is taken in by an elderly non-Jewish couple. Despite the risk, they take Sarah to her family's former apartment, where she discovers that her brother had died in the cabinet. A deeply traumatized Sarah survives the war and moves to the United States in the early 1950s. Jarmond finally discovers her whereabouts, only to learn that she had committed suicide in 1972. Julia also learns that her husband's family not only knew of the arrests but also of Michel's death.

The novel and film deal with multiple aspects of French collaboration. De Rosnay recounts the conditions of the Velodrome in graphic detail: the incomprehension and resignation of the prisoners, suicides, the filth and lack of water in the stifling heat. Striking too are her descriptions of the arresting policemen. They are all French. Germans barely appear in the novel or film. Sarah also encounters the callous indifference of not only most French policemen but also of ordinary French women and men. Yet as the portrayal of the brave family that rescues Sarah makes clear, *Sarah's Key* hardly condemns "the French." The willingness of a significant number of non-Jewish French men and women to risk their lives to protect Jews has a solid basis in fact.[12] And though de Rosnay's book does not deal with it, Jews in France were not passive in the face of their persecution. Jewish and non-Jewish welfare organizations were far more successful in helping Jews—especially children—than the storied Resistance, which remained focused on liberating metropolitan France, aiding the Allies, and impeding the forced deportation of French workers to Germany.[13]

Sarah's Key also offers insights into the trans-generational culture of silence and denial that can still be found in France and other countries with collaborationist pasts. The Julia character's initial ignorance of the roundup was reflective of de Rosnay's, who told an interviewer that growing up in the 1970s she had never been taught about it and needed a year to research its history. Though by the time de Rosnay was writing the book, French presidents had publicly addressed the country's complicity in the roundups, and there was no shortage of scholarly work available, the topic struck her as still being "shrouded by some kind of taboo." Hence, the focus on Bertrand and his family's conflicted, occasionally hostile, responses to Julia's increasingly disturbing discoveries.

More generally, the book and film invite debates on the relationship between the German occupiers, the Vichy regime, and ordinary French citizens. To what extent was the behavior of individuals—ranging from the most zealous antisemites to those who simply wanted to avoid trouble—influenced by the occupation and a new, undemocratic regime? The French policemen who arrested Jews were certainly engaged in a form of active collaboration, but to what extent did compulsion determine their actions? When Parisians shouted support for policemen as they herded terrified Jews into and out of the Velodrome, were they too engaging in a form of collaboration? And while coercion certainly played a role in collaboration, it was possible to choose resistance. Why did some take enormous personal risks to help Jews?

Then there is the question of memory. Most of us presume that lying about or covering up a painful past is morally problematic and corrosive to social harmony. But does ceaseless harping on past wrongs perpetuate grievances and deepen mutual hostilities rather than promote reconciliation and unity?[14] Here, too, the case of postwar France offers food for thought. One does not have to accept the stubborn denials of a Marine Le Pen to question the value of uncovering family secrets. Julia Jarmond faces a choice and chooses, at considerable personal cost, to disturb sleeping dogs.

Poland

In no other country has the memory of complicity in the Holocaust been more controversial than Poland, the geographic center of the genocide. In August 1939, Germany and the USSR signed a nonaggression pact and agreed to divide Poland between them. In September, their respective armies invaded and destroyed the Polish state. In advance of the German invasion of the USSR in June 1941, which would overrun the eastern half of Poland then occupied by the Soviets, the chief of the SS Reich Security Main Office, Reinhard Heydrich, ordered SS units to encourage "self-cleansing actions" by locals against Jews. He was pleased when Wehrmacht units followed suit.[15]

The Germans incited a wave of similar attacks that killed thousands of Jews in Lithuania, Latvia, Estonia, eastern Poland, and Ukraine. Heydrich did not want "self-cleansing actions" to continue beyond the initial phase of the occupation, but his reluctance did not prevent the Germans from relying on locals to locate, guard, rob, and transport Jews to ghettos and execution sites, and to kill them. Some were bribed or coerced, but as Norman Naimark put it, "there was no shortage of volunteers."[16]

Since the collapse of communist regimes in Eastern Europe, historians have learned a great deal about the extent of local complicity and the importance of the Gentile-Jewish side of Bartov's triangular relationship. The best-known "self-cleansing action" took place in the town of Jedwabne in northeast Poland. On July 10, 1941, residents of that town and nearby villages murdered Jedwabne's Jewish inhabitants, perhaps one thousand people or about half the town's population. German soldiers—who had authorized the massacre—stood by and took pictures, but did not participate.

The Polish-born historian Jan Gross provided this account in *Neighbors*, first published in Poland in 2000. Gross's analysis challenged communist and postcommunist memories of the war, which emphasized Poland's victimization and heroic resistance to the Nazis while placing the blame for the country's ordeal entirely on the Germans and Soviets. Gross also seemed to be challenging Poles' self-perception as a nation of rescuers. Contemporary Poles are, after all, justifiably proud that their ancestors account for the largest number of those identified by Israel's Holocaust memorial authority, Yad Vashem, as belonging to the "righteous among the nations" for risking their lives to protect Jews.[17]

Gross emphasized that the German occupation was the essential precondition for the massacre. But he focused on the Polish-Jewish dimension of the Holocaust and mined the darkest seams of Poland's wartime history. He revealed that the principal perpetrators had collaborated with the Soviet occupation in 1939 before collaborating with the Germans two years later, again with the Soviets in 1944, and then with the postwar Polish communist regime. He also stressed the deadly significance of the myth that Jews had welcomed the first Soviet occupation, benefited from "Sovietization," served the hated Soviet regime enthusiastically, and betrayed Polish resisters to the Germans. None of this, Gross stressed, was true.[18]

The Jedwabne case demonstrates that accounting for local contextualization and multiple causal factors is essential for understanding collaborator motivations. In Jedwabne, antisemitism was a necessary precondition for the pogrom but was operationalized by a series of unexpected, disruptive events. Hence the economic depression of the 1930s gave rural Poles an opportunity to blame Jews, whom they associated with both communism and capitalism. It also mattered that the local Catholic press was virulently anti-Jewish and that an antisemitic political movement was strongly represented in this part of Poland. As in other parts of Europe, greed was a motivating factor in the pogrom, but here the German occupation was crucial, as it made it possible to take Jewish property and personal possessions without fear of arrest.[19]

The trauma of multiple occupations was the most important catalyst. Between 1939 and 1944, the residents of Jedwabne were subjected to three occupations. The experiences of the 1939–1941 Soviet occupation and then German rule were especially traumatic. "Sovietization" badly disrupted the local economy, and Gentile and Jewish Poles alike were subjected to waves of deportations. The social fabric was badly frayed by the time the Germans arrived.

Once *Neighbors* caught the attention of the wider public in Poland, it provoked the most extensive and divisive controversy over local collaboration in any European nation. Many Poles, including some of Poland's most distinguished historians, considered the book an attempt to denigrate their country's good name and to justify restitution claims. They continued to accept the myths of "Jewish communism" and believed that if Poles had killed some Jews, this was understandable, given the depredations of traitorous Jews who had, allegedly, supported and benefited from communist rule.[20]

Yet the response to *Neighbors* also produced much that was positive. It provoked anguished soul-searching among conscientious Poles. Indeed, some students notice that Gross writes as a patriotic Pole and seems profoundly disturbed by his discoveries. In the year following the publication of *Neighbors*, most leading political figures accepted that Poles were responsible for the Jedwabne massacre, and Poland's president, Aleksander Kwaśniewski, issued a powerfully worded apology on behalf of the Polish nation in Jedwabne. *Neighbors* also prompted the new Institute for National Remembrance to publish a deeply researched multivolume study of the massacre that confirmed Gross's main conclusions. His work has also inspired a younger generation of Polish historians to investigate the Polish-Jewish dimension of the Holocaust in other parts of the country. Their work has revealed that the massacre, while an extreme case, was not unique in the region surrounding Jedwabne.[21]

On the day of Kwaśniewski's address in Jedwabne, an editorial in Poland's leading newspaper proclaimed that the debate over *Neighbors* revealed "Polish democracy [to be] on the road of truth and that truth serves democracy."[22] The recent surge in popularity of the nativist right in Poland suggested a less optimistic formulation: only that which serves to bolster national pride as defined by the ruling party is worthy of being labeled "truthful" and permissible to express in public. But the willingness of many Poles to insist that open, if painful, discourse about the past bolsters democracy has ensured—at least for now—that the debates sparked by *Neighbors* will continue within Poland.

Nazi Germany and Haj Amin Al-Husseini

My third case surprises students who are unaware of the Nazi regime's attitude toward Muslim lands and its relationship with Haj Amin Al-Husseini. His case is an important and, in many ways, unique one compared to other prominent collaborators.

Husseini was a Palestinian-born religious and political leader. Like others, he was a collaborator in multiple senses. Following World War I, the Ottoman province of Palestine was placed under British control by the League of Nations as a mandate. In 1921, British authorities appointed Husseini to the position of chief Sunni Muslim cleric of Jerusalem, or grand mufti. He became an active opponent of British rule during the outbreak of the Arab revolt in the mandate in 1936. Evading British arrest, Husseini spent two years in Iraq, where he supported an unsuccessful pro-Axis coup attempt in 1941. Italian officials rescued him in Persia and brought him to Rome. In November 1941, Husseini traveled to Berlin and met with a series of high-level Nazi leaders, including Adolf Hitler.[23]

Husseini's agenda aligned with that of the Nazi regime. He hated the British and sought Axis support for postwar Arab independence. He was also a fanatical antisemite and anti-Zionist. Years before his arrival in Berlin, Husseini had drawn on holy texts to identify Jews as an eternal and active enemy conspiring to destroy Islam, an accusation that comported with the Nazis' conspiratorial, racialist antisemitism. From 1941 to 1945, he collaborated energetically with the Nazis. His was the most important voice of an extensive propaganda operation aimed at influencing opinion in North Africa and the Middle East via Arabic-language radio broadcasts and leaflets. He also helped the SS recruit Bosnian and Albanian Muslims to special Waffen-SS units. His determination to block Jewish emigration to Palestine reached its deadliest point in 1943, when he put as much pressure as he could muster on German officials to prevent the deportation of some forty-five hundred Jews from Bulgaria, Romania, and Hungary to Palestine.[24]

For its part, the regime's support of Husseini formed part of what the historian David Motadel calls its "pro-Islamic stance." Hitler and Himmler admired Islam insofar as they considered it a fighting faith with an impressive record of imperial conquest. But there were practical reasons for courting Muslim opinion. At the height of their power in 1941, the Nazis controlled—and faced the imminent prospect of controlling—large and diverse populations of Muslims from North Africa to the Caucasus. Like the SS, the Wehrmacht made substantial efforts to recruit Muslims from Crimea and the north Caucasus and took other steps, such as opening mosques closed by the Soviets and authorizing the observance of religious holidays.[25]

Husseini remained loyal to Hitler until the war's end. He did not, however, share the fate of other prominent collaborators, and the Allies chose not to try him for war crimes. The pattern of multiple collaborations evident in parts of Eastern Europe can be observed in Husseini's experience. French occupation officials facilitated his postwar escape from Germany to France, where he offered to assist the French government in blunting anti-French sentiment in the Middle East and undermining the already tenuous British presence in the region. Despite his protected status, Husseini fled France and was granted asylum in Egypt.

I make a point of noting that Husseini's importance as a wartime collaborator is debatable. Like others, he was only valuable to the Germans to the extent that he could serve the regime's interests, and his ability to do so was limited. He controlled no territory and commanded no army. His was not the "voice of the Arabs," as Arab opinion about Nazi Germany and fascist Italy was not uniformly positive. It is unclear whether the Berlin broadcasts had any substantial impact on their listeners. Husseini's attempts to organize sabotage and intelligence-gathering operations in the Middle East failed. His determination to see thousands of Jews sent to death camps rather than Palestine is shocking, but in the end the decision was taken by the SS, not Husseini.

But I argue that his case is worth studying for a number of reasons. It focuses our attention on the motivations of collaborators, which were often localized, sometimes in line with German interests and sometimes not. In addition, a case could be made that no other collaborator was as important to the *postwar* world as Husseini. The mufti's resistance to Britain, his opposition to Zionism, his hatred of Jews, and his belief that Jews everywhere conspired to destroy the faith would inspire the ideologies and actions of the Muslim Brotherhood and its violent offshoots. His significance ultimately has less to do with his wartime collaboration and his postwar political activities, which were sharply curtailed by Israel's military victory in 1948, than with the long-term influence of the Nazi-Islamist synthesis he spent years propagating.

Conclusion

I want students to complete my courses with an understanding of the importance and complexity of collaboration in the Holocaust. Pedagogically, learning how to make informed comparisons may be the most valuable dimension of the case study approach. To suggest just a few examples: Vichy France is the classic instance of state-level collaboration, while in Poland there was no state at all. Yet complicity in the persecution of Jews was common in both places. Conversely, resistance to the Germans was far more extensive in Poland than it was in France, but the legacies of resistance movements in both countries has been marked by ambiguous—sometimes hostile—attitudes toward the fate of the Jews. It is essential, however, to point out the extent to which ordinary men and women across Europe who were not members of any resistance groups risked their lives to help Jews. Some memoir accounts and fact-based dramatizations, such as *Sarah's Key*, stress the importance of what I call the "rescue chain": the essential series of acts—from simply looking the other way to hiding someone—by individuals unconnected to both each other and the victim.[26]

Comparing how the memory of complicity played out in each country is similarly instructive. Though France was a mostly stable democracy after 1945, this did not ensure that the topic of collaboration could be discussed freely. One of the greatest documentaries dealing with collaboration, Marcel Ophüls's *The Sorrow and the Pity*, was banned from French television after its release in 1969. It was finally broadcast in 1981. The restrictions on what could and could not be said in public were, of course, far stricter in communist Poland, and the controversy surrounding *Neighbors* tells us something about the power of dictatorships to warp the historical record. But Poland has been a democracy for thirty years, and the intensity of the debate cannot be blamed solely on the legacy of communist rule. As in France, the "shroud of taboo" that compelled Tatiana de Rosnay to write *Sarah's Key* determined to a significant extent what could and could not be said by national leaders and historians, within the confines of small villages, and among families.

Finally, the case of North Africa and the Middle East may not seem as important as Poland or France. I use it in part because it is a good example of the limits of collaboration. Without question, there was a powerful congruence of interests between the Nazi regime and Haj Amin Al-Husseini. In the Middle East or in Europe, however, Germany's interests always predominated. But there is another reason to add the Middle East to the comparative mix: to impart students with an appreciation for the importance of contingency. There, it was only the defeat of German forces at El-Alamein in late 1942 that prevented the Nazis from taking control of Palestine and exterminating its Jewish population, making that battle not only one of the most important of the war but also of the history of the Holocaust. Ultimately, the unforeseeable course of the war determined the extent of the Final Solution's success or failure.

NOTES

1. Istvan Deak, *Europe on Trial: The Story of Collaboration, Resistance, and Retribution during World War II* (Boulder: Westview Press, 2015), 225. Also see Vesna Drapac and Gareth Pritchard, *Resistance and Collaboration in Hitler's Europe* (London: Palgrave Macmillan, 2017), and Götz Aly, *Europe against the Jews, 1880–1945* (New York: Metropolitan Books, 2020).

2. Omer Bartov, "Eastern Europe as the Site of Genocide," *Journal of Modern History* 80, no. 3 (September 2008): 571.

3. "People's Tribunals" in Hungary (1945-1949) were exceptional for the

attention given to perpetrators of crimes against Jews, as were Jewish Honor Courts convened across Europe and in Israel. See Ildikó Barna and Andrea Pető, *Political Justice in Budapest after World War II* (Budapest: Central European University Press, 2015), and Laura Jockusch and Gabriel N. Finder, eds., *Jewish Honor Courts: Revenge, Retribution, and Reconciliation in Europe and Israel after the Holocaust* (Detroit: Wayne State University Press, 2015).

4. Istvan Deak, Jan Gross, and Tony Judt, eds., *The Politics of Retribution in Europe: World War II and Its Aftermath* (Princeton: Princeton University Press, 2000), Timothy Snyder, *Black Earth: The Holocaust as History and Warning* (New York: Tim Duggan Books, 2015), 298–318, Anna Bikont, *The Crime and the Silence: Confronting the Massacre of Jews in Wartime Jedwabne* (New York: Farrar, Straus and Giroux, 2016).

5. Roni Stauber, ed., *Collaboration with the Nazis: Public Discourse after the Holocaust* (London: Routledge, 2011).

6. Bartov, "Europe as the Site of Genocide."

7. Julian Jackson, *France: The Dark Years, 1940–1944* (New York: Oxford University Press, 2001).

8. Susan Zuccotti, *The Holocaust, the French, and the Jews* (New York: Basic Books, 1993).

9. Zuccotti, *Holocaust, the French, and the Jews*, 252, 343–344; and Jackson, *Dark Years*, 360–363.

10. "Marine Le Pen Denies French Role in Wartime Roundup of Paris Jews," *Guardian*, April 9, 2017, https://www.theguardian.com/world/2017/apr/09/marine-le-pen-denies-french-role-wartime-roundup-paris-jews.

11. Tatiana de Rosnay, *Sarah's Key* (New York: St. Martin's Griffin, 2007); and *Sarah's Key* (dir. Gilles Paquet-Brenner, 2010).

12. Jackson, *Dark Years*, 363–370, Caroline Moorehead, *Village of Secrets: Defying the Nazis in Vichy France* (New York: HarperCollins, 2014); and Jacques Semelin, *The Survival of the Jews in France, 1940–44* (New York: Oxford University Press, 2018).

13. Bob Moore, *Survivors: Jewish Self-Help and Rescue in Nazi Occupied Western Europe* (New York: Oxford University Press, 2010); and Renée Poznanski, "Rescue of the Jews and the Resistance in France: From History to Historiography," *French Politics, Culture and Society* 30, no. 2 (Summer 2012): 8–32.

14. David Rieff, *In Praise of Forgetting: Historical Memory and Its Ironies* (New Haven: Yale University Press, 2016).

15. Timothy Snyder, *Bloodlands: Europe between Hitler and Stalin* (New York: Basic Books, 2010).

16. Norman Naimark, "Nazis and 'The East': Jedwabne's Circle of Hell," *Slavic Review* 61, no. 3 (Autumn 2002): 476–482.

17. Jan Gross, *Neighbors: The Destruction of the Jewish Community in Jedwabne, Poland* (Princeton: Princeton University Press, 2001).

18. Marci Shore, "Conversing with Ghosts: Jedwabne, Zydokomuna, and Totalitarianism," *Kritika: Explorations in Russian and Eurasian History* 6, no. 2 (Spring 2005): 345–374.

19. Gross emphasized the largely peaceable and productive prewar relationship between Jews and Gentiles in Jedwabne, but see Bikont, *The Crime and the Silence.*

20. Antony Polonsky and Joanna Michlic, eds., *The Neighbors Respond: The Controversy over the Jedwabne Massacre in Poland* (Princeton: Princeton University Press, 2004); and Laurence Weinbaum, "Where the Past Is Never Past: Holocaust Memory in Post-Communist Poland," in Stauber, *Collaboration with the Nazis,* 25–43.

21. Polonsky and Michlic, *The Neighbors Respond*; and special issue on the Holocaust in occupied Poland, *East European Politics and Societies* 25, no. 3 (August 2011).

22. Quoted in Weinbaum, "Poland," 31.

23. Zvi Elpeleg, *The Grand Mufti: Haj Amin al-Hussaini, Founder of the Palestinian National Movement* (London: Frank Cass, 1993).

24. Jeffrey Herf, *Nazi Propaganda for the Arab World* (New Haven: Yale University Press, 2009).

25. David Motadel, *Islam and Nazi Germany's War* (Cambridge, MA: Harvard University Press, 2014).

26. An important memoir account stressing the significance of the "rescue chain" is Françoise Frenkel, *No Place to Lay One's Head* (London: Pushkin Press, 2019), and Semelin, *The Survival of the Jews in France.*

Resistance and Rescue

L A U R A J. H I L T O N

To smuggle a loaf of bread—was to resist.
To teach in secret—was to resist.
To gather information and distribute an underground newsletter—
    was to resist.
To cry out warning and shatter illusions—was to resist.
To rescue a Torah scroll—was to resist.
To forge documents—was to resist.
To smuggle people across borders—was to resist.
To chronicle events and conceal the records—was to resist.
To extend a helping hand to those in need—was to resist.
To dare to speak out, at the risk of one's life—was to resist.
To stand empty-handed against the killers—was to resist.
To reach the besieged, smuggling weapons and commands—
    was to resist.
To take up arms in streets, mountains, and forests—was to resist.
To rebel in the death camps—was to resist.
To rise up in the ghettos, amid tumbling walls,
in the most desperate revolt humanity has ever known . . .

The poem "Resistance Is . . . ," written postwar by
Israeli poet Haim Gouri and Monia Avrahami, cap-
tures the multifaceted nature of Jewish resistance to Nazi oppression
during the Holocaust, including rescue.[1] Educators can use this primary
source to help students understand the broad array of actions that make
up Jewish resistance. It also introduces students to the larger historiographical issue of how scholars have framed these topics and how the explanations have changed over time and why.[2] By grounding discussion

in the scholarly debate about what constitutes resistance and why, educators can confront directly the surface-level, public understanding of both resistance and rescue.

Feature films such as *Schindler's List* and *Defiance* shape how students understand whether it was possible to offer resistance to the Nazis and their collaborators and whether rescue was possible. Yet, without historical context, these films skew understanding of how possible resistance and rescue actually were, in terms of geography, timing, the path of the war, and likelihood of outside assistance. Documentation of Nazi crimes, such as the Oyneg Shabes underground archive in the Warsaw Ghetto, offered resistance by collecting information, artifacts, and interviews, witnessing the persecution, and ensuring that the Jewish perspective of the events would exist in the future.[3] However, this form of resistance remains less known than its more classically heroic counterparts. In terms of individual or collective rescue efforts, students might know about Irena Sendler [Sendlerowa], who smuggled Jewish children out of the Warsaw Ghetto working with the Polish organization Zegota, or the S.S. *St. Louis*, turned away from America's shores in 1939 with 937 refugees onboard, or the escape of Danish Jews by boat into Sweden in the fall of 1943. They may have heard of diplomatic interventions such as Raoul Wallenberg's efforts to save Hungarian Jews from deportation in 1944 or Aristides de Souza Mendes's provisions of Portuguese visas to leave France from late 1939 to June 1940. Often educators use these stories to inspire and, especially in terms of those that succeeded, to reassure students that help did exist for Jews facing genocidal persecution. However, when such stories dominate a depiction of the Holocaust, it skews the stark reality that far more of the 700 million Europeans in territory controlled by the Nazis benefited from the persecution, deportation, and death of Jews than provided them with assistance.[4] The majority of Jews in Europe received no assistance from non-Jewish individuals, organizations, or governments, and at least 5.8 million of them died.

Historiography

Initially, scholars and educators focused almost exclusively on armed uprisings and partisan bands, such as the Warsaw Ghetto Uprising (April 1943), the Sonderkommando Uprising in Auschwitz (October 1944), and the actions of partisan bands in Belorussia.[5]

Armed resistance did occur, despite the immense logistical difficulties of lack of arms, training to use them, and assistance from non-Jewish populations. Over time, scholars documented additional armed rebellions in concentration camps, ghettos, and extermination camps, as well as partisan band and forest operations within Nazi-occupied Poland and throughout the territories claimed in the invasion of the Soviet Union.[6] Scholarship in the last two decades has documented even more acts of resistance, both armed and cultural, through the experiences of Jews within more than 1,140 ghettos.[7] Armed resistance is an important facet of teaching this topic. At the same time, it needs context, emphasizing the enormous difficulties that Jews faced and rooting each event in its specific geographic and temporal place, while being mindful not to glorify it over other forms of resistance.

By the 1970s, many scholars had widened the definition of Jewish resistance to include cultural, economic, political, educational, and spiritual responses to Nazi oppression, focusing on the concept of *amidah*, literally "taking a stand" or "standing up against." Yehuda Bauer defined Jewish resistance during the Holocaust "to be any *group* action consciously taken in opposition to known or surmised laws, actions, or intentions directed against the Jews by the Germans and their supporters."[8] In this expanded definition, collective actions taken to thwart the aims of the Nazis and their collaborators, to destroy Jewish lives and obliterate memory of their very existence, were resistance. Continuing to engage in spiritual activities, such as public worship (*minyamin*), education of children, the writing and production of underground newspapers, and engagement in Jewish cultural events, all of which the Nazis outlawed, constituted resistance in this sense and challenged the Nazis' attempt to eliminate Jews and their traditions and beliefs. Some scholars also define individual acts of defiance, for instance, writing "vengeance" on the wall in one's own blood or tearing up money on the edge of the execution pits to deprive the Nazis of further enrichment, as resistance.[9]

Many Jews understood resistance as *überleben*, surviving the war. Emil Fackenheim argues that resistance for Jews during the Holocaust became "a way of being," underlining how widespread resistance actually was, in this scholarly interpretation.[10] This expansion of what constituted resistance has not, however, remained uncontested. In his seminal work, *The Destruction of the European Jews*, Raul Hilberg asserted a tendency among Jews to avoid the use of force, stating that "preventative attack, armed resistance, and revenge were almost completely absent in Jewish exilic history."[11] Common images of Jews waiting to board trains to deportation in the east, or standing behind barbed wire after liberation, reinforce this perception of passivity in the face of destruction. If students raise questions such as "why didn't more Jews resist," explain how this displaces the blame onto the victims themselves. Helping students navigate these scholarly debates will enrich their own understanding of Jewish resistance to the genocidal aims of the Nazis.

Framework for Teaching Resistance and Rescue

Based on two decades of teaching at the collegiate level, this section focuses on five key, but often submerged, aspects of resistance and rescue that will encourage students to engage in critical thinking and move beyond emotional responses to the material: how Jewish resistance fits within the larger narrative of anti-Nazi resistance; the risks and illegality of many rescue attempts; the gendered construction of resistance; the importance of setting resistance and rescue within their specific time and place; and the ways in which resistance and rescue activities complicate the perpetrator-bystander-victim paradigm. Providing students with an informed and thoughtful framework for understanding resistance and rescue is essential, especially in terms of embedding these actions within the historical reality of World War II, Nazi occupation, and the Holocaust itself. It will help move students away from a simplistic and binary understanding of the Holocaust.

First, situate Jewish resistance within the larger story of resistance to the Third Reich. Explain to students that both Jewish resistance to Nazism and resistance by non-Jews to Nazism on behalf of Jews comprise a small portion of the overall resistance to Nazi Germany.[12] This is often difficult for students to grasp, because the Holocaust now occupies such a central place within American understanding of World War II. However, for many Europeans at that time, the war and occupation took center stage. Most anti-fascist resistance efforts and groups during the war focused on disrupting Nazi occupation, with an end aim of overthrowing it. They rarely provided Jews with assistance or prioritized helping them escape the Nazi grip. In addition, the relationships between the local population and the Nazi occupation varied greatly, which fundamentally shaped the levels and types of resistance that emerged. In some areas, local authorities, including police, worked directly with German occupiers; in others, Nazi control was more indirect. The topography of some regions and countries lent themselves more easily to resistance than others, especially places with thick forests, mountains, or isolated areas. Among other major obstacles to Jewish resistance, the Third Reich possessed "superior, armed power," the Jews were isolated from the larger European population, which made obtaining weapons even more difficult, and the Nazis employed purposeful deception to mask deportations. In addition, fierce and collective retribution, sometimes called "collective responsibility," exacted by the Nazis on populations that did resist, played a role.[13] Per Anders Rudling estimates that the Nazis engaged in at least 140 punitive operations that targeted entire communities (such as Lidice and Oradour-sur-Glane), in addition to smaller acts of reprisal.[14]

Second, explain that rescue activity was a dangerous form of resistance that necessitated breaking the law. When individuals made the decision to assist Jews, they knew they were engaging in illegal activities, and this had varying consequences if apprehended. In Poland, Nazi officials punished people who assisted Jews by executing them and sometimes their entire families. An October 15, 1941, law stated that all Jews who left their residences (i.e., ghettos) faced the death penalty; the Nazis applied this same punishment to anyone who assisted Jews. The Nazis widely publicized these executions and in many instances killed the person's entire family.[15] In the Netherlands by 1943, the standard punishment for assisting Jews was six months in a concentration camp; however, in France and Belgium, the Nazis never instituted a standard penalty.[16] In order to survive, many Jews had to engage in illegal acts on a daily basis, and some lived a completely falsified life, passing as non-Jewish. Therefore, rescuers and those receiving aid had to be on their guard constantly, which was exhausting. The tiniest thing could be a matter of life and death. In one story, Jews in hiding placed their lives and those of their rescuers in jeopardy when they offered to peel potatoes. A suspicious Polish official noticed that the peels were long and curly, the way that Jews peeled potatoes, rather than short, stubby strips, typical of non-Jewish Poles.[17] Explaining both the strain placed by the illegality of these acts and their potential punishments provides important context for why it was rare.

Third, provide gender analysis that explains how popular conceptions of resistance, focusing on armed and violent struggle, privilege resistance work normally conducted by men while downplaying the resistance work done often by women. Both Jewish women who "looked Aryan" and non-Jewish women successfully used the gendered ideas harbored by Nazis to act as smugglers of goods and people, couriers of information, and saboteurs.[18] They also often took the lead on social and cultural forms of resistance—for example, providing illegal education to Jewish children in ghettos. Jewish women who did not "look Jewish" could pass themselves off as non-Jewish natives, especially if they had the language skills and cultural shrewdness to do so. This was exceptionally difficult for Jewish men to do, due to their circumcision.

Fourth, teach how levels of resistance (both specific to assisting Jews and more generally anti-Nazi) varied over time and place.[19] The ability to successfully hide Jews or help them reach a safe haven had some early successes in 1939–1940, but incredibly restrictive conditions between 1941 and 1943 complicated these efforts. However, as the war fronts collapsed on all sides, rescue efforts rebounded. Countries such as France and Italy saw increased resistance as the tide of war turned. However, heightened urgency in the regions directly in the killing fields (Poland, Ukraine, Belorussia, and the Baltic States) spawned resistance once mass murder began in the summer of 1941. Uprisings in ghettos and camps reacted specifically to information about impending deportations or liquidations. In instances such as the revolts in Treblinka (August 1943) and Sobibor (October 1943), resistance was a last resort. Impending death at the hands of the Nazis and their collaborators led some Jews to choose how they would die, by offering resistance. Within border regions and more rural areas such as Le Chambon in France, assistance to strangers and acts of resistance were more likely to occur, due to topography, fewer informers, and a culture of providing for those in need, because no other resources existed. Demography also played a role, as the number of Jews who needed assistance had an impact on the likelihood of assistance occurring. It was easier to consider assisting eight thousand Jews in Denmark with escape to Sweden than to contemplate hiding literally millions of Jews in Poland who faced deportation to ghettos or extermination camps.

Lastly, delve into how stories of rescue and resistance transgress the perpetrator-victim-bystander paradigm, first proposed by Raul Hilberg.[20] Scholarship now encourages thinking about how individuals can overlap categories or move between them over the course of the Holocaust. It also uses more analytical terms, such as *collaborator*, *beneficiary*, and *rescuer*, rather than lumping everyone not a perpetrator or a victim into one very large category.[21] One who engaged in rescue could also be a perpetrator—for example, German engineer Hermann Friedrich Gräbe, who intervened multiple times to prevent the deportation of workers to a killing center and ultimately saved the lives of more than three hundred Jews.[22] Another example in this vein is Major Karl Plagge, a Wehrmacht officer who created a work camp outside of the Vilna ghetto and warned the Jewish workers of its impending liqui-dation as the Soviet Army approached.[23] In her writing on the Bielski brothers, leaders of a partisan band in Western Belorussia, Nechama Tec also questions these classifications, as the Bielskis were victims, rescuers, and resisters, saving approximately twelve hundred Jews.[24] Dogged historians and other scholars have unearthed these stories through research and oral histories, yet we will never know how many more are lost, as the secrecy demanded by Nazi occupation left behind a thin historical record. Resistance groups were loath to document their efforts since it incriminated them.

Rescue

Providing assistance to Jews seeking to escape the Nazis and their collaborators was an important element of resisting the Third Reich, and until recently information has focused almost exclusively on non-Jewish rescuers. Since Israel created it in 1953, Yad Vashem has been a key institution encouraging scholarship and documentation of rescue, focusing on non-Jewish rescuers. Yad Vashem has vetted and recognized more than twenty-five thousand non-Jewish rescuers, many of whose stories can be located on their website.[25] It established its own framework, interesting for students to consider, making a distinction between rescue and offering charity and excluding those who acted out of personal gain. Here too definitions include and exclude, linked to the earlier discussion of what constitutes resistance. In recent scholarship on rescue, the focus has shifted from concentrating almost exclusively on non-Jewish rescuers, organizations, and governmental efforts to one that now probes how Jews assisted other Jews (i.e., self-help).[26]

Since the 1980s, interdisciplinary scholarship, especially by sociolo-gists, has focused on seeking common characteristics among rescuers. The work of Nechama Tec, Eva Fogelman, and Samuel and Pearl Oliner are all central in this regard. Both Samuel Oliner and Tec survived the

Holocaust as children in hiding in Poland, and Fogelman's father survived as part of a partisan band in Belorussia, so their personal histories are intertwined with their subject matter. The Oliners developed the idea of an altruistic personality, based on interviews with more than 400 rescuers, 126 nonrescuers, and 150 survivors. Their research revealed four key characteristics of rescuers, many of which overlap with those identified by Tec and Fogelman: strong and cohesive family bonds; consistently close contact with Jews; strong sense of responsibility for the welfare of others; and identification with humanity as a whole.[27] Tec provides six key characteristics of rescuers: a strong sense of individuality; independence in thought and action; a history of offering help to those in need; seeing one's actions as necessary; spontaneous nature of assistance; and seeing Jews as humans (i.e., not as "other").[28] Fogelman conducted more than three hundred interviews as part of the Rescuer Project. She focuses on both individual characteristics (altruism) and situational factors, such as whether people were in proximity to those who needed assistance; whether the community trended toward providing help; economic ability to share; access to appropriate and safe shelter; and who was requesting aid.

In addition to delving into common characteristics of those who engaged in rescue, Fogelman borrows from the five-step process proposed by social psychologists Bob Latané and John Darley to realize actively that something is wrong; that due to this, people need help; then offering help; choosing how to help; and then actually helping.[29] Given that most people like to think that they would have assisted Jews, educators can use these stories to provoke more critical student thinking about their own behavior and encourage meaningful conversations about civic engagement. An excellent application of this framework is the example of Varian Fry, originally in France on behalf of the Emergency Rescue Committee (ERC) to rescue two hundred famous artists, intellectuals, and scientists. While he accomplished this goal, he continued his work far beyond the ERC initiative, eventually assisting more than four thousand Jews in fleeing France.[30] Fogelman outlines the main reasons that motivated people to offer assistance, including moral (conscience); close contact with Jews; being involved in an anti-Nazi network; having professional skills in need (e.g., medical care); and seeing children, as innocents, in need of assistance.[31]

Utilize a multileveled approach to explaining rescue, incorporating stories of those who rescued as individuals, those who operated as part of an indigenous network or organization, large-scale interventions or negotiations by international organizations, and finally rescue efforts officially made by diplomats (authorized or not) by their respective governments. These categories are permeable; that is, an individual may begin by spontaneously assisting a Jew in need and then become part of an organization. Include hiding Jews; providing Jews with papers, food, or employment in order to pass themselves off as non-Jews; enabling asylum (e.g., the British effort to bring ten thousand Jewish children to safety via Kindertransport); and thwarting the Final Solution by forestalling deportation or execution. With each of these, relate to students the factors that had an impact on whether rescue was possible. Deborah Dwork writes about the importance of prewar contacts (family friends, neighbors, business contacts), who sometimes offered key and initial assistance or hiding places and the difficulties in terms of logistics (finding safe hiding places, securing sufficient food); she reminds readers that it was very rare for entire families to be able to hide together.[32] Given that the story of Anne Frank hiding in Amsterdam is so well known, emphasize to students that she hid with her sister, her parents, three members of the Van Pels family, and Fritz Pfeffer and that hiding alone was much more common and incredibly lonely. Jews hiding themselves, by building bunkers to escape roundups, is another dimension of this.[33] In volume 1 of *Maus*, Art Speigelman explains in graphic memoir format the internal stress of being in hiding and provides depictions of the bunkers that his father constructed in Środula, which make excellent visuals for use with students.[34] Lastly, relate to students that no one knew how long this would last, and for many it stretched not just into months, but years, under tremendous psychological pressure.

Providing students with examples of individuals or small networks of people who hid or helped Jews survive introduces them to the complex variables in play and forces them to place it within the larger context.[35] An added intricacy is the different experiences that Jewish refugees faced compared with native Jews; the initial roundups of Jews in France in 1942 specifically targeted foreign and stateless Jews (see Steven P. Remy's chapter in this volume), driving a wedge between these two groups and making some French less likely to come to their aid. The Bulgarian government handed foreign Jews over to the Nazis but refused to hand over Bulgarian Jews. Foreign Jews also found themselves bereft of the contacts and networks to which native Jews may have had access. Lastly, while people may have been more likely to hide children, perceiving them as less threatening than an adult was, it is important to note that fewer than 15 percent of Jewish children survived the Holocaust.

Teaching students about networks that existed to hide Jews and provide them with necessary identification papers, ration cards, or employment provides a different but crucially important picture than the individual spontaneously helping a Jew in need. Some of these networks operated in connection with larger resistance groups while others were predominantly local or regional. Deborah Dwork provides an excellent overview of the Piet Meerberg group in the Netherlands.[36] Bob Moore explains the importance of Jews and non-Jews working together in Belgium, as a way of linking Jewish self-help, through organizations such as the Committee for the Defense of the Jews (CDJ) with non-Jewish networks that provided false papers, material aid, and hiding places.[37] The actions of Magda and Pastor Trocmé in Le Chambon and the villagers of the surrounding area provided safe haven for more than five thousand refugees fleeing Nazi persecution, including thirty-five hundred Jews. Inspired not only by their heritage of being a persecuted religious minority (Huguenots) but also by their disdain for Nazi occupation and the collaboration of Philippe Pétain's government in Vichy, approximately three thousand French clothed, fed, hid, educated, and provided forged documents to hundreds of people in need. Their geographic location also played a key role; being on a plateau with only one access road, villagers had ample warning when either the Vichy government or (later) German occupiers conducted raids. In addition, being a region where agriculture was a primary occupation, there were fewer issues with obtaining and distributing enough food than in a major urban area. In this region, breaking the law deliberately and refusing to ignore humans in need became a norm.

Although the international community twice convened conferences to discuss the fate of Jewish refugees (Évian in 1938 and Bermuda in 1943), in neither instance did governments extend meaningful offers of asylum. The scholarship on the lack of widespread asylum assistance between 1933 and 1945 is vast and often posited within narrower, national explanations. Providing emigration statistics, both in terms of from where refugees emigrated and to where they immigrated can provide a useful overview.[38] It also helps students understand how emigration transitioned into outright rescue once the war began in 1939, how it shifted when Germany outlawed Jewish migration in the fall of

1941, and how Jews who had immigrated to Western Europe were endangered as the Third Reich then invaded and occupied this region. An important facet of the emigration from Europe to Palestine, then under British mandate, was the British government's decision in May 1939, in response to the Arab Revolt of 1936–1939, to restrict visas to ten thousand per year for the next five years. In response, the Yishuv (Jewish communities of Palestine) sought Zionist youth with specific skills over other potential emigrants.[39]

With rescue efforts that involved both nongovernmental organization (NGOs), such as the American Jewish Joint Distribution Committee (AJJDC), and potential government interventions, teach students the layered factors that hampered Jewish emigration from Europe or to a safe haven within Europe. Provide them with multiple examples, and have students critically examine the factors at play. When teaching students about the roles played by both antisemitism and xenophobia in the case of the United States, make use of the Gallup public opinion polls from the late 1930s and through World War II,[40] especially those on whether the United States should alter its current immigration policies, which utilized quotas. Ask students about the ways in which the Great Depression (including persistently high unemployment in many nations) had an impact on public perception of refugees. Root these discussions about refugees and rescue operations firmly within the context of the global and all-consuming nature of World War II and ask students to consider how this hampered and postponed rescue efforts.

The path of the war and the Final Solution also intensified diplomatic rescue efforts, in multiple places, including Lithuania, Portugal, Italian-occupied Croatia, and Hungary. There are many examples of diplomats who made the decision to assist Jewish refugees, even when it clashed with their government's policies and wishes, which indicates that it was more possible than earlier scholarship maintained. Dutch diplomat Jan Zwartendijk worked with Chiune Sugihara, of the Japanese consulate in Vilna, to provide transit visas to reach Curaçao, a Dutch colony, which did not require entry visas. This enabled twenty-four hundred Jews to reach safety in Japan and eleven hundred to reach Palestine.[41] Aristides Mendes overstepped his authority as a Portuguese consul stationed in Bourdeaux, France, to issue thousands of visas to Jews seeking to flee Nazi occupation.[42] A fascinating and lesser-known example of rescue is the situation in Italian-occupied Croatia. Both Croatian members of the Ustaša (the Croatian Revolutionary

Movement) and the German military stationed in Croatia committed atrocities against Serbs and Jews in 1941. By 1942, large numbers of Jews had fled into the Italian-occupied portion of Croatia. Although Mussolini agreed to hand over the Jews to the Germans, his officials on the ground deliberately stalled the process. Despite continued pressure from German occupiers and Croatian nationals, the Italian military refused to hand over Jews within their zone for deportation. They provided identification documents to some Jews, claiming them as under the protection of the Italian government, and as they withdrew, they moved hundreds of Jews with them, to prevent their deportation and execution. Why would Germany's oldest, fascist ally Italy help Jews in need? Explanations center on feeling obligated to assist civilians, less antisemitism within Italy, conscience/morality, and a sense of nationalism, thwarting Germany's aims while feeling like a junior partner in the Axis alliance.[43] After Germany occupied Hungary (its former ally) in March 1944, Adolf Eichmann began plans to transport more than eight hundred thousand Hungarian Jews as quickly as possible northward to Auschwitz. The speed, ferocity, and thorough nature of this effort galvanized multiple people and organizations into action, including Raoul Wallenberg, a Swedish envoy who operated in Budapest between July and November of 1944, negotiating and bribing Arrow Cross members to cease pogroms and issuing protective "passports" to stop or slow deportations, helping to save between twenty thousand and twenty-five thousand Jews.[44]

Students often raise the question of how the United States responded, some of them believing that the United States entered World War II in order to stop the Holocaust. The historiography on this topic is vast and threaded with "what if" types of questions. It also is linked heavily with the questions of what did Americans and their government know and when. Mindful that this discussion, like many within the larger topic of resistance and rescue, can degenerate into what should have been done (backshadowing), educators should focus on what was done and why. Having students critique the responses of the international community without understanding the contemporary context provides them with the benefit of hindsight, which decision makers at the time did not have. Emphasize the major intertwined factors that shaped these decisions, including bureaucracy, inertia, antisemitism, lack of public concern, immigration quotas, concerns about national security, spies, and saboteurs, and the focus on winning the war. Key individuals and organizations to discuss include President Franklin Roosevelt, Assistant Secretary of State Breckenridge Long, the major American Jewish organizations, the July 1943 visit of Jan Karski, who brought firsthand information to Roosevelt and Supreme Court Justice Felix Frankfurter, and the creation of the War Refugee Board in January 1944.[45]

Classroom Engagement

The class period before I ask students to read and reflect on resistance, we work on defining what it was, based on student understanding. I have designed a quick activity for explaining the historiographies of resistance and rescue, while also pushing students to think about the assumptions that they bring to their understanding of the topic. I begin by handing out index cards and asking students to write down specific examples of resistance or types of resistance. I then collect the cards, read them aloud, and, as we move through the stack, ask if the example "belongs" with one I have already read. Students begin to sort the examples organically into categories. Once sorted, I write the examples and categories on the board and ask students to develop headings.

This exercise provides students with an initial framework for thinking about resistance and often provokes serious, informed conversation. I pick examples from across the board and ask what outside factors influenced the type of resistance or the specific event. For example, with the Warsaw Ghetto Uprising, students often ask what assistance (if any) the local, non-Jewish population provided and what direct links existed between the Polish resistance movements and Jewish resistance. They probe the timing of the uprising, linked with the accelerated liquidation of ghettos across Poland. They question the characteristics of those at the forefront, younger Jews, many of whom had already lost or been separated from their entire families. Some logistical concerns also surface. How could Jews inside a ghetto get access to weapons? How many had military training in weapons or strategy? If they had been successful, where would they have gone? One topic, which has surfaced every time I have used this exercise, is where suicide belongs, and if it is an act of resistance. Some students focus on the act and decision itself, stating that suicide was a form of resistance, since Jews chose to take their own lives, rather than face deportation and murder by the Nazis. Other students focus on the impact of the act and decision, arguing that it is not resistance, since it helped fulfill the Nazis' ultimate goal.[46]

Conclusion

At an academic conference, I once had a co-panelist state that she teaches resistance and rescue as the last topic. I believe that placing something so rare as resistance and rescue as the final lecture of the course or unit leaves students at the wrong ending point and encourages emotive rather than critical engagement with the topic. The Holocaust did not end with rescue and resistance. Indeed, as important as these efforts were to preserving life, they did not fundamentally alter the course of the Holocaust or World War II. Given the prominent role they play within postmemory of the Holocaust, it is essential to address them within the larger narrative arc of the course or unit thoughtfully and thoroughly.

NOTES

1. This poem is available in English here: https://www.facinghistory.org /resource-library/resistance-during-holocaust/resistance. The original Hebrew version is available on the website of the Ghetto Fighters House Museum, and is included in their documentary film, *Flames from the Ashes*, released in 1987. See http://www.gfh.org.il/eng/?CategoryID=61&ArticleID=73. Another innovative way to begin teaching resistance is to have students read or listen to songs written by Jews in the camps and ghettos. For examples, see Nick Strimple, "Music as Resistance," in Patrick Henry, ed., *Jewish Resistance against the Nazis* (Washington, DC: Catholic University of America Press, 2014), 319–338.

2. Robert Rozett provides a thorough overview in "Jewish Resistance," in Dan Stone, ed., *The Historiography of the Holocaust* (New York: Palgrave Macmillan, 2005), 341–363.

3. Samuel D. Kassow, *Who Will Write Our History? Rediscovering a Hidden Archive from the Warsaw Ghetto* (New York: Vintage, 2009).

4. Eva Fogelman, *Conscience and Courage: Rescuers of Jews during the Holocaust* (New York: Doubleday, 1994), xvi.

5. Rona Sheramy, "'Resistance and War': The Holocaust in American Jewish Education, 1945–1960," *American Jewish History* 91, no. 2 (June 2003): 287–313, explains that in the United States, educators in Jewish schools focused almost solely on stories of heroism and strength.

6. Yehuda Bauer, "Forms of Jewish Resistance during the Holocaust," in Michale Marrus, ed., *The Nazi Holocaust: Historical Articles on the Destruction of European Jews*, vol. 7, *Jewish Resistance to the Holocaust* (Westport: Meckler, 1989), 34–48, 39.

7. Geoffrey P. Megargee, ed., *The United States Holocaust Memorial Museum Encyclopedia of Camps and Ghettos, 1933–1945*, vol. 2, *Ghettos in German-Occupied Eastern Europe*, ed. Martin Dean (Bloomington: Indiana University Press, 2009).

8. Yehuda Bauer, "Jewish Resistance and Passivity in the Face of the Holocaust," in Francois Furet, ed., *Unanswered Questions* (New York: Schocken Books, 1989), 235–251, 237.

9. Both of these examples come from Dov Levin's monograph, *Fighting Back: Lithuanian Jewry's Armed Resistance to the Nazis* (New York: Holmes & Meier, 1985).

10. Richard Middleton-Kaplan, "The Myth of Jewish Passivity," in Henry, *Jewish Resistance against the Nazis*, 3–26, 18.

11. Raul Hilberg, *The Destruction of the European Jews* (London: W. H. Allen, 1961), 23.

12. For instance, the Westerweel Group in the Netherlands smuggled more than two hundred young Zionists across borders between 1942 and 1944. See Bob Moore, *Survivors* (Oxford: Oxford University Press, 2010), 64–67.

13. *Resistance during the Holocaust* (Washington, DC: United States Holocaust Memorial Museum, 1997), 5–7.

14. Per Anders Rudling, "The Khatyn Massacre in Belorussia," *Holocaust and Genocide Studies* 26, no. 1 (Spring 2012): 29–58, 29.

15. Fogelman, *Conscience and Courage*, 30.

16. Moore, *Survivors*, 366.

17. Fogelman, *Conscience and Courage*, 152.

18. On women who acted as couriers for the Jewish underground, see Liza Chapnik, "The Grodno Ghetto and Its Underground," especially 116–119; and Bronka Klibanski, "In the Ghetto and in the Resistance," especially 182–186, both in Dalia Ofer and Lenore Weitzman, eds., *Women in the Holocaust* (New Haven: Yale University Press, 1998).

19. An excellent and recent edited collection is Henry, *Jewish Resistance against the Nazis*.

20. Raul Hilberg, *Perpetrators, Victims, Bystanders* (New York: Harper Perennial, 1993).

21. In his recent work, Evgeny Finkel proposes a new typology of Jewish responses to the Holocaust, making distinctions between cooperation and collaboration, coping and compliance, evasion and resistance. See *Ordinary Jews: Choice and Survival during the Holocaust*, (Princeton: Princeton University Press, 2017).

22. For additional information, see David Scrase, "Gräbe," in Scrase et al.,

Making a Difference: Rescue and Assistance during the Holocaust; Essays in Honor of Marion Pritchard (Burlington, VT: Center for Holocaust Studies, 2004), 218–235.

23. Michael Good, *The Search for Major Plagge: The Nazi Who Saved Jews* (New York: Fordham University Press, 2006).

24. Nechama Tec, "Defiance," in Deborah Dwork, ed., *Voices and Views: A History of the Holocaust* (Lanham, MD: Rowman and Littlefield, 2005), 545–549.

25. Access online exhibits here: Yad Vashem, "Online Exhibitions," The World Holocaust Remembrance Center, https://www.yadvashem.org/exhibitions.html.

26. See Mordecai Paldiel, ed., *Saving One's Own: Jewish Rescuers during the Holocaust* (Lincoln: University of Nebraska Press, 2017), and Moore, *Survivors*.

27. Samuel P. Oliner and Pearl M. Oliner, *The Altruistic Personality: Rescuers of Jews in Nazi Europe* (New York: Free Press, 1987).

28. Nechama Tec, "Toward a Theory of Rescue," in Scrase et al., *Making a Difference*, 25–42, 37.

29. Fogelman, *Conscience and Courage*, 41–47.

30. Fry's story, and those of many other rescuers, are contained in Agnes Grunwald-Spier, *The Other Schindlers: Why Some People Chose to Save Jews in the Holocaust* (Stroud, Gloucestershire: History Press, 1988).

31. Fogelman, *Conscience and Courage*, 158–159.

32. Dwork, "Into Hiding," in Dwork, *Voices and Views*, 440–446.

33. See Havi Dreifuss, *Relations between Jews and Poles: The Jewish Perspective* (Jerusalem: Yad Vashem, 2017).

34. Art Spiegelman, *Maus: A Survivor's Tale; My Father Bleeds History* (New York: Pantheon, 1986), 110–113, 121–125.

35. Suzanne Vromen uses multiple examples of how Belgian nuns hid children in her monograph *Hidden Children of the Holocaust: How Belgian Nuns Helped Young Jews Survive the Nazi Terror* (Oxford: Oxford University Press, 2008).

36. Dwork, "Into Hiding," 446–450.

37. Bob Moore, "Integrating Self-Help into the History of Jewish Survival in Western Europe," in Norman Goda, ed., *Jewish Histories of the Holocaust: New Transnational Approaches* (New York: Berghahn, 2014), 193–208.

38. See, for example, the charts available in Donald Niewyk and Francis Nicosia, eds., *The Columbia Guide to the Holocaust* (New York: Columbia University Press, 2003).

39. Dina Porat, *The Blue and Yellow Stars of David* (Cambridge, MA: Harvard University Press, 1990).

40. See, for example, "Public Opinion," Americans and the Holocaust, United States Holocaust Memorial Museum, https://exhibitions.ushmm.org/americans-and-the-holocaust/topics/public-opinion.

41. Jonathan Goldstein, "The Kovno Connection," in Peter Hayes, ed., *How*

Was It Possible? A Holocaust Reader (Lincoln: University of Nebraska Press, 2015), 648–657.

42. Yehuda Bauer, "Rescue Attempts out of Lithuania," in Dwork, *Voices and Views*, 541–544.

43. Daniel Carpi, "The Rescue of Jews in the Italian Zone of Croatia," in Dwork, *Voices and Views*, 464–482.

44. Per Anger, "Wallenberg's Last Acts," in Dwork, *Voices and Views*, 462–464.

45. See Richard Breitman and Allan J. Lichtman, *FDR and the Jews* (Cambridge, MA: Harvard University Press, 2014); and Barry Trachtenberg, *The United States and the Nazi Holocaust: Race, Refuge, and Remembrance* (London: Bloomsbury, 2018). On the War Refugee Board, see Rebecca Erbelding, *Rescue Board: The Untold Story of America's Efforts to Save the Jews of Europe* (New York: Doubleday, 2018).

46. Konrad Kweit addresses this question of where suicide fits. See "Problems of Jewish Resistance Historiography," in Marrus, *Nazi Holocaust*, 49–69.

Life in the Aftermath

Jewish Displaced Persons

AVINOAM PATT

Some five months after the liberation in Germany, a group of young Holocaust survivors, barely removed from years of persecution and torture at the hands of the Nazi regime, moved to the estate of the virulently antisemitic Nazi propagandist Julius Streicher. As Streicher awaited trial in nearby Nuremberg, this group of young Zionists set about transforming his estate into an agricultural training farm or *hakhsharah*, in preparation for what they hoped would be their future lives in Palestine. The symbolic nature of the revenge exacted by the young survivors on Streicher's estate was unmistakable. However, the powerful political value of young Zionists inhabiting forty such training farms all over Germany would have profound implications beyond the satisfaction experienced by the members of Kibbutz Nili. In fact, the experiences of nearly 250,000 Jewish displaced persons living in Germany, Austria, and Italy after the war, constitute a remarkable, yet largely unknown chapter in the history of the Holocaust.

The Jewish displaced persons, or *She'erit Hapletah* (surviving remnant), emerged from the catastrophe of the Holocaust to form a vibrant, active, and fiercely independent community that played a prominent role in diplomatic negotiations ultimately leading to the creation of the state of Israel. This chapter examines the situation confronting Jewish survivors in the immediate aftermath of the war in Europe, the early organization of the surviving remnant in the Jewish displaced person (DP) camps, and the political, cultural, and social questions that affected the growing population of survivors in the DP camps of postwar Germany, Austria, and Italy.[1] Although frequently overlooked in courses on the Holocaust, the immediate aftermath of the war presents a fascinating period for examining the nature of Jewish responses to catastrophe, as survivors came to terms with the destruction of prewar communities, engaged in collective and individual mourning for lives lost, and charted a course for the Jewish future.

The Holocaust killed at least 5.7 million Jews or roughly two-thirds of the prewar European Jewish population. In 1933, approximately 9 million or 60 percent of 15 million Jews worldwide lived in Europe, 3.3 million in Poland alone. By 1950, only 3 million, or one-third of the prewar population, remained in Europe, and roughly two-thirds of those who remained in Europe in 1950 lived in the Soviet Union. The destruction of European Jewry shifted the center of gravity from Europe to the Americas, where over 50 percent of the world's Jewish population now lived (see Table 1).

For a brief period following the end of the war, however, a significant remnant of Europe's surviving Jewish community came to live in an entirely transitional situation, in the displaced persons camps of Germany, Austria, and Italy. Here they came to terms with being forced into exile from their prewar homes and with the destruction of European Jewish life and communities. Survivors engaged in complex processes of rebuilding their shattered lives involving prolonged periods of migration and life in transit. While standard periodization of the Holocaust concludes with the war's end in Europe in May 1945, the experiences of Jews in the aftermath of the war, both those living in the DP camps and those who attempted to rebuild destroyed communities, reveals that there is no neat division between the prewar, wartime, and postwar periods.

In an important sense, the large population of survivors gathered in the displaced persons camps of Germany, Austria, and Italy in the years 1945–1949 and who were much of the She'erit Hapletah, the "surviving" or "saved" remnant of East European Jewry, formed a community of Holocaust survivors that would never again be replicated. While survivors succeeded in creating (and re-creating) elements of prewar Jewish life that had been destroyed during the war, the DP period was a transitional moment, as the vast majority of survivors, unable to return to their former homes, longed for a solution to their stateless condition and hoped for resettlement in new homes and new communities

Table I. Jewish Population of Europe before and after World War II

Country	1933 population	1950 population
Poland	3.3 million	45,000
Romania	757,000	280,000
Baltic states	250,000	Approx. 25,000
USSR	2.5 million	2 million
Hungary	445,000	190,000
Czechoslovakia	357,000	17,000
Germany	565,000	37,000
Austria	250,000	18,000
Greece	100,000	7,000
Yugoslavia	70,000	3,500
Bulgaria	50,000	6,500
Great Britain	300,000	450,000
France	225,000	235,000
Netherlands	140,000	35,000
Belgium	65,000	25,000

Note: See United States Holocaust Memorial Museum, Holocaust Encyclopedia, "Remaining Jewish Population of Europe in 1945," http://www.ushmm.org/wlc/en/article.php?ModuleId= 10005687. According to the American Jewish Year Book, there were 11,532,630 Jews in world in 1951: 5,828,030 (50.6 percent) in the Americas; 3,463,500 (30.0 percent) in Europe, including Asiatic USSR and Turkey; 1,491,100 (13.0 percent) in Asia, of those 1.33 million of them in Israel; 694,000 (6.0 percent) in Africa; and 56,000 (0.4 percent)in Australia and New Zealand. See "World Jewish Population," American Jewish Year Book, http://www.ajcarchives.org/AJC_DATA/Files /1952_6_WJP.pdf.

around the world. In this brief postwar period, survivors set the agenda for forms of Holocaust commemoration, religious responses to the catastrophe, survivor politics, reconstruction of families, publishing, and documentation that would define the ways in which survivors carried their wartime experiences to new communities around the world. At the moment of liberation, however, it was by no means a foregone conclusion that this would be the case, or that the surviving population would even band together to form a collective identity as the She'erit Hapletah or "surviving remnant."

Beginning in the summer and fall of 1944, as Allied troops moved across Europe in a series of offensives against Nazi Germany, they began to encounter tens of thousands of concentration camp prisoners. Soviet forces were the first to approach a major Nazi camp, reaching Majdanek near Lublin, Poland, in July 1944. In the summer of 1944, the Soviets also overran the sites of the Bełżec, Sobibór, and Treblinka killing centers, which the Germans had dismantled in 1943 after the Germans and their collaborators had already murdered most of the Jews of Poland.

When the Soviets liberated Auschwitz, the largest killing center and concentration camp on January 27, 1945, they found only several thousand emaciated prisoners there, as the Nazis had forced the majority of Auschwitz prisoners to march westward (in what would become known as "death marches"). In the months that followed, Soviet forces also liberated camps in the Baltic States and Poland, as well as the Stutthof, Sachsenhausen, and Ravensbrück concentration camps. American forces liberated the Buchenwald concentration camp near Weimar, Germany, on April 11, 1945, a few days after the Nazis began evacuating the camp. They also liberated Dora-Mittelbau, Flossenbürg, Dachau, and Mauthausen. British forces liberated concentration camps in northern Germany, including Neuengamme and Bergen-Belsen, entering the Bergen-Belsen concentration camp, near Celle, in mid-April 1945. They found some sixty thousand prisoners alive, most in critical condition because of a typhus epidemic. More than ten thousand of them died from the effects of malnutrition or disease within a few weeks of liberation.

Upon Nazi Germany's unconditional surrender, hundreds of thousands of Jews throughout Europe remained in concentration and forced labor camps, in hiding, in the forests and in armed resistance units, and in the far reaches of the Soviet Union.[2] When Allied forces liberated camps in the German Reich, they encountered some eight million people whom they categorized as displaced persons (DPs)—that is, foreign nationals who needed Allied assistance and care before they could be repatriated to their countries of origin: forced and voluntary laborers, concentration camp inmates, and POWs, among them some ninety thousand Jews, survivors of Nazi labor, death camps, and death marches.[3]

Immediately following the defeat of Germany by the victorious Allied forces on May 8, 1945, millions of forced laborers, POWs, and

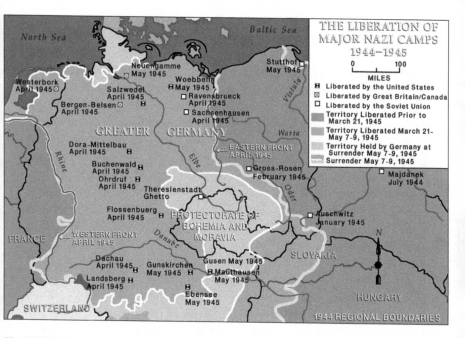

This USHMM map provides an overview picture of liberation. (https://encyclopedia.ushmm.org/content/en/map/liberation-of-major-nazi-camps-1944-1945)

other displaced persons flooded the roads of Germany in the desire to return home. According to Allied policy, a displaced person was defined "as any civilian who because of the war was living outside the borders of his or her country and who wanted to but could not return home or find a new home without assistance."[4] The Allies initially divided displaced persons into categories by place of origin and into those from enemy and Allied countries. As agreed to at Yalta in February 1945, the "Big Three" divided Germany and Austria into American, British, and Soviet zones of occupation, with a small French zone of occupation in southwest Germany. The majority of the Jewish population, perhaps some thirty-five thousand out of sixty thousand who survived the first weeks following liberation, were in the American zone of occupation in Germany, many of them around Munich.

Some liberated Jews made the choice to return to their countries of origin to search for family and determine what remained of their prewar homes,[5] while others refused repatriation (return to their country of origin). They knew that they had nowhere to return to because the Nazis and their collaborators had murdered their families, obliterated their communities, and looted their property. In general, Polish and Baltic Jews were the least likely to return to their home countries (especially where Soviet communism served as a deterrent to return), while Jews from countries such as Hungary, Romania, France, Belgium, the Netherlands, and, to a lesser extent, Greece, were far more likely to return to their countries following liberation. Later surveys of the Jewish DP population in the American zone of Germany corroborated this information. A survey of the 4,976 residents of the Jewish DP camp at Landsberg taken on October 1, 1945, indicated that 75.2 percent (3,740) of residents were Polish, while only 5.7 percent (283) were Hungarian and 3.3 percent (162) from Romania. A survey of residents of Feldafing taken at the same time indicated that a population drop from six hundred to four hundred from the summer to October 1945 was attributable to the sizable repatriation of Hungarian and Romanian Jews.[6]

By September 1945, the Allies repatriated some six million DPs.[7] Most of the millions of non-Jewish displaced persons, refugees, slave laborers, and POWs made the comparatively easy decision to return home. Roughly one million DPs, mostly East European nationals who feared repression for their collaboration with the Nazi regime or who simply refused to live under Soviet rule, refused repatriation. However, the Jewish DPs did not face such a clear decision; those unable to return to their prewar homes had become stateless.

Jewish DPs who made the decision to remain in Germany faced a choice: they could stay in the DP camp (generally German military barracks, former POW and slave labor camps, tent cities, industrial housing, apartments, hotels, or sanatoriums), at times continuing to be housed with wartime collaborators, or they could leave. One way to leave the DP camp was to settle in Germany permanently. Indeed, some of the liberated Jews chose to reconstitute prewar German Jewish *kehillot* (communities), although this was a choice that was more likely to be embraced by the fifteen thousand or so German Jews who had survived the war, many of whom had been in mixed marriages. Those who did choose to live in German cities faced an uncertain status and constant housing shortages.[8]

What were the most immediate needs that faced survivors in the aftermath of liberation? A thought exercise on the short-term, mid-range, and long-term needs of Jewish DPs can be a productive means of engaging students in thinking about what obstacles stateless Jews confronted in rebuilding their lives after the war, along with the resilience of the surviving population in advocating for themselves in the cruel reality that confronted them in the days, weeks, months, and years after the war.

Soon after liberation, Jewish survivors began to search for surviving family members almost immediately, although most Jews found that few had survived. Those survivors who remained in the DP camps faced deplorable conditions: poor accommodations, no plumbing, no clothing, rampant disease, continuing malnourishment, and a lack of any plan on the part of the Allies. Jewish chaplains serving with the American military were among the first Jews to encounter the survivors in the camps (along with the occasional Jewish Brigade soldier—a division from Palestine serving with the British Army).[9] While the American Jewish Joint Distribution Committee (JDC) sought to gain access to the camps as early as May 1945, the JDC's first organized group did not enter the American zone of occupation until August 1945, some three months later.[10] This meant that in the earliest stages after liberation, the survivors depended on the US Army and UNRRA (United Nations Relief and Rehabilitation Administration) for relief, and on a small group of Jewish chaplains who played an especially significant role in tending to the needs of the survivors. One particularly active chaplain, Rabbi Abraham Klausner, aided in the early political organization of the She'erit Hapletah and created a tracing service for survivors to find one another.[11] Klausner reported to his superiors in the United States on the situation facing Jews in postwar Germany after visiting thousands of DPs scattered across the American zone of occupation in the first month after liberation. He summarized his June 24, 1945, report to Philip Bernstein, executive director of the National Jewish Welfare Board committee on Army-Navy religious activities, stating, "Liberated but not free, that is the paradox of the Jew":

> There seems to be no policy, no responsibility, no plan for these . . . stateless Jews . . . Twelve hours a day I tell my lies. "They will come," I say. "When will they come?" they ask me. UNRRA, JDC, Red Cross— can it be that they are not aware of the problem? It is impossible . . . Of what use is all my complaining; I cannot stop their tears. America was their hope and all America has given them is a new camp with guards in khaki. Freedom, hell no! They are behind walls without hope.[12]

Organizing among themselves, Jewish DPs voiced their frustration in letters to military authorities and world Jewish organizations (such as the World Jewish Congress and the JDC), pleading for assistance from the US military government and UNRRA to rectify their miserable situation.[13] Expecting to be welcomed by the world with open arms, liberation was a rude awakening, as Jewish DPs continued to struggle to obtain bearable living conditions and yearned for contact with the rest of the Jewish world, which had still largely been denied access to the DP camps by military authorities seeking to establish order on the chaotic postwar situation.

With the JDC denied access to the military zone of occupation, survivors worked together with GIs and Jewish chaplains to organize help for themselves. Klausner met Zalman Grinberg, a doctor and a survivor from Kovno, who had commandeered part of a Benedictine monastery at St. Ottilien for use as a Jewish DP hospital after liberation, and who would become a close colleague in the rebuilding of Jewish life in postwar Germany during his early work in Bavaria.[14] As Grinberg wrote to the World Jewish Congress in May 1945, disappointment with the slow arrival of relief was evident: "It has been four weeks since our liberation and no representative of the Jewish world, no representative from any Jewish organization has come to be with us after the worst tragedy of all time, to speak with us, to give us help, and to lighten our burden. We must, ourselves, with our own diminished strength, help ourselves."[15] Chastened by the absence of any assistance from world Jewry, Grinberg and Klausner, with the assistance of other survivors and representatives from the Jewish Brigade, decided to take matters into their own hands, establishing the Central Committee of the Liberated Jews in the US Zone of Germany (CCLJ or ZK) on July 1, 1945, as the official representative body of the Jewish DPs.[16] The purpose of the Central Committee was to champion the interests of the Jewish DPs and to draw attention to their plight before the US Army and UNRRA just as other national groups of displaced persons had done. The CCLJ would eventually gain official US Army recognition as "the legal and democratic representation of the liberated Jews in the American zone" in September 1946. The Central Committee focused its work on the survivors' immediate needs, including food, shelter, medicine, and security, and addressed the question of emigration, soon reaching a consensus that Zionism represented the best solution for the stateless surviving population and that they should be encouraged to prepare themselves for immigration to Palestine at the earliest point possible.[17] The CCLJ appointed Rabbi Abraham Klausner honorary president and elected Dr. Grinberg as chairman of the executive committee. Josef Rosensaft, a survivor of Auschwitz and several other camps who had been liberated from Bergen-Belsen, became leader of the Central Committee of Liberated Jews in the British zone.[18]

The reports of continuing deprivation and poor organization of recovery sent by the DPs and Jewish chaplains eventually prompted American officials to take a greater interest in the problem of the displaced persons. President Truman dispatched Earl Harrison (dean of the University of Pennsylvania Law School and former US commissioner for immigration and naturalization) to survey conditions in the DP camps. In his scathing report back to Truman, Harrison concluded that we are "treating the Jews as the Nazis treated them except that we do not exterminate them." He proposed that Jews be separated in their own camps—until then they had been forced to live with other national groups and former collaborators—and, to resolve their refugee status, he proposed that one hundred thousand immigration certificates to Palestine be granted immediately to the Jewish DPs. Following Harrison's report, American authorities, under the leadership of General Eisenhower, worked to ameliorate conditions for Jewish DPs, moving Jews to separate camps and agreeing to the appointment of an adviser for Jewish affairs.

Over the course of 1945 and into 1946, with continued antisemitic violence, economic hardship, and increasingly restrictive new Communist regimes, many Jews, who were not liberated on German soil, escaped Poland and other Eastern European countries with the *Bricha* (Hebrew for "flight," a clandestine Zionist organization that conducted the underground immigration of European Jews to Palestine). They believed that there was no future for them in Europe and that entering the Western occupation zones of Germany would allow them to continue their route overseas.[19]

With the arrival of more than one hundred thousand Jews fleeing continued persecution and antisemitism in Eastern Europe with assistance from the Bricha, the Jewish DP population reached 250,000 in Germany, Italy, and Austria by the beginning of 1947. Approximately 185,000 were in Germany, 45,000 in Austria, and 20,000 in Italy. Young adults constituted a disproportionately high percentage of the surviving population: reports and surveys consistently estimated the proportion of Jewish DPs between the ages of fifteen and thirty at more than half and often above 80 percent of the total Jewish population.[20] In the absence of families, many survivors quickly created new families, as evidenced by the many weddings and the remarkable birthrate among the surviving population in the immediate postwar years. The nature of the surviving population also shifted as many more Jews who had survived the war in far-flung exile in the Soviet Union began to arrive in the DP camps. Upon repatriation to Poland, with the realization that their families, communities, and homes had been destroyed, they decided to move further west. Because the DPs were a population in constant transition—highly mobile, hoping for departure, waiting for immigration options, this notion of a postwar community of survivors was in flux—the She'erit Hapletah existed as a collective, but the individuals who composed it were constantly changing.[21]

While still living in a transitional situation, hoping for the possibility of emigration, DPs succeeded in creating a vibrant and dynamic community in hundreds of DP camps and communities across Germany, Italy, and Austria. With the assistance of representatives from UNRRA, the JDC, the Jewish Agency, and other organizations, they established schools throughout the DP camps. As the population of young people in the Jewish DP camps increased with the arrival of more Bricha "infiltrees," the educational system expanded, with most classes focused on preparing Jewish youth for a future in the Land of Israel, teaching Hebrew language, Jewish history, Jewish literature, and more. Despite some outside observers who objected to the concentration on Zionism, this approach reflected a consensus among Jewish DPs, who consistently articulated an emphatic and vocal desire to make Palestine the collective solution to the problem of Jewish statelessness, even for those who did not plan to go to Palestine individually.

The largest camps, including Landsberg, Feldafing, and Föhrenwald in the American zone of Germany and Bergen-Belsen in the British zone, boasted a vibrant social and cultural life, with a flourishing DP press, theater life, active Zionist youth movements, athletic clubs, historical commissions, and yeshivot testifying to the rebirth of Orthodox Judaism.[22] The DPs took an active role in representing their own political interests: political parties, mostly Zionist in nature—with the exception of the Orthodox Agudat Israel and the remnants of the Jewish socialist Bundist party still working to build a future for Jewish workers in the Diaspora—fought over camp committees and met at annual congresses of the She'erit Hapletah while advocating the immigration of survivors to Palestine. A flourishing DP press, along with a literary culture based in "Goles Daytshland" (the German Exile or Diaspora), also assisted in the creation of "imagined communities" for the survivors.[23] As evidenced by the creation of numerous theatrical troupes, a musical culture, a flourishing Jewish press, and a hunger for any form of entertainment, a unique form of Jewish humor in the DP camps was also a means of regaining a sense of normalcy after the war. As was the case during the war, this humor served as a coping mechanism to deal with suffering and trauma and to counter absurdities of the postwar situation. Jewish DPs were acutely aware of the intense irony of their continued existence in postwar Germany.[24]

Some among the survivors in the DP camps of Germany, Austria, and Italy (as well as the reconstituted communities in postwar Poland, Hungary, France, and elsewhere), realized they lived in a unique moment in time, where they had a short window of opportunity to document the atrocities of the war, before survivors dispersed around the globe to new homes. In the American zone of Germany, Moshe Feigenbaum and Israel Kaplan formed the Central Historical Commission, to gather individual testimonies that would become the foundation for the development of the field of Holocaust studies. These early collection projects, building on wartime documentation projects—most prominently Emanuel Ringelblum's *Oyneg Shabes* archive in the underground of the Warsaw ghetto—also created communities of shared wartime experience recorded and published in testimony projects. Although the intention was to chronicle a great variety of Holocaust experiences, the historical commissions often encountered a tendency among many survivors to privilege one Holocaust experience over the other and focus on stories of resistance or concentrate on the experience of Polish or Lithuanian Jews while neglecting the experiences of Jews elsewhere.[25] Likewise, survival in ghettos, camps, hiding, and partisan units appeared as the quintessential experiences under the Nazis, although a large portion of Jewish DPs had escaped Nazi occupation into the Soviet Union.[26] And some among the DPs preferred not to focus on prewar and wartime experiences at all, turning to the future. Posters in the

DP camps like the one depicted here worked to convince survivors that they had an obligation to "Remember what Amalek did to Thee! Collect and Record!"

Situating the most recent destruction in a series of catastrophic historical events that the Jewish people had also managed to survive (clockwise from top left: slavery in Egypt, the destruction of the temple(s) in Jerusalem, expulsion from Spain, and the Khmielnitsky Massacres of 1648–1649 in Ukraine), the historical commission reminded survivors that they had an obligation to "collect and record" their testimonies, both for the six million who had perished (note the number on the sheaf of pages pointed to by the skeleton) and to the future of the Jewish people, who would thus also "remember" this event.

The Zionist youth movements, with the assistance of emissaries from Palestine, created a network of at least forty agricultural training farms throughout Germany on the estates of former Nazis and German farmers, demonstrating their ardent desire for immigration to Palestine and performing an act of symbolic revenge against the Germans. As noted above, from an early point in time, the Jewish DP leadership espoused a strong Zionist position. In many cases, it was the surviving members of Zionist youth movements and political parties who undertook the self-help work and in turn became most active among those seeking to convince survivors to avoid a return to Eastern Europe. For the young Jewish survivors in the DP camps (primarily under the age of thirty-five), regardless of whether they had experience in a Zionist youth group before the war, such kibbutz groups emerged as attractive options, providing them with the camaraderie, support, and replacement "family" they so desperately craved. On the diplomatic level, the high visibility of the kibbutzim and hakhsharot (agricultural training farms) and their manifestations of Zionist enthusiasm demonstrated to outside observers a perceived state of "Palestine passion" on the part of the Jewish DPs.

For example, the DP youth pictured here on their way to work at Kibbutz Nili in Pleikhershof linked farming to revenge, finding satisfaction in working the land on Julius Streicher's estate while he stood trial in nearby Nuremberg. Students are often surprised by photos like this one, which challenge their preconceived notions of what "survivors" looked like, just one year after liberation. These are healthy, resolute, determined, happy young men preparing for their future lives in Palestine, and there could be no mistaking the symbolic value of this

"Remember what Amalek did to Thee! Collect and Record!" Central Historical Commission, Munich, US Zone of Germany, 1947. (Yad Vashem Archives M1P 685)

Members of Kibbutz Nili on the way to work in the fields, ca. 1946. (USHMM Photo Archives #30025)

(almost certainly staged) gesture by a kibbutz named "Nili," based on the acronym of the initial letters of the Hebrew verse "Netzach Yisrael Lo Yeshakker" ("the Strength of Israel will not lie"; I Sam. 15:29). The young men symbolically exacted their revenge on the "great Jew-hater," affirming the eternal presence of the Jewish people on the appropriated Nazi land, while reclaiming their bodies, their masculinity, and their work. The renaming of farm buildings and livestock with Hebrew names was part of a consciously symbolic revenge for youth empowered by membership in a kibbutz and the Zionist youth movement. While Zionism could allow them to transcend their current situation through a focus on the future, when they did face Germany and Nazism they were now armed with the tools to do so. At the same time, the young farmers could take pride in their collective accomplishments, as farming provided some tangible product for their time and efforts in Germany, as they waited for departure on Aliyah (literally "going up" or immigration to the Land of Israel). Indeed, in numerous ways, the demonstrations of a Jewish presence in postwar Germany, the baby carriages testifying to the "baby boom" in the DP camps, the focus on the education of Jewish youth, and the statement made by the survivors in Germany that "We Are Here" were a poignant affirmation of Jewish resilience and a defiant declaration that even after the destruction of the Holocaust, the Jewish people and the eternal Jewish spirit could not be eliminated.

The apparent importance of Zionism for the increasing numbers of arriving DPs confirmed the necessity of the Zionist solution for representatives of the Anglo-American Committee of Inquiry (AACI), created after the Harrison Report to come up with a diplomatic solution to the Jewish refugee problem in postwar Europe. After beginning their work in Washington and London in January 1946, members of the commission visited the DP camps and Poland to assess the Jewish situation beginning in February. Notwithstanding some concerns over Zionist propaganda, on April 20, 1946, the AACI recommended "(A) that one hundred thousand certificates be authorized immediately for the admission into Palestine of Jews who have been the victims of Nazi and Fascist persecution; (B) that these certificates be awarded as far as possible in 1946 and that actual immigration be pushed forward as rapidly as conditions will permit." This was the conclusion that the committee came to not only because of a lack of any other options but also because the committee genuinely believed that this was the truest expression of the Jewish DPs' desires. "Furthermore, that is where almost all of them want to go. There they are sure that they will receive a welcome denied them elsewhere. There they hope to enjoy peace and rebuild their lives."[27] The committee based these findings in part on surveys conducted among the DPs. However, the committee also firmly believed that based on what it had observed among the Jewish DPs, they were a group ardently preparing themselves for a Zionist future.

The Harrison Report served to link the resolution of the Jewish DP situation with the situation in Palestine, thereby elevating the diplomatic implications of the Jewish DP political stance. International observers from the Anglo-American Committee of Inquiry and the United Nations deemed DP Zionist enthusiasm central to the resolution of the political conflict over the land of Palestine. As their stay dragged on in Europe, DPs staged mass protests condemning the British blockade of Palestine and participated in the illegal immigration (aliyah bet) movement to Palestine, most noticeably in the Exodus Affair of 1947. In February 1947, the British referred the problem of Palestine to the United Nations, and following the drama of the Exodus Affair in the summer of 1947, and the work and report of the United Nations Special Committee on Palestine (UNSCOP), the United Nations voted for the partition of Palestine on November 29, 1947, recommending that the problem of the 250,000 Jewish Displaced Persons be dealt with through the partition of Palestine.

The announcement was greeted with great enthusiasm in the DP camps, and the Central Committee declared that "on the ruins of the Diaspora will arise the Jewish state, which will represent the most beautiful ideals of our people and will give the possibility to return the Jewish masses of the historical past and the coming future. With the help of the Jewish state the Jewish camps in Germany will be liquidated and the Jewish people will return to the family of free nations after 2000 years."[28] Following the passage of the UN partition plan (November 29, 1947) and the creation of the state of Israel in May 1948, approximately two-thirds of the DP population immigrated to the new state, with a sizable percentage of the younger segment participating in the fighting in the 1948 war. Most of the remainder immigrated to the United States, which had only become a realistic immigration option following passage of the Displaced Persons Act in 1948 and the amended DP Act of 1950, which authorized two hundred thousand DPs (Jewish and non-Jewish) to enter the United States. By 1952, more than eighty thousand

Jewish DPs had immigrated to the United States under the terms of the DP Act and with the aid of Jewish agencies. Almost all of the DP camps were closed by 1952, with the exception of Föhrenwald, which remained open until 1957.

How did Jews continue life in the aftermath of catastrophe? How did they cope with the destruction of family, community, and an entire civilization, while simultaneously attempting to chart a path for the future, living in an entirely uncertain present? Introducing students to the study of Jewish Displaced Persons not only challenges standard periodizations of the war but also forces them to consider the remarkable resilience of a population determined to continue life in the aftermath, to pay tribute to those who did not survive.

Notes

1. On defining Holocaust survivors after the war, see for example, Sergio DellaPergola, "Jewish Shoah Survivors: Neediness Assessment and Resource Allocation," in Dalia Ofer, Françoise S. Ouzan, and Judy Tydor Baumel-Schwartz, eds., *Holocaust Survivors: Resettlement, Memories, Identities* (New York: Berghahn Books, 2012), 293–314, 298–300.

2. Recent scholarship has shown that "liberation" from Nazi rule by Allied troops occurred in many different settings and circumstances and that only a few Jews experienced the stereotypical camp liberation in which emaciated yet enthusiastic camp survivors greeted Allied troops behind barbed wire. See Dan Stone, *The Liberation of the Camps: The End of the Holocaust and Its Aftermath* (New Haven: Yale University Press, 2015), and Leah Wolfsohn, *Jewish Responses to Persecution: 1944–1946* (London: Rowman and Littlefield, 2015), 53–80.

3. For a discussion of the number of Jews liberated from camps, see Stone, *Liberation of the Camps*, 19.

4. See discussion in Arieh Kochavi, *Post-Holocaust Politics: Britain, the United States, and Jewish Refugees, 1945–1948* (Chapel Hill: University of North Carolina Press, 2001), 14.

5. According to David Engel, the Jewish population of postwar Poland was in flux after the war, both due to the arrival of successive waves of refugees from the Soviet Union (and some returnees from Central Europe) and because of two great surges of emigration out of Poland. Although "between 266,000 and 281,000 Jews set foot on Polish territory at some time between July 1944 and July 1946, by mid-1947, however, only about 90,000 remained." See David Engel, "Poland," The YIVO Encyclopedia of Jews in Eastern Europe, http://www.yivoencyclopedia.org/article.aspx/Poland/Poland_since_1939.

6. Surveys of the Jewish DP population in the American zone of Germany from October 1945 corroborated this, indicating that the vast majority (as much

as 75 percent) of Jews who remained in Germany were in fact from Poland. YIVO Archives, New York, MK 488, Leo Schwarz Papers Roll 8, #1032–1037.

7. Stone, *Liberation of the Camps*, 19; and Anna Holian, *Between National Socialism and Soviet Communism: Displaced Persons in Postwar Germany* (Ann Arbor: University of Michigan Press, 2011), 3.

8. See Atina Grossmann, *Jews, Germans, and Allies: Close Encounters in Occupied Germany* (Princeton: Princeton University Press, 2007); and Ruth Schreiber, "The New Organization of the Jewish Community in Germany, 1945–1952" (PhD thesis, Tel Aviv University, 1995), 11.

9. For more on the Jewish Brigade, see Yoav Gelber, "The Meeting between the Jewish Soldiers from Palestine Serving in the British Army and *She'erit Hapletah*," in Yisrael Gutman and Avital Saf, eds., *She'erit Hapletah, 1944–1948, Rehabilitation and Political Struggle; Proceedings of the 6th Yad Vashem International Historical Conference, Jerusalem, October 1985* (Jerusalem: Yad Vashem, 1990), 60–80.

10. Yehuda Bauer, *American Jewry and the Holocaust* (Detroit: Wayne State University Press, 2017), 291. On the rescue work of Joseph Schwartz, see Ruth Baki Kolodny, *Ani Yosef Achichem* (I Am Joseph Your Brother: The Life and Work of Joe Schwartz) (Israel: Modan, 2010).

11. The term *she'erit hapletah* is biblical in origin and had been used during the war in the Yishuv to refer abstractly to the population of Jews who would survive the war; in the immediate aftermath of the war, the term would also be used in very concrete terms by the American Jewish chaplain Rabbi Abraham Klausner, who began to compile detailed lists of survivors he met in the camps he surveyed in the US Zone of Germany, publishing them under the series title *She'erit Hapletah*, a reference to the writings of the prophets, that there would be a "saving remnant" after the destruction. For a more detailed discussion of Klausner's role in the DP camps, see Avinoam Patt, "The People Must Be Forced to Go to Palestine: Rabbi Abraham Klausner and the Surviving Remnant in Postwar Germany," *Holocaust and Genocide Studies* 28, no. 2 (Fall 2014): 240–276.

12. June 24, 1945, report of Chaplain Abraham Klausner, "A Detailed Report on the Liberated Jew as He Now Suffers His Period of Liberation under the Discipline of the Armed Forces of the United States," Center for Jewish History, American Jewish Historical Society, Abraham Klausner papers, Box 3, Folder 11.

13. See Zalman Grinberg and Puczyc to OMGUS and UNRRA, July 10, 1945, YIVO Archives, DP Germany, MK 483, #340. Noting that many Ukrainians who had collaborated with the SS continued to be well fed, the Jewish prisoners, who had always received the worst nourishment, continued to be malnourished and were still without proper clothing.

14. Zeev W. Mankowitz, *Life between Memory and Hope: The Survivors of the Holocaust in Occupied Germany* (New York: Cambridge University Press, 2002),

31. For a transcript of the speech given by Zalman Grinberg at St. Ottilien on May 27, 1945, see YIVO Archives, LS, MK 488, Roll 13, Folder 104, #10–14.

15. YIVO Archives, DP Germany, MK 483, Reel 21. Dr. Zalman Grinberg, "Appel an den judischen Weltkongress," St. Ottilien, May 31, 1945. Klausner's requests for medical supplies for the newly formed hospital organized by Grinberg were met with replies of "materials unavailable" from the JDC, leading Klausner to secure supplies on his own through individual contacts in New Haven, Connecticut. See in Abraham J. Klausner, *A Letter to My Children: From the Edge of the Holocaust* (San Francisco: Holocaust Center of Northern California, 2002), 26.

16. The first CCLJ meeting took place in Feldafing DP camp, near Dachau. For more on the early and extensive involvement of American Jewish chaplains in the relief efforts and organization of DP institutions, see Alexander Grobman, *Rekindling the Flame: American Jewish Chaplains and the Survivors of European Jewry, 1944–1948* (Detroit: Wayne State University Press, 1993).

17. See Avinoam Patt, *Finding Home and Homeland: Jewish Youth and Zionism in the Aftermath of the Holocaust* (Detroit: Wayne State University Press, 2009), chapter 1.

18. On the experiences of survivors in the British zone, see Hagit Lavsky, *New Beginnings: Holocaust Survivors in Bergen-Belsen and the British Zone in Germany, 1945–1950* (Detroit: Wayne State University Press, 2002).

19. For more on the Bricha, see David Engel, *Ben shikhrur li-verihah: Nitsolei ha-Shoah be-Polin veha-ma'avak 'al hanhagatam, 1944–1946* (Tel Aviv: Am Oved, 1996).

20. From an early point following liberation it was evident that as much as half of the surviving population was under the age of twenty-five, and some 80 percent were under age forty. For example, a survey of Jewish DPs in Bavaria taken in February 1946 found that 83.1 percent of their number was between the ages of 15 and 40, with over 40 percent between 15 and 24, and 61.3 percent between 19 and 34 (YIVO Archives, MK 488, Leo Schwarz Papers, Roll 9, Folder 57, #581; Jewish Population in Bavaria, February 1946). A study by the American Jewish Joint Distribution Committee of Jews in the US Occupation Zone in Germany over one year after liberation found 83.1 percent between the ages of 6 and 44 (YIVO Archives, MK 488, LS 9, 57, #682; Jewish Population, US Zone Germany, November 30, 1946).

21. For a map depicting the DP camps, see "Major Camps for Jewish Displaced Persons, 1945–1946," Holocaust Encyclopedia, https://encyclopedia.ushmm.org/content/en/map/major-camps-for-jewish-displaced-persons-1945-1946. For an overview on the history of Jewish DPs, see, for example, Mankowitz, *Life between Memory and Hope*; Margarete Myers Feinstein, *Holocaust Survivors in Postwar Germany, 1945–1957* (New York: Cambridge University Press, 2010); Avinoam J. Patt and Michael Berkowitz, eds. *"We Are Here":*

New Approaches to Jewish Displaced Persons in Postwar Germany (Detroit: Wayne State University Press, 2010).

22. On the rebirth of religious life in the DP camps, see Judith Baumel, "The Politics of Spiritual Rehabilitation in the DP Camps," *Simon Wisenthal Center Annual* 6 (1989): 58–79.

23. Tamar Lewinsky points to the problem faced by authors in creating and re-creating Jewish culture within the unthinkable surroundings of "Goles Daytshland." See Tamar Lewinsky, "Dangling Roots: Yiddish Language and Culture in the German Diaspora," in Patt and Berkowitz, "*We Are Here,*" 308–334.

24. For more on this topic, see Avinoam Patt, "'Laughter through Tears': Jewish Humor in the Aftermath of the Holocaust," in Eli Lederhendler and Gabriel N. Finder, eds., *A Club of Their Own: Jewish Humorists and the Contemporary World*, Studies in Contemporary Jewry 29 (New York: Oxford University Press, 2016), 113–31.

25. For more on the Jewish historical commissions, see Laura Jockusch, *Collect and Record! Jewish Holocaust Documentation in Early Postwar Europe* (New York: Oxford University Press, 2012), chap. 4; and Natalia Aleksiun, "The Central Jewish Historical Commission in Poland 1944–1947," *Polin* 20 (2008): 74–97.

26. See Laura Jockusch and Tamar Lewinsky, "Paradise Lost? Postwar Memory of Polish Jewish Survival in the Soviet Union," *Holocaust and Genocide Studies* 24, no. 3 (Winter 2010): 373–399.

27. Anglo-American Committee of Inquiry, *Report to the United States Government and His Majesty's Government in the United Kingdom*, Lausanne, Switzerland, April 20, 1946 (Washington, DC: US Government Printing Office, 1946); see Lillian Goldman Law Library, Yale Law School, http://avalon.law.yale.edu/subject_menus/angtoc.asp (accessed July 21, 2019).

28. *Jidisce Cajtung*, December 2, 1947, reel 1, Jewish DP Periodicals Collection, YIVO Archives.

Postwar Trials and Justice

GABRIEL N. FINDER

According to the classic legal model, the state protects its own citizens and noncitizens residing within its borders from the criminal behavior of individual lawbreakers while it enforces and prosecutes violated norms of communal order. Moreover, it extends this protection and defense of communal norms to civilians or noncombatants of belligerent states during war. Nazi Germany upended this model. The Nazi state and representatives acting under its authority from the head of state, Adolf Hitler, on down—cabinet ministers, administrators, the police, the military, paramilitary organizations such as the SS, the personnel in concentration camps, to name but a few of these representatives—initiated and perpetrated atrocities on an unprecedented scale against its own citizens and the citizens of other states, primarily Jews but also many others, including handicapped people, Roma and Sinti (Gypsies), and Soviet prisoners of war. Karl Jaspers, the German philosopher, described Nazi Germany as a *Verbrecherstaat*, a criminal state, "a formulation," as Lawrence Douglas explains, that "demanded that the state be seen not as the defender of order but as the principal perpetrator of crimes, as the very agent of criminality."[1]

The challenges posed to the postwar international system of justice and national systems of justice alike in their confrontation with Nazi criminality were, therefore, formidable. As Mary Fulbrook writes, "Nowhere in post-Nazi Europe was legal reckoning with collective violence and state-sponsored crimes simple or straightforward."[2] That said, the postwar legal reckoning with Nazi-era crimes often, though not always, led to fundamental if not radical changes to domestic and international law and legal systems as a result of the confrontation with Nazi crimes

of atrocity. Indeed, Douglas speaks of the postwar emergence of a "jurisprudence of atrocity." The most famous legal innovation was the creation of a new species of criminal offense, "crimes against humanity,"
which found its first expression in the 1945 London Charter that established the International Military Tribunal (IMT) at Nuremberg, commonly known as the Nuremberg Trial.

Germany itself represents an interesting case of the potential of
domestic law to adjust to Nazi-era criminality. After World War II, the
West German legal system stubbornly refused to confront the distinctive quality of Nazi criminality and apply "crimes against humanity"
against alleged Nazi criminals. German law did not distinguish the
crime of murder from Nazi-era genocidal acts. German prosecutors
were required to prove each individual case of murder committed by a
defendant in a ghetto or concentration camp. Moreover, a murder conviction required proof of the defendant's racial animus or thirst for
blood. Under the circumstances, then, obtaining a conviction for murder in German courts demanded a very high bar of proof given the participation of the defendants in a collective enterprise in mass murder in
which their roles in individual acts of murder and their motives were
often far from transparent. Then, in 2010, a German court in Munich accepted prosecutors' novel "collective participation" theory in the trial
of John (Ivan) Demjanjuk. German prosecutors alleged that Demjanjuk,
extradited from the United States, had been a guard at the death camp
of Sobibor. The court ruled that Demjanjuk could be convicted as an ac-
cessory to murder since the prosecution had proved that twenty-seven
thousand Jews had been gassed to death during the period that he was
a guard at Sobibor and that he had served voluntarily. Although one
could argue that it was too little, too late, German law had evolved to
become a more effective instrument in dealing with Nazi-era crimes.[3]

Study of the postwar trials of Nazis[4] and of postwar justice invariably elicits a number of key questions ripe for discussion in a classroom: How many Nazis and which Nazis were tried and convicted?
Were the punishments of those who were convicted appropriate to
their crimes? Why were many Nazis able to evade punishment? To what
extent was the Nazi genocide of the Jews central to postwar trials? To
what extent did Jewish survivors contribute to the prosecution of Nazi
criminals? Taken collectively, these questions pointedly and ultimately
raise perennial questions: What is justice? How is it attained? How is it
measured? By whom? For whom? This chapter examines various facets

of these consequential questions through the prism of postwar trials for Nazi-era crimes.

The first question is almost invariably whether Nazi trials were "successful." But what would "success" or, for that matter, "failure" look like in this context? How does one even measure it? One possible measure is by how many Nazis were prosecuted and convicted. In purely quantitative terms, the numbers appear impressive at first blush. According to statistics compiled by Norbert Frei, European courts convicted about one hundred thousand Germans and Austrians of Nazi-era crimes after the war. The majority of these defendants— more than fifty-three thousand—were tried in Eastern Europe. (Figures exist for the Soviet Union, Poland, and Czechoslovakia. Since they do not exist for Hungary, Romania, or Yugoslavia, the number of convictions of Nazis in Eastern Europe is presumably higher.) West European courts, for their part, sentenced more than 3,900 former German and Austria Nazis.[5] Moreover, the four victorious Allies—the United States, the United Kingdom, France, and the Soviet Union—convicted an additional 8,812 German and Austrian Nazis in occupied Germany. That said, Rebecca Wittmann observes that between 1950, one year after West Germany had become an independent country, and 1962, the West Germans investigated thirty thousand alleged former Nazis, but they indicted only 12,846, tried 5,426, and convicted 1,399 while acquitting 4,027, a conviction rate of 25 percent. Furthermore, by all measures many sentences were not appropriate to the crime. Of Nazi defendants who were convicted, only 155 (15 percent) were convicted of being directly responsible for committing murder, and only 7 percent were convicted of crimes related to the killing of Jews.[6] (In contrast, East German courts convicted some forty-seven hundred Nazi defendants.)

Which Nazis were convicted? Many high-level Nazis were ultimately punished. Leading figures in the Third Reich such as Hermann Göring, president of the Reichstag and commander of the Luftwaffe, who until 1942 was the most important official in Nazi Germany after Hitler; Hans Frank, the governor general of the General Government, that part of occupied Poland not annexed directly to the Reich; and Arthur Seyss-Inquart, Reich commissioner of the occupied Netherlands, were convicted and sentenced to death at the 1945–1946 Nuremberg Trial. Göring committed suicide before his execution; Frank and Seyss-Inquart were hanged. Polish courts convicted Rudolf Höss, the commandant of Auschwitz; Jürgen Stroop, the SS general who led the final liquidation of the Warsaw Ghetto and the brutal suppression of the Warsaw Ghetto Uprising; Hans Biebow, the civil administrator of the Łódź Ghetto; Arthur Greiser, the Nazi governor of the Warthegau, the region in Western Poland annexed to Nazi Germany; and Amon Göth, the notorious commandant of the Płaszów concentration camp on the outskirts of Kraków, among others. Franz Stangl, commandant of the Sobibor and Treblinka death camps, was convicted in Germany. The Soviets tried and executed Friedrich Jeckeln, the SS officer who oversaw the mass murder of tens of thousands of Jews at Babi Yar, a ravine on the outskirts of Kiev, in September and October 1941 and Rumbala, outside Riga, in November and December 1941.

However, a significant number of prominent Nazis escaped punishment. Friedrich Übelhör, former regional president of the Łódź district, who issued the order for the establishment of the Łódź Ghetto, went missing in the final phase of the war. Otto Bovensiepen, the head of the Berlin Gestapo from November 1942 and one of several people responsible for the deportation of Berlin's Jews, was investigated only in February 1969, but his case was suspended the following year because of his purported poor health. Several infamous Nazis fled Europe, especially to Latin America, with the assistance of Catholic Church officials.[7] Josef Mengele, the notorious doctor who conducted human experiments on prisoners at Auschwitz, found refuge in Argentina, Paraguay, and, from 1960, Brazil until his death there in 1979. Hans Globke, instrumental in the drafting of the 1935 Nuremberg Laws, which stripped Jews of their German citizenship and made marriage and sexual relations between Jewish Germans and non-Jewish Germans a crime, and who had a hand in the expulsion of Jews from Germany and looting of their property, was never tried; indeed, he was one of German chancellor Konrad Adenauer's top advisers in the 1950s. Erich von dem Bach Zalewski, an SS general with blood on his hands as a result of his leading role in "anti-partisan" operations in the USSR and in the violent suppression of the 1944 Warsaw Uprising, was never tried for his World War II–era crimes. (He was convicted eventually for his part in the "Night of Long Knives," the officially sanctioned elimination of a radical Nazi faction in 1934.)

Were the punishments of the convicted appropriate to their crimes? Take the 1947–1948 Einsatzgruppen Trial, one of the twelve successor Nuremberg Trials conducted by American military authorities. (The official name of these successor Nuremberg trials, not to be confused with the IMT, was the Nuremberg Military Tribunals [NMT]). The defendants were all leaders of the SS mobile killing and security units, the Einsatzgruppen. They were charged with war crimes and crimes against humanity committed between May 1941 and June 1943 and of membership in a criminal organization. They all pleaded not guilty. They claimed that they acted legally, as soldiers, following orders. Although twenty-four were indicted, only twenty-two stood trial; one committed suicide in jail, while another was deemed incompetent to stand trial. In its verdict, the court found twenty of the defendants guilty on all three counts, and two guilty on count three (membership) alone. The lead defendant was Otto Ohlendorf, leader of Einsatzgruppe D, which beginning in June 1941 operated behind enemy lines in the USSR. His unit murdered ninety thousand Soviet civilians in a twelve-month period. In the end, fourteen defendants were sentenced to death, including Ohlendorf, two to life terms, and five received sentences that ranged from ten to twenty years. One defendant was released with time served. However, only four of the fourteen death sentences were eventually carried out in 1951. One defendant who received the death sentence was extradited to Belgium, where he received a further death sentence. The remaining defendants had their sentences commuted or were paroled. All of the convicted defendants still living were released from prison in 1958.[8]

Or take the 1963–1965 Frankfurt Auschwitz Trial. Twenty-two defendants were indicted; twenty were ultimately tried. They were of various ranks from high officials to privates; they had filled various functions from those responsible for the administration of the camp to members of the Political Department; doctors and medical orderlies; and camp guards who participated in selections and took part in gassing operations. Most operated at the main camp, Auschwitz I, only a few at Birkenau, Auschwitz II. In the end, six defendants were convicted of murder and received life in prison; eleven were convicted of aiding and abetting and received sentences ranging from fourteen years in prison for a high official to three and a half years in prison for an "ordinary" killer; three were acquitted. But the two highest officials indicted (Richard Baer, the last commandant of Auschwitz, died before the conclusion of the trial) were not convicted of murder but only of being accessories to murder. By 1989, three of the six defendants who had been sentenced to life in prison were released (the other three died in prison); all ten defendants who had been sentenced to prison terms of ten years or less had already been released by 1970.[9]

Indeed, many Nazis who committed serious crimes and received significant sentences were amnestied and released from prison in the 1950s and afterward. The reason for this was generally political. As Fulbrook observes, "In the Third Reich successor states, conflicts continued for decades between those seeking justice and those wanting to put an end to reckoning with the Nazi past."[10] The latter, officials and ordinary citizens alike, especially in West Germany, which was no longer under American military occupation, and in countries formerly aligned with Nazi Germany, were eager to sweep the past under the rug. Moreover, the new Germany and other postwar European governments, devastated by the war and now anxious to rebuild, required the skills of bureaucrats and technocrats, even politically tainted ones. Therefore, they championed the reintegration of former Nazis and their national collaborators into the reconstructed postwar national polities to the detriment of the pursuit or completion of full-fledged postwar justice.

One convicted defendant who returned to civilian life in 1952 after serving only five years of a twenty-year sentence was Dr. Herta Oberheuser. A dermatologist by training, she had been convicted in August 1947 by an American military tribunal of participation in medical experiments on nonconsenting female inmates, mostly Polish political prisoners, at Ravensbrück, a concentration camp primarily for women. She resumed her medical practice until her past was divulged and her medical license revoked. Oberheuser was one of only two German women tried in twelve trials conducted by American occupation authorities in Nuremberg. The other was Inge Viermetz, accused of deporting hundreds of Polish and Yugoslav children to Germany under the auspices of the SS Race and Settlement Office. The American court acquitted her. The Soviets (followed by the East Germans) convicted female guards from Ravensbrück, and a British military court tried sixteen female guards from Auschwitz and Bergen-Belsen in the fall of 1945, along with thirty-nine male defendants, convicting twelve of the female SS members and executing four of them, including the notorious Irma Grese. Before Grese oversaw the women's section of Bergen-Belsen, she had been placed in charge of the Hungarian women's camp at Auschwitz-Birkenau by Maria Mandl. Mandl was in charge of all women's sections at Auschwitz and female subcamps in the Auschwitz

Chief American prosecutor Justice Robert Jackson delivers the opening speech of the American prosecution at the International Military Tribunal trial of war criminals at Nuremberg. (Harry S. Truman Library, Provenance: Robert Jackson, Source Record ID: 72-880, USHMM)

complex and was implicated in the death and abuse of hundreds of thousands of women and children at Birkenau, the death camp, at which she participated in selections. At their trial of forty Auschwitz personnel in November 1947, the Poles convicted her, along with several other female guards, and sentenced her to death. Although thousands of women served the Nazi regime in various capacities, relatively few stood trial because they had not occupied leadership roles, and the Allies and countries formerly under Nazi occupation concentrated their efforts on men.[11]

Were the trials fair, even if the notion of fairness is interpreted rather broadly? Contemporary critics of the Nuremberg Trial accused the Allies of unfairly subjecting the Nazi defendant in the dock to "victors' justice." In one of the most touted opening statements made by a prosecuting attorney in the annals of legal history, Justice Robert H. Jackson, the US Supreme Court justice who was chief of counsel for the American prosecution at Nuremberg, sensitive to the trial's critics, exclaimed: "To pass these defendants a poisoned chalice is to put it to our own lips as well." One indication of fairness is the real possibility of acquittal, and three of the Nuremberg defendants were found not guilty. In contrast, historian Tomaz Jardim draws attention to the lack of due process at the trial of personnel who had served at the notorious forced labor camp Mauthausen—forty-eight defendants were executed, while three were sentenced to life in prison.[12] The trials of former Nazis conducted in the Soviet Union and Eastern Europe are often considered "show trials." Historian Alexander Prusin maintains that although Soviet trials of Nazi officials were designed to serve the Soviet regime's political and ideological purposes and exhibited certain patently unfair practices—defense counsel did not meet their clients until the trial and were not allowed to mount a defense in court, and confessions were often extracted as a result of abusive tactics such as sleep deprivation—they were conducted in line with Soviet law and yielded valuable historical information about Nazi atrocities on Soviet territory.[13] In the case of Poland, Prusin and I argue that trials of German and Austrian Nazis under the country's communist regime resembled Nazi trials in Western countries.[14]

If we move from the macro to the micro level, a clearer picture of postwar justice in specific contexts emerges. In this vein, Austria is illustrative. Austria established four special "people's courts," *Volksgerichte* (in Vienna, Graz, Linz, and Innsbruck), between 1945 and 1955 to put alleged Nazis on trial. The state attorney's office filed 28,148 indictments, which represented only a drop in the ocean—17 percent—of all investigations conducted of putative Nazi criminals. These indictments yielded 23,477 verdicts, resulting in 13,607 convictions and 9,870 acquittals, a 58 percent conviction rate, which might be deemed on the low side. Among the convictions, there were 43 death sentences, of which 30 were carried out; two of the convicted committed suicide before they could be executed. There were 29 sentences of life in prison. Otherwise, Austrian courts passed 269 sentences for between ten and twenty years, 381 for between five and ten years, 8,326 for between one and five years, and 4,559 for up to one year. In other words, 12,885 of the 13,607 convicted received sentences of between one and five years for their Nazi-era crimes. Moreover, up to 1955, only 108, or less than 1 percent, of the convictions were for crimes related to the Holocaust, that is, anti-Jewish crimes, ranging from Pogrom Night (Kristallnacht) in November 1938 to participation in the persecution and mass murder of Jews in ghettos and camps. The year 1957 marked the introduction of a policy of commuting sentences, thanks to which many convicted former Nazis were released before the completion of their sentences. After 1955, when the *Volksgerichte* were dismantled, there were only thirty-five trials of alleged Nazis in Austria; thirty ended in a verdict.[15]

Or take Auschwitz, which is a metonym for the Holocaust. Historian Aleksander Lasik estimates that 7,000 to 7,200 people served in the Auschwitz concentration camp complex and that 6,300 to 6,500 members of the Auschwitz concentration camp staff were still alive in May 1945. He concludes, however, that at most 15 percent ever stood trial in various countries. Moreover, of the some seventy thousand people who served on the staffs of thousands of Nazi concentration camps, the percentage of Auschwitz personnel brought before courts was relatively high as compared to the proportion of staff from other camps because of the symbolic importance of Auschwitz.[16]

The iconic postwar trial was the Nuremberg Trial. The four major victorious Allies—the United States, Great Britain, the Soviet Union, and France—indicted twenty-three defendants, all high-ranking Nazis from a cross-section of the Third Reich's political, military, diplomatic, and economic elite. (Ultimately, twenty-two were tried.) They were charged with conspiracy, waging aggressive war, war crimes, and crimes against humanity. The essential charge was the conspiracy to wage aggressive war. Nineteen defendants were found guilty. Twelve were hanged, three were sentenced to life in prison, two were sentenced to twenty years in prison, one was sentenced to fifteen years, and one was sentenced to ten years. Three were acquitted on all charges.

But was the Nuremberg Trial a "Holocaust trial"? That is to say, was it a trial at which the Nazi genocide of Europe's Jews was uppermost or near the top of the priorities of prosecutors and played a primary or highly significant role in the proceedings and in the judgment? Was it a trial that paid satisfactory attention to Jewish suffering (and heroism) and in which the Jewish fate under Nazi rule was thoroughly aired in open court? Scholarly opinion on this point is divided.[17] One indication that it was not is the fact that only three Jewish survivors of the Holocaust testified and that non-Jews provided testimony about the gassing of Jews at Auschwitz, even though Jewish witnesses were available. To be fair to the prosecution, Jackson referred to the Nazi genocide of Jews in his opening address, and American prosecutor William F. Walsh presented evidence of the Nazi persecution of the Jews, especially of the final liquidation of the Warsaw Ghetto in 1943.[18] Moreover, British prosecutor Sir Hartley Shawcross devoted his closing argument to Nazism's Jewish victims.[19] Finally, in its judgment, the tribunal made clear its sympathy for the Jewish victims of Nazi atrocities. "The persecution of the Jews at the hands of the Nazi Government has been proved in the greatest detail before the Tribunal," the court wrote. "It is a record of consistent and systematic inhumanity on the greatest scale." Not being in a position to enumerate all Nazi anti-Jewish crimes of which the prosecution had provided ample evidence, the court highlighted the mass shootings of Jewish civilian populations by SS Einsatzgruppen and the gassing of Jews at Auschwitz.

The court, however, rejected the prosecution's theory of the case that the persecution of the Jews was integral to the Nazis' common plan before the German invasion of Poland on September 1, 1939, to wage aggressive war. In the words of the judgment, "The Nazi persecution of Jews in Germany before the war, severe and repressive as it was, cannot compare, however, with the policy pursued during the war in the occupied territories. . . . The plan for exterminating the Jews was developed shortly after the attack on the Soviet Union [in June 1941]." Exemplary of this plan, in the tribunal's opinion, was the liquidation of the Warsaw Ghetto. The court ended its analysis of the "persecution of the Jews" with a reference to Adolf Eichmann's estimate, as recorded in an affidavit that was presented as evidence, that the Nazis' policy for the annihilation of Jews "resulted in the killing of 6 million Jews, of which 4 million were killed in the extermination institutions."[20]

It is often argued that, as opposed to the Nuremberg Trial, the first and perhaps only bona fide "Holocaust trial" was the 1961 Eichmann Trial in Jerusalem. Who was Adolf Eichmann? He claimed that he was just a pencil pusher. He was in fact a Nazi who pursued his assignment with zeal and even countermanded orders. He was assigned to Vienna to accelerate the emigration of Jews from Austria after the so-called annexation (Anschluss) in 1938; he coordinated the deportation of Jews across Europe to concentration and killing camps; and he was sent to Budapest in the spring of 1944 to organize the deportation of 430,000 Hungarian Jews to Auschwitz.

There were several unusual aspects to Eichmann's trial in Jerusalem, Israel, in 1961. He was tried under a law, the Nazi and Nazi Collaborator (Punishment) Law, passed in 1950 by the Israeli parliament, the Knesset. When Israeli legislators crafted the law they did not consider it likely that German Nazis and their non-Jewish accomplices would be tried under the law because the prospects of bringing them before a court in Israel were remote. In this regard, the law was a symbolic statement of Israel's collective memory of the Holocaust. Second, the 1950 law created a new species of criminal offense, "crimes against the Jewish people." Generally, criminal laws are drafted to be broad and inclusive, without establishing the specific identity of a perpetrator's victim or victims. Thus, the Allies at the IMT created crimes against humanity, without specifying any particular group of victims. After all, *humanity* is all-encompassing. The 1950 law included the offense of crimes against humanity. But Israeli legislators wanted to make two points. The first point was that Jews were the special targets of the Nazis' genocidal designs. Second, they were expressing their grievance that the genocide of the Jews was just one of several priorities for Allied prosecutors at the IMT and that charging the Nazis with crimes against humanity effectively submerged or shoehorned the suffering of European Jews into an undifferentiated amalgam of Nazism's victims.

There were other unusual aspects of Eichmann's trial. The Israeli law was passed in 1950, but Eichmann committed his alleged crimes between 1938 and 1945, raising the specter that the Israeli law was retroactive. Israeli prosecutors argued, and the judges accepted the argument, that justice demanded that Eichmann and other Nazis be held accountable for their atrocities regardless of when the law was passed, for the alternative—not to try them before a court of law—would be a travesty of justice and make a mockery of human decency. Second, Eichmann and other Nazis committed their crimes in Europe, not in Israel. Indeed, Israel hadn't even existed yet during World War II. A common principle of criminal law is the territorial principle, which holds that people suspected of crimes should be tried in national courts located in the territories in which the crimes were allegedly committed and that only national courts in countries where the crimes were allegedly committed can exercise jurisdiction to hear a case and reach a judgment. The Israeli prosecution made the claim, which the judges accepted, that Israel had an organic spiritual and political connection to the Jewish victims of the Holocaust, essentially that Israel represented the Jewish people, both living and dead, even before Israel existed.

Of course, the prosecution had more than enough documentary evidence to convict Eichmann under the 1950 law. But the prosecution, under Israeli attorney general Gideon Hausner, wanted to turn

Eichmann's trial into a didactic event for both a world audience and an audience of young native-born Israelis for whom Europe in the 1930s and 1940s seemed like light years away. According to Douglas, Hausner wanted to emphasize what Douglas calls "heroic memory." What is heroic memory? It was partly an emphasis on Jewish armed resistance to Nazism during the Holocaust. For this purpose, Hausner summoned to the witness stand legendary Jewish resistance fighters. It was, however, also partly an effort to shine a spotlight on the efforts of ordinary Jews just to survive, with their souls intact. The message that Hausner wished to convey through some one hundred Jewish witnesses was that the vast majority of Jews survived the Holocaust with dignity in spite of the Nazis' colossal effort to dehumanize them. As a result, the Jewish fate during the Holocaust was fully aired in open court and generated a national catharsis in Israel while deeply affecting the rest of the world. What this meant, however, is that very few of the witnesses actually observed or had dealings with Eichmann in the 1930s and 1940s and could testify directly about his actions and motivations or about the impact of his actions. For example, one could argue that the persecution and murder of Jews in death camps and concentration camps who were deported to them as a result of Eichmann's coordination of deportations by rail pointed to Eichmann's guilt. But the murder of Jews shot in ghettos by Einsatzgruppen had nothing to do with Eichmann. In other words, the testimony of only a few witnesses was legally relevant.[21]

Douglas calls the Eichmann Trial the "Great Holocaust Trial" in large measure thanks to the attention it enjoyed worldwide. It "served to *create* the Holocaust: it helped remove an episode of unprecedented atrocity from the silences of shame, unexamined horror, and purposeful avoidance and transform it into an episode of world historical significance and collective meaning."[22] But was the Eichmann Trial the first "Holocaust trial"? One could argue that the Einsatzgruppen Trial was the first trial to deal exclusively with defendants whose sole task was their participation in the genocidal murder of the Jews, since it focused almost exclusively on the Nazi genocide of the Jews. A major distinction between the Einsatzgruppen Trial and the Eichmann Trial is that the American prosecution at the Einsatzgruppen Trial, which was led by a young Jewish lawyer named Benjamin Ferencz, proved its case almost exclusively on the basis of documents and did not summon Holocaust survivors to testify. Indeed, Alexander Prusin and I argue that several trials of German and Austrian Nazis in communist Poland such as the trials of Rudolf Höss and Jürgen Stroop performed similar functions as the Eichmann Trial, as the defendants were key figures in the Nazi genocide of Jews, the Holocaust was at the center of the trials, and Jewish survivors were essential witnesses. To be sure, Polish trials paled in comparison on the global stage, but "if the Eichmann trial was the 'Great Holocaust Trial,' the trials of Göth, Stroop and other Nazis can be seen as prefiguring it."[23]

Especially for American students, the specific American legal response should be of utmost interest. At Nuremberg, the United States was first among equals, and the prosecution's main argument that all twenty-two Nazi officials in the dock conspired to wage aggressive war was an American initiative. The American prosecution also took the lead in presenting evidence of the Nazis' anti-Jewish crimes to the tribunal. Moreover, the United States mounted the twelve subsequent Nuremberg Trials and a large number of Nazi trials at the former Dachau concentration camp. To its discredit, the US government sheltered prominent Nazis or helped them vanish into thin air, while hundreds, maybe thousands, of Nazi collaborators were able to enter the United States after World War II after lying to investigators about their wartime activities. Congress, for its part, passed no law to try Nazi collaborators in US criminal proceedings (although the constitutionality of such an extraterritorial punishment may have been questionable). However, in 1979, Congress created the Office of Special Investigations (OSI) in the Criminal Division of the Department of Justice, charging it to identify former Nazi and Nazi collaborators who had been able to acquire residency in the United States or American citizenship after World War II through surreptitious means and to initiate civil proceedings to denaturalize and then either deport or extradite them. Between 1979 and 2020, OSI (part of the Human Rights and Special Prosecution Section since 2010) brought 133 such cases, prevailing in 109 of them. In addition, an amendment to US immigration law, the Holtzman Amendment, bars aliens who assisted in Axis crimes from entering the United States. Since 1980, OSI was responsible for preventing at least 175 such individuals from entering the country, putting suspects on a "watch list."[24]

Then there are the victims, the survivors of the Holocaust. Jews played an active role in the prosecution of Nazi criminals and not only at the Eichmann Trial. In the first place, they testified in a large number of trials. But they assisted in prosecutions in other important ways. Jacob Robinson, originally from Lithuania, was head of the Institute for

Jewish Affairs, a division of the World Jewish Congress, and in this capacity, he advised American prosecutor William F. Walsh in November 1945 while Walsh was preparing his presentation of Nazi anti-Jewish crimes to the IMT.[25] In Poland and in other countries Jews collected evidence for prosecutors, and Jewish historians who worked at the Central Jewish Historical Commission in Łódź and its successor, the Jewish Historical Institute in Warsaw, testified for the prosecution in Polish trials of Nazis.[26] Discussion of postwar justice should include the pursuit of Nazis. The most famous Nazi hunter was Simon Wiesenthal, but there were others, including Tuvia Friedman and the legendary couple of Serge and Beate Klarsfeld and their son, Arno, in France.[27]

Jews took part in postwar justice in another way—through the establishment of Jewish honor courts in several European countries and in displaced persons camps in Allied-occupied Germany and Austria. In the immediate postwar period, Jewish leaders across Europe, with the support of survivors in their communities, sought to put putative Jewish collaborators on trial. To this end, Jewish leaders in Poland, France, the Netherlands, and Germany, both in Berlin and in the displaced persons camps in the American zone of occupied Germany, established intramural honor courts to investigate Jews suspected of collaboration with the Nazis and, if the evidence warranted, to try them before a judicial panel of their Jewish peers.[28]

In the same spirit, Israel's 1950 Nazi and Nazi Collaborators (Punishment) Law authorized the country's criminal courts to try alleged collaborators. Although Eichmann was tried and convicted under the very same law in 1961, when Israeli legislators prepared and passed the law, what they primarily had in mind was bringing to justice, for betraying the trust of their fellow Jews, suspected Jewish collaborators among the new immigrants to Israel. Approximately forty trials of alleged Jewish collaborators were conducted in Israel between 1950 and 1972.[29]

To return, then, to the original question posed in this essay: Can postwar justice be deemed a success? In other words, did the postwar trials serve the cause of justice, sufficiently punishing perpetrators while vindicating the grievances of the victims? Most scholars are skeptical. Rebecca Wittmann's final assessment is typical: "Is rendering justice possible after a crime of such magnitude [as] the Holocaust? Can a legal system possibly come to terms with the atrocities committed by the Nazis and atone for the guilt of hundreds of thousands? The answer is obvious: no punishment exists that fits the crime."[30] Although whether these trials "succeeded" or "failed" is ubiquitous in the minds of students, not to mention scholars, recent historiography is more concerned with what Devin Pendas terms the "juridical politics of the past." "Questions of origin and development, of context and consequence"—these are the main questions posed by current studies of Nazi trials and of postwar justice.[31]

Lawrence Douglas shifts the conversation in a compelling way. Refracting postwar justice through the prism of Hannah's Arendt's controversial *Eichmann in Jerusalem*, Douglas comments on Arendt's conclusion that Eichmann deserved to hang, because just as he carried out a policy of "not wanting to share the earth with the Jewish people" and a number of other nations, so, too, "no member of the human race, can be expected to want to share the earth with you." Douglas interprets her words: "What is remarkable about these words is how they transpose her understanding of judgment as a 'sharing-the-earth-with others.' As the ultimate refusal to share the world with others, the crime of atrocity demands an act of restorative judgment that both speaks to the perpetrator and ejects him. Such a judgment corrects the 'pernicious . . . understanding . . . the common illusion that the crime of murder and the crime of genocide are essentially the same.'"[32] In other words, what ultimately mattered most in trials of Nazis was—and what matters most in trials of perpetrators of atrocities in general is—the very fact of passing judgment.

All things considered, one might ultimately generalize from the conclusion that Alexander Prusin and I found in the Polish context. Postwar justice in Poland (and elsewhere) was far from perfect, but, at the very least, as far as the trials of German and Austrian Nazis were concerned, "a certain justice was done."[33]

NOTES

1. Lawrence Douglas, "From IMT to NMT: The Emergence of a Jurisprudence of Atrocity," in Kim C. Priemel and Alexa Stiller, eds., *Reassessing the Nuremberg Military Tribunals: Transitional Justice, Trial Narratives, and Historiography* (New York: Berghahn Books, 2012), 276–295, quote on 277. For Jaspers's description and analysis of the *Verbrecherstaat*, see Karl Jaspers, *Wohin treibt die Bundesrepublik* (Munich: Piper Verlag, 1967), 21–22.

2. Mary Fulbrook, *Reckonings: Legacies of Nazi Persecution and the Quest for Justice* (New York: Oxford University Press, 2018), 206.

3. Lawrence Douglas, *The Right Wrong Man: John Demjanjuk and the Last Great Nazi War Crimes Trial* (Princeton: Princeton University Press, 2016).

4. I prefer the phrases *trials of Nazi criminals* and *trials for Nazi crimes* and the like to the conventional term *war crimes trials*. As Devin Pendas observes, *war crimes trials* is a flawed term. It is a highly politicized and inaccurate term of reference; furthermore, it has exculpatory undertones, for it implies that Nazi crimes were, *in potentia*, the equivalent of criminal acts committed by the Allies in the course of fighting and that all Nazi crimes were committed in the prosecution of conventional war. In fact, the Nazis' crimes were distinguished by their unprecedented scale and brutality, and the aim of these crimes was not to win World War II but to dehumanize and enslave civilian populations and to carry out genocide against them. See Devin Pendas, "Seeking Justice, Finding Law: Nazi Trials in Postwar Europe," *Journal of Modern History* 81, no. 2 (2009): 347–368, here 348n8.

5. Norbert Frei, "In der Tat: Die Ahndung deutscher Kriegs- und NS-Verbrechen in Europe—eine Bilanz," in Norbert Frei, ed., *Transnationale Vergangenheitspolitik: Der Umgang mit deutschen Kriegsverbrechern in Europa nach dem Zweiten Weltkrieg* (Göttingen: Wallstein, 2006), 31–32.

6. Rebecca Wittmann, *Beyond Justice: The Auschwitz Trial* (Cambridge, MA: Harvard University Press, 2005), 15. According to Frei, West German courts convicted 1,550 former Nazis between 1950 and 1959. Frei, "In der Tat," 31.

7. On the escape of Nazis to Latin America, see Gerald Steinacher, *Nazis on the Run: How Hitler's Henchmen Fled Europe* (Oxford: Oxford University Press, 2011).

8. Hilary Earl, *The Nuremberg SS-Einsatzgruppen Trial, 1945–1958: Atrocity, Law, and History* (New York: Cambridge University Press, 2009).

9. Wittmann, *Beyond Justice*; Devin O. Pendas, *The Frankfurt Auschwitz Trial, 1963–1965: Genocide, History, and the Limits of the Law* (New York: Cambridge University Press, 2006).

10. Fulbrook, *Reckonings*, 206.

11. Wendy Lower, *Hitler's Furies: German Women in the Nazi Killing Fields* (Boston: Mariner Books, 2013), 150–151. On Mandl, see Gabriel N. Finder and Alexander V. Prusin, *Justice behind the Iron Curtain: Nazis on Trial in Communist Poland* (Toronto: University of Toronto Press, 2018), 111–112, 120–123.

12. Tomaz Jardim, *The Mauthausen Trial: American Military Justice in Germany* (Cambridge, MA: Harvard University Press, 2012).

13. Alexander V. Prusin, "'Fascist Criminals to the Gallows!' The Holocaust and Soviet War Crimes Trials, December 1945–February 1946," *Holocaust and Genocide Studies* 17, no. 1 (Spring 2003): 1–30; also Alexander V. Prusin,

"The 'Second Wave' of Soviet Justice: The 1960s War Crimes Trials," in Norman J. W. Goda, ed., *Rethinking Holocaust Justice: Essays across Disciplines* (New York: Berghahn, 2018), 129–157.

14. Finder and Prusin, *Justice behind the Iron Curtain*, introduction and epilogue.

15. Claudia Kuretsidis-Haider, "NS-Verbrechen vor österreichischen und bundesdeutschen Gerichten: Eine bilanzierende Betrachtung," in Thomas Albrich and Winfried R. Garscha, eds., *Holocaust und Kriegsverbrechen vor Gericht: Das Fall Österreich* (Innsbruck: Studienverlag, 2006), 329–352. There were also several questionable dismissals of cases, acquittals, and sentences. For example, Franz Murer, the Nazi administrator of the Wilno ghetto, was acquitted in 1963 of seventeen charges. The architects of the crematoria at Auschwitz, Walter Dejaco and Fritz Ertl, were also acquitted, while Franz Nowak, responsible for the deportation of Jews from Austria to death camps, was finally sentenced after four trials to seven years in prison—not for his role in deportations from Austria but rather for his personal acts of violence during the deportations of Hungarian Jews to Auschwitz.

16. Aleksander Lasik, "The Apprehension and Punishment of the Auschwitz Camp Staff," in *Auschwitz, 1940–1945: Central Issues in the History of the Camp*, vol. 5, *Epilogue*, ed. Danuta Czech, Stanisław Kłodziński, Aleksander Lasik, and Andrzej Strzelecki (Oświęcim: Auschwitz-Birkenau State Museum, 2000), 99–117. According to historians at the United States Holocaust Memorial Museum, the number of Nazi camps exceeded forty-two thousand.

17. In the view of Michael Marrus, "Jewish issues were presented at various points in the prosecution's case and were woven into the evidence presented on all counts, especially war crimes and crimes against humanity." Michael Marrus, "The Holocaust at Nuremberg," *Yad Vashem Studies* 26 (1998): 5–41, here 15. In contrast, Donald Bloxham argues that the Allies' focus on war crimes and their perception that the Nazis' intent to wage "aggressive war" was at the root of all Nazi criminality prevented them from adequately representing the Nazis' distinctly anti-Jewish murder campaign in the proceedings. As a result, the overall effect of the prosecution's approach was to universalize Jewish victimhood. Donald Bloxham, *Genocide on Trial: The War Crimes Trials and the Formation of Holocaust History and Memory* (New York: Oxford University Press, 2010); also Donald Bloxham, "Jewish Witnesses in War Crimes Trials of the Postwar Era," in David Bankier and Dan Michman, eds., *Holocaust Historiography in Context: Emergences, Challenges, Polemics, and Achievements* (New York: Berghahn Books, 2008), 539–553. Lawrence Douglas occupies the middle ground in this debate. Douglas writes: "The prosecution's case was not primarily occupied with trying the defendants for extermination of the Jews of Europe but instead focused on the accuseds' roles launching and waging an

aggressive war. Still, the extermination of the Jews was importantly explored and condemned at Nuremberg." Lawrence Douglas, *The Memory of Judgment: Making Law and History in the Trials of the Holocaust* (New Haven: Yale University Press, 2001), 6.

18. See Gabriel N. Finder, "The Warsaw Ghetto Uprising at Nuremberg," *American Jewish History* 103, no. 2 (2019): 177–202.

19. Douglas, *Memory of Judgment*, 89–94.

20. International Military Tribunal, *Trial of the Major War Criminals before the International Military Tribunal, Nuremberg, 14 November 1945–1 October 1946*, 42 vols. (Nuremberg: International Military Tribunal, 1947),1:247, 249–250, 252–253.

21. On the Eichmann Trial, see Douglas, *Memory of Judgment*, chaps. 4–6; Deborah Lipstadt, *The Eichmann Trial* (New York: Schocken, 2011).

22. Douglas, *Memory of Judgment*, 6 (emphasis in original).

23. Finder and Prusin, *Justice behind the Iron Curtain*, 250.

24. On the OSI, see Douglas, *Right Wrong Man*, chap. 2; see also *United States Attorneys' Bulletin*, January 2006; and Rick Rojas and Richard Fausset, "The Mission to Hunt Nazis Has Become a Race against Time," *New York Times*, March 7, 2020. The most famous person placed on the "watch list" was Kurt Waldheim, former UN secretary general, while he was president of Austria in the 1980s.

25. Finder, "Warsaw Ghetto Uprising at Nuremberg," 194–200.

26. Finder and Prusin, *Justice behind the Iron Curtain*, chap. 5.

27. See Tom Segev, *Simon Wiesenthal: The Life and Legends* (New York: Doubleday, 2010); Beate Klarsfled and Serge Klarsfeld, *Hunting the Truth: Memoirs of Beate and Serge Klarsfeld*, trans. Sam Taylor (New York: Farrar, Straus and Giroux, 2018).

28. Laura Jockusch and Gabriel N. Finder, eds., *Jewish Honor Courts: Revenge, Retribution, and Reconciliation in Europe and Israel after the Holocaust* (Detroit: Wayne State University Press, 2015).

29. On Israeli collaborator trials, see Dan Porat, *Bitter Reckoning: Israel Tries Holocaust Survivors as Nazi Collaborators* (Cambridge, MA: Belknap Press of Harvard University Press, 2019); and Rivka Brot, *Ba-'azor Ha-'afor: Ha-kapo ha-yehudi be-mishpat* (Ra'anana, Israel: Lamda' 'Iyun, 2019), chaps. 5–6.

30. Rebecca Wittmann, "Punishment," in Peter Hayes and John K. Roth, eds., *The Oxford Handbook of Holocaust Studies* (Oxford: Oxford University Press, 2010), 524–539, quote on 537. See also Guenter Lewy, *Perpetrators: The World of the Holocaust Killers* (New York: Cambridge University Press, 2017), who characterizes the German prosecution of Nazi perpetrators as "flawed justice" (87) and contends that it was "not . . . a success story" (117).

31. Pendas, "Seeking Justice, Finding Law," 352.

32. Lawrence Douglas, "Arendt, German Law, and the Crime of Atrocity," in Richard J. Golsan and Sarah M. Misemer, eds., *The Trial That Never Ends: Hannah Arendt's "Eichmann in Jerusalem" in Retrospect* (Toronto: University of Toronto Press, 2017), 191–208, here 193–194.

33. Finder and Prusin, *Justice behind the Iron Curtain*, 251.

PART TWO

Sources, Methods, and Media for Teaching the Holocaust

Teaching
with Holocaust Diaries

Voices from the Chasm

AMY SIMON

Despite the enormous attention paid to Anne Frank's diary in primary and secondary Holocaust education, relatively little has been written about pedagogical approaches to teaching Holocaust diaries more generally. Chapters in Francine Prose's *Anne Frank: The Book, the Life, and the Afterlife*, Marianne Hirsch and Irene Kacandes's *Teaching the Representation of the Holocaust*, and Barbara Kirshenblatt-Gimblett and Jeffrey Shandler's *Anne Frank Unbound* have addressed issues stemming from the use of that ubiquitous diary in the classroom. However, the use of other important Holocaust diaries, even of young people, has largely gone unexamined. Perhaps because of the priority given to the difficult ethical questions that arise when teaching the Holocaust, and perhaps simply because diaries are largely absent from the curriculum, the majority of literature pertaining to teaching the Holocaust focuses on content and motivation rather than sources in general and diaries in particular. Furthermore, the scholarship on teaching Anne Frank's diary primarily addresses middle and high schools, rarely exploring the pedagogical role of the text at the university level.[1] This would suggest that the diary is primarily being taught at the secondary level and not as part of the higher education focus on the Holocaust that has exploded in the past twenty years.[2] Research into the Association for Jewish Studies syllabus archive supports this claim. Anne Frank's diary is only included in three out of the eighteen syllabi on offer there under the heading "Holocaust Studies, Antisemitism and World War II."[3] Examining the archive of syllabi available through H-German (the German section of the Humanities and Social Sciences Online website) reveals zero syllabi out of thirty-two under the heading "Nazi Germany/Holocaust" that include Anne Frank's diary. Even in courses with titles such as Children in the Shadow of the Swastika and Stolen Years: Youth under the Nazis in World War II, Anne Frank's diary does not make an appearance.[4] It seems safe to say that at the college level, Anne Frank's diary receives little attention. This is due perhaps to the perception that the diary is over assigned in earlier schooling, but also perhaps due to the pedagogical lack of interest in diaries as teaching tools more broadly, as evidenced by the fact that these syllabi do not generally propose teaching with other diaries either.[5]

Hundreds of diaries written by Holocaust victims, both Jewish and non-Jewish, have been translated into English and are therefore accessible to students in American classrooms. By and large, however, they seem to be missing from university-level Holocaust instruction. I have been using Holocaust diaries in my research and teaching for the past ten years and have found them to be some of the most important, impactful, and affective sources available. As texts written in close proximity to the events they describe, they offer perceptions and emotions often lost in postwar memoirs and testimonies of the Holocaust. Unaffected by later experiences and the long-term effects of memory and forgetting, they remind us of the myriad daily events that occurred during the Holocaust that often become subsumed in the broader story of persecution and death. Diaries also provide a description of daily chaos and confusion that provides important information about the carrying out of the Holocaust and its sometimes mundane but terrible effects on its victims. In short, Holocaust diaries provide invaluable information and perspective not available in any other type of source, making them necessary for serious university-level teaching about the Holocaust in all disciplines.

Although literary scholars, area studies academics, and historians all approach Holocaust diaries quite differently, I submit that the diary as a genre fits squarely in all of these fields. As a historian specializing in Holocaust studies, I have taught using Holocaust diaries in classes spanning three different academic fields and emphasizing three distinct ways of reading. This essay examines each of the three settings and classes in order to suggest a variety of ways of using and framing Holocaust diaries in the university classroom. This discussion also proposes answers to broader questions regarding these sources, such as: What genre do they fit into, and does their categorical fluidity help or hinder their educational use? Which courses are best suited to an examination of Holocaust diaries, and why? What kinds of knowledge do diaries contribute to Holocaust understanding that other sources do not? Finally, what are the limitations of using Holocaust diaries for teaching, and how do they compare with the benefits? I make clear that the educational benefits clearly outweigh any intellectual limitations; therefore, the careful selection and reading of diaries in college classrooms should become more widespread.

Literature of the Holocaust

The Literature of the Holocaust course I taught was a 300-level class situated in a Judaic studies program for which I was hired to teach as an expert in Holocaust studies. The enrollment varied from five to twenty students per semester, providing a seminar-style environment. I organized the readings in terms of temporal and experiential distance from the event. After a few theoretical readings, we started with texts written during the Holocaust, moving on to memoirs, then to fictional works written by survivors, then to fiction written by non-survivors. The diary we read was *The Diary of Dawid Sierakowiak*. I chose this diary primarily because of its poignancy and accessibility. The author's prose is straightforward and unadorned, making his meaning quite clear, and the entire diary runs only 250 pages, which includes many photographs, spaces, and section headings. Though this was a literature class, its situation outside of a literature or English department meant that the majority of students lacked experience in the close analysis of texts. Accessibility was essential, especially at the start of the semester. I also chose this diary because of the age and standing of the author. His youth had the potential to resonate with students not much older than he was at the time of writing (which it did, very much), and his position as someone outside the Jewish leadership hierarchy meant that his story represented experiences more similar to the majority of ghetto inhabitants than other well-known diaries such as Chaim Kaplan's or Adam Czerniaków's. Though many professors assign selections from various diaries to convey a certain historical point or in order to be able to compare texts to one another, I have always opted to assign diaries in their entirety. In fact, in this class as in others, I assigned this one diary, choosing the quality of prolonged examination to the quantity of different stories, voices, or interpretations.

With *The Diary of Dawid Sierakowiak*, as with the majority of Holocaust diaries, one of the most important aspects for learning is to see the changes over time; this can only be achieved through reading the whole text, from halcyon beginning to tragic ending. Sierakowiak's diary begins on June 28, 1939, before the start of World War II. Since he lived in Łódź, Poland, this early section of the diary details the experiences of a fifteen-year-old Jewish boy living a normal life. The first entries are carefree, but soon after his return from summer camp, Sierakowiak began writing about political developments. After the Nazis marched in and began their anti-Jewish decrees, Sierakowiak's life and diary spiraled downward, culminating in ghettoization and finally ending with the author's death. His diary provides a horribly vivid picture of a teenager gradually succumbing to hunger, depression, and disease. The shift from prewar freedom and comfort to wartime captivity and deprivation is one of the most important stories this diary tells. Many of the entries seem mundane, such as this one from April 15, 1941: "Two carts with carrots arrived in the ghetto today. I went with the policeman to the vegetable market for them. We won't apportion the load until tomorrow. Continuous clouds, rain, and cold wind; summer will pass this year in a single day."[6] However, the details provided throughout provide important information about daily life in the ghetto and its impacts on an underprivileged family. From this passage, the reader learns of the importance of food in the Łódź ghetto as well as the role of the Jewish police. The bad weather reminds the reader of how difficult it was to live with few resources, having to walk for miles in inadequate clothing and shoes, in terrible weather.

Furthermore, Sierakowiak's diary offers a view into the deterioration of the most intimate relationships as a result of the hardships Jews had to face. He charts his struggles with his father, whom he sees as selfish and greedy at the expense of others in the family and ultimately inept at taking action when his mother is finally rounded up. For example, on June 21, 1942, Sierakowiak wrote, "Mom hasn't received her coupons for food yet. Father insisted on weighing out his portion of sugar and butter, but Nadzia and I shared ours with Mom. As far as weighing and sharing portions is concerned, the situation is becoming critical at home. Naturally most of the trouble is caused by Father, who cheats at every opportunity (while considering himself the one who is being cheated)."[7] Because diaries are often written at the height of emotions, they reveal truths about perceptions and experiences not available through other sources and sometimes overlooked completely in the broader historiography. In this case, the reader learns that suffering does not always purify, and that it is incorrect to imagine Holocaust victims as better than others because of their terrible experiences. Sierakowiak suggests that severe distress can sometimes lead to quite the opposite. Thus, reading the whole diary is essential in order for students to understand "the gradual acquisition of knowledge and shifting of values that occur in life"—in this case, a life cut short by Nazi persecution.[8]

Because this was a seminar-style literature class, we spent a lot of time on this diary, examining it through a close analysis and discussion of the text. We spent each class period reading aloud and discussing in small groups lines from the diary that highlighted its most important themes, as determined both by the students and by myself. We also read with an eye toward the literary techniques that the diarist used to effectively describe his experiences and surroundings. We discussed the succinct style of the diary, hypothesizing why the author might have chosen such an approach to writing and what it might tell us about his personality, situation, and attitudes. This included a consideration of the physical deprivations of the ghetto and how difficult it may have been for the author to find paper, writing utensils, privacy, and even light in the evenings. I highlighted the most passionate moments in Sierakowiak's writings to draw students' attention to the experiences the author found most traumatic, and we discussed which types of incidents caused the emotional outbursts (such as the deportation of his mother). This type of analysis alerted us to the deprivations, home life, personal life, changing values and beliefs, and potentials for cultural and political resistance presented in Sierakowiak's diary. The richness of this diary and the very clear decline in the author's capabilities, motivation, and mental state over time make it a valuable piece to assign.

Addressing diaries as a primarily literary subject has a long history. Some of the earliest scholars to focus on the study of Holocaust diaries were professors of literature.[9] They included these works naturally as part of the canon of Holocaust literature, suggesting that the form of the diaries is at least as important as the content.[10] With the exception of a largely forgotten corpus of early historiography conducted by Holocaust survivors in Yiddish that made extensive use of Holocaust diaries, literary studies evaluated Holocaust diaries much earlier than did other relevant fields such as history.[11] However, it seems that diaries have largely disappeared from syllabi in the field of Holocaust literature. In fact, an assessment of sixty-five syllabi in literature, history, and communications departments on Holocaust subjects since 2012 reveals that the only diary assigned in literature classes was Anne Frank's diary, while history and communications classes used a slightly broader variety.[12]

Although I assigned the diary in part because of its effectiveness in communicating some of the experiential realities of the ghetto experience, it also functioned as an example of a form of literary response to the atrocity essential to the class's examination of the entire canon of Holocaust works, introducing questions about authenticity, the limits of language, and the difficulty of understanding. I thus used the diary to teach both *with* and *about* Holocaust diaries, emphasizing their role and function as purveyors of a specific type of firsthand knowledge about the event. We discussed how texts written during the Holocaust seem more authentic to postwar readers, even after an analysis of the limitations of their narrative structures and devices. As James E. Young has written,

> Even though the special authenticity and authority that attends all writing from within events might not confer an indisputable factuality on the victims' diaries, they do lend much greater weight to the significance of the interpretations implicit in these narratives. In this sense, the diaries assume importance far beyond whatever "facts" they could possibly deliver, for the interpretive truths reflected and constructed within these narratives may ultimately have constituted the bases for action taken by the writer and his community.[13]

Emphasizing this point challenged students in their beliefs about the historical factuality of Holocaust diaries and helped them focus on the "interpretive" truths the author revealed about himself and his situation, including how those observations impacted his future behaviors in the ghetto. We discussed his interpretations of events and the role that his limited perspective played in his perceptions. Thus, my students learned how to analyze the value of texts perceived as almost sacred in the postwar world—diaries written by those who perished during the Holocaust. With that analytical basis, they were better prepared to study and question other Holocaust representations written after the event.

History of the Holocaust

I have also taught *The Diary of Dawid Sierakowiak* in my History of the Holocaust classes, situated in the history departments of two different universities. Instead of the diary functioning in the time-line of the course at the beginning, representing the closest chrono-logical connection to the historical event, I situate the diary in this class historically. We read the diary at the point in the semester when we begin discussing ghettoization. It functions, as in the literature class, as a primary source, but this time for a different purpose. In the history class, we focus on content over form. Despite the distinct purpose, I continue to assign the entirety of the text, for the same reason as in the litera-ture class—the efficacy of the narrative is diminished by only reading excerpts. We do not read the diary to learn about a particular aspect of the Łódź ghetto, but rather to understand holistically the experiences of someone living within it.

As the History of the Holocaust class is a larger class with different goals than the literature class, the reading and use of the diary in the classroom takes on a different method and purpose. While I utilized a detailed reading of the diary's text in the literature class, in the history class of forty-five to eighty students, I use a small-group discussion model and pose overarching discussion questions. In this case, I begin the conversation about the diary by having groups of four students meet together to answer the question, "Based on reading *The Diary of Dawid Sierakowiak*, what were three of the most important aspects char-acterizing ghetto life?" After students complete a ten-minute discussion on this question, we reconvene as a whole and consider the question together. This beginning leads us into other historical questions that analysis of a diary can address.

Over the following three classes, we continue referring to the diary, focusing on what it can tell us about the experience of living in a Nazi-controlled ghetto. While in the literature class we spoke more about the individual author, his background, intellect, and writing style, in the history class we highlight the lifestyle he described—school life, terrible living conditions and illness, political organization, and rumor culture. The discussion of the book parallels class lectures on the beginning of World War II, the development of the system of ghettos throughout occupied Poland, and Jewish life in the major ghettos. It is meant to complement those broader historical lectures with a primary source that provides an emotional connection for students attending a larger class in which some can easily become anonymous and disinterested in the material. Providing the opportunity to discuss a private diary in small groups serves both to allow students a window into the historical reality of the Holocaust and to motivate them to continued participation and reading.

In this class, instead of serving as a foundational text, *The Diary of Dawid Sierakowiak* functions as one of a number of primary sources the students read. They read and evaluate Nazi documents such as the Nuremberg Laws and the Jäger Report, and they read other Jewish primary sources including Primo Levi's memoir, *Survival in Auschwitz.* While reading for content is a major part of the assignment, the diary also serves, along with these other texts, as an introduction for students to the professional study of history. We discuss the ways that historical events occurred, but also how scholars use a variety of contemporary sources to write history. We also read secondary historical works, notably Marion Kaplan's *Between Dignity and Despair* and Christopher Browning's *Ordinary Men.* Together, these texts allow students an understanding of the way that the Holocaust occurred, the reactions of perpetrators and victims to the events, and the ways that historians have interpreted the events after the war. Using Kaplan's and Browning's texts, which rely heavily on victim and perpetrator testimonies, demonstrates to the students the value of individual witnesses, among which Dawid Sierakowiak can be counted. Despite the differences in the ways I have taught Sierakowiak's diary in the literature and history classes, I have always adhered to James Young's conceptualization of testimony literature: "Rather than coming to Holocaust diaries and memoirs for indisputably 'factual' testimony, however, the critical reader might now turn to the manner in which these 'facts' have been understood and reconstructed in narrative: both as a guide to the kinds of understanding the victims brought to their experiences and to the kinds of actions they took on behalf of this understanding."[14]

Thus, in both classes, I have attempted to augment students' under-standing of Jewish experiences during the Holocaust through an em-phasis on the individual chronicle of a young man, and not only through reliance on broad historical narratives. I have sought to help them com-prehend the viewpoints of the people who suffered under the Nazi regime as well as their real and perceived options for survival and re-sistance through an analysis of a single Holocaust diary. Although some scholars have criticized the use of Holocaust diaries in the writing of Holocaust history, arguing that they present a narrow, biased, and in-complete view of the historical event, I contend that this critique proves irrelevant for the classroom. In each of the classes in which I have used Holocaust diaries, and in every syllabus that I have surveyed, educators situate Holocaust diaries among other sources. In literature classes, they appear alongside memoirs, fiction, and poetry; in history classes, they are read in conjunction with textbooks, monographs, memoirs, and other primary sources. Although one can critique the absolute "factu-ality" of such subjective sources, the diaries provide students with a perspective on the events of the Holocaust unavailable anywhere else. Understanding the ways that an individual victim chose to represent his experiences in the midst of the persecution and becoming emotionally invested in that individual through a look into his most private writing, students find the study of Sierakowiak's diary enormously powerful. The sympathy engendered through the connection students make with the author mitigates the distance between themselves and the historical moment, providing an educational experience unavailable by other means.

The Holocaust in American Memory

The third class in which I have taught using Holocaust diaries is called The Holocaust in American Memory. I have taught this class as a 200-level seminar in a Judaic studies program and most re-cently as a senior seminar in the social relations and policy major at James Madison College at Michigan State University. The major is ex-plicitly historical and comparative, looking at social relations in the United States and internationally, over time, and is situated within a public affairs residential college. This is indeed quite a unique space in which to offer a Holocaust-themed class (mine is the only one in the curriculum), and the motivations for and ways of analyzing sources must be different from those in a traditional literature or history classroom setting.

The purpose of the class is to examine, chronologically, the development of Holocaust memory in the United States over time from memorializations occurring during World War II until today. The course emphasizes the connections between Jewish and other victim groups as well as relationships between minority groups and the United States government in their attempts to create a number of Holocaust memorial projects including the United States Holocaust Memorial Museum. It traces public discourse about the Holocaust in Jewish and non-Jewish venues through the 1950s until today, requiring students to analyze the role of the Holocaust in public memory in the United States.

To this end, I assign *The Diary of a Young Girl* by Anne Frank as well as the 1959 film adaptation of the diary.[15] We also frame our discussion with several articles on the reception of both the film and the diary.[16] Many students have read the diary in school, sometime between fourth and twelfth grade. This provides a productive opportunity for them to reexamine the text from an adult perspective. Instead of focusing on the form, content, or emotional impact of the diary, as in the other classes discussed here, we examine its central role in forming America's memory of the Holocaust. Thus, this is another site in which I teach both *about* and *with* diaries in the classroom. We discuss how Anne Frank's diary became so popular and ingrained in secondary curricula across the country, as well as what kind of stories educators have told about the Holocaust through their use of this diary. The purpose of the assignment is to encourage students to critique the uses and abuses of Anne Frank's diary in both Holocaust education and memory. Ultimately, we seek to answer the questions, "Why has Anne Frank's diary been so attractive to the American public, and how has it been used to highlight certain aspects of Holocaust history while silencing others?" Students come away from the class with a new understanding of the political uses of historical texts and how these texts have been employed in shaping public memory.

Clearly, the goals here are significantly different from the previously discussed goals in the literature and history classes. Though we read the diary, we are not primarily concerned with questions of authentic voice, historical facts, and the constraints of the author. We discuss, instead, the aspects of the diary that have most often been emphasized in public discourse on the text—the author as a teenager undergoing typical teenage problems with family and friends; the author as an aspiring writer; the author's precocious personality; the author's apparent lack of Jewish identity; and the author's propensity to look for the good in people. We take each of these commonly held beliefs about the diary and challenge them with the text itself, often concluding that the public narrative surrounding the text does not bear out a careful reading of the entire diary. We find, rather, that people have accentuated the parts of the diary they prefer to discuss at the expense of some of the more complicated issues it suggests. Anne Frank cannot be described as a teenager reacting to her situation in typical ways because her situation was radically different from that of most people her age. The fact that she did not write about Judaism all of the time does not mean that she did not do it quite thoughtfully and meaningfully at others and that she did not understand the particular role of Jewish suffering throughout history. And finally, the undue focus on the phrase highlighted in the 1959 movie, "In spite of everything I still believe that people are really good at heart" erases all of the doubt, depression, and complex emotions Frank struggled with throughout her diary.[17]

In addition to its overuse in the precollege curriculum, I do not teach *The Diary of a Young Girl* in my other classes because it does not address the most difficult situations of deprivation and suffering that most Jews faced in the ghettos (and later camps). Because Anne Frank's diary breaks off before she dies in a concentration camp, students can read it without learning about the depths of horror Jews endured during the Holocaust. Instead, reading the diary, and particularly viewing the film, can leave students feeling hopeful and optimistic about human nature, despite the history of the Holocaust and Anne Frank's own fate. Our reading of the diary in this class reminds us of the ways that focusing on the "redemptive narratives"[18] of the Holocaust obliterates the most horrific experiences that the majority of European Jews faced, and it pushes us to question and criticize those who have done this in our public life.

This essay highlights only two of the hundreds of published and translated Holocaust diaries available for use in the college classroom, revealing that much more can and should be done with them. Although I argue that using shorter diaries in their entirety should be a preferred method for teaching with Holocaust diaries, I do realize that many teachers do not have enough time to do this. To that end, a number of excellent collections of excerpts of especially children's diaries exist that could be used to achieve some of the same learning goals as the ones I pursued in these classes, especially Alexandra Zapruder's compilation, *Salvaged Pages*.[19]

In particular, comparing diaries written at the same time in different places can demonstrate to students the vastness of the project to destroy the Jews and Jewish reactions to it. As a visiting lecturer in several university classrooms, I have had students read entries from January 1941 in the diaries of Victor Klemperer, Emanuel Ringelblum, and Etty Hillesum, without context.[20] From there, they discuss the excerpts in small groups and try to answer questions such as "Who is the author?" "When is the author writing?" "What is the author's purpose in writing?" "What facts do we learn from the text?" "What is the mood of the diary?" The students usually do a good job of analyzing these texts but are also surprised by the timing and sometimes the identity of the authors. They realize that these Jewish individuals, a man in Dresden, a man in the Warsaw Ghetto, and a woman in occupied Amsterdam, all suffered persecution at the hands of the Nazis, but that their daily experiences and reactions to that persecution depended on their place, gender, education, and age. Many students in this activity as well as in the other classes become particularly interested in the differences between male and female voices in the diaries, and a few have taken up this question in larger research projects. Exercises like this are accessible to instructors who may have only one class to cover the material, but are still quite effective, as they provide glimpses into the inner world of Holocaust victims and how to read primary sources.

This chapter emphasizes the importance of presenting students with voices from within the historical event of the Holocaust and the ways these voices have impacted our comprehension of it ever since. It also provides several examples of how instructors can and should incorporate these texts into their classes. The immediacy and emotional power of these writings is essential to a deep understanding of the experiences of those who suffered and died during the Holocaust, and though we must be careful and thoughtful in how we contextualize and teach them, the educational benefits are well worth the effort.

NOTES

1. A notable exception is Pascale Bos, "Reconsidering Anne Frank: Teaching the Diary in Its Historical and Cultural Context," in Marianne Hirsch and Irene

Kacandes, eds., *Teaching the Representation of the Holocaust* (New York: Modern Language Association of America, 2004), 348–359.

2. How often Anne Frank's diary is currently being taught at these levels remains an open question, as no systematic analysis on the topic exists at this time. An informal 2017–18 survey of sixty-five university students in Michigan revealed that 63 percent had read the diary as part of a middle or high school curriculum. This suggests that the diary is still important in these classrooms, though not universally taught.

3. "AJS Directory of Course Syllabi," Association for Jewish Studies, https://netforum.avectra.com/eweb/DynamicPage.aspx?Site=AJS&WebCode =syllabi (accessed September 30, 2017).

4. "Syllabus Database," H-German, https://networks.h-net.org/node /35008/pages/49659/syllabus-database (accessed October 1, 2017).

5. Approximately one-quarter of the syllabi examined here listed some part of a diary as part of the required reading.

6. Dawid Sierakowiak, *The Diary of Dawid Sierakowiak: Five Notebooks from the Lodz Ghetto*, ed. Alan Adelson, trans. Kamil Turowski (Oxford: Oxford University Press, 1996), 80.

7. Sierakowiak, *Diary*, 188.

8. Steven E. Kagle, *American Diary Literature, 1620–1799* (Boston: Twayne, 1979), 15.

9. Lawrence L. Langer, *The Holocaust and the Literary Imagination* (New Haven: Yale University Press, 1975), and *Using and Abusing the Holocaust* (Bloomington: Indiana University Press, 2006); Alvin Rosenfeld, *A Double Dying: Reflections on Holocaust Literature* (Bloomington: Indiana University Press, 1980); David Roskies, *Against the Apocalypse: Responses to Catastrophe in Modern Jewish Culture* (Cambridge, MA: Harvard University Press, 1984); James Young, *Writing and Rewriting the Holocaust: Narrative and the Consequences of Interpretation* (Bloomington: Indiana University Press, 1988).

10. David Roskies, "The Holocaust according to the Literary Critics," *Prooftexts* 1, no. 2 (May 1981): 211.

11. Philip Friedman, *Roads to Extinction: Essays on the Holocaust* (New York: Conference on Jewish Social Studies, Jewish Publication Society of America, 1980); Isaiah Trunk, Israel Kaplan, Bernard Mark, and Artur Eisenbach in the journal *Bleter far Geshikhte*, 1945 to 1950.

12. This study used the websites listed above as well as a group of fifteen syllabi presented by college professors at the 2013 Jack and Anita Hess Faculty Seminar at the United States Holocaust Memorial Museum. History and communications faculty in this study assigned selections from eight different diaries.

13. James E. Young, "Interpreting Literary Testimony: A Preface to Rereading Holocaust Diaries and Memoirs," *New Literary History* 18, no. 2, *Literacy, Popular Culture, and the Writing of History* (Winter 1987): 419.

14. Young, "Interpreting," 406.

15. Anne Frank, *The Diary of a Young Girl: The Definitive Edition* (New York: Bantam Books, 1997); *The Diary of Anne Frank*, directed by Frankie Glass and George Stevens (1959; Los Angeles: 20th Century Fox, 2004), DVD.

16. Leshu Torchin, "Anne Frank's Moving Images," in Barbara Kirshenblatt-Gimblett and Jeffrey Shandler, eds., *Anne Frank Unbound: Media, Imagination, Memory* (Bloomington: Indiana University Press, 2012), 93–136; Willy Lindwer, *The Last Seven Months of Anne Frank* (New York: Pantheon, 1991), 12–34, 90–110; Judith Doneson, "The American History of Anne Frank's Diary," *Holocaust and Genocide Studies* 2, no. 1 (January 1987): 149–160.

17. Undated entry between July 15 and 21, 1944, in Frank, *Diary*, 328.

18. This term *redemptive narratives* has been popularized in Holocaust studies by Dominick LaCapra, *Representing the Holocaust: History, Theory, Trauma* (Ithaca: Cornell University Press, 1994).

19. Alexandra Zapruder, ed., *Salvaged Pages: Young Writers' Diaries of the Holocaust* (New Haven: Yale University Press, 2002). See also Laurel Holliday, ed., *Children in the Holocaust and World War II: Their Secret Diaries* (New York: Pocket Books, 1995); Jacob Boas, ed., *We Are Witnesses: Five Diaries of Teenagers Who Died in the Holocaust* (New York: Henry Holt, 1995).

20. Victor Klemperer, *I Will Bear Witness: A Diary of the Nazi Years* (New York: Random House, 1998); Emanuel Ringelblum, *Notes from the Warsaw Ghetto: The Journal of Emmanuel Ringelblum* (New York: Schocken Books, 1974); Etty Hillesum, *Etty: The Letters and Diaries of Etty Hillesum, 1941–1943* (Grand Rapids, MI: William B. Eerdmans, 2002).

Strategies
for Teaching the Holocaust
with Memoirs

JENNIFER GOSS

To teach with memoirs is to allow students to view the Holocaust through another lens that complements and enhances the classroom. A memoir is a text based on the experience of the writer; therefore, memoirs of Holocaust survivors give access into an individualized account unique in its perspective. Unlike an audiovisual testimony, which is very "in the moment" of delivery or a diary that is written as events unfold, a memoir is typically a more polished recollection that has the advantage of tying events together and including moments that the writer feels most crucial to their story.

Memoirs engage students by offering insight into the writer's experiences and their processing of those experiences. This additional layer gives the reader an intimate link to an individual who has experienced an era of history. It allows students to think not only about the events that occurred but also about the impact of those events on an individual and the feelings experienced by that individual during the era and afterward. Many times due to the nature of a survey course, history focuses on statistics as much or more than it does on individuals. Memoirs allow students to translate those statistics into people and deepen understanding as to why this study is crucially important to understanding the past and present. Memoirs can cultivate empathy as well as provide a valuable perspective on how factors such as geography or gender can impact one's experience.

There is the common misconception that in order to include memoirs, they must be included in full form. Yet the opposite is true; in many circumstances, educators can incorporate memoir excerpts successfully in conjunction with an existing course framework. This chapter shares strategies to accomplish this in high school and postsecondary courses.

A Brief History of the Holocaust Memoir

The first identifiable "Holocaust memoirs" were published prior to the end of World War II. One notable early memoir is *Escape from the Pit*. Written by a young Polish Jewish teenager, Renya Kulkielko, it tells her experiences in several ghettos and work camps including the Będzin and Warsaw ghettos followed by her life "hiding on the outside" disguised as a Catholic teenager and working as a courier in Warsaw for the resistance. The work was published in 1944 in Haifa, which Kulkielko reached after a harrowing escape following an arrest by the Gestapo.[1] The text is also an early illumination of aid as Kulkielko received assistance from a mixed group of Poles, Jews, Russians, and Germans on her journey through Slovakia, Hungary, and Turkey. It was published in the United States in 1947.

One Year in Treblinka by Jankiel Wiernik was also published in 1944, both in the United States and abroad.[2] Wiernik initially survived due to his trade—carpentry. The book recounts his experiences in the Treblinka death camp.[3] His work as a carpenter provided an in-depth glimpse of the horrors perpetrated within the walls of one of six killing centers during the era of the Holocaust. Between Treblinka's opening in July 1942, approximately eighty kilometers north of Warsaw, and its closure in November 1943, it is estimated that the total number of victims range between 870,000 and 925,000.[4] Wiernik, one of fewer than seventy survivors of the camp, detailed his own experiences amid reports on the suffering of the victims and the inner workings of the camp administration that he observed during his year there.

In 1945, three Polish prisoners—Tadeusz Borowski, Janusz Nel Siedlecki, and Krystyn Olszewski, published a collaborative work, *We Were in Auschwitz*. The text is a series of short stories depicting prisoner life in the camp system. Although the writers were not Jewish, they illuminated some of the challenges faced by Jews and Roma/Sinti in the camp system. The book received mixed reception; on one hand, its aesthetic cover design featuring blue/gray stripes akin to a camp uniform and Siedlecki's number caught the eye of readers, but the contents, abruptly direct and shocking in nature, repelled those same readers.[5] The text would serve as a launching point for Borowski's career as a controversial chronicler of the era of the Holocaust with the inclusion of his short story entitled "This Way to the Gas, Ladies and Gentleman."

The publication of these works in a time when the world was recovering from the war's horrors is one of the reasons these works are lesser known than others that have become canonical in the realm of Holocaust memoirs. Other memoirs written during this era, many in displaced persons camps at the behest of historical commissions composed of survivors, would not see formal publication for many decades, if ever. For many of the early works that were published, their rush to the press also led to styles that may have been less marketable—such as *Escape from the Pit*, whose compelling narrative is diminished by a coarse and challenging style.

A select few works published in the war's immediate aftermath had the fortune of better style, editing, and publication, therefore gaining quicker footholds. Today many remain firmly planted within the field including Olga Lengyel's *Five Chimneys* (1945), Seweryna Szmaglewska's *Smoke over Birkenau* (1946), and Viktor Frankl's *Man's Search for Meaning* (1946). All deserve consideration for work with students because of their varied, yet immediate, reflection on experiences of the era.

The most canonical work of a Holocaust survivor, Elie Wiesel's *Night*, was first published in English in 1959. Today, it is recognized as the first bestseller in the realm of Holocaust memoirs. *Night* was originally written in Yiddish, which Wiesel categorized as the language of those who perished. Its original draft of over one thousand pages was trimmed to 116 pages in its first English iteration. Wiesel's work was also retitled from . . . *And the World Remained Silent* to *Night* and its tone moderated to make it more marketable to American audiences.[6] Wiesel's stark yet detailed language draws readers into the world of Auschwitz and the terrors beyond while also bringing the reader into the fold of his family with a detached sense of emotion that still leads readers to care about their outcome. Still, its path to its current status was slow. It was not until 1985 that it gained widespread traction following Wiesel's criticism of President Ronald Reagan's visit to Bitburg Cemetery. Although *Night* has not outsold Anne Frank's diary in the realm of Holocaust works, it has set the standard for memoirs.

Today, the number of published Holocaust memoirs is difficult to identify, but the numbers likely stretch high into five figures. The range of experiences of Holocaust survivors are vast, and published memoirs span across every aspect. Individuals who experienced persecution under the Nazis but who managed to flee before the outbreak of World War II have written works. Other published works show experiences of individuals who spent time in ghettos, labor camps, or death camps, while others focus on experiences of those who survived in hiding or by passing as Aryans "hiding in the open." Some works provide a rich exploration of prewar or postwar life including immigration outside of Europe, while others focus very specifically on the Holocaust era. What is a boon for publishers has become a challenge for educators: *How does one possibly determine what to use in one's classroom?*

Beginning Steps

The first step in determining which memoir(s) to use is to answer a fundamental question in teaching any topic—what is my rationale? Knowing one's rationale is a crucial component in teaching as it guides the material and methods an educator employs. In order to establish a rationale for teaching the Holocaust, two veteran Holocaust educators and scholars, Stephen Feinberg and Samuel Totten, recommend considering the following:

- Whom am I teaching?
- Why am I teaching them about the Holocaust?
- Why at this time?
- And with what materials?[7]

Once one answers these questions, this information can be used to guide selection of an appropriate memoir(s) for students. One of the biggest influences lies within the second question, "Why am I teaching them about the Holocaust?" One's goals for the course will be the primary factor in guiding selection of an appropriate text(s) although it is also beneficial to take into account the level of readers within the class. Unlike typical academic texts, memoirs exist at varying reading levels, and background research helps create a successful reading experience for students. Selecting several memoirs with varied reading levels and allowing choice between them or creating differentiated activities provides access to all students and leads to increased engagement and understanding. Those at the secondary level may find it beneficial to identify a student's SRI (Scholastic Reading Inventory) level so that students can identify books within their appropriate Lexile level.

As this chapter is not intended to be a "must-use" list of content, it does not delve into a specific list of memoirs to use in one's class. There are certainly memoirs that have extensive supporting materials; however, the strategies included in this chapter can be adapted for use with any variety of memoirs. Examples cited simply show possibilities for the educator; however, the list of options is expansive.[8]

In the event one assigns a single memoir for reading, it should be a text that both correlates with course teachings and expands upon them. For example, if the focus of one's course is the wartime experience, it would be beneficial to bring in a piece that also includes a focus on the prewar and postwar experiences. *Maus I* and *Maus II* are two richly illustrated graphic memoirs that go beyond the wartime experience of Vladek Spiegelman as told to his son, Art Spiegelman. As the story is both that of Vladek and his son, it bridges between a survivor's account and testimony of the second generation. Another work with a rich prewar account is Judith Magyar Isaacson's *Seed of Sarah*, which not only brings in a female perspective during the war but also the story of a Hungarian Jewish child who speaks of her postwar experiences in a reflective fashion. These works help expand the typical survey offering in a fashion that could lead to additional discussion and research.

Regardless of the approach chosen, it is vitally important to provide proper context. Since a memoir focuses on the experience of one individual, context is crucial to understand how this experience fits into the larger realm of the Holocaust. Secondary source pieces can provide this context. The United States Holocaust Memorial Museum (USHMM) and Yad Vashem, the Holocaust memorial in Israel, both have excellent resources to broaden understanding of what occurred during the Holocaust outside of the memoir's universe. Another solid resource is the Echoes & Reflections interactive timeline, which can be beneficial in providing context to students.[9]

This chapter specifically examines the following approaches to utilizing memoirs:

- In excerpted form with the support of primary and secondary source documents.

- In full form, with both in-class and out-of-class activities that can be tailored to one's classroom.

Using Memoirs in Excerpted Form

This first section of approaches uses a variety of memoirs to demonstrate ideas for using memoirs in excerpted form. These approaches are modeled using memoir segments that span the chronology of the Holocaust experience but are not all-inclusive. Strategies can be adapted to fit any aspect of this era.

Method One: Using Excerpts to Teach across the Holocaust

One way to use memoir excerpts is through a stations-based approach, designed to explore a specific aspect of the Holocaust or to span the Holocaust experience if one has only a limited amount of time. This method involves setting up various points in the classroom where students can examine related resources. The number of stations can vary; typically between four and six stations are most effective. The average length of time spent at each station should range from five to ten minutes depending on resource length, class size, and class length. At each station, the educator shares a memoir excerpt and asks students to read and unpack the excerpt while discussing it with peers. This type of activity works well to orient students to different voices from the Holocaust in a short amount of time. The focus of each station can vary, or the educator can choose to use the same questions across each station to compare and contrast different excerpts along common themes. The latter approach is less labor intensive on the front end and is a good way to initially use this method.

One of the often-overlooked aspects of the Holocaust experience is a study of life in the ghettos. An example of this activity centered on ghetto experiences is described below and provides an opportunity to study diverse experiences that spanned the system of ghettoization in Nazi-occupied Europe. For further reading on the topic of the ghettos, please see Martin Dean's chapter in this volume. This activity could include the following excerpts:

1. *All but My Life*, by Gerda Weissman Klein—chapter 11, pp. 78–81 (revised edition, 1995)

2. *Night*, by Elie Wiesel—pp. 11–16 (2006 edition)
3. *Remember, My Child*, by Itka Zygmuntowicz—chapter 4, pp. 45–47 (2016 edition)
4. *On Both Sides of the Wall*, by Vladka Meed—chapters 32 and 33, pp. 194–197 (2003 edition)
5. *Courage Was My Only Option*, by Roman Kent—chapter 7, pp. 63–65 (first edition, 2008)
6. *The Pianist*, by Władysław Szpilman—chapter 1, pp. 11–13 (Picador edition, 2000)

Students rotate among stations focusing on the same essential questions:

1. What does this individual's experience tell us about life in the ghettos?
2. What unique aspects of the experience does this account share?
3. What aspects does this account have in common with other accounts studied?
4. What questions would you ask this individual based on the excerpt you have read?

Stations can also layer in other primary and secondary source materials if time permits.

Method Two: Pairing Memoirs with Primary Sources

Another way to provide context is to pair memoirs with primary source selections. Learning about the horrors of Kristallnacht from a memoir is powerful, but pairing the text with photographs and film footage from the period enhances it. This technique can be used throughout the teaching of an entire memoir or, as in the previous activity, can be done in excerpted fashion. For educators who are accustomed to the traditional read-and-discuss method, this approach can be implemented in a piecemeal fashion to further engage students in a discussion.

An example of this method involves using the transport scene from Wiesel's *Night*. This segment depicts the family's resettlement from the Sighet ghetto to Auschwitz. It takes place in spring 1944, a point in time when most of Europe's Jews had already perished in the Holocaust. Providing additional context to this segment can be beneficial because, while Wiesel's examination of the event is powerful, it focuses on the starkest of details that fifteen-year-old Wiesel was aware of at that time.

To broaden understanding of deportation, pair the excerpt with the four primary source documents to bookend both components of the train transport experience. The first resource is a list of instructions that address the deportation of the Jews of Pfalz, Germany, in 1940.[10] It provides instructions for those responsible for the transport, namely local police, in a direct and clinical fashion. This document allows insight into the preparation for deportation and its implementation. From here, students explore Salitter's report; available through Unit 9 of Echoes & Reflections, a popular collection of resource materials created through a collaboration of the Anti-Defamation League, the University of Southern California (USC) Shoah Foundation, and Yad Vashem.[11] Salitter's report is the report of a German official, Captain Paul Salitter, about the December 1941 transport of 1,007 Jews from Dusseldorf, Germany, to Riga, Latvia. It provides a glimpse of the "process" that accompanied the very painful experience of deportation for Jewish victims. This document in conjunction with the accompanying testimony of Hilde Sherman, a Jewish victim on that exact transport, provides additional depth to Wiesel's account of his deportation.

To identify the continuation of the process after the transport culminates, examine the Auschwitz Album, a collection of photographs taken by a German SS officer stationed in Auschwitz in spring 1944. This extensive album captured the arrival of a transport of Hungarian Jews during the period in which Wiesel and his family arrived in Birkenau. The photographs add visuals to the experience that Wiesel depicts in *Night*, with the only major difference likely being his nighttime arrival in the camp versus the daytime arrival of the individuals captured in the photographs.

The Auschwitz Album was donated to Yad Vashem in 1980. Its history and additional resources are highlighted on Yad Vashem's website, along with additional uses beyond pairing with this excerpt.[12] (See the photo and discussion in Valerie Hébert's chapter in this volume.) The album shows a range of components of the process of arrival in the camp, as well as the final moments of those who were chosen to be gassed while they were awaiting their fate in the woods behind the gas chambers and crematoria.

In pairing these resources with *Night*, students can consider the following questions:

- What are the strengths of Wiesel's narrative when looked at as a sole source?
- How is this narrative strengthened by additional text and audiovisual resources?
- Which additional components does Salitter's report add? Hilde Sherman's testimony? The Auschwitz Album?
- What other items should one consider in conjunction with these pairings?

Another type of primary source one can pair with memoirs is visual history testimony (VHT), commonly known as an audiovisual recording. There are numerous collections of VHT that exist for access in English and other languages, making it a powerful resource not only for applications in history and English courses, but also for those who want to educate about the Holocaust in foreign language courses. The most notable collection exists within the archives of the USC Shoah Foundation, which contains more than fifty-three thousand testimonies of Holocaust survivors, liberators, and rescuers.[13] More than two thousand of these testimonies are available to educators through their digital platform, IWitness.[14] The remainder are accessible, in part, through their main site and at special access points at institutions around the world. The USHMM in Washington, DC, also has a collection of testimonies, many of which have excerpts online. Yale's Fortunoff Archive also possesses a collection of testimonies, and many other local Holocaust resource centers have access to such pieces. Additionally, many of these institutions are now making testimony excerpts available in podcast form.

Visual history testimony (see Margarete Myers Feinstein's chapter in this volume) brings memoirs to life using the voice of the memoir's author or of an individual with a shared or similar experience. For many students, reading words on a page is a limiting experience, but pairing the reading with VHT brings a different perspective to the students, reengaging them or invigorating their interest in the printed page. Additionally, this pairing allows students to discuss how VHT is delivered "in the moment" whereas a memoir is the result of editing and revision that can alter reader perception of the event. VHT also often evokes a different form of emotional response.

This pairing can occur in direct conjunction with a reading (i.e., reading a passage then listening to a segment of VHT) or as a separate pre-reading or post-reading activity. Some suggestions of possible pairings are listed here:

1. Arrival in Auschwitz: Pair pp. 27–34 of *Night* with the testimony of Ellis Lewin from Echoes and Reflections Unit 5: The Final Solution[15]
2. Life in the camps: Pair pp. 66–70 of *Survival in Auschwitz* by Primo Levi with the testimony of Itka Zygmuntowicz from Echoes and Reflections Unit 5: The Final Solution (Testimony Clip #2)[16]
3. Liberation: Pair pp. 213–218 of *All but My Life* with 30:00–36:20 of *One Survivor Remembers*[17]

Unpacking Memoirs in Full

Reading complete memoirs and discussing them is also a valuable experience. In my own classroom, students have approached the experience of reading the entire memoir in one of three ways.

1. Through book discussion groups
2. Through interschool book blogs
3. Through a critical analysis paper or discussion

Each of these approaches has its own merits, but all share a core belief that it is one thing to ask a student to read and summarize a text; it is another to ask the student to do so in a critical fashion with peers.

The first approach allows freedom of choice for students to select a text within a group of texts. In recent years, my class choices have included the following: *Night*, *Maus I & II* (read as a pair), *Remember, My Child*, and *All but My Life*. These works offer varying perspectives on the Holocaust and provide the opportunity for students to read them collectively in order to discuss them as small groups. The discussed techniques also work with a single class read; however, in this setting it can be more challenging to give all students the opportunity to adequately discuss and unpack the reading. This is easier to facilitate in small groups.

In small groups, students do not receive a text-specific set of questions as this can make the experience too much of a "read and find" event versus a deeper analysis. For each segment of assigned reading, students do the following:

- Discuss the segment read and explain a passage that was particularly meaningful in moving the story forward.
- Identify specific components of this segment of the story that reaffirm or further illustrate something learned in class.
- Explain a specific component of this segment of the text that illuminated something new about this facet of the Holocaust or caused you to examine it in a different light.
- Postulate what you think may happen next and explain your reasoning.

These questions, while "cookie-cutter" in nature, do not elicit cookie-cutter responses. They cause a deeper dive into the text not only to come up with an answer but also to find evidence that is supported by prior learning to justify the answer shared with their peers. In addition to students responding to the questions, this format allows them to create a dialogue among the group in response to their own answers to the questions, citing similarities and differences between their responses.

Educators can take different approaches to utilizing this method. Depending on class size, groups can meet simultaneously while the educator moves from one group to another to monitor student responses. Students can be asked to create an exit ticket rating their own participation in a discussion. Discussions could also be scheduled in conjunction with other work so that the educator can monitor one group at a time.

Method Two can be used for a common text or, as in Method One, with small group texts; additionally, it can be utilized across geographic limitations. For example, I have asked students to blog about a text utilizing the Art Spiegelman books *Maus I* and *Maus II,* in conjunction with a colleague in California. During the first half of the semester, students read *Maus I* and then tackled the second text during the second half.

In addition to having the students reflect on the reading, additional insight can be offered on the topic by including links to other primary and secondary source material that relate to the blog topic. For example, in addition to reading chapters 4–9 of *Maus I*, students responded to the following prompt:

After reading part 1 of *Maus*, you are aware that Vladek is sharing memories with his son Artie. Watch this YouTube video: https://www .youtube.com/watch?v=J7WLk-KVYM4.

After watching the video and reading *Maus*, comment on Vladek's memories of life before WWII, citing specific evidence from the text. Do his memories appear REALISTIC or IDEALISTIC?[18]

Students are required to write a response of three to five paragraphs and then respond in at least one substantial paragraph to two class-mates from the partner school. Educator grading and expectations for this activity are flexible.[19] This activity also works well in a discussion board format within the context of either a traditional or hybrid course.

The third suggested approach for whole-text reading involves solo student analysis. This approach offers the most flexibility for educators who are unable to include discussions or additional activities within class time. Students choose books individually, through either a campus library, bookstore, or online outlet, and read them by an assigned deadline. This allows for self-paced reading and allows students to collectively reflect on the experiences of a variety of individuals during this era.

At the end of the allotted time, students can complete their analysis in one of three formats—in a presentation (full-class or one-on-one format), in a video blog, or in paper format. Again, the choices here are best determined by each educator considering factors unique to their own setting. Regardless of the format, educators can ask students to include the following components and answer the guiding questions:

- A *brief* summary of the plot
- A thorough analysis of how well the piece reflects the appropriate time period including but not limited to:
  - Flow of narrative
  - Correspondence to historical items discussed in class
  - Additional insights obtained from the text
  - Connections to other works studied (primary and secondary sources)
- Supporting research to validate analysis (at least three sources *other than the text itself*—these sources should be journal articles or professional commentary on the issue(s) addressed in your paper)
- A discussion on readability—How does the writer shape the narrative to engage the reader? Did he or she succeed? Why or why not? Would you recommend this work to someone else

seeking to learn about this period of history? Why or why not? Consider that readability can be critically important to engaging the reader to explore a period of history from a different angle and perhaps with greater interest than a documentary or lecture.

- Why do you think the creator chose to represent this piece in history? Why did you select this piece? What did you learn from it?

This approach suits most traditional college classrooms. Some educators provide a curated list of texts for review, while others give students additional freedom to select a text that interests them. If one chooses the latter approach, it is recommended that the students be given guidelines in areas such as page number and experience group (Jewish survivors, Roma/Sinti survivors, political victims of Nazi persecution, those in hiding, those who experienced life in a camp or ghetto, etc.).

Conclusion

In the end, how one teaches with memoirs must fit one's rationale and classroom setting. The approaches suggested in this chapter can be adapted to most classrooms; however, you know the individual needs of your students and your time constraints. Alternating approaches that may fit within your timeframe can be a helpful way to determine the best approach on a longstanding basis.

As we are in a time of increasing technological change, it is likely new ways to engage students in the process of reading memoirs will emerge in the future. For example, the Azrieli Foundation, known for publishing survivor memoirs, recently released an interactive platform for students to read memoirs accompanied by images and video. The platform features the memoirs of dozens of survivors and allows users to interact free of charge with stories in a groundbreaking fashion.[20]

Teaching with memoirs has a powerful impact on connecting students to the past in a unique fashion. It is the job of an educator to provide students with a path to understand this complex historical period of the Holocaust through the addition of context and supplementary resources. When asked why he wrote, Elie Wiesel once responded, "For the survivor, writing is not a profession, but an occupation, a duty."[21] As educators, it is our duty—our responsibility—to ensure that we share firsthand accounts along with the teaching of content, for it is in those stories that the voices of the past truly live and resonate with students forever.

NOTES

1. Renya Kulkieloko, *Escape from the Pit* (Baltimore: Shaftek Enterprises, 2012). See also Leah Wolfson, *Jewish Responses to Persecution* (Lanham, MD: Rowman & Littlefield, 2015), 377.

2. Jankiel Wiernik, *One Year in Treblinka: An Inmate Who Escaped Tells the Day-to-Day Facts of One Year of His Torturous Experiences* (Plano, TX: Normanby Press, 2015). See also David Cesarani and Eric J. Sundquist, *After the Holocaust: Challenging the Myth of Silence* (Abingdon, Oxon: Routledge, 2012), 207.

3. Treblinka I was a forced labor camp located a mile away; the death camp was known officially as Treblinka II.

4. "Treblinka," United States Holocaust Memorial Museum, www.ushmm .org/wlc/en/article.php?ModuleId=10005193.

5. Ruth Franklin, *A Thousand Darknesses: Lies and Truth in Holocaust Fiction* (New York: Oxford University Press, 2013), 37–38.

6. See Naomi Seidman, "Elie Wiesel and the Scandal of Jewish Rage," *Jewish Social Studies*, n.s. 3, no. 1 (Autumn 1996): 1–19.

7. Samuel Totten and Stephen Feinberg, *Essentials of Holocaust Education: Fundamental Issues and Approaches* (New York: Routledge, 2016).

8. For assistance in locating possible memoirs, you may wish to consult the United States Holocaust Memorial Museum's annotated bibliography at https://www.ushmm.org/collections/bibliography.

9. See "Timeline of the Holocaust," Echoes & Reflections, https:// echoesandreflections.org/timeline-of-the-holocaust/ (accessed December 5, 2019).

10. This document can be found in P. Sauer, ed., *Dokumente ueber die Verfolgung der juedischen Buerger in Baden-Wuerttemberg durch das nationalsozialistische Regime, 1933–1945* (Documents on the persecution of the Jewish citizens of Baden-Wurttemberg by the National-Socialist regime, 1933–1945), vol. 2 (Stuttgart, 1966), 236–237.

11. Further information and resources from Echoes & Reflections are available at www.echoesandreflections.org.

12. The Auschwitz Album can be located on Yad Vashem's site, http:// www.yadvashem.org/yv/en/exhibitions/album_auschwitz/index.asp.

13. To learn more about the USC Shoah Foundation's collection, please visit https://sfi.usc.edu. See Margarete Myers Feinstein's chapter in this volume on teaching with survivor testimonies.

14. IWitness is accessible at https://iwitness.usc.edu.

15. Ellis Lewin's testimony is available at http://echoesandreflections.org/unit-5/?state=open#content.

16. Itka Zygmuntowicz's testimony is available at http://echoesandreflections.org/unit-5/?state=open#content.

17. The film *One Survivor Remembers* is available at United States Holocaust Memorial Museum, https://www.ushmm.org/remember/days-of-remembrance/resources/one-survivor-remembers.

18. See Rene McVay, "Memory," Cross Country Connections—Blogging about Books, September 26, 2017, http://crosscountryconnections.blogspot.com/ (accessed January 4, 2018).

19. Essentially, this exercise asks students to examine whether the recollections capture the reality of what happened or whether they are tinged with nostalgia. The longer publication *MetaMaus* is also an outstanding resource for students and educators utilizing Spiegelman's works as it dives deeper into Vladek's testimony and Art's creation process combined.

20. For further information please see Azrieli Foundation, http://memoirs.azrielifoundation.org/recollection#home | view-all.

21. Elie Wiesel, "Why I Write: Making No Become Yes," *New York Times Book Review*, April 14, 1985.

Teaching Holocaust Literature in the Twenty-First Century

VICTORIA AARONS

I'm making my pencil its pledge.
ABRAHAM SUTZKEVER,
"1980"

Make for yourself a teacher.
MISHNA,
PIRKEI AVOT, 1:6

The "pledge" to give voice to the Holocaust, as the survivor and Yiddish poet Abraham Sutzkever writes, is an imperative that echoes throughout the literature of those who experienced firsthand the events of the Nazi genocide. Such an imperative to tell their stories speaks to the vital necessity to make their many voices heard, an act of defiance against silence, indifference, and historical amnesia. Through an array of literary forms and approaches, these writers establish the scaffolding for the ethical engagement of reader and witness in the calculation of devastating loss—the loss of individuals, of communities, and of the civilizing principles of humanity. For the survivor, as Primo Levi wrote, "The need to tell our story to 'the rest,' to make 'the rest' participate in it, had taken on for us, before our liberation and after, the character of an immediate and violent impulse."[1] The felt obligation, the necessity, to give testimony to the reality of the legislated, systematized efforts to eradicate the world of the Jewish people, as well as others deemed "undesirable" by the Third Reich—Roma/Sinti, homosexuals, political dissidents, and others persecuted for their "difference"—shapes the writing of those who experienced the events and thus bears witness to the traumatic imprint of the Holocaust. In "Why I Write: Making No Become Yes," survivor Elie Wiesel explains: "The only role I sought was that of witness. . . . I knew the story had to be told. Not to transmit an experience is to betray it."[2] Despite both the perceived limitations of language and the oft-cited dictum issued by Theodor W. Adorno, though later qualified, that "to write poetry after Auschwitz is barbaric,"[3] there exists a significant and expanding body of literature that responds to the events of the Holocaust—that period from 1933 to 1945, from book burnings, increasing anti-Jewish laws, and acts of legislated violence to the Final Solution and its aftermath—making imperative the continuing legacy of the Holocaust.

Such attempts to memorialize and to give voice to those who experienced the Holocaust, those who suffered at the hands of the Nazis, their collaborators and bystanders, extend beyond direct eyewitness testimony to subsequent generations of post-Holocaust writers who are deeply invested in the continuing expression of individual and collective Holocaust histories and memory. As novelist Joseph Skibell cautions, "If you don't tell that story, it disappears, and even if you do tell it, it might just disappear anyway."[4] In the long and rich tradition of Jewish literature and lore—both written and oral—storytelling frames experience and gives meaning to past events as a measure of interpretive engagement with that history. In concert with eyewitness accounts, subsequent generations of post-Holocaust writers carry memory into the future in an attempt to reckon with that history, to articulate the enormity of the Holocaust, and to speak to the imperative of remembering its continuing weight and consequences for our lives. Those writing from an ever-increasing temporal and geographical distance from the events of the Holocaust return to narratives of the past in order to bridge the gap, the temporal and affective divide, between "proximity" and "distance," as memoirist Daniel Mendelsohn puts it, that is, between the diminishing memories of the past and the immediate concerns of the present age, before time and opportunity have eroded such memories.[5] Thus, teaching the literature of the Holocaust to a generation coming of age in the twenty-first century creates an opportunity to re-engage, with a new generation of students, the moral and interpretive resonances of this still growing body of literature.

There are, of course, many ways "to get there," a variety of fruitful ways to structure a course designed to introduce students to the literature of the Holocaust: chronologically, historically, or topically. The approach I take is largely generational (although such a focus necessarily follows a basic chronological pattern). Essentially, I structure the course around three varying generational and perspectival approaches that guide reading and discussion: (1) eyewitness accounts, that is, writers who themselves experienced the Holocaust, who lived through the immediacy of events and their aftermath; (2) *second-generation* writers, the children of survivors and others whose own lives and identities were shaped significantly by the eyewitnesses and who published works in the latter part of the twentieth century; and (3) *third-generation writers*, the generation of the grandchildren as well as those who write from a third-generational perspective, that is, those writers who have published in the early decades of the twenty-first century and whose imaginations of events surrounding the Holocaust frame and engender their narratives. The reference to *generation*, then, in this context is familial as well as cultural. Taken together, these generations of *witnesses* create, as psychologist Eva Fogelman posits, a "phenomenal intergenerational dialogue."[6] I attempt to construct, through a range of temporalities, geographies, and voices, the breadth of expression and the extension of memory as we move farther in time from the events of the Holocaust. An approach that engages the ongoing evolution in Holocaust literary representation suggests not only the developing genre of Holocaust literature but also the extended aftershocks, the ways in which the events of the Holocaust—the fact of the Holocaust—casts its tentacles into each subsequent generation.

Generation is thus a fruitful way to demonstrate the elasticity, the fluidity, and the ongoing attempts to shape our expanding response to the legacy of the Holocaust. To this end, I include readings by those writers who have a direct or indirect familial link to survivors and victims of the Holocaust, but also those who do not, all of whom return to the Holocaust through the reach of their imagination—lived or invented. The course is thus designed to introduce different voices and genres in order to demonstrate the wide variety of modes of representation as well as the richness of literary expression: works by men and women written in English and in translation from different geographical regions, including short stories, poems, memoirs, diaries, novels, plays, and graphic narratives. In what follows, I give some examples of texts that I have found effective in demonstrating the range of literary representation. In brief, the course asks the following question: How does distance—temporal, geographical, and experiential—with each passing generation shape our response to the Holocaust?

In response to apprehensions about the elision of memory and of the lessons of history, concerns that the past will be overshadowed, eclipsed by the exigencies and catastrophes of the current age, continuing generations of writers evoke the legacy of the Holocaust in an attempt to preserve the stories of the past, even as such memory wanes. We are soon approaching a time that will see the end of direct survivor testimony, and thus the transmission and extension of the continuing legacy of the Holocaust becomes increasingly imperative, as Mendelsohn puts it, before "it's too late," before forgetting takes the place of memory. As scholar Gerd Bayer suggests, "As time moves away from World War II, memory takes on a different quality as it becomes transformed from direct witnessing and the resulting testimonials to archival and mediated forms of remembering that carry the responsibility of firmly embedding the Holocaust in the cultural memory of later generations."[7] In this literature, memory is shaped by the imagination.

The literature that approaches the Holocaust by those who did not directly experience the events complicates its transmission. Generations of writers who write after survivor testimony must navigate stories heard, or recorded, or that exist on the borders of a diminishing cultural consciousness in combination with archival research, documented accounts, historiography, and the imagination, all in an effort to re-create and reanimate those narratives of the past, "as if," the Guatemalan Jewish writer Eduardo Halfon, the grandson of a survivor of Auschwitz, paradoxically proposes, "you could speak the unspeakable."[8] In other words, the challenge for post-Holocaust generations, increasingly so, involves accessing stories of the past, locating the means of articulating that which cannot be expressed adequately in words, but nonetheless finding the language with which to re-create what one, finally, cannot know completely. Marianne Hirsch describes the position of those who write from indirect, secondhand experience as one of "'Postmemory' . . . the relationship that the 'generation after' bears to the personal, collective, and cultural trauma of those who came before. . . . Postmemory's connection to the past is thus actually mediated not by recall but by imaginative investment, projection, and creation. . . . These events happened in the past, but their effects continue into the present."[9] The shift from eyewitness testimony to an imaginative projection of events, places, and even people becomes the means for transmitting the potentially lost objects of Holocaust representation.

Such complexities in the extended transmission of memory for generations increasingly removed from the Holocaust have not deterred literary expression. Indeed, despite concerns regarding the unspeakable, inarticulable, and "untranslatable" nature of the Holocaust, there remain, as Berel Lang suggests, "those variations on the unspeakable that cover also the indescribable, the unthinkable, the unimaginable, the incredible—[that] come embedded in yards of writing that attempt to overcome the inadequacy of language in representing moral enormity at the same time that they assert its presence."[10] Thus, we find now, over seven decades since the end of the war and the liberation of the concentration camps, and well into a new millennium, a profusion of literary attempts to reenact and to give voice to the Holocaust: novels, short stories, semiautobiographical accounts, memoirs, poetry, graphic narratives, biographical portraits, and other distinct and overlapping modes of expression that contribute to a rich and fluid genre of Holocaust literature.

As Geoffrey Hartman has proposed, there are now "three generations . . . preoccupied with Holocaust memory. They are the eyewitnesses; their children, the second generation, who have subdued some of their ambivalence and are eager to know their parents better; and the third generation, grand-children who treasure the personal stories of relatives now slipping away."[11] Thus, we find ourselves at a point in time in which Holocaust literary representation has expanded to include an ongoing dialogue among a range of generations of writers for whom the Holocaust is not "past history." In his Nobel Prize acceptance speech, novelist and survivor Imre Kertész said the following:

> The problem of Auschwitz is not whether to draw a line under it, as it were; whether to preserve its memory or slip it into the appropriate pigeonhole of history; whether to erect a monument to the murdered millions, and if so, what kind. The real problem with Auschwitz is that it happened, and this cannot be altered—not with the best, or worst, will in the world. . . . Whenever I think of the traumatic impact of

Auschwitz, I end up dwelling on the vitality and creativity of those living today. Thus, in thinking about Auschwitz, I reflect, paradoxically, not on the past but the future.[12]

The Holocaust, then, belongs not only to the past, but also to the future, to the ongoing moral and ethical calculation of the meaning of the Holocaust and its unraveling implications for the worlds in which we live.

As I have proposed elsewhere, Holocaust literature might be thought of as constituting its own genre, one that draws upon and is shaped by the longstanding Jewish traditions of midrash and lamentation.[13] Midrash is a hermeneutic process of interpretive commentary on Hebrew Scripture, stories told that attempt to explain and extend scriptural texts. The literature of the Holocaust might be thought of as the performance of a kind of contemporary midrash, that is, interpretive expressions that comment on and respond to the "text" of the Holocaust, stories that extend themselves through retelling and reinterpretation and thus demonstrate their enduring relevance and historical resonance. As Sandor Goodhart argues, "As an interpretative method, midrash . . . is a story told in response to a gap or tear or a break in a prior or previous text in such a way that constitutes a material extension of that earlier text."[14] Midrash in Holocaust narratives interpretively responds to the gaps and fissures created by the silences of time and distance. Midrash thus responds to openings for moments of projected continuity and amplification, an invitation to carry the weight of memory into the present. Lamentation, another important mode of expression that informs Holocaust writing, has its origins in the Hebrew Book of Lamentations, the prophet Jeremiah's elegiac expression of mourning and moral reckoning. Together, these two ancient forms of expression create potentially responsive moments of engagement both in the classroom and in solitary reading.

Together, midrash and lamentation create a genre of rupture, a literature that enacts and thus participates in the very dislocation and devastation that it attempts to transmit. As Goodhart puts it, "Midrash . . . does more than just respond to a perceived gap in the text; it performs that dislocation itself; it echoes the dislocation that is already a part of the primary narrative to which it is responding."[15] As midrash performs and comments on the events it pulls into the present, lamentation contributes to the tone and tenor of mourning and the extended calculation of such loss. It is through a genre of rupture that Holocaust

literature—in a wide variety of forms and from a range of voices—
hopes to respond to the enormity of the trauma of the Holocaust and
engage the reader in an act of midrashic interpretation and understanding. As Israeli novelist David Grossman has put it, "books are the place
in the world where both the thing and the loss of it can co-exist," stories
"which have to be told again and again because that is the only way to
assemble the traces of identity and fuse the fragments of a crumbled
world."[16]

Thus, engaging in thoughtful discussion of the events leading up to,
during, and in the direct aftermath of the Holocaust, as well as its continuing resonance and relevance, involves a trialogue among writer,
reader, and teacher in preserving memory and articulating the narratives of the past, but also, significantly, in carrying that history and its
stories forth, in teaching the Holocaust to others. The challenge, then,
for those of us who teach courses in Holocaust studies, especially to
generations for whom the Holocaust is an increasingly remote event
in time, involves actively engaging our students in the material so that
the texts our students read, as Bayer proposes, "bridge the gap to the
present, thereby making traumatic events of the past relevant for the
present."[17]

This is, of course, no easy task given the subject matter; students,
not surprisingly, recoil in defense at the horror and extreme suffering
they encounter in the pages of the literature we assign. Furthermore,
we have the additional challenge of teaching generations of students
who, very simply, read less and less closely. Thus, the course must be
structured in such a way that provides both depth and a comprehensive overlay of the myriad of complex expressions of Holocaust testimony. Because there is such a wide swatch of material to cover, the
challenge is less a matter of *what* to include than it is *what not* to include.

In other words, each semester, as I am thinking about the course's
design, I ask myself the following: What, simply given time restraints
as well as constraints on what our students reasonably can absorb, am I
omitting? (This question is particularly confounding for those who cannot devote an entire semester to Holocaust literature.) Where are the
gaps in a syllabus that aims to convey the enormity of the Holocaust
and, at the same time, emphasize the limitations in representation?
How do we balance the historical background our students need to
have with the literary texts? As child survivor Ruth Kluger writes, "We
all splash in dark waters when it comes to the past, to this past."[18] We

do so because of the myriad of complexities inherent in the subject, including understanding how such an event as the Holocaust could have taken place among a cultured, highly educated population, but also because we want to get it right. That is, we want to remain faithful to history and to the ethical and moral implications of past actions on our present age. As Edmund de Waal asks in *The Hare with Amber Eyes*, the story of his extended family's Holocaust legacy, "What is remembered and what is forgotten?"[19]

I ask myself this question every time I teach Literature of the Holocaust, a course I offer each year to undergraduates at the private liberal arts university where I work. The point of departure, as I think about the contours of my class, is the following: What do I want students to get from such a course, and how might I best facilitate it? Very simply put, I want my students to appreciate not only the magnitude of the collective destruction of the Nazi era and the threat to humanity at large, but also the consequences of such devastation on an individual scale. In other words, I want my students to come away from the course with an appreciation for the ways in which the Holocaust changed the fabric of the civilized world, and, significantly, that the victims targeted by the Nazis were not mere abstractions. They were individuals— mothers, fathers, children, doctors, artists, teachers, and students not unlike themselves—whose individual lives were shattered. An abstraction, of course, is not an individual. While the Holocaust was a collective experience, a wide-scale rupture felt globally, it was also an individual, personal rupture that called upon individuals to navigate the horrors that came to define their lives.

This is what Primo Levi asks us to recognize when he describes the night before deportation when, in the midst of collective panic and despair and the certainty of impending death, the mothers "stayed up to prepare the food for the journey with tender care, and washed their children and packed the luggage. . . . Nor did they forget the diapers, the toys, the cushions and the hundred other small things which mothers remember and which children always need. Would you not do the same?" Levi asks. "If you and your child were going to be killed tomorrow would you not give him to eat today?"[20]

A literature that introduces our students to the lives of ordinary people in the midst of the extraordinary—both in terms of the cataclysmic conditions suffered and the acts of courage and fortitude in the face of such atrocities—brings them, to the extent possible restricted by the limits of representation, *inside* the experience. To be sure, our students are more than familiar with the generalities, with dates and numbers. But, as Reuven Malter, the narrator of Chaim Potok's novel *The Chosen*, admits, "I just couldn't grasp it. . . . I couldn't begin to imagine six million . . . murdered. . . . It didn't make any sense at all. My mind couldn't hold on to it, to the death of six million people."[21] The final calculation of vast numbers, as Mendelsohn, writing decades after the end of the war, puts it, is an ineffective contender when up against "the limits of the mind. Six million is an unimaginable number . . . you don't grasp it. The mind needs contours that it can imagine."[22] I want my students to appreciate both the immensity of the Holocaust as it gained momentum over time and also the specificity, individuals who may have been lost to history, but whose stories are reanimated in the wide range of literature that responds to those events.

I sometimes wonder whether such a design may be overly ambitious, an attempt to cover far too much in one brief semester. Each semester, I struggle with the question of what texts to include and what I can reasonably omit without diminishing the impact of the course. I want my students to appreciate the various forms of expression, the directions from which writers approach the complex and deeply disturbing subject of the Holocaust. As Kluger insists, these are "stories which shouldn't even exist to be told," yet these "stories have no end"; they extend and unfurl throughout time.[23]

An additional challenge in designing the course is the matter of historicizing the literature. This is a curious generation of students. They might be said to suffer from "Holocaust fatigue." Yet, while they have seen any number of films and documentaries or visited museums and memorials, their knowledge of the developing moments leading up to and enacting the Final Solution is at times shockingly limited. They know the public version, the abstraction, but little in the way of detail about the systematic legislation of laws, ghetto formation, "euthanasia" measures, appropriation of property, deportation, concentration camps and killing camps. On the one hand, the course cannot be all things. This is, after all, a course taught in the English Department on the literature of the Holocaust; it is not a history course. On the other hand, the distinction is misleading because our students need the historical context to make sense of the literature that they read; they need a framework for understanding. As Dan Bar-On posits, "There is, of course, a 'historical' truth (what happened), but there are also several 'narrative' truths (how someone tells what happened)."[24]

Thus, I begin the course with a general lecture that introduces the students to the basic historical facts of the Holocaust. While, as I say, my students know the "basics"—who did what to whom, when, where, and how—they do not know the nuances, the particulars of that history as they unfold; they do not know the history of antisemitism leading up to the rise of the Third Reich; they are unaware of pre-Holocaust Jewish life; they are largely uninformed about ghetto and concentration camp formation; Auschwitz, for most of them, is a stand-in appellation for the general experience of the Holocaust, and even though a surprising number of my students have visited concentration camps, they do not experience them as part of a larger picture.

Beyond establishing background context, then, I let the readings open themselves up to history. In other words, the points of history and the factual data emerge through the literature. For example, when introducing ghetto life, we read the short story "The Lemon," written by Prague-born Arnošt Lustig, a survivor of Auschwitz. This story demonstrates the dire conditions of the ghetto through the eyes of two young boys who have lost members of their families and who attempt to survive amid the claustrophobic contours of the ghetto walls: disease, starvation, and devastating loss. When we discuss deportation, we read, among other texts, Charlotte Delbo's prose poem, "Street for Arrival, Street for Departures." The semiautobiographical narrative, "This Way for the Gas, Ladies and Gentlemen," by Tadeusz Borowski, opens up the discussion to the heinous logistics of transport and the landscape of horror upon arrival at the concentration camps and killing centers. This text introduces recurring terms such as *Muslim* or *Muselmann* (a prisoner destroyed physically and spiritually, with neither the will nor strength to continue living), *kapo* (prisoner functionary in a concentration camp assigned to supervise forced labor), and *Schutzstaffel* (SS, Defense Squadron, the Nazi elite guard, bodyguards responsible for the murder of enemies of the Third Reich). When we talk about women's experiences in the camps, for example, we read Sara Nomberg-Przytyk's short stories "Esther's First Born," and "The Block of Death." Teaching Elie Wiesel's classic *Night* presents the occasion to discuss the systematic closing in on Jewish communities and the succession of anti-Jewish laws and decrees in Hungary: incarceration, liquidation of property, identification, ghettoization, seclusion, deportation, death camps.

Contextualizing historical realities within the narrative frame gives a "face" to history. Situating such events and moments that demonstrate the escalation of persecution and actions leading to mass annihilation introduces the complexities and intricate design and execution of genocide. Rather than a singular event, the Holocaust was an accumulation of events and actions, deliberately executed against a vulnerable population. Approaching the subject of the Holocaust requires an active process of reading and discovery. This is a history that, as one of the late novelist Ehud Havazelet's characters puts it, "was no longer something to be recalled from a distance—it was there in front of him, to walk into if he dared."[25] Thus, first setting up the broad strokes of that escalating period of time that we refer to as the Holocaust and then moving into the specifics when the individual texts give rise to them creates the kind of balance that gives our students the opportunity to engage with the literature in thoughtful and responsible ways.

There are two very useful anthologies that include a number of texts that I consider essential to the design of the course: *Truth and Lamentation: Stories and Poems on the Holocaust*, edited by Milton Teichman and Sharon Leder (University of Illinois Press, 1994), and a more recent volume, *Writing in Witness: A Holocaust Reader*, edited by Eric J. Sundquist (SUNY Press, 2018). Both anthologies contain key readings that introduce historical moments and terms as well as a variety of forms of testimony. *Truth and Lamentation* is a collection of short stories and poems written during and after the Holocaust, including eyewitness accounts as well as writings by "witnesses through the imagination," to borrow a term from Holocaust scholar S. Lillian Kremer.[26] One of the many strengths of this volume is the range of geographies, cultures, and languages (in translation) from which the editors draw. The anthology also includes both Jewish and non-Jewish writers, recognized writers and others less well known. I have also found that the wide range of poems that are included provides a structured way to introduce the language of poetry and thus counteract some of the anxieties about reading poetry, which, to many of my students, is a far less comfortable and familiar genre than is, say, the short story. When I teach poems, I introduce rhetorical tropes and patterns (tropes of omission such as the ellipsis, metaphors, and metonymic figures) that attempt to create the very rupture that they evoke. Having students read the poems out loud helps them hear the ways in which ordinary language is juxtaposed to the images it creates.

There is very little overlap between *Truth and Lamentation* and *Writing in Witness*, and the two anthologies complement each other well. *Writing in Witness* is a collection of written testimony by survivors and direct eyewitnesses, including a wide distribution of languages and perspectives (men, women, and children, Jews and non-Jews), and genres, including primary texts, diary entries, letters, eyewitness accounts, memoirs, poems, and stories. Writing by those who experienced the atrocities and whose attempts to preserve the memory of the Holocaust fills the pages of this volume with searing testimony. The various forms of testimony suggest the range of expression but also the complexities in transmission. Both anthologies include excellent introductions to guide the reading, as well as useful biographical information about the writers, and both allow for a discussion of genre and various modes of representation as well as providing an instructive way into the subject of the Holocaust. These are valuable resources, primary and secondary sources that have the added benefit of introducing a wide range of short pieces that are manageable given the time constraints of the class period.

I supplement these two anthologies with several memoirs and novels that mark important moments and perspectives, including Elie Wiesel's *Night*, Primo Levi's *Survival in Auschwitz*, Joe Kubert's graphic novel of the Warsaw Ghetto Uprising, *Yossel: April 19, 1943*, and Edward Lewis Wallant's classic *The Pawnbroker*, which might be considered the "first" Holocaust novel written in America, published in 1961, an important year for Holocaust consciousness and awareness.[27] While this is not a course on film, I do include excerpts from Leni Riefenstahl's production of *Triumph of the Will*, Alain Resnais's 1956 French documentary *Night and Fog*, and the 2001 BBC/HBO film *Conspiracy*, directed by Frank Pierson, a dramatization of the Wannsee Conference in 1942, a meeting among Nazi officials, including Reinhard Heydrich and Adolf Eichmann, that put the Final Solution into horrifying motion, an occasion magnified by the matter-of-fact tone with which those present discuss the logistics of mass murder. Of course, anyone reading my list above who knows this field will be keeping a mental tally of how much I have necessarily left out, a process that itself enacts the anxiety of the question, "What is remembered and what is forgotten?" and offers a perspective on the inevitable, morally charged issue of Holocaust memory.

When I teach Primo Levi's "Shema," a poem that evokes the ancient Hebrew prayer of testimony to God's singularity (Deuteronomy 6:4-9; 11:13-21; 15:37-41) and stands as sentry to his memoir *Survival in*

Auschwitz (included in *Truth and Lamentation*, 488), I show it to be a midrash on the ancient prayer of the Shema (Deuteronomy 6:4), one that turns the original text of affirmation and faith into a calculation of the failure of humanity and a warning about the erosion of memory and testimony.[28] Another example of a contemporary midrash is W. D. Snodgrass's concrete poem, "Heinrich Himmler Reichsfuehrer SS—8 April 1945," a dramatic monologue written in the bureaucratic voice of Himmler in the form of a memorandum on graph paper. The individual letters of the words are isolated in the individual squares of the grids, thus enacting its own state of terrifying rigidity and ordered commands and the chaos of an unbalanced mind fueled by hatred; the poem thus performs fragmentation and rupture (*Truth and Lamentation*, 276). Dan Pagis's stunning minimalistic prose poem, "Written in Pencil in the Sealed Railway-Car," through its tropes of omission and elision, re-creates absence and presence (*Truth and Lamentation*, 491). Here the speaking voice, an anonymous woman, Eve, in the cattle car with her son Abel en route to her death, is aborted in the anticipated horror of her impending death. Pagis's poem consists of a fragmented sentence cut off in mid-expression and thus anticipates the very erasure of life that it enacts. The silence at the poem's end, the broken line, "tell him that i," performs erasure in the diminishment created by the lowercase *i* and the violence implied by the silencing of voice. Another example of a text that performs the loss and dislocation that it evokes is the 2006 graphic memoir by Miriam Katin, *We Are on Our Own*. Katin, a child survivor who, together with her mother, spent a year in hiding in the Hungarian countryside, through the juxtaposition of text and image draws the fragmentation and destabilizing of time and the erosion of memory. She reenacts the traumatic moments of their experience as the panels dissolve into an expression of confusion and fear.

Holocaust narratives committed to responsible representation, that is, narratives that are faithful to the realities of history, create the conditions for discomfort and unease; they create a language and a landscape of rupture, of discursive disequilibrium, and of narrative disjunction. Thus, such attempts to evoke the enormity of the Holocaust on a collective and individual level in order, as Wiesel once put it, to bring the reader "to the other side," to engage the reader in responsible and thoughtful contemplation of both the events and their extended implications, must enact the very conditions they evoke.[29] The course can't do everything, but it must demonstrate the range, the elasticity, and the imperative of bearing witness as well as the limits of such representation to extend and exact memory and testimony into the future. The literary representation of the Holocaust, as it moves into the third and now fourth generations of post-Holocaust writers, offers a rich terrain to reanimate that which was irretrievably lost. The course I teach on the literature of the Holocaust thus concludes not with the end of the war and the liberation of the concentration camps, but with the future, with future generations and the continuing legacy of the Holocaust.

Notes

1. Primo Levi, *Survival in Auschwitz: The Nazi Assault on Humanity*, trans. Stuart Woolf (1958; New York: Touchstone/Simon & Schuster, 1996), 9.

2. Elie Wiesel, "Why I Write: Making No Become Yes," *New York Times Book Review*, April 14, 1985, 13–14.

3. Theodor W. Adorno, "Cultural Criticism and Society," in *Prisms*, trans. Samuel and Shierry Weber (Cambridge, MA: MIT Press, 1967), 34.

4. Joseph Skibell, "Ten Faces," in *My Father's Guitar and Other Imaginary Things* (Chapel Hill, NC: Algonquin Books, 2015), 209.

5. Daniel Mendelsohn, *The Lost: A Search for Six of Six Million* (New York: HarperCollins, 2006), 88.

6. Eva Fogelman, "Third Generation Descendants of Holocaust Survivors and the Future of Remembering," *Tablet Magazine*, May 1, 2008, http://www.jewcy.com/religion-and-beliefs/third_generation_descendents_holocaust_survivors_and_future_remembering (accessed January 8, 2013).

7. Gerd Bayer, "After Postmemory: Holocaust Cinema and the Third Generation," *Shofar* 28, no. 4 (Summer 2010): 116.

8. Eduardo Halfon, "The Polish Boxer," in *The Polish Boxer*, trans. Daniel Hahn, Ollie Brock, Lisa Dillman, Thomas Bunstead, and Anne McLean (New York: Bellevue Literary Press, 2012), 84.

9. Marianne Hirsch, *The Generation of Postmemory: Writing and Visual Culture after the Holocaust* (New York: Columbia University Press, 2012), 5.

10. Berel Lang, *Holocaust Representation: Art within the Limits of History and Ethics* (Baltimore: Johns Hopkins University Press, 2000), 18.

11. Geoffrey Hartman, "Shoah and Intellectual Witness," *Partisan Review* 1, no. 1 (1998): 1.

12. Imre Kertész, "Nobel Lecture: Heureka!," trans. Ivan Sanders, The Nobel Prize in Literature 2002, http://www.nobelprize.org/nobel_prizes/literature/laureates/2002/kertesz-lecture-e.html (accessed June 21, 2018).

13. See Victoria Aarons, "A Genre of Rupture: The Literary Language of the Holocaust," in Jenni Adams, ed., *The Bloomsbury Companion to Holocaust Literature* (London: Bloomsbury, 2014), 27–45.

14. Sandor Goodhart, "'A Land That Devours Its Inhabitants': Midrashic Reading, Emmanuel Levinas, and Prophetic Exegesis," *Shofar* 26, no. 4, special issue, Emmanuel Levinas and Jewish Thought: Translating Hebrew into Greek (Summer 2008): 18.

15. Goodhart, "'Land That Devours Its Inhabitants,'" 20.

16. David Grossman, *Writing in the Dark*, trans. Jessica Cohen (New York: Farrar, Straus and Giroux, 2008), 13.

17. Bayer, "After Postmemory," 120.

18. Ruth Kluger, *Still Alive: A Holocaust Girlhood Remembered* (New York: Feminist Press, 2001), 19.

19. Edmund de Waal, *The Hare with Amber Eyes* (New York: Farrar, Straus and Giroux, 2010), 17.

20. Levi, *Survival in Auschwitz*, 15.

21. Chaim Potok, *The Chosen* (1967; New York: Simon & Schuster, 2016), 169.

22. Andrew O'Hehir, "Finding *The Lost*," Salon, December 14, 2006, http:// www.salon.com/2006/12/14/mendelsohn_3/ (accessed September 23, 2013).

23. Kluger, *Still Alive*, 83, 40.

24. Dan Bar-On, *Fear and Hope: Three Generations of the Holocaust* (Cambridge, MA: Harvard University Press, 1995), 10.

25. Ehud Havazelet, "To Live in Tiflis in the Springtime," in *Like Never Before* (New York: Farrar, Straus and Giroux, 1998), 239.

26. S. Lillian Kremer, *Witness through the Imagination: Jewish American Holocaust Literature* (Detroit: Wayne State University Press, 1989; reprint ed., 2018).

27. The year 1961 was the year of the trial in Jerusalem of Adolf Eichmann, the Nazi war criminal responsible for the deportation of millions of victims to ghettos, concentration camps, and killing centers. In 1960, Eichmann was captured by the Mossad (Israel's intelligence organization) in Argentina and brought to trial in Israel in 1961. He was sentenced to death and hung in 1962. The trial was widely covered.

28. For further discussion of this devastating poem and its midrashic possibilities see Victoria Aarons, "Memory, Conscience, and the Moral Weight of Holocaust Representation," in Simone Gigliotti, Jacob Golomb, and Caroline Steinbberg Gould, eds., *Ethics, Art, and Representations of the Holocaust: Essays in Honor of Berel Lang* (Lanham, MD: Lexington Books/Rowman & Littlefield, 2014), 183–198.

29. Wiesel, "Why I Write," 13.

The Grey Zone
of Holocaust Education

Teaching with Film

ALAN S. MARCUS

When I first saw *Schindler's List* (1993) in the theater, I was stunned at how "real" it made the Holocaust seem. As a second-year high school teacher, I rushed to show it as soon as it was available. In my haste, I did not consider how the graphic images might upset students. I did not realize how much historical context I should provide. I was naive to think that the film itself could teach my students. Only after many years of reflection, experience, and research did I realize how much work is required to use film effectively to teach history and how complicated it is to teach the Holocaust with film.

History teachers are faced with many dilemmas when planning Holocaust lessons: How can students learn about such an important, difficult, and morally complex event in limited time? Which goals are paramount in learning about the Holocaust—knowing the facts, dates, and people? Influencing the actions of individuals? Preventing future genocide? Memorializing the victims? And what resources will best support these goals? In this chapter, I advocate for the inclusion of Hollywood feature films as a critical resource for teaching the Holocaust. (The term *film* is used throughout the chapter to mean Hollywood-style feature films only and not documentaries.) First, I discuss many of the dilemmas facing teachers who incorporate film in their Holocaust education curriculum. Second, I present two cases of using film to teach the Holocaust: one secondary teacher who includes more global perspectives and another who focuses on developing empathy and examining people's roles. The chapter is guided by theoretical and empirical scholarship but ultimately is grounded in practical ideas for secondary teachers as well as postsecondary classrooms.

The Influence and Use of Holocaust Films

Outside of Holocaust survivors, film is arguably one of the principal influences on Holocaust awareness and education compared to other sources. In 1978, the miniseries *Holocaust* was shown on television and was a catalyst for public discussion. Then, in 1993, *Schindler's List*, directed by Steven Spielberg, reinvigorated interest in the Holocaust by the public and educators. The film, shown again in theaters on the twenty-fifth anniversary in 2018, is a powerful teaching tool when used effectively. Since then, dozens and dozens of Holocaust films have been released. However, the potential educative quality of these films varies greatly.

Films are tied with firsthand accounts for the most commonly used source to teach the Holocaust in schools. Sixty-nine percent of teachers in the United States report using film (feature and documentary) to teach about the Holocaust, whereas 76 percent of teachers in England use feature films to teach the Holocaust.[1] *Schindler's List* is one of the most commonly shown films, with 26 percent of teachers in the United States reporting they use the film when teaching the Holocaust and another 11 percent showing *The Pianist*.[2] Another study of teacher practices in England reports similar findings, with *Schindler's List* as the most used Holocaust film by teachers.[3] Regrettably, *The Boy in the Striped Pajamas* (2008) is also being shown frequently. In the United States it is the third most used Holocaust feature film (almost 10 percent of teachers) while in England, it is also a popular film for teaching the Holocaust.[4] *The Boy in the Striped Pajamas*, as discussed later, is an extremely inappropriate film to use for educational purposes.[5] Teacher familiarity with these films is now essential, and it is crucial that teachers employ very careful pedagogical thinking if the power of this genre in the classroom is to be realized.

No one source can completely represent the experiences of people in the Holocaust. Yet teachers must find ways to best represent the horror of the Holocaust. Among the wide range of types and formats of sources that offer some insight into the Holocaust such as memoirs, survivor testimony, government documents, photos, diaries, and so forth, Hollywood feature film is one of the most engaging and accessible, offering a wide range of perspectives and touching on many of the ethical dilemmas and complexities of the Holocaust.

Rationale and Model for Teaching History with Feature Films

Feature films are audio and visual representations of the past that can motivate students to want to learn more. They can support efforts to connect the past and the present and also examine cause and effect. Feature films are also viewed in large volumes by students outside of the classroom, and teachers can take advantage of students' familiarity with the medium. In addition, films can bring the past to life in powerful ways and represent alternate perspectives.

Taking advantage of films' unique qualities, teachers need to use film for much more than as a secondary source where students "learn" specific facts about an event or person. Particularly for Holocaust education, teachers can use films in more sophisticated and effective ways such as developing empathy, illuminating underrepresented perspectives, bringing the past to life, and tackling difficult history.[6] First, Holocaust films can be very valuable for developing historical empathy. Given the oft-cited goals of Holocaust education to prevent future genocide and decrease stereotyping and racism, developing empathy is significant. For example, *Europa Europa* (1990), the true story of a German Jewish teenager, successfully helps students connect to the character and immerses the viewer in issues of identity, stereotyping, racism, and survival.

Holocaust films can also expose students to underrepresented perspectives. Textbooks and curriculum regularly focus on perpetrators and victims. Often left out are resisters, rescuers, collaborators and other roles, and particularly the fact that many people don't fit neatly into one role. A film such as *Defiance* (2008) provides students with an in-depth look at one group of resisters and shows that many people did fight back, while also rescuing Jews.

Additionally, teachers can use films to bring the Holocaust to life. *Schindler's List* is a powerful way to better understand life in ghettos and concentration camps through its realistic sets, clothing, sound effects, and the actions of its characters. Finally, teachers can consider the Holo-caust as difficult history due to the suffering of those involved, the moral complexity of people's actions, and the trauma some experience in studying the Holocaust. In particular, films can help students under-stand the moral complexity of the Holocaust. A film such as *The Grey Zone* (2001) examines the role of the Sonderkommando and the ways in which they were victims, resisters, and collaborators all at once. As pris-oners and forced laborers, they were victims. In many cases, they saved lives and actively fought back, making them resisters. And though not voluntarily, they can be viewed as collaborators as they worked in the death camps, forced to dispose of the corpses of victims in gas chambers and crematoria.

Challenges and Dilemmas in Teaching the Holocaust with Feature Film

There are a number of unique challenges to teaching the Holocaust in general and specifically with using film. Key issues that teachers should consider include thinking about the Holocaust as "dif-ficult" history, the dilemmas of using graphic content, how to choose appropriate films, and thinking about film as a form of evidence.

The Holocaust, Film, and Difficult History

History as a discipline, and films that tell the stories of the past, attract audiences through narratives, by using real and fictional characters with engaging stories, and with an emphasis on conflict. With many events, the past involves violence, injustice, or other emotionally power-ful ordeals viewed as sensitive or ones that could inflict trauma and elicit emotional reactions. Films provide one of the most powerful me-diums through their visual, audio, and character and narrative elements that can promote an affective and emotional response in an audience. Thus films are powerful for engaging audiences, but they also can create difficult and traumatic moments when audiences experience these repre-sentations of the past—moments that are often intentional so audiences are "entertained" or their understandings of the past are challenged.

The Holocaust is particularly challenging to teach, and Holocaust films can be especially difficult to use. The difficultly arises because of the trauma experienced by those involved, the potential graphic content, the complexity and scope of the event, and the broad range—and quality of—available films. The challenges of using film for Holocaust education can be thought of as both affectively and conceptually difficult history. Affectively difficult history occurs when events dealing with conflict, violence, death, identity, and other trauma are perceived by some students as sensitive, disturbing, and uncomfortable.[7] History becomes conceptually difficult when informal and formal learning experiences reveal the fluid, dynamic, challenging, and contested nature of historical interpretations and concepts.[8] Teaching the Holocaust through films in ways that consider affectively and conceptually difficult history can help teachers more successfully draw on the difficult history for engagement and empathy, while managing the difficult history so students are not traumatized.

The Holocaust, Film, and Historical Empathy

One of the most important historical thinking practices, particularly for studying the Holocaust, is empathy.[9] Historical empathy is best defined by Barton and Levstik, who identify empathy as having two elements: caring and perspective recognition. Caring includes a more affective process of recognizing the experiences of others emotionally and physically while also recognizing that it is impossible for them to truly understand what those experiences would have been like. Caring involves caring *about* the past and *for* the past. Barton and Levstik explain that "empathy without care sounds like an oxymoron. Why would anyone expend energy trying to understand historical perspectives if they had not care or concern for the lives and experiences of people in the past?"[10] Film can enhance perspective recognition through narratives that expose underrepresented points of view and help explain the thinking, experiences, and decisions of those in the past. Film also promotes caring through its powerful audiovisual medium and carefully constructed character-driven narratives. By including empathy as an important goal for Holocaust education, educators promote what Salmons says is critical, which is that we complicate students' thinking and illustrate that those involved—victim, perpetrators, bystanders, rescuers, and others— are multidimensional and not just distinctly black or white heroes or villains.[11]

Studying the Holocaust presents an incredible range of topics and morally intricate issues. Its scope is vast—the number of people impacted by the event; the variety of capacities of those involved such as collaborators, bystanders, resisters, rescuers, and so on; the geographic area covered; and the incredible diversity of experiences such as the Kindertransport, liberating a concentration camp, the Sonderkommandos, and the Warsaw Ghetto. The Holocaust also evokes complex moral issues. It is difficult for students intellectually and emotionally to understand what happened and particularly the idea that a modern society and state could systematically attempt to wipe an entire group of people from existence. The Holocaust offers "maybe the most important moral lessons we stand to learn as human beings."[12]

The Challenges of Graphic Content in Films

One of the most significant ways in which teaching the Holocaust with film is difficult is the potential graphic nature of representations of the Holocaust, particularly the Holocaust as seen in film (e.g., images of dead or naked bodies, torture of victims, depictions of killing, language used by perpetrators). While an effective film to use, *Schindler's List* presents a barrage of graphic images that can traumatize viewers. Teachers must grapple with what ages—or maturity levels—can best handle graphic content and what type of content is necessary for meeting curricular goals. Whether—and how much—graphic film content to include is dependent on the specific context and should be determined by the teacher's goals, the maturity and background of the students, school and community norms, and other resources used in the lesson. Film exacerbates the challenge posed by graphic content because films present narratives through a combined visual and audio narrative that includes special effects to bring the past alive and evoke an emotive response from viewers.

For some teachers, the Holocaust cannot be fully understood without learning about the trauma of victims, at least in part through graphic content. Other teachers worry that graphic content is used simply for the shock value rather than to legitimately understand the past or that their students simply can't handle the graphic content. I ask teachers and my students to consider the following questions when deciding whether to use film with graphic images for Holocaust education and how to use a film. Not all of these may apply to each context, and some teachers may weigh certain of these items more than others.

- Does the film meet goals for the lesson?
- What is the maturity level of my students?
- What prior life experiences do students have that may impact how they will react to graphic images?
- Does the film show any dead or mutilated bodies?
- Does the film create or promote historical empathy?
- Does the film reinforce widely held beliefs/truths?
- Does the film provide important evidence of the past?

Choosing Appropriate Films

Teachers are faced with many films from which to choose and little time to research films. The primary driver should be a teacher's goals for using a film and for teaching the Holocaust. Working from previous scholarship, I propose eight guidelines with questions teachers can ask of a film.[13] Few films will meet all of the criteria, but the criteria can be used to evaluate a film's potential. See the list at the end of this chapter for recommended Holocaust feature films.

Criteria	Questions to ask
Establish lesson goal	Is the film the best possible source to meet the lesson goals?
Determine the film's ability to develop historical empathy	Does the film appropriately develop historical empathy? With which characters does the film want the viewer to empathize and why?
Assess if historical figures are represented accurately and shown to be complicated multidimensional figures	In what ways are historical figures overly distorted into near perfect heroes or evil villains? Do the representations of historical figures complicate our understanding of the past?

Evaluate the ways in which the film depicts alternative perspectives on history in contrast to what students might otherwise see in their textbooks or regular lessons	In what ways does the film reinforce or challenge traditional historical narratives? Does the film present the historical experiences of marginalized groups that might otherwise receive little attention?
Determine whether the political, social, and ideological values reflected in the film overly distort the historical narrative or if they can be effectively used as part of the activities with the film	What political or social values are reflected by the film and which are disparaged or ignored? In what ways does the time period in which a film was made influence the narrative or perspectives? At what point do the political, social, or ideological influences on a film distort the past so it is unusable?
Verify the film's adherence to the historical record and ascertain the reliance of the film on historical evidence and scholarship	How well does the film match the historical record? Is the film factually accurate, and does it also stay true to the spirit of past events and people? How well does the film (or the writing/producing of the film) use historical evidence and scholarship— primary sources, historian's expertise—to support the narrative, character development, and visual re-creation of the past?
Establish that any fictional elements in the film enhance, and not distort, the history presented	Does the film overly distort the past with fictional elements, condensing of time, composite characters, or politically overt messages? Do the fictional elements add to or take away from the useful pedagogical perspective or power of the film?
Determine availability of other resources to use with the film	Are primary sources, other films, or other resources available that allow the film to be part of a broader lesson or unit?

Part of choosing films is to eliminate mis-educative films. One such film is *The Boy in the Striped Pajamas*, which can be a perilous film to use for Holocaust education.[14] The film is about eight-year-old Bruno, a German boy who lives next to an extermination camp where his father is the commander. Bruno sneaks away from the house to explore and finds the camp; across the wire fence, he befriends Shmuel, a Jewish prisoner his age. The film is historically inaccurate, narrow in perspectives presented, misleading, and based on fiction, not evidence. The film misrepresents the Holocaust and perpetuates myths. While teachers like the lack of graphic imagery and the potential connections to characters the age of their students, the film has not just small inaccuracies but gross distortions that can alter the way we view the Holocaust in problematic ways. One of the film's biggest problems is the lack of voice for Holocaust victims who are underrepresented by Shmuel, the Jewish boy in the film, with homosexuals, Romani, the disabled, and political prisoners altogether invisible. Victims have no agency, and the film does almost nothing to educate about victims' suffering or resistance.[15] British historian David Cesarani describes how unrealistic the film is because it "justifies the post-war claim of Germans that they knew nothing about what happened to the Jews . . . the book is full of Germans who know nothing and, if they do, heartily disapprove. This is not fable; it is fiction in the worst sense of the word."[16] Germans here are not perpetrators, but victims themselves. There are also specific inaccuracies such as deaths from Zyklon B poison gas being instant versus the reality of taking ten to twenty minutes of suffering to kill. Also, Bruno and Shmuel could never have met so frequently and for so long. The outright falsehoods combined with distortions of the truth make the film terrible to use to teach about the Holocaust. The one exception could be if teachers ask students to evaluate the distortions in the film and think about the film as a source to be critiqued, rather than a reliable source of factual information.

Film as Evidence and Testimony

Films act as both primary and secondary sources. As primary sources they are evidence of the time period in which they were created. They reflect societal norms and values, events of the time, and the messages of their directors, producers, and actors. Films can additionally be used as secondary sources to learn about the Holocaust, bringing the past to life by helping the audience see and hear the past. Thus, as primary and secondary sources, and in the ways they bring the past to life, films act as evidence of the Holocaust. There are of course inherent issues with feature films such as compressed storylines to fit a two-hour narrative, composite characters representing larger groups of people, and the pressures of providing entertainment aimed at profit.

But the benefits of films—development of historical empathy, bringing the past to life, using films as primary and secondary sources—outweigh the drawbacks.

Films are already one of the most used sources to teach about the Holocaust. As the age of live Holocaust survivors and live testimony comes to an end, what will fill the space left behind? In many cases, it could be that film fills the void. It is possible that films will become the "evidence" that replaces live survivors alongside video testimony and the children of survivors, particularly in trying to engage students. Like Holocaust survivors, films offer powerful narratives, but nothing can replace the power, sway, and respect garnered from a live survivor. In terms of evoking emotion, films present a viable second choice, yet one that should be used with caution.

Cases of Using Film to Teach the Holocaust

Here I present outlines of two cases of using Holocaust films. The cases are not meant to be fully fleshed-out lessons ready to be implemented, but rather outlines that can be adapted to specific class-room contexts. While both cases describe secondary teachers, the goals, big ideas, and types of activities could be easily adapted for university classrooms with added rigor.

Case I:
Film as a Means to Provide More Global Perspectives on the Holocaust

In the United States, US and world history, including the Holocaust, are most commonly taught from an American point of view. While this is to be expected, the marginalization of non-US national viewpoints is problematic given that the Holocaust is a global event that primarily occurred in non-American geographical, political, and military spheres and can only be fully understood in that context. As described earlier, one of the key challenges to teaching the Holocaust includes its complexity and scope. Teaching with non-American feature films adds an important dimension that expands the scope of Holocaust perspectives while providing opportunities to unpack the Holocaust's complexity.

Non-American films—films made in and from a variety of na-tions and national perspectives outside of the mainstream Hollywood system—can provoke students to explore global perspectives, to evaluate less-familiar sources of evidence, and to recognize alternative and competing interpretations of the Holocaust. When included alongside American perspectives, non-American films provide a richer historical context and promote a more ethno-relative worldview—a worldview that allows for "the experience of one's own beliefs and behaviors as just one organization of reality among many viable possibilities."[17]

This case looks at the lessons of Mr. Thackeray, who teaches a twelve-day unit on the Holocaust following a ten-day unit on World War II more broadly, in his global studies course with high school sophomores and juniors (an admittedly luxurious length of time for these units).

Mr. Thackeray's Unit: Holocaust Film and Global Perspectives

Unit Goals

- Students will explore multiple global perspectives of the Holocaust.
- Students will investigate the value of studying history from various national points of view.
- Students will evaluate the role of films in learning about the Holocaust.

Unit Overview

Due to the previous unit the students already have a solid background on WWII including knowledge of key people and events and significant work on the geography of WWII. The Holocaust unit begins with a history of antisemitism in Europe over hundreds of years and the German government policies during 1933–1939. Mr. Thackeray uses a combination of short interactive lectures and primary source analysis. Next the students have to conduct research on topics related to the content of the films including the role of the Catholic Church during WWII and the counterfeiting operations of the Nazis. The research is well scaffolded with specific resources, questions, and tasks, but there is also room for student inquiry, where they can pose questions, find evidence, and draw conclusions. Finally, Mr. Thackeray shows three films with an emphasis on the non-American perspectives they bring. For the final assessment students choose one of the three films (their choice) and answer the following questions: (1) How does this film help you understand the Holocaust? (2) How have your views of the Holocaust changed or stayed the same? (3) How might this film be different if told from an American point of view? (4) Are films a good way to learn about the Holocaust?

Films Shown

- *Europa Europa* (1990) follows Solomon Perel, a German Jewish teenager, who gets separated from his family during the Holocaust. Solly hides his identity to survive by pretending to be an Aryan German. His wartime experiences include fleeing from Germany to Poland, hiding in a Soviet Union orphanage until the Germans invade, serving in the German army after being captured, and enrolling (not by choice) in a Hitler Youth school. The film is a true story based on Solly's autobiography, and it won a Golden Globe Award for best foreign language film. It is a joint French, Polish, and German film production.
- *Amen* (2002) is based on a true story. The key events are grounded in the experiences of SS Lieutenant and chemist Kurt Gerstein, who created the Zyklon B pellets to disinfect soldiers' drinking water. He uncovers the Nazis' use of the pellets to create gas for mass murder of Jews. He is opposed to the German extermination policy and sets out to slow down use of the pellets. As part of his efforts he enlists the support of a priest (a fictional character created to represent his contacts with the Catholic Church more broadly). *Amen* is a French, German, and Romanian film that won an Academy Award for Best Screenplay and is based on a 1963 play.
- *The Counterfeiters* (2007), an Austrian and German film, is a true story about Jewish prisoners that provides a narrow but incredibly rich exposure to previously unexplored narratives. The film tells the story of a group of counterfeiting experts and those with skills that support counterfeiting who are forced by the Nazis (Operation Bernhard) to counterfeit the British pound and American dollar or be killed. *The Counterfeiters* won the Oscar for best foreign language film.

Activities with Film

First Mr. Thackeray shows *Europa Europa*. As additional preparation, students receive a map of Europe, and Mr. Thackeray reviews key locations where Solly travels during the film. Students use the map while watching to better understand the geography of the events. While viewing, students complete two activities. First, they fill in a timeline of key events involving Solly, so by the end they have a visual of key moments in the film and a reference. Second, Mr. Thackeray stops the film at numerous turning points. Students have to predict what they expect to happen and why. When possible, they need to provide evidence or connect to prior knowledge. At each prediction point pause, they review the accuracy of their responses at previous prediction points. Mr. Thackeray also leads whole class discussions each time the students predict. Postviewing, there is a whole class discussion, drawing on the turning points in Solly's life with a focus on issues of identity. The students also discuss places where an American point of view could alter the film. Finally, students consider how the film compares to other sources as "evidence" of the Holocaust.

Next the students view *Amen* to flip the perspective from a German Jew to a German SS officer. For this film Mr. Thackeray also stops the film for discussion at numerous points. At these stopping points, he uses scenes from the film as a starting point and asks students to analyze various primary sources that build on key ideas in the film. The sources add depth to the ideas in the film and promote more in-depth discussion. Sources used include the film's controversial film cover image (a Christian cross merged with a Nazi Swastika); photos of the real Gerstein, trial testimony from SS soldiers about the gassing of prisoners; Pope Pius XII's Easter Message in Vatican City in 1941; a 1942 letter from Myron C. Taylor, FDR's personal representative to the Vatican, to the church detailing the killing of Jews in Eastern Europe; and Gerstein's 1945 sworn written testimony he wrote for Allied forces. By the end of the viewing, the class has already extensively discussed the film. As a wrap-up, students have two structured debates. The first is over the question, Should Gerstein be tried as a war criminal? The second debate question is, During the Holocaust would you consider the Catholic Church collaborators, bystanders, or something else? There is also discussion about where American points of view could alter the film.

Finally, the students view *The Counterfeiters*. Mr. Thackeray previews the film and provides background information on the three main characters: Solomon, Herzog, and Berger. The students are assigned one of the three characters to "shadow." For the character shadow, students keep track of the actions and beliefs of their character. At the end of the film, the students meet in groups of three with each character represented. Using a large Venn diagram with three intersecting circles, the groups fill in the diagram for character's beliefs and character's actions. This is followed by a whole class discussion of the characters. Each student then chooses one "freeze frame" image from the film to answer: What master image best represents the film? This is followed by small group and whole class discussion about their choices plus an analysis of the film as a historical document.

Mr. Thackeray covers many of the traditional elements of the Holocaust as background, with an emphasis on helping students consider how non-American points of view can help them both better understand the Holocaust and think about bias in the study of history more broadly. By emphasizing ethno-relative worldviews, his students are better positioned to understand the impact of the Holocaust on individuals. His focus on more global perspectives carries on in other units in his class.

Case 2:
Film to Develop Empathy and Explore People's Roles in the Holocaust

Holocaust education is often narrow in its coverage with a focus on victims and perpetrators more so than on other groups such as resisters, collaborators, rescuers, survivors, bystanders, and liberators. Feature films provide the opportunity to engage students in understanding these marginalized perspectives, within the context of exploring the Holocaust as difficult and morally complex history.

The second case is Ms. Simon's use of film to help students better understand the moral complexity of the Holocaust through people's roles (collaborators, resisters, etc.) and to develop empathy by exploring multiple perspectives and helping students personally connect to the past. The use of films occurs during a seven-day Holocaust unit within the study of World War II in her eleventh-grade US history class, which has a block schedule with ninety-minute periods.

Ms. Simon's Unit: Holocaust Film to Understand Moral Complexity and Develop Empathy

---

Unit Goals

- Students will investigate the moral complexity of people's roles in the Holocaust.
- Students will analyze the beliefs and actions of people during the Holocaust.
- Students will probe connections between people's actions during the Holocaust and the role the students can play in society today.

Unit Overview

Teaching the Holocaust is not normally covered in the school's US history course, but Ms. Simon believes in its importance. First she provides an admittedly rushed and "barely adequate" one-day lecture overview of the Holocaust to equip students with a basic understanding of the rise of Nazis; the series of state-sponsored actions against the Jews, the disabled, homosexuals, communists and other groups; and the establishment of ghettos, camps, and the Final Solution. Ms. Simon then uses a series of diary and memoir excerpts, read and analyzed for homework and during several classes, to help students understand the wide range of roles people played during the Holocaust (survivors, collaborators, bystanders, rescuers, etc.). She places an emphasis on the ways in which many people don't fit neatly into one role. Finally, parts of three films are viewed to further understand these roles and evaluate the moral complexity of the Holocaust. For a summative assessment, students are tasked with writing a letter to one of the main characters in one of the films. They are told to pick someone whom they either liked or disliked, connected with, wanted to speak to, or had some feelings about. Students can write the letter from the time period in the film or from today's perspective. They also separately explain why they chose that person, what they wanted to say, and why. Next, students exchange letters with a classmate (facilitated by Ms. Simon) and write a response to the classmate's letter from the perspective of or as if they are that character. Finally, the class discusses where in today's society they see people acting in similar ways (e.g., stereotyping, bullying, resisting) and how they as individuals can make a difference.

Films Shown

- *Schindler's List* (1993) is based on the true story of Oskar Schindler, a businessman and war profiteer who changed from caring primarily about making money to using his factories to save Jews from death at concentration camps. Directed by Steven Spielberg, it won seven Academy Awards including Best Director and Best Picture.
- *The Grey Zone* (2001) narrates the experiences of a group of Jewish Sonderkommando (special unit) in the Auschwitz concentration camp in October 1944. The Sonderkommando were prisoners forced to assist the camp's guards in exterminating their fellow prisoners. This included preparing victims for the gas chambers, removing the bodies, and placing the bodies in the crematorium ovens or in large, outdoor burning pits.
- *Defiance* (2008) is another film grounded in real events. *Defiance* presents the experiences of the three Bielski brothers who shelter Jews—men, women, and children—in the forests of Poland and Belorussia and actively resist the German occupiers.

Activities with Film

First, students watch *Schindler's List*. Prior to the film Ms. Simon reviews the locations in the film on a map. Rather than provide a long-list of fact-based questions, Ms. Simon asks her students to do two tasks. First, they are to keep a film journal where they record what they see as important events in the film and where they write their own personal reactions—intellectual and emotional. Second, they are to keep in mind the following questions:

- How does Oscar Schindler change throughout the film? In what ways was he similar and different by the end of the film?
- What strategies did individuals and families use to cope with the brutality and death around them and to survive?

Ms. Simon carefully monitors her students for emotional stress and always ends the film ten minutes before the end of class to allow students to decompress and recompose. After the film, students work in small groups to discuss how Schindler changed during the film and how individuals and families coped. They identify moments in the film when characters were faced with moral dilemmas, and they discuss the choices they made. Finally, Ms. Simon leads a whole class discussion that asks, Who is the hero of the film? And also, where in the film are various roles are portrayed (perpetrators, liberators, survivors, rescuers, bystanders, resisters, collaborators, victims)? This builds on the earlier work with diaries and memoirs.

Next students watch excerpts from *The Grey Zone*. Given time constraints, Ms. Simon does not show the entire film. The clips focus on the moral dilemmas raised by the film through characters' actions and how these actions resulted in characters filling multiple roles (e.g., victim and collaborator; perpetrator and rescuer; collaborator and resister). Scenes include Jewish prisoners saving their own lives by working as Sonderkommando, decisions about whether to save someone's life while risking one's own life, plans for resistance and rebellion, whether to sacrifice or risk some lives for the greater good, and so on. Each scene is followed by class discussion of the dilemmas. Ms. Simon is careful to have students attempt to understand the perspective of the characters rather than to judge them from a presentist perspective.

Last, students view clips from *Defiance*. Prior to viewing, Ms. Simon asks the students to list three "defining characteristics" of what people need in order to retain their humanity and to keep these in mind when viewing the film. Next, students view clips, similar to those from *The Grey Zone*, that show characters grappling with moral dilemmas. Scenes include whether the partisan group should focus on hiding and protecting refugees, whether they should actively fight, whether they should seek revenge from those who betrayed them, and if and how they should cooperate with the Soviets. After the viewing, students discuss the similarities and differences between the three brothers—the decisions they made and why, and their role during the Holocaust. They also discuss the following question:

- In what ways did the characters in these three films retain and lose their humanity?

Sometimes Ms. Simon will replay a scene for the students to analyze if it helps to support the discussion.

Ms. Simon packs a lot into seven days of class that challenge students to respond outside of their comfort zone. She uses both a whole film and clips from films to develop students' historical empathy, expand their understanding of people's actions during the Holocaust, and explore the moral complexity of the Holocaust.

Conclusion

Teachers must grapple with the many challenges of teaching the Holocaust and using film to teach the Holocaust. The suggestions in this chapter are intended to provide guidance and a starting point, but teachers need to adapt this guidance and these activities based on their goals and classroom context. Films do not teach, but when used thoughtfully, they are a phenomenal teaching tool.

Holocaust Feature Films to Consider Using with Students

Amen (2002)

Angry Harvest (1985)

Au Revoir Les Enfants (1987)

Bent (1997)

The Black Book (2006)

The Book Thief (2013)

The Counterfeiters (2007)

Defiance (2008)

Denial (2016)
The Devil's Arithmetic (1999)
Divided We Fall (2007)
Downfall (2004)
Europa Europa (1990)
Everything Is Illuminated (2005)
Fateless (2005)
The Grey Zone (2001)
Ida (2013)
In Darkness (2011)
Judgment at Nuremburg (1961)
Life Is Beautiful (1997)
Operation Finale (2018)
The Pianist (2002)

The Reader (2008)
Run Boy Run (2013)
Sarah's Key (2010)
Schindler's List (1993)
The Shop on Main Street (1965)
Son of Saul (2015)
Sophie's Choice (1982)
Sophie Scholl (2005)
Sunshine (1999)
Train of Life (1998)
Uprising (2001)
Wakolda (2013)
The Zookeepers Wife (2017)

Notes

1. M. B. Donnelly, "Educating Students about the Holocaust: A Survey of Teaching Practices," *Social Education* 70, no. 1 (2006): 51–54; Alice Pettigrew, Stuart Foster, Jonathan Howson, Paul Salmons, Ruth-Ann Lenga, and Kay Andrews, *Teaching about the Holocaust in English Secondary Schools: An Empirical Study of National Trends, Perspectives and Practice* (London: Centre for Holocaust Education, 2009), 1–127.

2. Mark Gudgel, "A Mixed-Methods Study of the Use of Film by American Secondary School Educators in Teaching about the Holocaust" (PhD diss., Regent University, 2015).

3. Pettigrew et al., *Teaching about the Holocaust.*

4. Gudgel, "Mixed-Methods Study"; Pettigrew et al., *Teaching about the Holocaust.*

5. Alan S. Marcus, "Teaching the Holocaust through Film," *Social Education* 81, no. 3 (May/June 2017): 172–176.

6. Alan S. Marcus, Scott Alan Metzger, Richard J. Paxton, and Jeremy D. Stoddard, *Teaching History with Film: Strategies for Secondary Social Studies*, 2nd ed. (New York: Routledge, 2018).

7. Ben Walsh, David Hicks, and Stephanie van Hover, "Difficult History Means Difficult Questions: Using Film to Reveal the Perspective of 'the Other' in Difficult History Topics," in Jeremy D. Stoddard, Alan S. Marcus, and David Hicks, eds., *Teaching Difficult History through Film* (New York: Routledge, 2017), 17–36.

8. Walsh, Hicks, and van Hover, "Difficult History Means Difficult Questions."

9. Sam Wineburg, *Historical Thinking and Other Unnatural Acts: Charting the Future of Teaching the Past* (Philadelphia: Temple University Press, 2001).

10. Keith Barton and Linda Levstik, *Teaching History for the Common Good* (New York: Routledge, 2004), 228.

11. Paul Salmons, "Teaching or Preaching? The Holocaust and Intercultural Education in the UK," *Intercultural Education* 14, no. 2 (2003): 139–49.

12. Simone Schweber and Debbie Findling, *Teaching the Holocaust* (Los Angeles: Torah Aura Productions, 2007), 1.

13. Marcus, "Teaching the Holocaust through Film."

14. Marcus, "Teaching the Holocaust through Film."

15. David Cesarani, "Striped Pyjamas," *Literary Review*, October 2008, https://literaryreview.co.uk/striped-pyjamas.

16. Cesarani, "Striped Pyjamas," 359.

17. Milton J. Bennett, "Becoming Interculturally Competent," in Jamie Wurzel, ed., *Toward Multiculturalism: A Reader in Multicultural Education* (Newton, MA: Intercultural Resource Corporation 2004), 62.

Survivor Testimonies and Interviews

M A R G A R E T E   M Y E R S   F E I N S T E I N

Oral histories and testimonies offer many advantages for students of the Holocaust. They also present challenges. Used properly, however, survivor interviews can engage students and open up new avenues of inquiry. Studies of many topics (such as family relationships, spiritual resistance, and sexuality) can be enriched by oral history. Some experiences, such as revenge acts and wartime rape, are often absent from the written record. Survivors often hesitate to discuss sensitive topics in print but are more willing to disclose them in the context of an interview with a sympathetic questioner. Video recordings of oral history interviews (sometimes referred to as *testimonies*) also offer the benefit of allowing us to see the interviewee's facial expressions and body language, which add levels of meaning to the spoken word. The ways in which survivors organize their memories during an interview can provide insights that a conventionally composed, revised, and edited memoir cannot (see Jennifer Goss's chapter in this volume). This chapter discusses the advantages of incorporating survivor testimonies and interviews into the classroom, provides guidance for how to prepare students to use personal narratives as historical sources, shares insights into analyzing testimonies, suggests classroom activities, and identifies useful resources.

Testimonies as Historical Documents

Survivor oral testimonies give a human face to the victims as well as to the survivors of genocide. The academic tone of textbooks often does not convey the violence and the personal tragedies cloaked by terms such as *liquidation of the ghettos* or *selection*. Personal narratives can give students a better understanding of the effects of events and the variety of responses that were available to the victims and how the responses varied over different times and places. The human dimension, the significance of individual decisions, the moral conundrums, and the lifesaving or life-destroying impact of happenstance confront students in ways that textbooks cannot. Many students will be able to empathize with the survivors, many of whom were the students' age at the time of their persecution. By engaging the students, survivor interviews and testimonies promote learning. Students better retain course information, become more interested in research, and participate more readily in classroom discussions.

Preparing to Use Testimonies

Instructors should identify the learning outcomes for using recorded survivor oral histories. Perhaps there are particular topics of research that are best found in testimonies, or maybe the goal is to highlight historiographical issues or research methods. Teachers will want to make clear to students why they are using oral histories to study the Holocaust. The USC Shoah Foundation offers "Using Visual History Testimony in the Classroom" on its website to provide educators with assistance in developing classroom activities using visual history testimony.[1] Depending on access to technology, the teacher can choose from published oral histories and digital archives that provide access to survivor and witness interviews. Many of the archives offer curricular advice designed for grades 7 through 12. Often these lesson plans are easily adapted to college-level assignments.

Before introducing survivor interviews into the classroom, instructors will want to prepare students by providing the appropriate context. Students need to know the general history of the Holocaust and to have familiarity with major events related to World War II. Class time should also be devoted to familiarizing students with key historiographical interpretations of the Holocaust and with the types of sources historians use, so that students can appreciate how the questions asked and the sources used shape historical understanding.[2] Sources created by the perpetrators, for example, might help explain the bureaucratic system of the Nazi state, but they cannot tell us how the victims understood their circumstances or how they struggled to survive. With background knowledge, students will be better able to evaluate how particular interviews contribute to knowledge of the Holocaust.

Analyzing Testimonies and Interviews

It is important to teach students how to analyze interviews and testimonies. As with any historical document, the researcher must ascertain how the video or transcript was created and what circumstances influenced the shape it took. If the interview was conducted on behalf of an archive or institution, it could be useful to know the mission of the originating agency, since that could influence the selection of interviewees and the questions asked. If the testimony is the result of a criminal trial, then there are issues of potential self-incrimination as well as the constraints of the legal proceedings that would privilege certain information over other. An attorney at trial might not be interested in how a survivor felt about something since it did not pertain to the case, but in an oral history interview that might be salient. Both the structure and dynamics of the interviews as well as personal and contextual factors that shape memories need to be considered when analyzing personal narratives.

The Interview

Students should consider how oral history might differ from a diary or memoir as a source. Unlike a diary that is written in close proximity to events, both oral history and memoirs are created after the fact, which permits the survivor to place events into a larger framework and to reinterpret their significance with the benefit of hindsight. At the same time, they also introduce issues of memory, which can emphasize some experiences and repress others. While a diary is usually intended as a private document with personal significance, an oral history or memoir is intended for a wider audience and its perceived interests. Writing a diary is a solitary endeavor, but oral histories and published memoirs are created in collaboration with an interviewer or an editor.[3]

The role that the interviewer adopts affects the way in which the narrative develops. For example, the Fortunoff Video Archive for Holocaust Testimonies trained interviewers to allow the survivors (whom it calls *witnesses*) to take the lead in telling their stories. The interviewers were to listen and to clarify, asking open-ended questions to allow the witnesses to shape their narratives and posing follow-up questions for time, place, and additional information. This approach allows survivors freedom to organize their narratives whichever way is most meaningful to them and to make connections thematically or across time. These interviews are particularly useful for researchers wanting to study memory and psychology. The Visual History Archive of the Shoah Foundation Institute encouraged its interviewers to follow a chronological format. If a survivor followed a train of thought to connect an experience to one that came earlier or later, the interviewer was instructed to bring the narrator back to the timeline. As a result, some survivors had their narratives interrupted and redirected. The emphasis on chronology serves to structure the narrative in a readily understandable sequence, restricting meandering detours, but it also interferes with the free flow of memories.

Instructors will want to encourage students to consider how the relationship between the interviewer and interviewee (also known as the *subject* or *narrator*) can influence the narrative. If the interview was conducted by a family member of the interviewee, then that might influence the survivor's willingness to discuss some subjects. Parents might want to protect their children from the harsher elements of their experiences or might be more concerned with presenting themselves in a positive light than when talking with a professional (or student) interviewer. If the narrator is uncomfortable with the interviewer, then some information may be withheld. If there is a strong rapport between the two, then the interviewee may volunteer more information and be more willing to discuss difficult experiences.

The genders of the interviewer and narrator are also worth noting. Female survivors might be more willing to discuss sexual assault, abortion, and other sensitive topics with a woman than with a man. The circumstances of the interview also influence the retrieval of memories. The era in which the interview was conducted could influence what a person remembers or the significance she or he attributes to a memory. What is remembered or emphasized during a period of calm and prosperity might be different than what is recalled during a period of increasing antisemitism or economic crisis. Recent events could trigger memories. For example, one interviewee recalled that when Menachem Begin was elected prime minister of Israel, she overheard members at a

B'nai Brith meeting saying that Begin had blood on his hands from his time in the Irgun. Suddenly a repressed memory surfaced of the time she had thrown a stone at a Hitler Youth, hitting him in the head, causing him to fall to the ground. She had fled the scene and heard the siren of the ambulance but did not know the extent of his injuries. She now wondered whether she too has blood on her hands. The discussion about Begin had prompted the memory. Had the interview taken place prior to that discussion, she would not have been able to tell the story of her act of retribution.

Memory

Once the factors that influenced the production of the interview or testimony have been taken into consideration, students should examine the elements that shaped how the survivor's memories were encoded. Various filters influence memories. For example, the memories of a child survivor will be different from the memories of an adult. Children do not have an awareness of the wider world that can help them interpret their experiences in the same way as an adult. Child survivors were often left out of adult conversations and could only guess as to the reasons for events. For example, children whose parents sent them to safety in England on what was known as the Kindertransport almost uniformly felt abandoned or rejected by their parents. For the parents, however, it was usually an agonizing, loving choice that they hoped would allow their children to escape persecution. With hearing only the perspective of such a child, a student might falsely conclude that parents of Kindertransport children were callous.[4]

In a similar fashion, students should be aware of how political and religious affiliations may have shaped the experiences and also the memories of survivors. For example, German antisemites often sought out Orthodox men who wore beards and earlocks for humiliation and beatings. Religiously observant or politically active Jews occasionally found a support network of fellow inmates who shared their religious or political beliefs, providing psychological benefits and assistance in the struggle for survival. Some ultra-Orthodox Jews interpreted the Holocaust as God's will and a sign of God's displeasure with modern Jewry, while some other Jews interpreted the Holocaust as proof that God did not exist or was dead. These different perspectives can lead the former to emphasize the providential nature of events and the latter to focus on human agency. Political ideology could also lead survivors to interpret events to conform to their worldview. Zionists might explain things as the result of Jews not having a homeland, while communists might blame the machinations of an anachronistic feudal class.

Emotions and expectations can also shape a person's interpretation of events. Many survivors, for example, state that the Poles or Ukrainians were worse than the Germans in their treatment of Jews. Instructors should encourage students to consider whether this was objectively true or whether this was a perception influenced by their neighbors' betrayal of them. Since survivors had not necessarily expected kindness from the German occupiers, betrayal was not a factor; thus, the behavior of the locals may have felt more hurtful than that of Germans. Gender also can influence experiences and how they are remembered. For example, women often recall the humiliation of having their body hair shaved upon arrival at Auschwitz. Men rarely mention it. Some scholars initially concluded that only women had been shaved. In fact, both men and women had their body hair shaved, but it was almost only women who chose to discuss it. This difference in remembering sheds light on issues of gender, while also cautioning us about the limits of oral histories as sources.[5]

The knowledge that memories are subjective and that their retrieval can be shaped by many factors could lead students to discount their validity as historical sources. It is important to remind students that scholars have shown that a survivor's central memories remained stable over time, with only slight variations in what a survivor remembered or chose to discuss at various times.[6] Also, the use of multiple interviews or testimonies helps to identify fundamental truths, screening out distortions created by personal, individual perspectives. Neuroscientist Daniel Schacter observes that videotaped interviews with Holocaust survivors "can help to ensure that forgetting and distortion—which can infiltrate any individual rememberer's story—are counteracted by the overwhelming truths that emerge from core elements that are shared by numerous rememberers."[7] When used carefully, survivor narratives can provide important information about events and about the meanings survivors attribute to events and experiences.[8]

Activities and Resources

The Library of Congress offers guidelines for analyzing oral histories that are useful in facilitating active learning.[9] Students are led through the reflection process. First they are to observe what they see and hear in the interview including unfamiliar terms, accents, and background noises. Next they are to reflect, speculating about the purpose of the oral history, what they can tell about the narrator and the narrator's point of view, and how hearing a firsthand account affects the emotional impact of the material. Finally, the students are to ask questions that will lead them to more observations. Follow-up activities can make these thoughts more concrete and serve as the basis for integrating oral histories into other course material and assignments. Students begin by writing a brief summary of the interview. Then they speculate about what the interviewer and the interviewee each hoped to accomplish in the oral history and whether they succeeded in their goals. Finally, based on what they have already learned, the students assess whether the oral history supports, contradicts, or adds to what they already understood about the Holocaust.

Depending on school resources, instructors may prefer to use published interviews or testimonies. David P. Boder's *I Did Not Interview the Dead* contains seven complete transcriptions of his 1946 interviews with Holocaust survivors in the Displaced Persons camps in occupied Germany.[10] Although out of print, this volume is available at some libraries and online as an electronic resource. Transcripts (in the original language and in English translation) and sound recordings (there are fifteen in English) are available on the *Voices of the Holocaust* website (http://voices.iit.edu/). The advantage of these interviews—that they are close to the event and demonstrate the difficulty survivors initially had in interpreting and communicating their experiences—is also the disadvantage, since many references are unexplained and require the reader to have rather extensive knowledge of the Holocaust in order to make sense of them. Donald Niewyk in his book *Fresh Wounds* provides edited versions of thirty-four interviews from Boder's collection.[11] While the editing makes them easier for students to read and comprehend, they are filtered versions of the originals. For those instructors wanting to focus on the experiences of women, Lore Shelly provides edited accounts from women survivors of Auschwitz in *Auschwitz— The Nazi Civilization.*[12]

Postwar war crimes trials provide a different perspective on survivor accounts. Transcripts of the trials include testimony by survivors and other witnesses. The testimonies are designed to gain the convictions of specific accused war criminals and thus convey only a small portion of the survivors' experiences. The Library of Congress website

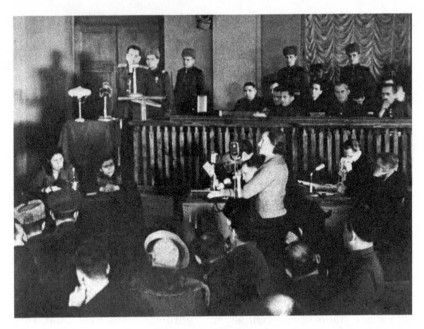

Dina Pronicheva, a Jewish survivor of the Babi Yar massacre, testifies about her experiences during a war crimes trial in Kiev. (USHMM Photo Archives, #86215, courtesy of Babi Yar Society)

gives access to the complete transcripts of the Nuremberg Trials.[13] The first volume contains basic pretrial documents, the judgment, and sentencing. Subsequent volumes hold transcripts of the daily court proceedings. The PDF can be searched by keywords to help locate Jewish witnesses and others. Harvard Law School has made available four transcripts from the Nuremberg Trials that are searchable by key words.[14] Searchable transcripts of the Bergen-Belsen Trial of 1946 in the British zone of occupied Germany are also available online.[15]

Some archives have made available online video recordings of oral history interviews with survivors and other witnesses. The Fortunoff Video Archive for Holocaust Testimonies houses more than forty-four hundred videotaped survivor and witness interviews. Excerpts from some of the interviews are available on YouTube. On the archive's website, there is a page for Edited Programs that provides links to excerpts of individual testimonies and to thematic programs incorporating survivor testimonies on a particular topic, which might be especially useful for teachers.[16] The edited testimonies run for fifteen to thirty minutes each. Thematic programs consist of films based on interviews from the collection that cover a variety of topics from "Parallel Lives," dealing with experiences similar to those of Anne Frank to "Future Imperfect," discussing the impact of the Holocaust on survivors' future lives and their families. One such film, *Witness: Voices from the Holocaust*, uses historical film footage along with oral histories from liberators, bystanders, Hitler Youth, and survivors to tell the history of the Holocaust. It has a companion book and teacher's guide. The teacher's guide provides suggested topics for journal entries, classroom discussion, and research papers. Excerpts from some of the interviews used in the various films are available online.

The United States Holocaust Memorial Museum (USHMM) is actively conducting and collecting survivor interviews, thousands of which are available online. The website for the museum's Jeff and Toby Herr Oral History Archive contains a link to search the collection as well as a link to guidelines for conducting interviews.[17] Within the collection, it is possible to search for testimonies that discuss key events, key cities, key concentration camps, or key ghettos; however, it is not possible to search within individual testimonies. Over two thousand of the testimonies have been transcribed. The museum also has available on its website excerpts from forty-eight survivor interviews in its First Person Podcast Series.[18]

An interesting classroom exercise to demonstrate the value of nonverbal cues and vocal inflections is to divide students into two groups. One group reads the transcript of a selected interview, while the second group views the video of said interview. (A large class could be divided into three groups, with the third group only listening to the audio of the interview.) Each group reports on what they learned from the interview, and then the class compares the strengths and weaknesses of each medium for conveying information and knowledge of survivor experiences.

A highly useful classroom tool is IWitness from the USC Shoah Foundation.[19] The USC Shoah Foundation has collected more than fifty thousand videotaped testimonies from Jewish Holocaust survivors, other victims of Nazism, liberators, and aid workers. It is now incorporating videos from other organizations, as well as interviews from other genocides. Over fifteen hundred interviews related to the Holocaust, the Armenian genocide, and the genocide of Rwandan Tutsis are currently available for classroom use through IWitness.

Educators can easily open an IWitness account and then invite their students to join a class group. Instructors and students may use keyword searches to find segments of testimonies that pertain to a particular experience or place. It is possible for the instructor and students to create their own documentaries using video clips and other resources on the site. Instructional videos on the site inform users about ethical considerations involving editorial choices in the use of testimonies. Instructors need to be explicit about how a film assignment would be assessed. Rubrics for video assignments are available online. Some elements for assessment can be the concept (relevance to class, clarity of purpose), content and organization (variety and strength of evidence, ethical/appropriate use of interviews, logical sequence of events and explanations), quality of the video (well edited, smooth transitions, good sound, appropriate musical soundtrack). Another possibility is to require students to edit a testimony for length, perhaps to fifteen or thirty minutes, and then to explain their editorial choices. Assessment would include evaluation of the extent to which the student editor respected and remained faithful to the meaning and intent of the narrator.

Creative expression can develop students' emotional intelligence in relation to the Holocaust as well as mastery of content. Survivor testimonies can serve as a stimulus for creative expression through drama, visual arts, dance, and music. After reflecting on a particular interview or collection of interviews, each student could select an excerpt from an oral history to perform as a monologue. The student would also explain why she or he chose that particular section. A variation would be for the instructor to assign a limited number of interviews from which students could choose their excerpts, ensuring that multiple students will perform selections from the same interview. Students would then discuss why they chose different (or similar) parts of the interviews for their monologues, in order to explore how our personal experiences or interests affect the ways we hear testimony and evaluate its significance to us. A group project could involve students selecting excerpts from different interviews on a particular subject to put them into conversation with one another. Topics could include hunger in the ghetto, family relationships, and decisions about flight and resistance. This assignment encourages students to be sensitive to the variety of experiences and to individual responses to them. The students would perform the conversation and reflect on how their choices influenced the narrative: Did they try to lead the conversation in a particular direction? Did they want to leave a particular issue unresolved or to suggest a solution?

Creating visual artworks offers another means for students to express their response to the material. Students should be encouraged to think symbolically and metaphorically when designing their piece. Inspired by the oral histories, students could each create a model of a Holocaust memorial along with an artist's statement explaining its significance and its connection to the testimonies. IWitness has classroom activities designed by educators. One of them, "Art in the Face of Death," provides guidelines for introducing students to art produced during the Holocaust and by Holocaust survivors and then leading students to create their own artwork.

IWitness also provides instructions for teachers to create their own activities. Activities focus on particular issues or experiences (such as stereotypes and homecoming) and contain clips from oral histories along with questions and essay prompts to guide the students. Students are able to share their responses and to comment on their classmates' postings, while instructors can easily provide individual feedback to students using the website. For instructors who are using feature films in the classroom, such as *Denial* and *1945*, the site also provides activities and discussion guides.

Although time is running out to interview survivors of the Holocaust, it may be possible to interview child survivors or children of survivors (also known as *second generation*). Instructors should determine the purpose of the assignment in advance and create an appropriate standard of assessment. Perhaps the interviews themselves are the goal with the intent of establishing an archive in the school library. Perhaps the interviews are to be the basis of a historiographical paper or a central source for a research paper on a specific aspect of Holocaust history. Giving a grade to an interview may be difficult, since some things are beyond a student's control. It would be reasonable, however, to assess the student's background research for the interview, the quality of the prepared questions, and the extent to which the student followed best interview practices during the interview.

Best practices guidelines from the Oral History Association (OHA) are available online.[20] As mentioned above, the United States Holocaust Memorial Museum offers guidelines designed specifically for oral history interviews with Holocaust survivors, including suggested questions.[21] The Second Generation Project at Manhattan College has posted suggested questions for interviewing children of Holocaust survivors.[22] All of these guidelines can be easily adapted to interviews with other groups. The OHA and USHMM guidelines provide instructions for all stages of the interview process from the preliminary interview through the use and storage of recordings.

While the assignments suggested here have focused on historical knowledge, oral histories are useful in other disciplines. Students of foreign language can watch testimonies recorded in the language of study. They can listen for spoken vocabulary, for cultural values, for accent and dialect. Literature students can compare oral history narratives to literature they are reading in class both for content and for methods of narrative construction.

Survivor testimonies and interviews are powerful tools for engaging students in study of the Holocaust. Classroom use of oral histories can develop students' emotional intelligence, strengthen their media literacy, expand their understanding of the impact of the Holocaust, and promote their critical thinking skills. Through working with survivor testimonies and interviews, students can gain a deeper appreciation for the way in which history is constructed and for the value of personal narratives in that process.

NOTES

1. "Using Visual History Testimony in the Classroom," USC Shoah Foundation, http://iwitness.usc.edu/SFI/Data/EducatorData/Using-Testimony-in-Classroom.pdf (accessed December 15, 2017).

2. Donald L. Niewyk, ed., *The Holocaust: Problems and Perspectives of Interpretation*, 4th ed. (Boston: Wadsworth, 2011); Yehuda Bauer, *Rethinking the Holocaust* (New Haven: Yale University Press, 2001).

3. See Lawrence L. Langer, *Holocaust Testimonies: The Ruins of Memory* (New Haven: Yale University Press, 1991), esp. 18–21.

4. *Into the Arms of Strangers* (2000), a documentary of the Kindertransport, incorporates video testimonies of survivors with historical film footage.

5. Pascale Rachel Bos, "Women and the Holocaust: Analyzing Gender Difference," in Elizabeth R. Baer and Myrna Goldenberg, eds., *Experience and Expression: Women, the Nazis, and the Holocaust* (Detroit: Wayne State University Press, 2003), 23–50. On gendered narrative construction, see Ruth R. Linden, *Making Stories, Making Selves: Feminist Reflections on the Holocaust* (Columbus: Ohio State University Press, 1993).

6. See Christopher R. Browning, *Collected Memories: Holocaust History and Postwar Testimony* (Madison: University of Wisconsin Press, 2003), esp. 44–47.

7. Daniel L. Schacter, *Searching for Memory: The Brain, the Mind, and the Past* (New York: Basic Books, 1996), 305.

8. Margarete Myers Feinstein, "Hear the Voices: The Need for Personal Narratives in Holocaust Studies," *CSW Update Newsletter*, May 2010, 27–33, http://escholarship.org/uc/item/3jw7t3vg (accessed October 27, 2017). See also Christopher Browning, *Remembering Survival: Inside a Nazi Slave-Labor Camp* (New York: W. W. Norton, 2010).

9. "Teacher's Guide: Analyzing Oral Histories," Library of Congress, http://www.loc.gov/teachers/usingprimarysources/resources/Analyzing_Oral_Histories.pdf.

10. David P. Boder, *I Did Not Interview the Dead* (Urbana: University of Illinois Press, 1949).

11. Donald L. Niewyk, ed., *Fresh Wounds: Early Narratives of Holocaust Survival* (Chapel Hill: University of North Carolina Press, 1998).

12. Lore Shelley, ed., *Auschwitz — The Nazi Civilization: Twenty-Three Women Prisoners' Accounts* (Lanham, MD: University Press of America, 1992).

13. "Trial of the Major War Criminals before the International Military Tribunal," Military Legal Resources, Library of Congress, https://www.loc.gov/rr/frd/Military_Law/NT_major-war-criminals.html (accessed December 15, 2017).

14. "Nuremberg Trials Project," Harvard Law School Library, http://nuremberg.law.harvard.edu (accessed December 15, 2017).

15. Online version of Raymond Phillips, ed., *Trial of Josef Kramer and Forty-Four Others* (The Belsen Trial) (London: Hodge, 1949), http://www.bergen belsen.co.uk/pages/Trial/TrialFront/TrialFront_01.html (accessed December 15, 2017). To view only the trial transcript, visit http://www.bergenbelsen.co .uk/pages/TrialTranscript/Trial_Contents.html.

16. "Fortunoff Video Archive for Holocaust Testimonies," Yale University Library, https://fortunoff.library.yale.edu/excerpts/ (accessed December 19, 2019).

17. Jeff and Toby Herr Oral History Archive, United States Holocaust Memorial Museum, https://www.ushmm.org/collections/the-museums-collec tions/about/oral-history (accessed December 19, 2017).

18. First Person Podcast Series, United States Holocaust Memorial Museum, https://www.ushmm.org/information/visit-the-museum/programs -activities/first-person-program/first-person-podcast.

19. IWitness, USC Shoah Foundation, http://iwitness.usc.edu/SFI.

20. "Best Principles and Practices," Oral History Association, October 2009, http://www.oralhistory.org/about/principles-and-practices/ (accessed December 20, 2017).

21. *Oral History Interview Guidelines*, United States Holocaust Memorial Museum, https://www.ushmm.org/m/pdfs/20121003-oral-history-interview-guide.pdf (accessed December 8, 2017).

22. Martha A. Frazer, "L'Dor V'Dor: The Second Generation Project," The Holocaust, Genocide and Interfaith Education Center at Manhattan College, June 2010, http://www.hgimanhattan.com/second_generation_project/ (accessed November 27, 2017).

Teaching with Photographs

V A L E R I E H É B E R T

Are we the better for seeing these images? Do they
actually teach us anything?

SUSAN SONTAG, *REGARDING THE PAIN OF OTHERS*

To understand and teach the Holocaust requires courage to face all its remnants, as painful and unset-
tling as they are. Photographs, because of their easy availability and
transcendence of language and geography, are one of the most accessible sources. Similar to memoirs and testimony, photographs excel at
personalizing experience. Six million is an abstract figure. A photograph
of four men and a boy about to be shot is "painfully specific."[1] This
specificity is not merely referential. Photographs originating in the pre-
digital age are materially connected to their subjects, for it was their reflection of light on light-sensitive film that created the image.[2] They are
visual echoes.

However, the facts of a photograph are often difficult to authenticate.
Frequently the image has become detached from the photographer and
the caption (if ever there was one). The who, what, when, and where of
a photograph's content can only be surmised. Further still, the meaning
of the photograph, its why, is highly unstable. A perpetrator may have
aimed his camera at a cringing victim in order to deepen the humiliation
of their persecution and to flaunt Nazi power. But the same photograph
is also evidence of Nazi barbarism, an indictment of the antisemitism it
initially celebrated. Susie Linfield in *The Cruel Radiance* discusses the
malleability of a photograph's meaning in the context of Henryk Ross's

"Ghetto policeman's family, 1940–1944." Łódź, Poland. (Photographer: Henryk Ross, 35 mm cellulose nitrate negative; Art Gallery of Ontario, 2007/1988.13; Gift from the Archive of Modern Conflict, 2007)

images of the Łódź ghetto. Employed as a photographer in the statistics department for the production of official portraits and identity cards, etc., he secretly recorded all aspects of ghetto life and the Nazis' destruction of fellow Jews.[3] In a few of these photos, we see nourished bodies, intact clothing, smiles, affection. One of them depicts a ghetto policeman with his wife and baby, likely photographed in 1942.[4] This was around the time the Nazis deported the ghetto's children and elderly to be gassed at Chełmno, indeed with ghetto police help. This family were undoubtedly prisoners of Nazi power, but they benefited from it as well. This child was alive because the father served Nazi demands. Still, within two years, they too were likely all murdered.[5]

This image and the others Ross made of the Judenrat and Ghetto Police with their families are the visual counterpart to Primo Levi's essay "The Gray Zone," his final rumination on Nazi evil, which, he tenderly explains, intertwined guilt and innocence and bound the impulse for survival to moral corruption.[6] A passing consideration of the Holocaust plots good and evil easily and distinctly. However, the deeper one looks the more these categories blur and combine. Rather than push us away from the meaning of the Holocaust, this tangle of opposites brings us closer to the alienating truth of this history. Ross's photographs prod viewers in irreconcilable directions: do we see traitors who were "monstrously indifferent to others or victims tragically ignorant of their own impending fate? Do we exult the few who were saved if only for a short time and at a terrible price?"[7] More simply put: Do these photographs show us something inspiring or nauseating? Linfield concludes: "To look at these photos is to be twisted by such questions, and to know that the answers to them are necessary to seek and yet impossible to find."[8]

Teaching the Holocaust with photographs requires tolerance for ambiguity and sober expectations. Perhaps because they represent suffering so viscerally, so precisely, we want them to explain why people suffer or how we should respond to suffering. But only people can answer these questions. Photography is a process, and the images are products: simply another tool that can be put in service of this or that agenda. They can enlighten or mislead. They are another way, like literature, art, philosophy, theology, or history, through which we explore the human condition. They are no more advantageous or deficient a mechanism through which we contemplate the joys, mysteries, and tragedies of our experience. In this way, in looking at Holocaust photographs, we honor Primo Levi's request that we "consider that this has been."[9] Final judgments are impossible. They are beside the point.

Some have argued that photographs in their limited and shifting meanings are fatally flawed as sources for authentic insight. In *Camera Lucida*, Roland Barthes wrote that photographs prove little more than that the scene existed, and that any other meaning is extraneous, and further still that in time they block memory, becoming countermemory.[10] The Weimar-era critic Walter Benjamin feared that "the simplicity of the photographic world would obscure the complexity of the human world."[11] His contemporary Siegfried Kracauer declared: "the photograph annihilates the person," their story diminished and hidden "as if under a layer of snow."[12] Claude Lanzmann, director of the incomparable documentary *Shoah*, vehemently rejected incorporating archival photographs, charging that they would "kill . . . evocation."[13] Susan Sontag called photography "knowledge at bargain prices—a semblance of wisdom."[14]

In *Regarding the Pain of Others*, her 2003 reconsideration and retraction of many of the conclusions advanced in her influential 1977 work *On Photography*, Sontag suggests that as opposed to their characterization as reductive and static, photographs are an invitation to pay attention, to reflect, and to learn.[15] Photographs are neither simple nor dispensable scraps of the human story, but rather gateways to nuanced analysis of even our most painful pasts. Their ambiguity and openness to interpretation *are* their pedagogical strength. As educators, it is our task to train minds to think critically, to cultivate the ability to see things from many angles, to notice subtle distinctions. As the Ross example demonstrates, photographs help us do this. At the same time, the flexibility of photographic evidence, while it may expand our understanding of this history, also demands caution and restraint in reading it. Its plasticity has limits, and attributing any meaning to photographs is as unhelpful as rejecting all of it.

Below is an overview of the kinds of Holocaust photographs that exist and why, as well as their particular advantages and challenges as teaching tools. A summary of the key positions in the literature on Holocaust and atrocity photography serves to guide us in engaging with the ethical questions this source poses. To be clear, this chapter focuses on how to use photographs effectively and responsibly *within* a course on the Holocaust. It assumes the provision of the general historical context. Photographs in isolation, although not meaningless, have limited didactic power. Some images exemplify issues with little outside reference; in most cases they need the support of related sources to be fully appreciated. Examples included here illustrate this. Further, consideration is limited to wartime photographs (e.g., those taken by perpetrators and witnesses and images of Jews in distress), as these documents of existential extremity present us with thorny ethical questions about their place in the classroom. The photographic record is longer and more varied than the collections I reference. Roman Vishniac's haunting pictures of prewar Polish Jews capture fragments of life on the edge of the abyss. Postwar survivor portraits are a testament to the courage to reclaim life and identity in the stunned aftermath. Most of the images discussed here depict suffering and loss with harrowing literalness. A selection of Yaffa Eliach's collection of six thousand photos of shtetl dwellers from Eishyshok, Lithuania, form a three-story "Tower of Faces" in the heart of the United States Holocaust Memorial Museum. The vast majority of the people in these pictures perished. In showing bar mitzvahs, weddings, picnics, and family get-togethers, they demonstrate that we can confront that heartrending loss not only by viewing dead bodies but also by looking at life in all its magnificent familiarity.

Sybil Milton estimates that there are more than two million Holocaust photos in archives in over twenty countries.[16] The actual number is unquantifiable: soldiers on all sides, SS and police personnel, occupation officials, civilian witnesses, and victims took photographs. Notwithstanding periodic Nazi bans and the seizure of photographic equipment, people continued to make personal mementos and trophies.[17] Countless of these remain in private albums and attics across Europe and beyond. The largest category of Holocaust photographs consists of official and private images taken by Germans.[18] Every army division included a *Propaganda Kompanie*: generously equipped frontline documentary photographers and filmmakers who chronicled the progress of the war. Soldiers also brought cameras to the front for personal use. In 1995 a research institute in Hamburg mounted an exhibit entitled *Vernichtungskrieg: Verbrechen der Wehrmacht 1941–1944*, which exposed the German Army's participation in ideologically motivated crimes. Its core evidence was official and souvenir photography of atrocities against racial and political enemies: mass shootings, hangings, and squalid conditions in POW camps, among other horrors. In their number and consistency, the images forced public reckoning with the long-denied truth of the military's complicity in Nazi aims.[19] In occupied areas, it was common for soldiers and occupation staff to visit Jewish ghettos, cameras in hand.[20] Notable here are the collections taken by Joe Heydecker and Heinrich Jöst in Warsaw and Walter Genewein in Łódź. Significant too are the infamous Stroop Report photographs, which documented the destruction of the Warsaw ghetto post-uprising.

Auschwitz, Buchenwald, Mauthausen, Sachsenhausen, and Stutthof each contained an *Erkennungsdienst* where photographers and lab assistants produced mug shots and images of medical experiments, suicides, and executions. Photographs of camps in operation are unevenly representative, so although we have thousands of pictures of Auschwitz, there are few known images of Chełmno and Sobibór, and none of an actual gassing.[21] Regarding Auschwitz, the Lili Jacob and Karl Höcker albums are particularly important.[22] The first contains 193 photographs documenting the spring 1944 arrival at Birkenau of several Hungarian deportations. Jacob was one of the deportees. She survived the initial selection, forced labor, transfer to other camps, and was ultimately liberated at Dora. While recuperating in former SS barracks there, she discovered the album in a bedside table. Amazingly, she recognized herself, family members, and friends in its pages. She presented the album as evidence at the Frankfurt Auschwitz trial in the 1960s and later donated it to Yad Vashem. The collection contains the only known photographs of selections at Birkenau and documents all the steps toward murder, short of the gassing itself. The Höcker album offers a fascinating parallel narrative. This collection comprises 116 photos taken during the last six months of Auschwitz's operation, the same period represented in the Jacob album. Höcker, adjutant to the camp's commandant, Richard Baer, assembled it. It chronicles visits and ceremonies and, perhaps most disturbing, senior and rank-and-file personnel enjoying sun, blueberries, and sing-alongs at the nearby SS retreat Solahütte.[23] It is essential viewing for anyone interested in probing perpetrator identity.

Western Allied liberators took the second largest collection of photographs. Each US Army Signal Corps had twenty photographers, thirty filmmakers, and twenty darkroom technicians using mobile equipment. Images appeared in British and American newspapers within twenty-four hours of being taken.[24] For about six weeks in spring 1945, they were inescapable. Their searing content (emaciated prisoners behind barbed wire, corpse-laden train cars, bodies stacked like cordwood) combined with their ubiquity, defined memory of the Holocaust.[25] Some observers see this as problematic. Mauthausen, Buchenwald, Ohrdruf, Bergen-Belsen, Dachau, among others, were sites of horror to be sure, but as Hannah Arendt remarked, these images skewed the public's understanding of the anti-Jewish campaign. Most Jews, after all, died in the east of bullets and poison.[26] There are fewer photographs of the death camps at the time the Allies encountered them. The Nazis had dismantled Treblinka, Sobibór, Chełmno, and Bełżec before the war's end. The Soviets came upon Majdanek and Auschwitz, and valuable images of those liberations exist, but overall the Soviets had fewer photographers and less equipment.[27]

The smallest collection originates with victims and resisters. This group faced particular challenges in documenting what they saw. For example, in occupied Poland, the Nazis shut down or commandeered photographic materials factories, processing labs, and publication houses.[28] The Polish underground recognized photography as a crucial weapon of resistance, but photos taken under these circumstances meant that quality varied widely. Sometimes prints were crudely retouched, such as by outlining figures in pencil. It made them appear doctored, suspect. The same photograph might also be distributed by multiple organizations (in secret, with attendant complications), resulting in the single image acquiring numerous interpretations. Only sometimes did they arrive with identifying captions.[29] Of particular significance in this category are the four photographs taken at Birkenau—indeed within meters of the gas chamber complex—by a member of the *Sonderkommando* and smuggled out in a toothpaste tube with the help of the Polish underground. Two show corpses about to be burned on an open pyre, one shows naked women on their way to the gas chamber, and the last, treetops on an angle, suggests the frenetic conditions of the photographs' creation. When the four images were exhibited in Paris in 2001 in the show *Mémoire des Camps*, it ignited heated debate over their propriety and meaning. Among the most aggrieved assessments was the diagnosis that since the images "can't tell us everything, then they must tell us nothing."[30] Art historian Georges Didi-Huberman was their strongest defender, seeing in them the prisoner-photographer's rejection of helplessness. He writes: "The photographs were snatched from a world bent on their impossibility."[31] It bears emphasis: the very existence of photographs, not just their content, matters.

The motives for taking photographs vary. Resisters, sympathetic bystanders, and victims possibly wished to document, inform, or provoke a response. Mendel Grossman, who sought to preserve evidence of the Łódź ghetto, declared that some of his subjects *wanted* to be photographed in their humiliation as an indelible mark on posterity.[32] Perpetrators and unsympathetic bystanders may have deployed the camera to assert racial supremacy or political dominance or to reinforce antisemitic ideology. We see this in the case of photographing the vile condition of ghetto dwellers who appeared to confirm stereotypes about Jewish subhumanity. Perhaps it was a defense mechanism against horror or, conversely, a fascination with atrocity with or without willing participation in the violence. There was most certainly a prurient voyeurism in photographing naked women during and after sexual attacks or moments before they were shot. The latter exemplifies the intersection of ideological and gendered violence. Of course, any combination of these motives could be activating the photographer's impulse and change with subsequent clicks.

Often photos are undated and their authors anonymous.[33] In *Photographing the Holocaust*, Janina Struk discusses what is commonly referred to as the 1943 Śniatyn Death Pit photo (facing page). It remains debatable when and where it was actually taken.[34] It captured a scene replayed countless times across Eastern Europe when Jews and other "undesirables" were rounded up, stripped, and shot into mass graves by Nazis and their collaborators. It shows four men and a boy, naked. Two are at the pit's edge, an old man stands slightly back, and another man and a boy are walking towards the pit. The beards suggest Jewish orthodoxy. There are another eight men, in various uniforms and civilian clothes. Some hold guns. One, motioning about something, appears to be looking at the photographer. The photograph was not likely taken surreptitiously or hastily: it is sharp and composed; the camera would have had to be adjusted for light and focus. It *could* have been staged. The photo exists in isolation; we don't have preceding or subsequent frames. Perhaps intervention in the scene was slight, the process of murder slowed down for the benefit of the camera. But even a staged photograph has meaning. Someone wanted to preserve this scene. Albeit without names, date, place, or knowledge of the intention behind it, it shows *something*. Moreover, it exists within a wider historical context about which we know a lot. Teaching this historical context alongside the photograph allows us to make educated hypotheses. Photos in their ambiguity and flexibility still tell a story, and the spectrum of possibility is instructive.

The image lends itself to several interpretations. It could be celebrating the breach of taboos: the murder of the very young and the very old, public nakedness (the shame of which is amplified by the other figures who remain clothed). It could be a trophy immortalizing a moment of complete dominance. The contrast between naked and clothed bodies magnifies the power imbalance, as does the calm stance of most of the dressed men who surround the pit. Guns are held one-handed, pointing down. This is midprocess, not a rampage. They appear secure in their positions. The nakedness intensifies the others' vulnerability.

German police and auxiliaries in civilian clothing prepare to execute naked Jewish men and boys who are being lined up at the edge of a mass grave. May 11, 1943, Śniatyn, Poland (present-day Ukraine). No photographer recorded. (USHMM Photo Archives, #98091, courtesy of Jacob Igra)

We see fear in the bodies of the man leaning back from the pit and in the tensed shoulders of the old man, who still wears one shoe.

Of course, these very same features are also an indictment of the crime, visual layers of savagery. The photograph's original meaning rests with the photographer's motive, but its subsequent one lies in the perspective of the viewer and the context in which it is seen.[35] A scholar bent on historical specificity might be frustrated by the impenetrability of the photograph's *actual* provenance and motive, but the interpretations summarized above are not mutually exclusive. The same document can have divergent meanings. This is not a marker of unreliability or dubiousness. Truth can be present even where facts are not.

A thread running through the literature on atrocity photography contends that however impactful or revealing photographs may be, in their number and easy access, they quickly numb and debilitate the viewer's senses. The problem Sontag identified in *Regarding the Pain of Others* was not that people remember awful pictures; it is that they remember *only* through these pictures. This calcification of memory impedes other forms of understanding.[36] The argument exists on the same continuum as the compassion fatigue theory.[37] To be sure, there is no shortage of horrific Holocaust photographs, and in the digital age, no means of stemming their circulation. There are also patterns to Holocaust and other atrocity images: bodies in mass graves, mug shots, emaciated prisoners behind barbed wire, children in distress. They are familiar. Cornelia Brink argues that the images are "paralyzing," Barbie Zelizer and Carolyn Dean, that they are "desensitizing."[38] Zelizer takes the argument further. In *Remembering to Forget*, her analysis of Allied liberation photographs, she argues that they served a vital function in the waning months of the war and early postwar period, in that they supplied a quasi-language to communicate the Nazis' unprecedented crimes before we had words to describe them. However, in her view, these photographs, as reductive and circumscribed as they necessarily were, and in combination with their ubiquity and repetition, ultimately displaced authentic, comprehensive memory of the events and truncated our ability to respond to subsequent calamities.[39] Maggie Nelson, in *The Art of Cruelty*, makes a similar point: "Obsessive contemplation of our inhumanities can end up convincing us of the inevitability of our badness, we do ourselves a disservice by staying riveted to the *ad nauseum* proof that humans have always steadily pursued the bloody business of genocide, war, and terrorism."[40] She warns that if we don't turn our attention away, we risk so alienating ourselves that we are driven to either more violence or apathy.

Susan Sontag, too, sees the incapacitating effect of looking: "The vast photographic catalogue of misery and injustice throughout the world has given everyone a certain familiarity with atrocity, making the horrible seem more ordinary—making it appear familiar, remote ('it's only a photograph'), inevitable. At the time of the first photographs of the Nazi camps, there was nothing banal about these images. After thirty years, a saturation point may have been reached. In these last decades, 'concerned' photography has done at least as much to deaden conscience as to arouse it."[41] It is a common argument, but a peculiar one. Holocaust photographs do not cancel each other out. They merely, like bodies, stack up. One does not find the same accusation leveled at Holocaust memoirs. Having read 100 of them, is the 101st automatically less compelling? Would we counsel our students to read less, for fear that these sources would, in their indigestible number and unavoidable duplication of certain facts, diminish their appreciation for the significance of the event and blunt their response to it?

Jews from Subcarpathian Rus undergo a selection on the ramp at Auschwitz-Birkenau. May 1944, Auschwitz, Poland. (Photographer: Bernhardt Walter / Ernst Hofmann; USHMM Photo Archives, #77241, courtesy of Yad Vashem)

There is, on balance, so much to be gained from teaching with photographs. They do a lot in a little time and space. Compare the investment needed to read a words-only document against the density of information we acquire at a glance through the frame. Moreover, a photograph presents this information simultaneously, another quality that distinguishes it from written forms.[42] To describe an event, one can only discuss one element at a time. This imposes sequence and, unwittingly, hierarchy; it separates parts of the experience from each other. Photographs, on the other hand, are unordered composites; the eye is free to move around; we can take in various elements at once. Neither perspective nor focal point is absolute. We can shift between the whole and its parts. Consider how a photograph of a deportation arriving at Birkenau (above) reflects more closely the chaos and confusion that survivors describe of their first moments after being thrust out from the trains. The people, all ages, Jewish and non-Jewish, camp functionary and prisoner, crowded, moving in different directions, the terrain, the architecture, and the boxcars. Just as the experience was lived in a multilayered bewildering simultaneity, so also does the photograph capture this more accurately than words can.

As much as images capture the commotion of a complex scene, they also slow history down. In *Regarding the Pain of Others*, Sontag observes: "the force of a photograph is that it keeps open to scrutiny instants which the normal flow of time immediately replaces."[43] This is its advantage over film, its closest visual relative. Indeed, the suspension of time is necessary for the analysis that seeks to take all the information in and then refract divergent interpretations. Moreover, the richness of a photograph's content is multiplied when set against other sources. Sybil Milton called for reconciling the photographic record with the written one. For example, images of deportations from towns and cities across Europe present opportunities to analyze the behavior of bystanders who sometimes appear in the background.[44]

Linfield remarks that photographs taken by Holocaust perpetrators reveal that "not everyone is ashamed of the same things."[45] This may seem a facile observation, but there is depth here: photographs are another category of evidence of antisemitic hatred, our ability to dehumanize others, and our capacity for cruelty. Their provenance is ideology in action. The act of taking the photograph is the perpetrator's own testimony, and it says more about the perpetrator than they may have noticed. The abject condition of the subject captured on film is a consequence of the same hatred or indifference that moved the photographer to trip the shutter. Put another way, the photographs are the *acting out* of cruelty, not just *evidence* of cruelty; tangible artifacts of hatred, not just its mirror reflection.[46] Sontag writes: "even if [the atrocious images] are only tokens and cannot encompass the reality to which they refer they still perform a vital function. The images say: This is what human beings are capable of doing, may volunteer to do, enthusiastically, self-righteously. Don't forget."[47]

Some of the photographs discussed here are horrifying to behold: violence, vulnerability, and terror frozen in time. For all the pedagogically valuable aspects of these images, their sensitive content demands contemplation of the ethical implications of projecting them on screens in our classrooms. If they are nearly unbearable to look at, we should refine the reasons why we should. Reading a photograph for its opposing messages (for example, about Nazi triumph *and* Nazi evil) enriches our students' ability to think about this history in a more complex way. So too does familiarizing them with the arguments for and against looking at these images cultivate a more reasoned and principled opinion regarding these images' place in the public sphere.

Objections to using photographs of the Holocaust range from the sweeping generalization exemplified by Andrea Liss, who concludes that since the Holocaust is essentially incomprehensible, so too must we accept that photography is not a means of understanding, to the very specific grievance exemplified by Gertrud Koch, who states that the Nazi perspective is indissoluble from the image.[48] If it was taken from a fascist viewpoint, it cannot be viewed otherwise. Just as Nazi ideology was based on lies, so the photos that correspond to these delusions are "meaningless images—incapable of imparting knowledge or truth."[49] Criticism also centers on the nature of photography itself. Barthes writes that any photograph is violent, even if it does not show violent things, because "it fills the sight by force, and because in it nothing can be refused or transformed."[50] In her influential 1977 book *On Photography*, Sontag emphasized the predatory aspects of the practice.[51] She declared: "there is an act of aggression in every use of the camera," and photographing someone is "a semblance of rape."[52] The language we use to describe the process seems to confirm her assertions: we *take* a photo, we *capture* an image, we *shoot* a subject. For Marianne Hirsch, the idiomatic becomes literal. She notes, despairingly, "victims in Holocaust photographs were shot before they were shot."[53] At risk, too, is that photography can transform ugliness into beauty. In this, Sontag built upon the sentiment of Walter Benjamin, who cautioned that photos "aestheticize misery."[54] Of the famous 1943 Stroop Report image of the Warsaw ghetto boy with arms raised, Sontag writes that it is a "beautiful photo." Although it "conveys distress, it ends by neutralizing it."[55] Struk reiterates the point that photographs, isolated from their context, can be regarded as works of art: beautiful, comforting, and uplifting instead of the "fragments of a cruel history" that they are.[56]

The sentiment holds to a point. Ross's photograph of the ghetto policeman's family savoring life and love in the midst and as a function of their fellow ghetto prisoners' murder illustrates this. The image looks like the happy snapshots most of us possess in old family albums. However, this impression withers to anguish once we understand the hideous circumstances of its provenance. Has the photograph betrayed us or does it possess an invaluable truth? The persistence of joy amid horror *is* beautiful. At a minimum, the child pictured is innocent, as innocent as those who were killed. Can we not tolerate the intellectual challenge of seeing life and death, beauty and tragedy simultaneously? Isn't this the very thing that keeps us tethered to the notion of humanity through even our most tormented histories?

Returning to certain scholars' refusal to see anything redemptive in these kinds of images: we know that during the Holocaust the camera itself could be a weapon of intimidation. Nazis commonly made Jews pose during persecution or in the final moments before their murder. These images in their immutability extend the violence in perpetuity. The subjects did not give consent nor did they ever see themselves in that position. We the observers occupy the same vantage point of the photographer. Simply to view the image replicates the power imbalance.[57] Indeed, the reenactment can be taken even further. Struk was sharply critical of an exhibit at Birkenau that used a photograph of an old woman and children walking toward the gas chamber (another from the Jacob album). Curators had enlarged the image and placed it on the very path where they had been photographed. Struk writes: "They have been condemned to tread the path to the gas chamber forever, returning their image to Birkenau is their final humiliation." And we the viewers are complicit in this, "we collude with the . . . degradation."[58]

It is not only that degradation captured on film radiates out, absorbing and transforming our gaze into unwitting participation. The display of violated bodies (clothed or not) has often been labeled pornographic. The anxiety runs deeper than the taboo of exhibiting nakedness; it is the suspicion that what should repulse might actually titillate.[59] Carolyn Dean calls the consequence of such imagery "the exhaustion of empathy . . . a morally distorted perception of suffering"; David Campbell: "the violation of dignity."[60] Against these provocative objections, Linfield draws an astute distinction between the exploitative and obscene spectacle of broken bodies and atrocity images that in spite of their explicit content still preserve the victim's dignity: "pornography reveals something that strangers should not see and whose worth is diminished when they do. But photographs of suffering people—of the body in pain—are the revelation of something that *ought not exist*." Moreover, it may indeed be our moral obligation to look, since secrecy only exacerbates the damage persecution causes.[61]

Although photography is a form of acquisition, the photographic record is partial, particular images are stained by Nazi ideology, and the victims' humiliation and terror remain suspended in the photographs' permanence, these truths do not disqualify them as having valuable lessons to teach. We know a lot about the context of these photographs, and even the basic components equip us with a critical faculty with which to engage them. Linfield gently reminds us, and Levi before her, that the Holocaust is not a story of Jewish triumph. Examples of heroism and moral incorruptibility can be found, but most Jews died, and their suffering was grotesque. Heinrich Jöst, who wandered the Warsaw ghetto and who, by virtue of his German identity, uniform, and "moral vacancy," got up close to his subjects and captured their

A man on the street plays the violin in the hope of receiving food or for money. September 19, 1941, Warsaw, Poland. Jöst's original caption reads: "This man played the same sound on his violin again and again. His eyes followed me, but whether out of fear or because he hoped to receive a coin I do not know." (Photographer: Heinrich Jöst; USHMM Photo Archive #32299, courtesy of Guenther Schwarberg)

An undertaker in the Warsaw ghetto's Jewish cemetery on Okopowa Street lifts the body of a woman for Heinrich Jöst to show him how little it weighs. September 19, 1941, Warsaw, Poland. Jöst's original caption reads: "The dead were not heavy, as one corpse-bearer showed me—although I had not asked him to—in front of the buildings of the Jewish cemetery." (Photographer: Heinrich Jöst; USHMM Photo Archive #32221, courtesy of Guenther Schwarberg)

wretchedness in precise and unflinching detail, documented "a crucial set of realities . . . [the images'] cruelty is their truth."[62] Linfield continues: "his photos show us a process of spiritual and physical disintegration. . . . It is an ugly thing to contemplate, but we do not honor the victims by being too delicate, too respectful, to look."[63]

Remember too, that it was the Nazis' intention to destroy not only the Jews but also their memory and the evidence of their destruction.

The existence of photographs and our ongoing engagement with them undermine that goal. Our revulsion to them is natural; that they still repulse may be reassuring. Turning away is tempting, but misguided. We frame the wrong subject when we aim our criticism at the evidence instead of the cause of the suffering caught on film.[64] We better serve this history when we help our students understand the difference.

NOTES

1. Opening epigraph: Susan Sontag, *Regarding the Pain of Others* (New York: Picador), 92. Susie Linfield, *The Cruel Radiance* (Chicago: University of Chicago Press, 2010), 22.

2. Cornelia Brink, "Secular Icons: Looking at Photographs from Nazi Concentration Camps," *History and Memory* 12, no. 1 (2000): 140.

3. Robert Jan van Pelt, "Lodz and Getto Litzmannstadt: A Historical Introduction," in Maia-Mari Sutnik, ed., *Memory Unearthed: The Lodz Ghetto Photographs of Henryk Ross* (New Haven: Yale University Press, 2015), 204.

4. Sutnik, *Memory Unearthed*, 25–26.

5. Linfield, *Cruel Radiance*, 78. See also Janina Struk, *Photographing the Holocaust* (London: I. B. Tauris, 2004), 86.

6. Primo Levi, *The Drowned and the Saved* (New York: Knopf Doubleday, 1989).

7. Linfield, *Cruel Radiance*, 78.

8. Linfield, *Cruel Radiance*, 78.

9. Primo Levi, "Shema," in *Collected Poems*, trans. Ruth Feldman and Brian Swann (London: Faber and Faber, 1992), 9.

10. Roland Barthes, *Camera Lucida* (New York: Farrar, Straus and Giroux, 2010), 87 and 90; and Struk, *Photographing the Holocaust*, 211.

11. Walter Benjamin in Linfield, *Cruel Radiance*, 18.

12. Siegfried Kracauer in Linfield, *Cruel Radiance*, 18–19.

13. Claude Lanzmann in Linfield, *Cruel Radiance*, 92.

14. Susan Sontag, *On Photography* (New York: Picador, 2001), 24.

15. Sontag, *Regarding the Pain*, 117.

16. Sybil Milton, "Photographs of the Warsaw Ghetto," in Museum of Tolerance Online Multimedia Learning Center, *Simon Wiesenthal Center Annual* 3, chapter 15, 1997, http://www.museumoftolerance.com/education/archives-and-reference-library/online-resources/simon-wiesenthal-center-annual-volume-3/annual-3-chapter-15.html (accessed July 2018).

17. On Nazi-issued prohibitions on photography, see Judith Levin and Daniel Uziel, "Ordinary Men, Extraordinary Photos," *Yad Vashem Studies* 26 (1998): 7; Judith Keilbach, "Photographs, Symbolic Images and the Holocaust: On the (Im)possibility of Depicting Historical Truth," *History and Theory* 48,

no. 2, theme issue 47, "Historical Representation and Historical Truth" (May 2009): 65; Struk, *Photographing the Holocaust*, 35, 70–71, 86.

18. Linfield, *Cruel Radiance*, 68.

19. See the exhibit catalog, Hannes Heer et al., *The Germany Army and Genocide* (New York: New Press, 1999).

20. David Crew, "What Can We Learn from a Visual Turn? Photography, Nazi Germany and the Holocaust," *H-German Forum: German History after the Visual Turn* (September 18, 2006); and Linfield, *Cruel Radiance*, 68.

21. Linfield, *Cruel Radiance*, 68.

22. Israel Gutman and Bella Gutterman, eds., *The Auschwitz Album* (New York: Berghahn Books, 2003); and Alec Wilkinson, "Picturing Auschwitz," *The New Yorker*, March 10, 2008, https://www.newyorker.com/magazine/2008 /03/17/picturing-auschwitz (accessed July 2018).

23. United States Holocaust Memorial Museum, "Auschwitz through the Lens of the SS: A Tale of Two Albums," https://www.ushmm.org/wlc/en /article.php?ModuleId=10007436; and Paul Lowe, "Picturing the Perpetrator," in Geoffrey Batchen, Mick Gidley, Nancy K. Miller, and Jay Prosser, eds., *Picturing Atrocity: Photography in Crisis* (London: Reaktion Books, 2011), 189–198.

24. Struk, *Photographing the Holocaust*, 129.

25. Sontag, *Regarding the Pain*, 24 and 89.

26. Sontag, *Regarding the Pain*, 84; and Keilbach, "Photographs, Symbolic Images and the Holocaust," 61.

27. Struk, *Photographing the Holocaust*, 139.

28. Struk, *Photographing the Holocaust*, 35.

29. Struk, *Photographing the Holocaust*, 37–38.

30. Linfield, *Cruel Radiance*, 88.

31. Georges Didi-Huberman in Linfield, *Cruel Radiance*, 90; Didi-Huberman, *Images in Spite of It All* (Chicago: University of Chicago Press, 2008); Susan Crane, "The Special Case of Four Auschwitz Photographs," *Postmodern Culture* 19, no. 1 (2008).

32. Mendel Grossman, *With a Camera in the Ghetto* (New York: Schocken Books, 1977).

33. Struk, *Photographing the Holocaust*, 202.

34. Struk, *Photographing the Holocaust*, 7.

35. Sontag, *On Photography*, 106; and Brink, "Secular Icons," 149.

36. Sontag, *Regarding the Pain*, 89.

37. See David Campbell, "The Myth of Compassion Fatigue," in Liam Kennedy and Caitlin Patrick, eds., *The Violence of the Image* (London: I. B. Tauris, 2014), 97–124.

38. Brink, "Secular Icons," 144; Carolyn Dean, *The Fragility of Empathy after the Holocaust* (Ithaca: Cornell University Press, 2004), 1; and Barbie Zelizer, *Remembering to Forget* (Chicago: University of Chicago Press, 1998), 202.

39. Zelizer, *Remembering to Forget*, 158.

40. Maggie Nelson, *The Art of Cruelty* (New York: W. W. Norton, 2011), 7.

41. Sontag, *On Photography*, 20–21. Sontag's reference to "thirty years" reflects the publication date of her work.

42. Sidra Ezrahi, *By Words Alone* (Chicago: University of Chicago Press, 1980), 4.

43. Sontag, *Regarding the Pain*, 111–112.

44. Sybil Milton, "Images of the Holocaust, Part II," *Holocaust and Genocide Studies* 1, no. 2 (1986): 194.

45. Linfield, *Cruel Radiance*, 67.

46. Linfield, *Cruel Radiance*, 67, 70.

47. Sontag, *Regarding the Pain*, 115.

48. Andrea Liss, *Trespassing through Shadows* (Minneapolis: University of Minnesota Press, 1998), 124.

49. Gertrud Koch in Linfield, *Cruel Radiance*, 70. See also Susan Crane, "Choosing Not to Look: Representation, Repatriation, and Holocaust Atrocity Photography," *History and Theory* 47, no. 3 (2008): 321.

50. Barthes, *Camera Lucida*, 90.

51. Sontag, *On Photography*, 4, 11, 14.

52. Sontag, *On Photography*, 6, 24.

53. Marianne Hirsch in Crane, "Choosing Not to Look," 311.

54. Walter Benjamin in Linfield, *Cruel Radiance*, 18.

55. Sontag, *On Photography*, 109.

56. Struk, *Photographing the Holocaust*, 98.

57. Linfield, *Cruel Radiance*, 69; and Crane, "Choosing Not to Look," 311.

58. Struk, *Photographing the Holocaust*, 215–216.

59. Sontag, *Regarding the Pain*, 95.

60. Dean, *Fragility*, 20; and Campbell, "The Myth," 101.

61. Linfield, *Cruel Radiance*, 41.

62. Linfield, *Cruel Radiance*, 82, 85.

63. Linfield, *Cruel Radiance*, 85.

64. Linfield, *Cruel Radiance*, 30.

Teaching the Holocaust in Museums

DANIEL GREENE

The Holocaust is an overwhelming topic. We might be overwhelmed in one sense of the word by how quickly new information about the Holocaust proliferates. Books, websites, memoirs, and films are released at such a rate that it seems impossible to keep up. Moreover, we might be overwhelmed by the struggle to understand how this tragedy could have happened and the toll it took on individual people, including six million Jewish victims and millions of others. This latter sense of being overwhelmed by the Holocaust is one we are more likely to see our students experience as they confront this history, often for the first time, in the classroom. One foundational challenge, as historian Peter Hayes notes in his book *Why? Explaining the Holocaust*, is to make sure that these overwhelming aspects do not become reasons for disengaging; treating the Holocaust outside the realm of historical inquiry; or calling it "'unfathomable,' 'incomprehensible,' and 'inexplicable.'"[1] Learning about the Holocaust in museums can be a profoundly valuable way for students to face this challenge, leaving them with new understandings of both the narrative and the significance of Holocaust history.

Make no mistake: visiting exhibitions about the Holocaust still might overwhelm, intellectually and emotionally. Many Holocaust museums pack their exhibitions (and their websites) with much more information than museumgoers can digest in one visit. In most museums, the sheer size of exhibitions and limitations of visitors' time and interest make viewing every object, media display, and didactic text in the galleries impossible. For example, *The Holocaust*, the permanent exhibition at the United States Holocaust Memorial Museum (USHMM) in Washington, DC, fills some thirty-six thousand square feet of gallery space, and museum surveys estimate that visitors spend an average of between ninety minutes and two hours moving through it, though some certainly spend far more time. It is important to help our students understand that they are not expected to read and retain all the information in exhibitions that tell the history of the Holocaust, especially considering that they will be on their feet for most of the time as they do so. Yet many museums are not forthcoming enough about this with their visitors, and some museumgoers, therefore, may feel an expectation to try to digest all the content presented or may be sheepish about not doing so. Putting these expectations aside is akin to teachers freeing themselves from the burden of "coverage" in survey history courses.[2] Once museumgoers free themselves from expectations of lingering over all the content they encounter in a gallery, they can interact with museum presentations in ways that remain memorable and educationally valuable. To do so, students need to be cognizant of how and why museums present history.

Preparing for a Museum Visit

Students will find visiting a Holocaust museum a much more rewarding endeavor if they are prepared well by their teachers in advance. This preparation might span from the mundane to the intellectual. Logistical questions—whether about location, security procedures, agenda for the visit, or other details—will help students, especially those who do not have much experience visiting museums, know what to expect. Sometimes, students become upset by having to pass through security scanners and check their backpacks when they arrive, for example, or when they learn that they cannot use selfie sticks in exhibition spaces. This sets a negative tone for a visit, and educators can avoid such issues by taking some time to help students understand what their visit to the museum will entail. Moreover, students might perceive field trips in general as a chance to "let loose," behaving in ways that would be inappropriate in the context of a Holocaust museum. Teachers might address this tension in advance by being clear with students about behavioral expectations in a Holocaust museum, rather than assuming students will understand these expectations without being told. Most museums' websites contain information that educators can use to help prepare students for all aspects of their visits, and it is worth consulting, even though most of it may seem basic.

Beyond these practicalities, students must be ready intellectually for their visit to a Holocaust museum. Engagement in the classroom with the history of the Holocaust is critical preparation for a visit. Without some basic understanding, students will not be able to critically consider the choices made by the museum in presenting this history, which requires a higher level of cognitive skill. Many of the other chapters in this book will be useful in this regard, as will the vast secondary literature on the Holocaust, some of it written with high school and college students in mind. Many museums offer content specifically designed for classroom use, too, and their websites are likely to include educational guides or lesson plans keyed to exhibition content. They also might post web-based versions of exhibitions including audio, visual, or other media programs that are included in exhibition displays. Even if teachers preview this material, they should use caution in showing students too much of this content that they will also see during a museum visit, for fear of lessening the impact when they encounter it within the museum's walls. Teachers may also benefit from visiting the museum before the class trip, if it is feasible.

Moreover, educators should engage students who are preparing to visit Holocaust museums in thinking about how learning in museums differs from classrooms. In both settings, students will be confronting difficult material, but in a museum, this experience may be more immersive. Curators and exhibition designers seek to create spaces that support the historical content being conveyed. These environments cannot reproduce the horror and confusion of experiences in ghettos or concentration camps (nor should they try); however, they can be more visceral experiences than discussing the Holocaust in a classroom. In exhibition galleries, students likely will see graphic photographs or moving footage of atrocities, sometimes in large-scale or life-size imagery. Viewing these images in museums is a different experience than looking at them in books, on the web, or projected on a screen in a classroom. Seeing this material or listening to testimony by Holocaust survivors who endured such hardships might produce emotional reactions, which is entirely understandable.

Questions to Consider in Museums

The eight questions that follow will lead students to a better understanding of the history of the Holocaust as well as the museums' educational intent in presenting this history to vast and diverse publics. As they think about these questions, it is critical for students to keep in mind that museums are not neutral arbiters of historical content. Instead, exhibitions are the result of careful consideration, debate, and reasoned judgment by curators and other museum staff. Teachers should discuss these questions with students or ask students to consider them with their peers as they walk through exhibitions. (Topical conversations about exhibition content in the gallery should be encouraged!) Each question includes some commentary below it that might help shape productive discussions.

Many museum visitors—students and others—tend not to understand that everything they encounter in museum spaces is the result of choices made by museum staff, often by curators, but also by educators, designers, conservators, registrars, digital developers, and others. In other words, museum exhibitions result from decisions made by people with agency, who face the challenge of presenting complex topics in limited space. Students should be encouraged to recognize and discuss these choices, not only with a goal of evaluating them but also as a way to think deeply about the curatorial intent of the museum. So, "Did you like this exhibition?" usually will be a less effective question for students than "What is the exhibition's historical argument?" Framing questions in language that surfaces choices also might be effective: "Why do you think the museum decided to present this topic in this way?"

These eight questions will help guide teachers and students through their engagement with museum exhibitions. Teachers might choose to present these questions to their students prior to the museum visit and return to the questions in classroom discussion following the visit.

Is there a title, curatorial statement, or an opening text
that frames the exhibition?

Exhibitions typically use few words to address visitors directly. Most text in exhibitions instead describes individual objects on display,

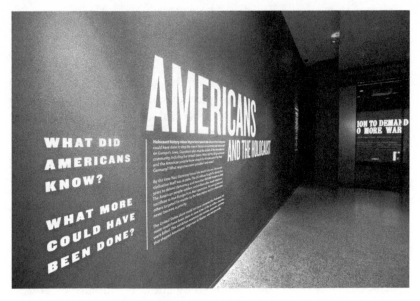

Entrance to *Americans and the Holocaust*, a special exhibition at the United States Holocaust Memorial Museum. (Photographer: Joel Mason-Gaines; USHMM)

answering: Who created this? When? What is it called? Who owns it? How does it relate to the overall theme of the exhibition?

In contrast, the title of an exhibition as well as its opening text may address different categories of questions, such as: What is this exhibition about? Is there an overall lesson that the museum hopes to communicate to visitors? Why is the subject significant, either historically, at this moment in time, or both? Is there some controversy about the topic that the exhibition seeks to address?

These are big questions that curators will address in a short text panel—usually around 150 to 250 words. Reading these opening text panels, therefore, might only take a couple of minutes at the most. Spending some time considering their tone and main points can provide a solid foundation for visitors' experiences in the gallery. Skipping them entirely might leave visitors at sea, making navigation through the galleries much more difficult.

Consider one example. The opening text for *Americans and the Holocaust*, a special exhibition at the United States Holocaust Memorial Museum, refocuses visitors' attention geographically, explaining that even though the Holocaust took place in Europe, there are important

American aspects to this history. It also raises difficult questions about what Americans knew about Nazi Germany's persecution and murder of Jews as well as what more Americans might have done to prevent it. It explains that Americans made great sacrifices to defeat Nazism during World War II and asks why rescue of Jews never became a priority for the US government. It sets the stage for helping visitors to the exhibition think about the "motives, pressures, and fears that shaped Americans' responses to Nazism, war and genocide."[3] The text, therefore, provides a framework for visitors' experiences in the gallery and lets them know what to expect.

What is the first "moment" in the story?

Not all exhibitions open with a curatorial statement. Some dispense with opening text entirely and use another technique to bring visitors into the history, whether a film or some other type of immersive experience.

For example, visitors to the USHMM's permanent exhibition, *The Holocaust*, enter an elevator that takes them to the fourth floor. While on the way up, they hear the voice of an American soldier recounting his confusion as he enters a concentration camp. The elevator door opens and visitors see a large photomural showing American soldiers in 1945 encountering atrocities committed by the Nazi regime. (This experience speaks directly to the question of why a Holocaust museum belongs on the National Mall by adding an American perspective to the story from the outset.) The opening audio clip heard on the elevator implicitly raises the key question answered in the exhibition: "How did this happen?" The approach here is to begin the exhibition with a moment at the end of the historical narrative (liberation of concentration camps in 1945) and then very soon after rewind to the beginning of the story (the Nazi rise to power in 1933). Visitors move through chronologically once the seed of the "How did this happen?" question has been planted by showing the "ending" of the history as the first element in the exhibition.[4]

Every exhibition takes its own approach, yet curators spend a good deal of intellectual energy deciding what the first moment of the exhibition should accomplish. Whether it conveys the big ideas of the exhibition, asks a difficult question that the exhibition will explore, or introduces a subject that might not be well known to most visitors, these first moments are critical expressions of curatorial intent. Even in

Holocaust museums, these moments need to be engaging enough to interest visitors and keep them from turning around and walking out the gallery doors without seeing the exhibition.

Teachers can prompt useful discussions with their students by asking: Why do you think the exhibition started the way it did? Or, What do you think the curator wanted us to be thinking about the moment we walked into the gallery?

Is the exhibition organized chronologically, thematically, or some other way?

Curators can arrange exhibitions in many different ways, though most Holocaust-related exhibitions tend to be either chronological or thematic. (These two approaches are not mutually exclusive, but one usually takes precedence over the other.) Students may not initially be aware of such curatorial choices, but once educators highlight the approach, they can then prompt students to think about how and why either a chronological or thematic structure serves the overall purpose of the exhibition.

Organizing principles of the exhibition likely are chosen to best support the overall curatorial intent. Many exhibitions that provide a survey history of the Holocaust—usually beginning with the Nazi rise to power and ending either with postwar trials that sought to bring perpetrators to justice or with a reference to genocides that have occurred since the Holocaust—are presented chronologically. One advantage of this structure is that it allows curators not only to communicate what happened but also to help visitors understand how, as historian Doris Bergen explains, "The Holocaust happened step by step."[5] A careful chronological approach to the story of the Holocaust can effectively push against the misguided notion that once Hitler became chancellor of Germany, mass murder of Jews was inevitable. It wasn't. Effectively presenting the step-by-step changes in Germany—whether Nazi Germany's increasing militarism and territorial expansion within Europe before war began in 1939 or its persecution of Jews before mass murder began in 1941—can help museum visitors "read history forward," encouraging them to empathize with historical actors who lived through the horrors of Nazism, rather than to judge them for not seeing what was coming. (For more on this issue, see the chapter in this volume by Russel Lemmons and Laura J. Hilton.) One possible shortcoming of a rigidly chronological structure is that it might appear to visitors as more of a chronicle or timeline ("And then this happened, and then that happened . . .") rather than an engaging narrative with interpretive significance.

Thematic approaches to Holocaust exhibitions may be more suitable in exhibitions that do not seek to provide comprehensive coverage of Holocaust history. Thematic exhibitions might focus on events in one geographic location (a single ghetto or concentration camp, perhaps); or one event (the Olympics in Berlin, or the conference at Wannsee where the Nazi regime planned the so-called Final Solution to the Jewish question); or biographical treatments of an individual or group. A challenge for thematic exhibitions is that while they do not have the burden of full coverage, they still need to root the given theme in a historical context. Visitors to thematically organized exhibitions should pay attention to how the framing of the story being told contextualizes the specific focus.

How does the exhibition text lead visitors through the gallery?

Museum professionals often complain that visitors to exhibitions do not read text. The essence of their frustration might stem from the large gap between the time they invest writing interpretive text and object labels and the time that visitors spend engaging with the text. Though artifacts and media programs in exhibitions might be more attractive to many visitors, exhibition text provides signposts about the history being told, helping visitors better understand both the organization of the exhibition and its significance.

It is not realistic to assume that any visitor to the exhibition will read all the text in the galleries. (The scripts for exhibitions in roughly five thousand square feet of gallery space at the USHMM often exceed one hundred pages.) Nonetheless, educators should teach students to be aware of the hierarchy of text in galleries. One key here is teaching students how to be visually literate to the cues being used by exhibition designers, who might treat section headers or "headlines" within exhibitions in ways that set them off and make them easily readable. These headlines usually communicate something essential about that part of the exhibition: the subject, the argument, or a question to consider. Museum text below these headlines often resembles journalistic writing more than academic writing in that curators try not to "bury the lede," meaning that the text emphasizes the most important points first—perhaps acting on the assumption that some visitors will not read a text panel all the way to its end. Teachers might prompt students (especially those who are not prone to reading in exhibitions) to walk through the galleries and note all the exhibition headlines throughout; often what emerges clearly is the exhibition outline, with its chapter headings and subheadings.

Are there iconic artifacts in the exhibition? What are they?
How are they displayed?

One of the most exciting aspects of visiting museums is the opportunity to see historic artifacts. Educators should encourage students to look closely at these objects. Introductory questions such as "What is this?" or "Who did this belong to?" are not too basic, because they often provide a foundation for deeper inquiry. In thinking about the role of artifacts in exhibitions, students might need some prompting in two specific areas: the role of iconic artifacts—the signature objects associated with the Holocaust such as train cars, yellow stars, and piles of shoes, for example—in Holocaust museums and the treatment of individual objects.

Consider train cars, which have become ubiquitous in many Holocaust museums and often are used to evoke the horrific conditions in which the Nazi regime deported Jews eastward to their deaths in concentration camps and killing centers. These trains are icons, as religious studies scholar Oren Baruch Stier explains. They have meaning based on their history and context, but it is often their representational or memorial meaning that affects visitors in more significant ways.[6] Stier's examination of train cars in multiple Holocaust exhibitions reveals that the authenticity of the object (answering: Was this *specific* car used to deport Jews?) is less important for most museums that displaying a train car "of the type" used to deport Jews.

At the USHMM as well as in other Holocaust exhibitions, visitors are given the option of walking a path that leads through the train car itself, or taking an alternative route provided for visitors who may find entering the boxcar too emotionally difficult. Train cars have become iconic for many reasons, no doubt their sheer size being one of them. (The USHMM's top floors had to be built after hoisting the train car into place, as there was no way it could have been installed, whole, after the museum building was fully constructed.) Although iconic artifacts like this provide memorable moments in museum exhibitions, there is a danger that they misrepresent the history of the Holocaust. Not all Jews who died in the Holocaust experienced deportation in train cars like the ones shown, for example. Teachers should help students interrogate how curators have chosen to use iconic artifacts such as train cars, asking how they serve the overall goals of the exhibition, as well as whether they might work against those goals.

Smaller objects also can be icons of Holocaust history: victims' eyeglasses, suitcases, or personal effects collected by the Nazis at killing centers, for example. Victims' shoes are often displayed to chilling effect in museums. And whether to display the hair shorn from the victims in the killing process has been the subject of some controversy, raising difficult ethical questions for museum professionals.[7] Students in museums might be prompted to pay attention to whether these artifacts are "lumped" in massive piles or "split" and displayed individually. Confronting hundreds of pairs of eyeglasses or shoes might convey the enormous number of victims (though only symbolically), but displays like this may work against telling specific stories of individuals. One pair of shoes or one refugee child's teddy bear might be just as poignant and memorable if used to tell an individual's story. Teachers might prompt students to think about the curatorial intent of choosing to group artifacts together or split them apart and to consider why such choices may have been made.

How is media used in the gallery?

Just as visitors should be attuned to how texts and artifacts function in exhibitions, they should be prompted to ask when and how media supports the narrative. Audiovisual media might include footage and sound presented as a historic artifact with little mediation by the museum, or as highly edited and produced content with museum narration, or something along a continuum in between.

Consider two uses of historical footage in USHMM's special exhibition *Americans and the Holocaust*. In a section of the exhibition on American protests against Nazism in 1933, a video program (without audio) on a repeating loop shows historic footage of anti-Nazi rallies and marches in multiple American cities. Images of newspaper headlines from 1933 are superimposed on this footage in order to locate visitors in place and time and provide some information about what they are seeing. The intended effect is to show visitors almost ambiently that some Americans across the country chose to protest Nazism during the first months after Hitler became chancellor of Germany.

By contrast, a longer media program near the start of the exhibition includes seven minutes of footage from American newsreels dating between 1934 and 1938. The program opens with scripted museum voice-over narration that explains what newsreels are, especially that they were a key source of information that shaped how Americans understood the world during the 1930s. This newsreel footage communicates the intensity of American antisemitism and isolation from world affairs. One section of the newsreel compilation uses "Inside Nazi Germany," a 1938 *March of Time* episode, to help visitors understand that Americans who went to the theater in that year could have learned a lot about the Nazi regime's persecution of Jews. Onscreen text in this program, written by the curator, helps visitors understand what they are seeing in each clip and why it is significant. This program is presented in a small theater, with benches that encourage visitors to linger there a bit longer. Unlike the unmediated protest footage, the newsreel theater with voice-over narration directly tells visitors what the program is intended to convey.

Our increasingly digital world, of course, does not stop at exhibition gallery doors. Media programs in galleries also include elements that invite interaction by visitors and give curators opportunities to reveal information over time in different ways. Digital interactives might provide more experiential moments as well: at a re-created lunch counter at the Center for Civil and Human Rights in Atlanta, Georgia, for example, visitors confront, in a highly mediated way, the frightening harassment that those who participated in sit-ins during the civil rights movement endured. Holocaust museums have been more reluctant to include interactives that put the visitor in the narrative or simulate the experiences of Holocaust victims. Appropriately so. But interactives can be used to great effect to reveal information about individuals over time and add layers to an individual's story in ways that keep visitors interested.

It is difficult to predict where new technologies will lead museum practice, but artificial intelligence and virtual reality already play important roles in many museum exhibitions. Students who were "born digital" may be less impressed than older generations at the use of technology, but they still should be reminded to think about curatorial intent around the use of technology, as well as to ask why media or digital components were employed, and in service of what educational end.

Are first-person testimonies included in the exhibition?

Exhibitions might also include first-person testimony by Holocaust survivors, military veterans, or others who lived through this history. *The Holocaust*, the permanent exhibition at the USHMM, features a film called *Testimony* just before the end of the exhibition. The experience of watching it is intimate and personal, as survivors tell their stories of the Holocaust not at the macro level of politics but at the very personal level of hunger, aid from or betrayal by neighbors, and fear. As historian Edward Linenthal notes, *Testimony* is organized "around themes of resistance, rescue, and defiance."[8] It reminds visitors of the personal toll that these events took on individuals.

Some students might be reluctant to analyze critically such emotional survivor testimonies. But they should be encouraged, as with all elements in the exhibition, to think about the curatorial intent. Teachers might ask: Which sections of the exhibition are told through narratives of living witnesses? Do decades of remove between the events themselves and the retelling of the events matter, and if so, how? Who is included in those testimonies—Holocaust survivors, bystanders, or even perpetrators? Who is not included? Does the testimony distance visitors in time somehow, or does it make the history seem more immediate to hear the experiences through witnesses' memories?

How does the exhibition end?

Museum visitors should think about the closing moment of the exhibition in similar ways as the opening moment. Students should be prompted to ask: What is the last thing the exhibition asks visitors to consider? Does it close with a quotation, a question, testimony, or a film? Does the closing moment reflect back on what has been seen in the gallery or propel the visitor forward, either with a difficult question or with a reference to the present? Is there an opportunity for visitors to give feedback to the museum and in what way? Remember, no choices made by curators in the gallery are inevitable. So, teachers and students should ask why the exhibition ends the way it does.

Consider an invented (but hopefully illustrative) example. Imagine an exhibition chronicling the life story of Anne Frank, perhaps the most famous victim of the Holocaust. (There have been many such exhibitions.) At one extreme, a curator could choose to close the exhibition with the most-often quoted passage from her diary: "I still believe, in spite of everything, that people are truly good at heart."[9] As Alexandra Zapruder explains, the "positive and hopeful" message of this passage is "repeated again and again" as people search for something redemptive from this tragedy.[10] An alternative, much more bleak ending to such an exhibition would be to "locate" visitors at Bergen-Belsen, perhaps by using a photomural of the camp in spring 1945, near the time Anne Frank died there. Between these extremes, of course, are many options, including contextualizing Anne Frank's experiences among the 1.5 million children killed by the Nazi regime, or among diarists during the Holocaust, or in contrast to voices of young writers in genocides after the Holocaust. (See Amy Simon's chapter in this volume on using diaries, including Anne Frank's.) However a curator chooses to end an exhibition, the ending often expresses the museum's claims to the subject's significance.

The Future of Holocaust Museums

Although this chapter has focused almost entirely on how to engage with museums within exhibition galleries, many Holocaust museums also provide opportunities to speak to survivors in formal or informal settings. This is an opportunity that is fleeting, now more than seventy-five years since the end of World War II, and one that should not be missed. Survivors volunteer at many Holocaust museums, sometimes stationed near information desks or elsewhere. Many museums also have regularly scheduled public programs with survivors, such as the "First Person" series at the United States Holocaust Memorial Museum—hour-long conversations with survivors in a museum auditorium. Teachers who bring their classes to Holocaust museums might try to schedule such trips with opportunities to talk to survivors in mind or contact museum staff in advance to see if a private discussion with a survivor is possible. Dialogues with survivors tend to be one of the most memorable ways for students to learn about the history of the Holocaust.

Holocaust museums face a critical challenge in coming years, when there will no longer be any living Holocaust survivors. Recorded testimony, however, endures. Some museums are addressing the passing of survivors by employing relatively new technologies in museum galleries. The Shoah Foundation and Illinois Holocaust Museum and Education Center, for example, have partnered to mount a "holographic Survivor Story Experience," where visitors can interact with a three-dimensional hologram of a survivor powered by machine learning. (See Margarete Myers Feinstein's chapter on visual history in this volume.) These experiences can be effective and memorable, though they are not able to fully replicate intimate, personal conversations with living witnesses to Holocaust history. The presence of Holocaust survivors, which has so profoundly motivated the existence of Holocaust museums and shaped them as institutions, will be impossible to replace. This will be one of the most critical challenges Holocaust museums face in the coming years. Another topic to watch in the decades ahead will be whether and how Holocaust museums choose to incorporate the histories of other genocides that have occurred since the Holocaust, even assuming that Holocaust history will remain at most institutions' cores. Although these challenges in the years ahead will be formidable, Holocaust museums have become a part of the permanent cultural landscape in many regions of the United States over the past generation. They provide many valuable opportunities for learning about the Holocaust in engaging and enduring ways that do not occur in the same way through books, websites, other educational resources, or in a traditional classroom setting.

Notes

1. Peter Hayes, *Why? Explaining the Holocaust* (New York: W. W. Norton, 2017), xiii. Hayes writes: "Incomprehension is the default position in the face of the enormity of the Holocaust, even though that stance blocks the possibility of learning from the subject."

2. Lendol Calder, "Uncoverage: Toward a Signature Pedagogy for the History Survey," *Journal of American History* 92, no. 4 (March 2006): 1358–1370. Calder writes "that the typical coverage-oriented survey is a wrongheaded way to introduce students to the goodness and power of history" and optimistically claims that, for teachers, "the mystique of coverage is abating" (1359).

3. *Americans and the Holocaust* opened at the United States Holocaust Memorial Museum in Washington, DC, in April 2018. An online version of the exhibition may be accessed at ushmm.org/americans. The exhibition content in the museum gallery is not identical with the online presentation.

4. On these and other decisions that went into the USHMM's exhibitions, see Edward T. Linenthal, *Preserving Memory: The Struggle to Create America's Holocaust Museum* (New York: Penguin Books, 1995).

5. Doris L. Bergen, *War and Genocide: A Concise History of the Holocaust*, 3rd ed. (Lanham, MD: Rowman & Littlefield, 2016), 1.

6. Oren Baruch Stier, *Holocaust Icons: Symbolizing the Shoah in History and Memory* (New Brunswick: Rutgers University Press, 2015), 3.

7. On this debate among the original curatorial team at USHMM, see Linenthal, *Preserving Memory*, 211–216. After much debate, the curators decided to display a photograph of human hair, not the hair itself.

8. Linenthal, *Preserving Memory*, 253.

9. Anne Frank, *The Diary of a Young Girl: The Definitive Edition* (New York: Doubleday, 1995), 332. The entry is dated July 15, 1944. The sentence before the well-known passage is rarely quoted, perhaps because it complicates Anne Frank's thinking: "It's a wonder I haven't abandoned all my ideals, they seem so absurd and impractical. Yet I cling to them because I still believe, in spite of everything, that people are truly good at heart."

10. Alexandra Zapruder, *Salvaged Pages: Young Writers' Diaries of the Holocaust* (New Haven: Yale University Press, 2002), 5.

Memorials, Monuments, and the Obligation of Memory

STUART ABRAMS

No day shall erase you from the memory of time.

VIRGIL

Without memory, there is no culture. Without memory, there would be no civilization, no society, no future.

ELIE WIESEL

S hould the way in which we study the Holocaust, and other genocides for that matter, differ from the way in which we analyze any other historical event? Is there something that happened in the middle of the twentieth century that goes beyond that which we should consider traditional history? The manner in which twenty-first-century high school and college students "remember" the Holocaust is often in an indirect, imagined, and fantasized way. Today's students are even further removed from the events of the Shoah than the immediate postwar generation had been. Nonetheless, "without memory," Wiesel noted in his 1986 Nobel Peace Prize acceptance speech, "our existence would be barren and opaque, like a prison cell into which no light penetrates; like a tomb which rejects the living."[1]

Tom Lantos, the only Holocaust survivor to have ever served in the United States Congress, was often quoted saying, "The veneer of civilization is paper thin. We are its guardians, and we can never rest."[2] The study of memorials, monuments, and museums offers a unique educational opportunity to use memory as an effective tool to help move students along the road, as Lantos said, "to a more civilized world." As educators, we must strive to instill in our students the belief and the tenacity that they can and that they must be the carriers of noble ideals and human dignity for future generations. Has the world learned from history to the degree that genocide, mass murder, and other forms of human suffering have been eradicated in any substantial way? No. Have the irrational emotions associated with racism, xenophobia, and antisemitism yet been extinguished? Not yet. As educators, as human beings, we must never give up. I suspect the events witnessed in Charlottesville in 2017 or in Pittsburgh in 2018 can sometimes cause us to lose hope and feel, to some degree, like failures as educators. We must never give up on our students.

Some of the memorials discussed in this chapter were designed to exist long after their creators have passed from this earth; it is equally true that our students will be the messengers to a time that many of us shall not see. Therefore, we must leave in their capable hands all the skills necessary to bring to future generations the message, not of despair, indifference, and hate, but rather the message of hope, renewal, and love. Students often seem to be most captivated by the direct encounter with a survivor, a living artifact from the past. Nonetheless, we are sadly but regularly confronted by the reality that there exists an ever-decreasing number of eyewitnesses to the Holocaust. Therefore, we search for new, compelling, and insightful ways to help students grasp the ungraspable.

This chapter examines how educators can use memorials as an instructive and captivating tool not only to study the power of history and memory but also as tools for a better understanding of the Holocaust. Likewise, the study of memorials asks students to consider how societies choose to remember the past. At the conclusion of this chapter, I share an assignment that attempts to offer students the opportunity to discern their own appreciation and awareness of the indecipherable in their own idiosyncratic way by challenging them to design their own memorial.

Memorial artists in Germany and throughout Europe, the United States, and elsewhere are tormented, vexed, and stimulated by the complexities this reality creates. Monuments and memorials serve as statements of how a collective group, a society, a state, chooses to remember its brightest hours and its darkest moments. As we know, however, collective memory functions differently in different places at different times. Nations and peoples who perceive themselves as victims will embrace one form of memory, while artists in countries responsible for persecution will be forced to wrestle with entirely different challenges. As James E. Young asks, "How does a state incorporate shame into its national memorial landscape? Under what memorial aegis, whose rules, does a nation remember its barbarity? Where is the tradition for a memorial . . . when combined remembrance and self-indictment seem so hopelessly at odds? [. . .] How do former persecutors mourn their victims? How does a nation reunite itself on the bedrock memory of its crimes?"[3]

The study of the Holocaust offers educators the challenge of sharing with students an unprecedented event in the history of humanity, and frequently within a limited amount of time. How can we teach our students to examine the complexities of the Holocaust and analyze the myriad of emotional responses to it, while developing the critical thinking skills such as independent thinking, personal autonomy, and reasoned judgment in both thought and action that are essential in order to drill down and investigate the moral decision making often associated with the victims, perpetrators, bystanders, and rescuers of the Shoah? Art has frequently played an important role in helping fight against intolerance of different cultures, racism, and other forms of unjust societal segregation. Alongside the desire to educate our students, the study of memorials, monuments, and museums can act as a shield against hate, indifference, and denial. In this age of information, there is no shortage of Holocaust educational materials and historical examples that we can choose to bring into the classroom. Three-dimensional abstract representations of the Holocaust in the form of memorials challenge students to interpret the deeper meaning of the catastrophic events of the Shoah in a manner that can help make sense of the overwhelming information presented before them.

The study of memorials also asks students to consider the multiple ways in which humans create memory, through art, language, music, physical space, and more. To offer but one example, when teaching about the massacre at Babi Yar, the ravine outside Kiev where more than thirty-three thousand Jews were massacred in late September 1941, I have often recruited colleagues from both the language arts department and the music department at my school to help in the discussion relative to the events at Babi Yar. This interdisciplinary approach to the study of a historical event is both educational and poignant. Having the history teacher describe the events leading up to the massacre in the ravine outside of Kiev, while the language arts teacher works with students to deconstruct Yevgeni Yevtushenko's poem "Babi Yar" (written in 1961 to protest the Soviet state's refusal to identify Babi Yar as a site of mass killing), as the music teacher conveys the power of Shostakovich's Symphony #13 (based on that same poem), is a powerful introduction to one of the horrific sites of mass killing that defines the Shoah.[4] At the same time, this exercise forces students to consider the multiple ways in which memory of a place and an event can be shaped. Holocaust memorials, monuments, and museums can serve as not only unique teaching resources but also as contemporary and engaging entry points for students to begin a study of the Holocaust.

Experiential Learning in the Classroom

> It's a big rock telling people what to think; it's a big form that pretends to have a meaning, that sustains itself for eternity, that never changes over time, never evolves—it fixes history, it embalms or somehow stultifies it.[5] (James E. Young, interview, Yad Vashem)

One could argue that the purpose of memorials and monuments is to keep, through inanimate objects, history alive. Typically, memorials are conceived as structures or markers designed to remind people of a loved one; monuments are statues, buildings, or other structures dedicated to that person. Memorials and monuments (while some distinguish between these two terms, for my purposes I use them interchangeably) reflect, in part, the ways in which communities and individuals have determined the manner in which they choose to remember.

All across the globe, artists have created memorials and monuments to commemorate the Holocaust. Legal scholar Martha Minow asks, "Should such memorials be literal or abstract? Should they honor the dead or disturb the very possibility of honor in atrocity? Should they be monumental, or instead disavow the monumental image, itself so associated with Nazism? Preserve memories or challenge as pretense the notion that memories ever exist outside the process of constructing them?"[6]

As James E. Young and others have argued, however, memorials perform a paradoxical function: once we assign monumental form to memory, we have, to some degree, divested ourselves of the obligation to remember. Memorials function as a type of prosthetic memory device.[7] The public knows the memorial will perform the remembering for them; thus, ironically, they are absolved of the obligation to remember. Some memorials thus also wrestle with the problem of absence, not by creating a new structure but by creating countermemorials that force visitors to consider what has been lost, what has disappeared. Having students wrestle with the meaning of statements of this nature helps foster the development of the necessary intellectual adroitness that will be required as one moves along in the study of memorials, monuments, and museums.

It is a daunting decision as to where to begin a critical analysis of memorials, monuments, and museums. As an introduction, I often look at the seemingly uncomplicated monument located in Devanter, Netherlands, in remembrance of Etty Hillesum titled Disturbed Life. Esther "Etty" Hillesum (1914–1943) is the adult, journal-writing counterpart to Anne Frank. In her diary, which she kept from March 1941 until she was interned in Westerbork in October 1942, where she remained along with her family until they were deported to Auschwitz in September 1943, Hillesum continued to find meaning in life, despite its absurd nature: "God is not accountable to us, but we are to Him. I know what may lie in wait for us. . . . And yet I find life beautiful and meaningful."[8] A Dutch artist, Arno Kramer, created Disturbed Life, a monument in memory of Hillesum, ultimately murdered at Auschwitz. This small yet distinct monument offers some clues into some of the frequently used themes displayed in other monuments. Why is there a split or crack in this monument? Is this an example of an artist's attempt, despite the physical limitations, at representing themes such as disruption, absence, privation, or loss? This is an interesting and compelling point for students to ponder. Similar "splits" can be found in other memorials (e.g., the Bełżec Memorial in Poland) as well as in the specific designs of museums such as the United States Holocaust Memorial Museum.

Disturbed Life, monument to Etty Hillesum, Deventer, Holland. (Photographer: Gou-wenaar, June 30, 2015; https://commons.wikimedia.org/wiki/File:20150630_Het_verstoorde_leven_door_Arno_Kramer_Deventer.jpg)

In order to enable students to understand the importance of context, starting with two Holocaust memorials in the United States before moving to the monuments in Europe accomplishes this outcome. Context for memorials, monuments, and museums is an essential component if students are to be able to understand, interpret, and critically evaluate these artistic creations. For example, it should come as no surprise that the theme of the United States Holocaust Memorial Museum on the National Mall in Washington, DC, introduces visitors to an American perspective on the Holocaust by first employing the gaze of the American liberators through audio and photography. In Israel, on the other hand, Moshe Safdie's Memorial to Deportees, a cattle car hanging over the Judean Hills at Yad Vashem, juxtaposes the memory of millions of lives abruptly cut short with the fact of Israel's existence.[9]

The first "American" memorial I examine with my students is the New England Holocaust Memorial, founded by Stephan Ross, designed by Stanley Saitowitz, and erected in Boston in 1995. Located, not

The New England Holocaust Memorial in Boston, Massachusetts, was founded by Stephan Ross, a Holocaust survivor, and designed by Stanley Saitowitz. It was erected in 1995. Each tower symbolizes a different major Nazi extermination camp. (Photographer: Beyond My Ken, August 16, 2017 / ; https://en.wikipedia.org/wiki/New_England_Holocaust_Memorial#/media/File:2017_New_England_Holocaust_Memorial_from_west.jpg)

by accident, on the Freedom Trail at a noisy and busy intersection in downtown Boston, near Faneuil Hall along with many other treasures of American history, the site of this memorial is quite distinct. The site offers a unique opportunity for reflection on the meaning of freedom and oppression and on the importance of a society's respect for human rights.[10]

The design utilizes uniquely powerful symbols of the Holocaust. Boston's Holocaust Memorial features six luminous glass towers, each fifty-four feet high. The towers are lit internally to gleam at night. They are set on a black granite path, each one over a dark chamber, which carries the name of one of the principal Nazi death camps. Smoke rises from charred embers at the bottom of these chambers. Six million numbers, etched in glass in an orderly pattern, suggest the infamous tattooed numbers and ghostly ledgers of the Nazi bureaucracy. Evocative and rich in metaphor, the six towers recall the six main death camps, the six million Jews who died, or a menorah of memorial candles.[11]

Look at these towers, passerby, and try to imagine what they really mean—what they symbolize—what they evoke. They evoke an era of incommensurate darkness, an era in history when civilization lost its humanity and humanity its soul. . . . We must look at these towers of memory and say to ourselves, No one should ever deprive a human being of his or her right to dignity. No one should ever deprive anyone of his or her right to be a sovereign human being. No one should ever speak again about racial superiority. . . .

We cannot give evil another chance.[12]

Another important American memorial is the Miami Holocaust Memorial called A Sculpture of Love and Anguish, designed by Kenneth Treister. It is composed of a series of vignettes with an outstretched arm reaching nearly fifty feet into the sky. One hundred and thirty life-sized figures cast in bronze are integrated into a larger garden and park designed by the sculptor. The first sculpture at the beginning of the journey through the memorial depicts a mother and two snuggling children, fearful as the first signs of the Holocaust appear. Ultimately, the visitor arrives at the sculpture, which seems to represent a scene from hell, frozen in bronze. Students tend to have their own interpretation of this giant outstretched hand with a number symbolizing the tattoos branded on prisoners. Some see despair, while others see hope, or a last grasp for life. The final sculpture depicts the same mother and two children seen at the outset of the installation . . . now dead. The hope is that students will be moved by curiosity and interest to do further research and begin to contemplate how killers killed, how the victims perished, all while the beautiful city of Miami enjoyed *serenity*. With the hotels being full and the beaches crowded, will students ultimately wonder, how come? Newspapers all across the country, the *Miami Herald* included, reported the events; and yet somehow it made no difference. How come?

Are memorials, monuments, and museums sufficient as tools of remembering? Are they simply a substitute or, more importantly, an obstacle to action? The Holocaust Memorial in Miami reflects the challenge of simultaneously remembering and representing the Holocaust as if fully "remembering" the event is even possible. While memorials are designed to inspire memory, it is impossible for an individual to remember an event she or he never actually experienced.

Graphic artists such as Art Spiegelman force us to consider the impossibility of fully transferring memory from one generation to the next. Although this transfer of memory might be impossible, by creating

Miami Beach Holocaust Memorial. (Photographer: Daniel Di Palma, September 23, 2017; https://commons.wikimedia.org/wiki/File:Miami_Beach_-_South_Beach_Monuments_-_Holocaust_Memorial_25.jpg)

books such as *Maus,* Spiegelman may also be seen as complicit in creating the illusion that by simply visiting a memorial, reading a book, and letting it do the memorial work, the reader or visitor has done enough. Art Spiegelman's *Maus: A Survivor's Tale* is not a single story at all but two stories told simultaneously that show how the past and present can exist side by side.[13] (See the discussion in Victoria Aarons's chapter in this volume.) Students benefit from seeing Vladek's (the father) and Art's (the son) imaginative record of that same story and can examine the simultaneity of past and present on the illustrated page. *Maus* offers much for students to contemplate about the Holocaust in a way that is both educational, surprising, and appealing, while also illustrating the dilemmas of creating art to represent the Holocaust.

After discussing Spiegelman's visual representations of testimony with students, I introduce the unique photographic memorial style of Shimon Attie, whose work richly highlights the effect of time on humans, nature, and everyday normal life, particularly life in Europe. Shimon Attie's archival photographic images of the past projected onto otherwise amnesiac sites of history is another example of Young's "texture" of memory. Attie attempts to reanimate present-day sites with his memory of what happened there. Attie hopes that, once seen, the images of these projections will always haunt these sites by haunting those who have seen his projections.[14] In Attie's eyes, even the designs of household items can recall the times of their origin and, by extension, the households from which they were torn. Projecting images of the past onto sites in the present is a compelling way to demonstrate the many layers of time. "I wanted to give this invisible past a voice, to bring to light, if only for some brief moments."[15]

Students find the Vanishing Monument: The Monument against Fascism in Hamburg-Harburg fascinating. Esther Shalev-Gerz and Jochen Gerz designed the countermonument and installed it not in a well-manicured park-like setting but rather in a busy public square in the center of the commercial district of Hamburg, Germany.[16] The Gerzes' challenge was to create a memorial that would function not as a prosthetic device absolving the public from the obligation of memory. In fact, their desired outcome was just the opposite. The artists made it crystal clear that "what we did not want was an enormous pedestal with something in it presuming to tell people what they ought to think."[17] Their goal was to utilize a countermonument design in such a way that it would spur visitors to action and transform passive memory into active memory. Students must also be asked to consider the ways in which they can reorganize memory and learning from passive acquisition of knowledge into informed action.

The memorial is a three-foot-square obelisk rising forty feet into the sky. A temporary inscription near its base invited "citizens of Hamburg, and visitors to the town, to add their names here to ours. In doing so, we commit ourselves to remain vigilant. As more and more names cover this twelve-meter-tall lead column, it will gradually be lowered into the ground. One day it will have disappeared completely, and the site of the Harburg monument against fascism will be empty. In the end, it is only we ourselves who can rise up against injustice." A stylus was attached to the corners of the square in which visitors could sign their names as a defiant voice against fascism and the rise of neo-Nazi sympathies. As five-foot sections of the obelisk became covered with names and all other types of graffiti, the square would be lowered into a chamber below ground revealing a fresh five-foot area for new names and comments. Ultimately, there would be no five-foot sections left, and the entire monument would be lowered into the underground chamber. Having visitors participate and therefore become part of the monument helped transfer the onus of memory onto their shoulders, requiring them to remember for themselves.[18] As with most monuments, memorials, and museums, however, things do not always go precisely as planned, and controversy often follows. Fears rose that the memorial would reflect a grotesque microcosm of German society forty-five years after the event. Perhaps that is precisely what the artists hoped to achieve; a true and accurate reflection of German society while returning the burden of memory of the Holocaust to us all.

It would seem to be hard to imagine any monument to the victims of the Holocaust being any more controversial than that of Guenther Demnig's brass-topped cobblestones known as *Stolpersteine* or "stumbling stones," which for years have served as memorials to Holocaust victims throughout Germany and more than a dozen other European countries.[19] Since Demnig first began his art project in the mid-1990s, the project has mushroomed. As of October of 2018, there are somewhere in the neighborhood of seventy thousand of these commemorative bricks in dozens of cities and towns across Germany and more than twenty other European nations, making "the Stolpersteine project the world's largest decentralized memorial in the world." For 120 Euros, anyone can sponsor a stumbling stone. Demnig believed that the stumbling stones would become a more personal memorial to the victims of Hitler's Germany. He came to rely on residents and students, in addition to religious and secular groups, to research the "last address of choice of victims of the Nazi regime." The stones give the name of the victims, date of birth, and information about what happened to them. For example, it might indicate the date they were deported, which concentration camp they were taken to, and when or where they died, if such details are known. "I think the large Holocaust memorial in Berlin will always remain abstract. You have to make a decision to visit it. But not with the stumbling blocks. Suddenly they are there, right outside your front door, at your feet, in front of you." Demnig's creative genius makes it clear that everybody passing the Stolpersteine in the first place is responsible, individually and independently, for remembering.[20]

The brick project has its critics. One example that merits mention is the fact that neo-Nazis were removing Stolpersteine and then putting in their own Stolpersteine to memorialize Germans who were murdered by immigrants.[21] However, the main complaints once again are that the bricks only highlight victimhood, and that when people, dogs, and bikes trample over the names of the dead, some argue, they are victimized a second time. In Munich, city officials and a large influential Jewish group rejected the project. In fact, they banned the bricks, arguing that they desecrated the memory of the victims. Charlotte Knobloch, leader of the city's Jewish community and former president of the Central Council of Jews in Germany, said they were not respectful of the victims they intended to honor. "People murdered in the Holocaust deserve better than a plaque in the dust, street dirt and even worse filth," she said.[22]

Quoting the Talmud, a Jewish text of rabbinical teachings, the home page of Demnig's website reads, "A person is only forgotten when his or her name is forgotten."[23] He further argues that to read what is engraved on the stones requires the onlooker to bow as if showing the respect and reverence the victims so rightly deserve. Another compelling point that argues against the misplaced criticism is the Stolpersteine make clear the six million Jews slaughtered were all individuals. Wrapping our heads around the number six million is impossible for all. The stumbling blocks make it clear that it was one plus one . . .

Memorials as an Introduction
to the Thematic Approach

The only limitation to the manner in which we can incorporate memorials into an overall teaching strategy is our own creativity. For example, monuments can effectively be used to introduce specific themes relative to Holocaust and genocide studies such as resistance and rescue. (See the larger discussion of these issues in Laura J. Hilton's chapter in this volume.)

Janusz Korczak was a distinguished Jewish doctor and revered educator, arguably Poland's most renowned children's advocate. When, in 1940, the Warsaw ghetto was formed, Korczak was forced by a Nazi edict to relocate his orphanage into quarters that one might expect to find under ghetto-like conditions. During the years that the orphanage existed, he used all of his influence, charisma, and energy to allow the children to live life in a manner as dignified as possible. The children were fed, clothed, and, despite the ban on education in the ghettos, educated. Even with opportunities for him to escape the ghetto and live in relative safety on the "Aryan side," Korczak resisted these overtures and would not leave without his children. On Thursday August 6, 1942, the Germans deported Korczak, his assistants, and the two hundred children from the orphanage to the *Umschlagplatz* (transit point) and then to the slaughterhouse Treblinka. Following the path of Janusz Korczak from the Warsaw ghetto to the Umschlagplatz, to the cattle cars, to the final destination of Korczak and his children at Treblinka allows many opportunities to incorporate memorials to illuminate and enrich student learning. Restoring the identity of one individual whose name is the only name carved into a stone at Treblinka may help students better understand the unknown numbers of victims deported to Treblinka whose names have been lost or forgotten.

Bebelplatz is a public square at Unter den Linden Boulevard in the Mitte district in Berlin. Once planned as a jewel of Prussian humanistic enlightenment, in a cruel twist of fate this square is better remembered today as the venue for the Nazi's first official book-burning bonfire on May 10, 1933 (see Ilana Offenberger's chapter in this volume). It is impossible not to recognize that this event occurred in the shadows of one of Germany's greatest universities, Humboldt University, where Karl Marx had once been a student of Hegel's. Describing what this action meant and how it would be perceived as a dire warning to Nazi opponents is of significant and noteworthy importance. Joseph Goebbels, Nazi minister for popular enlightenment and propaganda, began in 1933 an effort to "synchronize" culture with Nazi ideology. Goebbels had a strong ally in the National Socialist German Students' Association (Nationalsozialistischer Deutscher Studentenbund, or NSDStB). In a symbolic act of ominous significance, on May 10, 1933, university students burned upward of twenty-five thousand volumes of "un-German" books. These works of so-called subversive writers were set alight with the purpose of destroying the "Jewish mind and the whole rotten liberalist tendency."[24]

The memory of this event is symbolically kept alive by a memorial monument known as Bibliothek (sunken library) by Mischa Ullmann. If one were attempting to introduce themes such as the rise of totalitarian regimes, Hitler's rise to power, the patterns of and path to genocide, indoctrination, or the promotion of ultranationalistic fervor, this memorial with its underground library and its empty bookshelves can be a most powerful and persuasive introduction to these themes.

Material Culture and Memorials

Educators charged with teaching about the Holocaust and other genocides are faced with the same obstacle: limited time to convey the complexities and details necessary for our students to completely comprehend, if possible, the disturbing and alarming proceedings of the Shoah. When asked, after visiting the United States Holocaust Memorial Museum, many people will tell you that the most moving exhibit that they saw were "the shoes." Big shoes. Little shoes. Women's shoes and men's shoes. Ballet shoes. Children's shoes. If we can discover the story behind just a single pair of shoes, it will often make for a significantly more powerful bond between the individual and the event. *Empathy* refers to the ability to relate to another person's pain vicariously, as if one has experienced that pain themselves. While it might seem impossible to truly empathize with survivors, personal accounts help unravel the various complexities associated with anyone trying to comprehend the horrors of the past. Students, like all of us, find it difficult to grasp the idea of six million victims. However, we all can understand and absorb a story with one individual and their family.

Closure Activity

It can be challenging to bring context and closure to a unit that utilizes memorials as the vehicle for considering the responsibility and obligation of memory. The assignment I created asks students to create their own memorial. They first must choose a country and a person or an event. The next step is for them is to decide if the perspective of their memorial is to be from that of a perpetrator, victim, or rescuer.

Here are a few things students must consider when creating their memorial:

- How can you incorporate in your memorial that the obligation of memory will rest with the visitor to the memorial, not the memorial itself?
- In our discussions, we have observed the challenges of prosthetic memory; what, by your light, will resonate with the visitor after they have seen and experienced your memorial?
- How will your memorial challenge the visitor to carry the responsibility of memory with them into the future?
- Will your memorial reject traditional monuments and be conceived in a way to challenge the very premise of the monument?
- Finally, speculate about the future of your memorial: what will its relevance be in five, ten, twenty-five, and fifty years?

Over the years, I have been fortunate to visit with my students many of the countries of Central and Eastern Europe where one can touch, feel, see, and sometimes even smell the memorials and monuments that many have only seen in pictures or discussed in class. It is difficult to find the words to articulate the power and profound impact visiting these places can have. You cannot help but be changed forever when seeing the iron shoes along the Danube, walking in and out of the stelae on the undulated ground of the Holocaust memorial in Berlin, or stepping onto the hallowed graveyards of Treblinka and Birkenau.

The benefits and academic merit of study tours can be immeasurable. Students are presented with and forced to consider a completely new global perspective. Unfamiliarity and separation from home are great incubators for thought. New experiences allow students to question one's preconceived ideas. The enriching experience of educational travel encourages students to expand their worldview, witness a new way of life, and better understand people, history, and culture. Finally, the relationships and connections made between material discussed within the four walls of a classroom and personal relationships students have with people from home force a reevaluation of the subject. There's no education quite like the lessons learned from travel.

Even for those students who do not have the opportunity to travel with a teacher or a class to visit a memorial, the challenge of designing one's own memorial forces them to think critically about the dilemmas that confront an artist attempting to create meaning out of tragedy and destruction. How does one make sense of the inexplicable with minimal time, space, and resources? How to convey meaning that will resonate far into the future? At the very least, students will be forced to think twice before walking past the next memorial or monument they see and consider the meaning of the monument before them.

NOTES

1. Elie Wiesel, Nobel Prize Acceptance Speech, 1986, https://www.nobel prize.org/prizes/peace/1986/wiesel/26054-elie-wiesel-acceptance-speech -1986/.

2. See, for example, Lantos Foundation, https://www.lantosfoundation .org/thefoundation/.

3. James E. Young, *At Memory's Edge*: *After-Images of the Holocaust in Contemporary Art and Architecture* (New Haven: Yale University Press, 2000), 7.

4. For the text of the poem "Babi Yar," see, for example, https://www-tc .pbs.org/auschwitz/learning/guides/reading1.4.pdf.

5. See "Excerpt from Interview with Professor James E. Young," May 24, 1998, Shoah Resource Center, International School for Holocaust Studies, https://www.yadvashem.org/odot_pdf/Microsoft%20Word%20-%203659 .pdf.

6. See "Visual Essay: Holocaust Memorials and Monuments," chapter 11, "The Holocaust and Human Behavior," Facing History and Ourselves, https:// www.facinghistory.org/holocaust-and-human-behavior/chapter-11/visual -essay-holocaust-memorials-and-monuments (accessed February 21, 2019).

7. The term is used to somewhat different effect in Alison Landsberg, *Prosthetic Memory*: *The Transformation of American Remembrance in the Age of Mass Culture* (New York: Columbia University Press, 2004).

8. Etty Hillesum, *An Interrupted Life*: *The Diaries, 1941–1943* (New York: Henry Holt, 1996), 150. The diaries were only published posthumously in 1981. Hillesum was murdered in Auschwitz on November 30, 1943.

9. See "Yad Vashem Memorial to the Deportees," The Moshe Safdie Archive, McGill Library, http://cac.mcgill.ca/moshesafdie/fullrecord.php?ID= 10833&d=1.

10. On July 2, 2019, young Jewish activists in Boston set forth from the site of the New England Holocaust Museum to protest the Trump administration's Immigration and Customs Enforcement policies toward detainees, using the site of the memorial as a symbolic call to action.

11. The documentary film *Etched in Glass* includes further details on the creation of the memorial. James E. Young, *The Texture of Memory* (New Haven: Yale University Press, 2000), also includes a detailed analysis of the memorial. In 2017, vandals damaged the memorial, but the broken panes of glass were replaced.

12. Elie Wiesel, https://www.nehm.org/the-memorial/.

13. James E. Young, "The Holocaust as Vicarious Past: Restoring the Voices of Memory to History," *Judaism: A Quarterly Journal of Jewish Life and Thought* 51, no. 1 (2002): 666–699.

14. Young, "Holocaust as Vicarious Past."

15. See discussion in Young, "Sites Unseen: Shimon Attie's Acts of Remembrance, 1991–1996," in *At Memory's Edge*, 62–89.

16. See Esther Shalev-Gerz, "The Monument against Fascism," Hamburg-Harburg, Germany, 1986, http://www.shalev-gerz.net/?portfolio=monument -against-fascism.

17. As cited in Young, *At Memory's Edge*, 130.

18. See Young, *At Memory's Edge*, 130.

19. Gunter Demnig, http://www.stolpersteine.eu/en/home/.

20. See Eric Westervelt, "Stumbling upon Mini Memorials to Holocaust Victims," May 31, 2012, NPR, https://www.npr.org/2012/05/31/153943491 /stumbling-upon-miniature-memorials-to-nazi-victims (accessed July 17, 2019).

21. Feargus O'Sullivan, "Vandals Are Attacking Berlin's Powerful City-wide Holocaust Memorial," CityLab, November 16, 2017, https://www.citylab .com/life/2017/11/berlin-stolpersteine/545990/.

22. Jas Chana, "Plan for Holocaust Memorial 'Stumbling Stones' Takes a Tumble," Tablet Magazine, August 5, 2015, https://www.tabletmag.com /scroll/192696/plan-for-holocaust-memorial-stumbling-stones-takes-a-tumble.

23. Demnig, http://www.stolpersteine.eu/en/home/. While no specific Talmudic source is provided, it is possible Demnig is citing Tractate *Megillah* 3:2, "R. Chiyya in the name of R. Yochanan: 'If the name of the owner was incised on the object, it is as if the name of the owner [who has donated it] will never be forgotten from the object.'"

24. See description at "Bebelplatz," Berlin.de, https://www.berlin.de/en /attractions-and-sights/3561138-3104052-bebelplatz.en.html (accessed July 17, 2019).

Why Should We Teach the Holocaust Today and Tomorrow?

R OBERT H ADLEY

For those who teach the Holocaust, the question of its inherent importance is often an assumed reality. For many teachers, student interest in the topic was a driving force to teach the topic and one that drove many teachers to create entire courses of study on the topic. This was certainly true of my own evolution as a Holocaust educator starting first in alternative education; it was the one topic that grabbed students' attention and kept them engaged. Student interest consistently drove me to explore deeper into this history and to widen my scope of scholarship into other genocides with which I was not familiar when I first started my journey. I never questioned teaching the topic or why I would continue to teach it going forward.

When I first confronted this question in preparation for writing this chapter, I eagerly worked up my best pat response as to why teaching this topic today was of vital importance and that the continuation of genocide into the twenty-first century demanded we confront this horrific chapter in our history. In creating my class, an optional advanced government class, my focus was largely based on the impact of individual choice. In evaluating authors such as Christopher Browning and work on modern genocides from Samantha Power and John Prendergast,[1] I was always struck by the power of the individual as agents of choice. This became the guiding framework for the class and a theme to which my students and I returned throughout the course. Stemming from my frustration with students who took a rather fatalistic view of the Holocaust as being something so powerful that individuals could not make a meaningful impact against its sea of hate engulfing the world, I adorned my walls with portraits of everyday individuals whose choices made a positive impact in the past and those who do so today. One of my primary focuses in this advanced civics class for seniors was to engage the role of a citizen in a democracy and convey that each person played a significant role in maintaining the democracy for everyone. This is what made the course such a powerful learning experience for students.

In the following pages, I explore some of the key issues confronting teachers incorporating the study of the Holocaust into their curriculum. Teachers must first understand their rationale for teaching it, which determines the structure of how they teach it. Many teachers seek relevance by incorporating a study of modern genocide alongside the Holocaust, drawing comparisons and dealing with the question of its uniqueness. Some seek to engage their students by inspiring activism and community engagement in an effort to make "Never Again" a reality. Still others probe whether the Holocaust is a proper vehicle to teach moral leadership, asking students to wrestle with moral ambiguities and engage human behavior on a critical level. I also explore how many teachers integrate genocide studies into their rationale, bringing up the issue of comparison and the uniqueness of the Holocaust. Some teachers use survivor testimony to teach the Holocaust to give voice to those the victims and to honor those who survived it. Lastly, our desire to ensure the topic is taught has also led a number of states to seek a mandate on its inclusion into our state standards, posing the question of the effectiveness of mandating the topic as a means of ensuring our students learn this history. Teachers must question the simple inclusion and incorporate meaningful best practices into our classrooms.

Rationale

In my nearly twenty years of teaching the Holocaust, I have come to understand that teachers approach the Holocaust from a vast array of perspectives and disciplines. Many of my colleagues teach this subject in English and language arts, psychology, economics, geography, history, religion, and ethics as well as art, music, and even science. The list continues to grow as more teachers find the relevance in incorporating the subject into their field of study. Understanding their goals and their desired outcomes from teaching the Holocaust must be central in understanding why teaching this topic is relevant today and will remain so into the future.

It was only in 2001 that I first had serious educational training on teaching the Holocaust. Upon arriving at the United States Holocaust Memorial Museum (USHMM) that summer, I was confronted by a stack of books, piled so high I could barely see over the top of them while seated. As an educator, I was initially filled with excitement at the incredible free offering of books, prior to my realization of the sheer density of the topic on which I was about to embark. From the very beginning of the teaching fellowship, we were asked the essential question of why we were teaching the Holocaust. I do not think I had a very adequate answer at that moment, presuming that this was simply a topic that was important to teach. Dan Napolitano, our fellowship director, took us through primary guidelines for teaching the Holocaust but prefaced the discussion by framing it through the lens of one's rationale.[2] In the room, we had sixteen language arts teachers, seven social science teachers (including myself), one English as a Second Language teacher (or ESL), and one religion teacher. It was clear that teaching this topic was different from anything else I was teaching my students.

Having a solid rationale is critical in creating an effective Holocaust curriculum and to answering the question of why you are even teaching the topic. Many teachers attempt to teach the Holocaust as if it is just another unit, having no rationale beyond it being the next topic to cover on the syllabus or even in the content standards. In attempting to ascertain why educators teach this subject and why it should be taught, we must be grounded in a better sense of how teachers perceive the significance of the topic today.

Approaches

There are many approaches teachers use in framing their study of the Holocaust, from grounding their study focusing on discrimination as a broader theme (i.e., exploring the historical antecedents of antisemitism) and connecting it to examples from today. Others use the framework of the Holocaust to explore the concept of genocide more broadly, exploring events such as slavery and the treatment of Native Americans in this context or contemporary genocides in places such as Rwanda, Darfur, and Syria. There are many ways to create relevancy in teaching the Holocaust, which is why teachers continue to gravitate to it.

Unfortunately, every year we read and hear stories of teachers making some of the worst pedagogical choices in attempting to teach the Holocaust, from lessons designed to have students promote alternative uses for death camps to attempting to have students debate whether the Holocaust even happened.[3] For many of these teachers, the Holocaust was simply a prop intended to teach a larger lesson or skill, used in part because of its upsurge in popularity. What is often lacking is a cogent rationale grounded in best practices in teaching the history of a challenging topic like this. This then pushes us to refine our question to say, Why is teaching the Holocaust *well* important today?

Just as Holocaust education was poised to explode in the late 1970s, eminent historian of the Holocaust Henry Friedlander predicted the quandary of an influx of Holocaust education without thought into our classrooms, stating, "The problem with too much being taught by too many without focus is that this poses the danger of destroying the subject matter through dilettantism."[4] The danger of teaching the Holocaust as the popular subject of the moment is that it is fleeting when not engaged with meaningfully. Holocaust studies professor at Northwestern University Peter Hayes writes in his seminal work *Why*, "We have to approach the record neither in awe nor in anger if we hope to learn anything valuable, rather than merely to have our preconceptions confirmed or our righteousness aroused."[5] Attempting to take a shallow dive into the pool of the Holocaust can in fact do more harm than good with our students. Maintaining longevity of effective Holocaust education in our schools will in part require more teacher training in the subject to truly ground the work in history.

Teacher Training

One of the larger challenges facing Holocaust education today is not one of access, resources, time, or even the ubiquity of standardized testing, but instead quality instruction. The key question for the next generation of teachers is that of best practices that truly target their goals. Teachers rarely question if they should teach the Holocaust, but still far too few have accessed sufficient training to handle the topic. Purdue University education professor and USHMM fellow David Lindquist notes, "teachers should receive highly focused and specific training in teaching the Holocaust that considers both the history and the pedagogy of the event."[6]

In attempting to ascertain why teaching the Holocaust is important today, we must look at how teachers are being prepared to approach this topic. I believe in doing so we also get a glimpse into where we are going in the field of Holocaust education and teachers continuing to develop their rationales. Teacher seminars such as the Olga Lengyel Institute conduct five- to ten-day seminars allowing teachers to dig deeper into the curriculum and discover new approaches to teaching the subject. In one of those seminars conducted in Farmington Hills, Michigan, teachers John Farris and Corey Harbaugh started and ended their seminar by asking the teachers to write their rationale statements. The exercise was fruitful for teachers as they had to meaningfully reflect on why they broached the subject in the first place, but more importantly to the teachers, they also reflected on how the seminar impacted their thinking in reframing their approach for the following year. As trainers, we always hope that teachers incorporate new ideas into their classrooms in some way, but this exit ticket approach employed by the teachers gave them a greater glimpse of where this integration might be going. The following is an example of a post-reflection on his rationale statement written by teacher Greg E.:

Holocaust education goes much further than just a series of events and a final death toll. Every character involved in the Holocaust has a unique and loaded story. My students need to understand that the lessons from the Holocaust can apply in all walks in life. My students need to understand that we can learn important lessons from the Holocaust and apply those lessons to the future . . . Moving forward, my mission is to provide the information and multiple perspectives needed for my students to understand all the concepts. My mission will be to provide a diverse set of sources, primary and secondary, in a way that allows my students to question and think critically . . . These skills include critical thinking, questioning what they see, social justice, and many more.

While I certainly will guide my students in their thinking, I want them to shape their own views and ideas. When we bring these views and ideas together in the classroom, it will be one more step towards becoming a responsible citizen in our society.[7]

Greg's perspective hit on many of the key lessons on which the seminar focused, such as using primary source documents and helping students think critically about the subject. Greg also clearly states that a goal of his is the application of lessons about the Holocaust on students' lives. Coming to terms with the sheer weight of that rationale will have a profound impact on how he designs his curriculum and add relevance to students who often see history as unrelated to their lives.

Others focused their rationale on transference through the acquisition of essential skills such as analysis, pointing to their goal of getting their students motivated to become "agents of change." This goal impacts how they plan their unit, as the material used will be aimed at a much larger purpose of civic engagement in working to prevent actions that lead to hatred and genocide.

These rationale statements provide a sense of where teachers are heading today in the development of their Holocaust curriculum. It is important to note that targeted professional development gave these teachers the opportunity to refine their goals, focusing on their curricular needs and, most importantly, the student. Far too many teachers still need of this level of training to help them process critically the challenges of teaching the Holocaust effectively.

The Issue of Uniqueness in the Classroom

One of the great debates in Holocaust education that lies at the heart of how teachers devise their rationale statements is framed on how we see the event itself. For many years, the Holocaust was a unique event in human history, transcending any labeling to account for the horrors of the time. In the 1979 report to the president on the Holocaust, the President's Commission on the Holocaust makes the case for uniqueness from early on, stating, "The Holocaust was a crime unique in the annals of human history, different not only in the quantity of violence—the sheer numbers killed—but in its manner and purpose as a mass criminal enterprise organized by the state against defenseless civilian populations."[8] This definition, while certainly holding elements of truth, left the Holocaust outside the bounds of comparative analysis. Clearly, the events of the Holocaust are unique in time and place and in some ways method as well. However, the commission further complicates our ability to connect the Holocaust to our students by stating, "The universality of the Holocaust lies in its uniqueness: The Event is essentially Jewish, yet its interpretation is universal."[9] For many teachers, placing it in a unique Jewish context challenges their ability to find relevance in teaching it to a largely non-Jewish classroom.

From the earliest days of the United States Holocaust Memorial Museum, the museum stepped into the middle of the debate on the uniqueness of the Holocaust by creating the Committee on Conscience, whose ostensible aim was to make "Never Again" a living goal of the museum.[10] The conflict of maintaining the legacy of memory and the vigilance of calling out the warning signs of genocide today certainly play a role in teacher training and development at the USHMM. Early on, the committee held a strong presence on the genocide occurring in Darfur, Sudan. Most teacher trainings contained some aspect of programming from handing out pamphlets to holding full sessions on how to teach the genocide. The teachers' rationale statements were evolving with the museum as it was responding both to its own committee as well as an outgrowth of student activism through organizations such as STAND (Students Taking Action Now: Darfur) on high school and college campuses throughout the world.[11] Today that vision created the Simon Skjodt Center for the Prevention of Genocide, leading to some excellent exhibits on ongoing genocides as well as being a warning system for the US government on issues of genocide prevention.

Comparative Genocide in the Classroom

Many teachers today couple Holocaust education inside a framework of Holocaust and genocide studies. For them, integrating genocide studies into a larger unit on the Holocaust proved a positive addition rather than a distraction from its core purpose and fit well into their rationale for teaching the unit. Educators such as Joe Karb and Drew Beiter studied this approach with their eighth-grade classroom in Springville, New York, integrating two periods in a twelve-period unit on studying other genocides such as Armenia, Cambodia, Rwanda, and Darfur. Student outcomes, as seen through their projects measured at the end of the unit, were satisfying to the teachers' goals. "Their responses also indicated a broader understanding of why studying the Holocaust is important, one that reflects the social awareness and moral leadership so important to our pluralistic society."[12] Some teachers still maintain strict segregation of study between the Holocaust and other genocides, unwilling to risk the potential for comparison. Some teachers fear that in placing them together in the same context, students will compare one worse than the other, creating a hierarchy in their minds based on numbers alone.

Does educating students about other genocides complement Holocaust education? Or is the inverse true? A 2010 study by the International Holocaust Remembrance Alliance concludes, "A clear and well-informed understanding of the Holocaust, the paradigmatic genocide, may help educators and students understand other genocides, mass atrocities, and human rights violations."[13] This might prompt a follow up question: Does teaching about other genocides help teachers and students better understand the Holocaust? This does not argue that genocide education be mandated in our schools, but it makes a clear connection between the Holocaust and other genocides, which will by its own intent push teachers to reevaluate their own rationales and thus shift how we teach the subject moving forward. It may in fact help students to demystify the Holocaust when they recognize that genocide is a part of the human condition, not inevitable, but a product of choices made by individuals.

Current trends show teachers using more integrated approaches, which invariably impacts the goals and objectives of the unit they are teaching. For many, still pressed for curriculum time, using an integrated approach has downsides, such as what they leave out in the study of either the Holocaust or other genocides. When I excitedly put together my semester-long class on the Holocaust, I felt I was missing key pieces and having to make hard choices about what I could include in the time I had. Attempting to cram in too much may bring teachers back to a superficial exploration of the Holocaust and other genocides. Teachers must always find how their approach fits into the larger goals in their own discipline. How schools continue seeing the value in integrating the Holocaust into a larger genocide context is an unknown, and the pressures connected with standardized testing may well further compartmentalize teachers' approaches to unit design. What remains clear, however, is the best teachers will continue to capitalize on those "teachable moments" as they arise as students and teachers alike attempt to find meaning in their study of the Holocaust.

Mandates

The need for training teachers provokes the inevitable question of whether states should mandate Holocaust education in their schools. Some states, such as New Jersey and Illinois, were early adopters of mandates. While the trend grows as more states add a mandate for Holocaust education, even with the mandates, the issues facing effective Holocaust education persist. Most teachers agree this should be taught, so a mandate in and of itself does not address the central issue of effective teacher training. Karen Shawn, education professor and noted Holocaust educator at Yeshiva University, notes: "One would suppose that directives for statewide Holocaust education would help, not hinder, the cause of Holocaust education. However, the directives are aimed at the wrong audience. They require only students to learn about the Holocaust. There are no mandates or requirements for teachers to enroll in accredited courses in Holocaust history, literature, or pedagogy. Thus the vast majority of educators, through no fault of their own, currently lack the basic skills necessary to implement state mandates with professional integrity."[14] While many more educational training opportunities now exist for teachers than when that statement was written, it is also true that this has nothing to do with the mandates that states have implemented. Almost none of the mandates included any funding for teacher training and perhaps most tellingly, no real tools for assessing the effectiveness of the mandate have ever been developed, let alone implemented.

In recent years, the push to mandate Holocaust education has only intensified. With the recent successes in Michigan, Connecticut, and Rhode Island of mandating Holocaust and genocide education, other states are poised to act. Events such as the antisemitic attack in a Pittsburgh synagogue that left eleven Jews at Shabbat service dead have become a catalyst for some to rethink and include it in their standards. In Oregon, fourteen-year-old Claire Sarnowski of Lake Oswego took it upon herself to pursue a mandate, accomplishing more than all her predecessors to date in getting a bill to the floor of the state senate for debate in the 2019 session.[15] Claire made the connection early on as to why the Holocaust was important to teach and to learn. She did not do so because she had any familial or religious connection to the event, but as a human, connecting to other humans. Her story only amplifies the power of why teaching this topic well is so incredibly important.

Moral Dimensions of Teaching the Holocaust

Another area of concern that teachers face is Holocaust fatigue and student indifference to the plight of others. For some this means that multiple well-meaning teachers have broached the topic over the course of a student's education without any meaningful coordination between educators and across disciplines as to how to scaffold the student learning experience in the classroom. Some students shut down if teachers do not carefully guard against the horror and or shock through careful consideration of materials that are age appropriate and focus on the student's individual needs. John Roth, professor emeritus at Claremont McKenna College, argues about the slide of indifference and the dangers that imposed on all of us: "The truth about the Holocaust cannot be approached unless one grasps the fact that twentieth-century states may progressively squeeze the individual into obedience devoid of dissent. . . . What happened seems inescapable, individual responsibility recedes, and, as a consequence, trust in the world suffers. Such a deterministic outlook is as dangerous as it is easy, for it is the stuff of which indifference is made. The truth about the Holocaust cannot be taught unless indifference is resisted."[16] How teachers combat this issue will in a large way determine the impact of Holocaust education today and its relevance into the future. The question becomes how will this be done moving forward. The purpose of this chapter is not an effort to articulate a full answer to this question. Some insights, however, are important for us to consider when asking ourselves why the Holocaust is and will continue to be relevant in our schools. Mary Gallant, education professor at Rowan University, and Harriet Hartman, professor of sociology, make it clear that Holocaust education cannot be stuck looking purely to the past: "for Holocaust education to be truly meaningful it must apply the lessons of the past to our plans for the future."[17]

One of the basic beliefs in Holocaust education is that it will bring about some moral good as a result. Simone Schweber, Goodman Education Professor at the University of Wisconsin–Madison, explains it well: "Underpinning the consensus around its import is the widespread belief that education about the Holocaust, by virtue of its subject matter alone, is a venue for instilling moral values."[18] This is a warning to educators that the Holocaust is not a magic elixir for all ills that students face in the classroom, such as bullying. It is quite possible that students come out of a poorly constructed lesson or unit on the Holocaust no better off than when they came in, perhaps even worse if teachers do not use best practices. It is critical that teachers effectively evaluate what the student is taking away from a lesson and that it lines up with their intended goals.[19]

It is important for educators to guard against oversimplification of history to make a point about the issues that plague us today. This delicate balance is an ongoing quandary for history teachers most of all. Paul Salmons brilliantly upsets the apple cart in our haste to teach the "moral lesson." He notes that Western education models have long included elements of moral education, noting that they "have underpinned the values of Western society for centuries. And yet it was from that same society that the Holocaust sprang."[20] It is critical that our students' thinking be complicated. Students desperately want the simple answer that we have trained them to give, that racism and antisemitism is bad, got it, moving on. However, any honest reflection of the Holocaust reveals deep levels of complexity and moral ambiguity. We do our students no favor in ignoring the "gray zone."

Exploring the moral complexity is what makes the history of the Holocaust "sticky" for students. Asking deep meaningful questions, which for many students will be the first time they have been asked such questions, is what makes the Holocaust such a powerful educational experience. I assigned each of my students a journal that was central to my class. It became a sort of safe space for students to reflect deeply, either textually or graphically, what they were feeling as well as mundane things like taking notes. My students routinely went home from class with their journals and engaged family members and friends about the questions they confronted in class, and many of them wrote about the challenges they confronted in answering them. The study of the Holocaust was different for our students. It was their need to confront this history, unlike any other event, that created the energy throughout the unit. It is fundamentally students that drive the importance of why we teach the Holocaust, and it is through them that teachers will continue to find its relevance.

Throughout this chapter, I focus on teachers' rationales for teaching the Holocaust. Understanding those rationales helps us understand how the Holocaust is truly important in today's classrooms as they give us a glimpse into why teachers are taking on this topic. Teaching approaches and reasons for teaching the Holocaust have evolved, incorporating other genocides and even human rights education in greater numbers over the last twenty years. I fully expect this trend to continue as the next generation of educators will explore this history, find meaning, and impart the history to their students. They will do so with many technological tools that we are only now exploring, but they will remain grounded both in the immense archive of primary source documents as well as the trove of survivor testimonies they left behind. Professional development will play a key role in preparing teachers to implement effective instruction well into the future. New museums, such as the one recently opened in Portland, Oregon, and one recently reopened in Dallas, Texas, join the many museums along with the USHMM in helping lead this effort.

What will keep the Holocaust relevant well into the future is the interplay between the teacher and the student to explore these difficult lessons together to help form meaning today. Is the Holocaust relevant today? Is it important to teach in our schools? These were never really in doubt. We have answered that call with an emphatic yes! What remains ahead is to teach this history well. If history has taught us anything, it is that failing to do this will have clear and profound consequences for us all.

Notes

1. Samantha Power's seminal work *"A Problem from Hell": America and the Age of Genocide* is a great resource for educators teaching modern genocide, whereas *Not on Our Watch: The Mission to End Genocide in Darfur and Beyond* by Don Cheadle and John Prendergast is a practical handbook on activism focused during the genocide in Darfur. Christopher Browning's *Ordinary Men* remains a powerful shift in thinking regarding choices made by perpetrators during the Holocaust.

2. Samuel Totten and Stephen Feinberg, *Teaching and Studying the Holocaust* (Needham Heights, MA: Pearson Education Company, 2001), 9–10.

3. Beau Yarbrough, "Exclusive: Holocaust Denied by Students in Rialto School Assignment," *San Bernardino (CA) Sun*, July 11, 2014, https://www.sbsun.com/2014/07/11/exclusive-holocaust-denied-by-students-in-rialto-school-assignment/ (accessed March 11, 2019).

4. Henry Friedlander, "Toward a Methodology of Teaching about the Holocaust," *Teachers College Record* 80, no. 5 (1979): 520–521.

5. Peter Hayes, *Why? Explaining the Holocaust* (New York: W. W. Norton, 2017), 325.

6. David Lindquist, "A Necessary Holocaust Pedagogy: Teaching the Teachers," *Issues in Teacher Education* 16, no. 1 (2007): 21–36.

7. Corey Harbaugh, "Michigan Holocaust Educators Network 2017 Summer Conference" (Seminar, Holocaust Memorial Center, Farmington Hills, July 2016).

8. "Report to the President: President's Commission on the Holocaust," US Department of Health, Education and Welfare, National Institute of Education, September 27, 1979.

9. "Report to the President."

10. Irving Greenberg, "Remembrance and Conscience: Transcript," United States Holocaust Memorial Museum, https://rabbiirvinggreenberg.com/wp-content/uploads/2014/06/12.5.01-Remembrance-and-Conscience.pdf (accessed December 18, 2019).

11. STAND, Students Taking Action Now on Darfur.

12. Joseph D. Karb and Andrew T. Beiter, "From the Holocaust to Darfur: A Recipe for Genocide," *Journal of Inquiry and Action in Education* 2, no. 1 (2009): 57–73, 70.

13. Task Force for International Cooperation on Holocaust Education, Remembrance and Research, "2010 Education Working Group Paper on the Holocaust and Other Genocides," The International Holocaust Remembrance Alliance, https://www.holocaustremembrance.com/sites/default/files/EWG_Holocaust_and_Other_Genocides.pdf (accessed July 10, 2017).

14. Karen Shawn, "Current Issues in Holocaust Education," *Dimensions: A Journal of Holocaust Studies* 9, no. 2 (1995): 15–18.

15. Deborah Moon, "Survivor and Teen Team Up to Push Holocaust Education," *Oregon Jewish Life*, October 30, 2018, http://orjewishlife.com/holocaust-survivor-and-teen-team-up-to-push-holocaust-genocide-education/ (accessed November 1, 2018).

16. John K. Roth, "On Losing Trust in the World," in R. C. Schank and R. P. Abelson, eds., *Scripts, Plans, Goals and Understanding* (Hillsdale, NJ: L. Erlbaum, 1988), 165.

17. Mary Gallant and Harriet Hartman, "Holocaust Education for the New Millennium: Assessing Our Progress," *Journal of Holocaust Education* 10, no. 2 (Autumn 2001): 1–28, 6.

18. Simone Schweber, *Making Sense of the Holocaust: Lessons from Classroom Practice* (New York: Teachers College Press, 2004), 6.

19. An interesting debate among Holocaust educators centers on the book *The Boy in the Striped Pajamas*. The book is used a great deal, especially at the middle school level, primarily because it is so impactful with students. Sadly, teachers don't evaluate what that impact really is and mistake it for a deeper

understanding of the Holocaust, which it clearly isn't. See discussion of the film in Alan Marcus's chapter in this volume.

20. Paul Salmons, "Universal Meaning or Historical Understanding? The Holocaust in History and History in the Curriculum," *Teaching History* no. 141, special issue, "Holocaust" (December 2010): 57–63.

Contributors

Victoria Aarons has published more than seventy articles and book chapters and is the author or editor of *A Measure of Memory: Storytelling and Identity in American Jewish Fiction; What Happened to Abraham: Reinventing the Covenant in American Jewish Fiction; The New Diaspora: The Changing Landscape of American Jewish Fiction; Bernard Malamud: A Centennial Tribute; The Cambridge Companion to Saul Bellow; Third-Generation Holocaust Narratives: Memory in Memoir and Fiction; Third-Generation Holocaust Representation: Trauma, History, and Memory; New Directions in Jewish American and Holocaust Literatures; The New Jewish American Literary Studies;* and *Holocaust Graphic Narratives: Generation, Trauma, and Memory.*

Stuart Abrams teaches genocide studies, psychology, history, and human rights education at Avon High School. He is the recipient of numerous awards: the Joseph Korzenik Fellowship for excellence in Holocaust Education from the Greenberg Center at the University of Hartford (1996), a Museum Teacher Fellowship from the United States Holocaust Memorial Museum (2000), Avon School District's Teacher of the Year (2009–2010), the Prudence Crandall Memorial Human and Civil Rights award from the Connecticut Education Association (2011), and the inaugural Simon Konover award in Recognition for Excellence in Holocaust Teaching (2016). He serves as an organizer and presenter at the University of Hartford's annual Holocaust Educators Conference for middle and high school teachers each fall. Under the USHMM's sponsorship, Mr. Abrams served as an organizer and presenter at the Belfer Next Step Conference for the Northeast Region held at Skidmore College in Saratoga, New York, in 2007.

Waitman Wade Beorn is a historian of the Holocaust and genocide as well as a digital humanist. He is currently working on a comprehensive monograph on the Janowska concentration camp in Lviv. Dr. Beorn serves as a senior lecturer in humanities at the University of Northumbria. Previously, he was the inaugural Blumkin Professor of Holocaust and Genocide Studies at the University of Nebraska–Omaha and the executive director of the Virginia Holocaust Museum. He is the author of *Marching into Darkness: The Wehrmacht and the Holocaust in Belarus* (2014) and *The Holocaust in Eastern Europe: At the Epicenter of the Final Solution* (2018).

MARTIN DEAN received a PhD in European history from Queens' College, Cambridge. He has worked as a researcher for the Special Investigations Unit in Sydney, Australia, and as the senior historian for the Metropolitan Police War Crimes Unit in London. As an applied research scholar at the US Holocaust Memorial Museum, he was a volume editor for *The Encyclopedia of Camps and Ghettos*. His publications include *Collaboration in the Holocaust* (2000) and *Robbing the Jews* (2008), which won a National Jewish Book Award in 2009. He is based in Washington, DC, and works as a historical consultant for the Babyn Yar Holocaust Memorial Center and as an adviser on film documentaries.

JONATHAN ELUKIN is an associate professor of history at Trinity College in Hartford, Connecticut. He received his PhD from Princeton University. He works in several fields, including the history of Jewish-Christian relations in medieval Europe; the history of law and kingship in the Middle Ages; early modern and modern historiography about Jews and Judaism; and the history of antisemitism. His first book is *Living Together, Living Apart: Rethinking Jewish-Christian Relations in the Middle Ages* (2007). His essays have appeared in the *Journal of the History of Ideas* and other edited volumes of essays on the Middle Ages and Jewish history.

MARGARETE MYERS FEINSTEIN is a senior lecturer in Jewish studies at Loyola Marymount University and received her PhD in history from the University of California, Davis. She is interested in the legacies of Nazism, the topic of her books *Holocaust Survivors in Postwar Germany* (2010) and *State Symbols: The Quest for Legitimacy in the Federal Republic of Germany and the German Democratic Republic* (2001) and numerous articles. Feinstein is currently using survivor testimonies to investigate retribution against Germans after the Holocaust.

GABRIEL N. FINDER is a professor in the Department of Germanic Languages and Literatures and former Ida and Nathan Kolodiz Director of Jewish Studies at the University of Virginia, and he is an associate editor of the journal *Holocaust and Genocide Studies*. His teaching and research interests include the Holocaust, Holocaust-related trials, and the rebuilding of Jewish life in Europe after the Holocaust. Most recently, he is coeditor with Laura Jockusch of *Jewish Honor Courts: Revenge, Retribution, and Reconciliation in*

Europe and Israel after the Holocaust (2015), a 2016 National Jewish Book Award finalist in the Holocaust category; coauthor with Alexander V. Prusin of *Justice behind the Iron Curtain: Nazis on Trial in Communist Poland* (2018); and coeditor with David Slucki and Avinoam Patt of *Laughter After: Humor and the Holocaust* (2020).

JENNIFER GOSS holds an MA in Holocaust and genocide studies from West Chester University of Pennsylvania. She has worked as a high school social studies teacher since 2002 and currently teaches in Staunton, Virginia, where her course load includes an elective in Holocaust and genocide studies. In the evenings, Jennifer teaches courses in United States history and world civilizations at Blue Ridge Community College. In addition to her work in the classroom, she is a USHMM Teacher Fellow '10 and serves as a facilitator for several programs, including the Anti-Defamation League's Echoes and Reflections program. In 2012, Jennifer produced the student-created, Emmy-nominated documentary *Misa's Fugue* with colleagues, and in 2016 she coauthored the memoir *Remember, My Child* with survivor Itka Zygmuntowicz.

DANIEL GREENE is president and librarian at the Newberry Library in Chicago and an adjunct professor of history at Northwestern University. He curated *Americans and the Holocaust*, a special exhibition that opened at the United States Holocaust Memorial Museum in Washington, DC, in 2018. Greene's book *The Jewish Origins of Cultural Pluralism* (2011) won the Saul Viener Book Prize in American Jewish history.

ROBERT HADLEY works as a teacher trainer in Bethel, Alaska, helping prepare native Yupik students for a career in teaching. He worked as a consultant with the USC Shoah Foundation training teachers on integrating testimony into their curriculum after teaching history and Holocaust studies for twenty years near Portland, Oregon. He was a United States Holocaust Memorial Museum fellow in 2001 as well as a Holocaust Educators Network fellow with the Olga Lengyel Institute. He currently codirects the annual Oregon Holocaust seminar. He holds master's degrees in secondary education from Western Oregon University and one in Holocaust and genocide studies from Gratz College.

VALERIE HÉBERT is an associate professor of history and interdisciplinary studies at Lakehead University in Orillia, Ontario, Canada, offering courses on European history, the Holocaust, and the photography of human rights violations and international conflict. She has received research fellowships from the Social Sciences and Humanities Research Council of Canada,

Hebrew University, and the Mandel Center for Advanced Holocaust Studies at the United States Holocaust Memorial Museum. She has published on the Nuremberg Trials, Rwanda's Gacaca Tribunals, and the Holocaust's influence on human rights discourse. Currently, she is writing about photographs documenting the mass shooting of Jewish women and children in Eastern Europe during World War II.

LAURA J. HILTON is a professor of history at Muskingum University in New Concord, Ohio. She earned her PhD in modern European history from The Ohio State University. Her research focuses on the postwar period of Germany, 1945–1951, in particular the interactions among Germans, refugees, Displaced Persons, and Allied occupiers. Recently, she has published articles in *German History*, *Jahrbuch des International Tracing Service*, *Holocaust and Genocide Studies*, and *The History Teacher* (forthcoming). She has authored a chapter in *Food, Culture and Identity in Germany's Century of War* and is currently working on a monograph centered on the rumor culture in postwar Germany.

RUSSEL LEMMONS is a Distinguished Professor of History at Jacksonville State University in Alabama. He earned his PhD from Miami University. The author of two books—*Goebbels and Der Angriff* and *Hitler's Rival*—he is also a coauthor of *The Holocaust Chronicle*. His articles and reviews have appeared in numerous scholarly publications. The recipient of grants from Fulbright, the German Academic Exchange Service, the United States Holocaust Memorial Museum, and several other scholarly organizations, he is currently writing a biography of Rupert Mayer, S.J., a Roman Catholic priest who resisted National Socialism.

ALAN S. MARCUS is an associate professor in the Department of Curriculum and Instruction at the University of Connecticut and is a UConn Teaching Fellow. His scholarship focuses on museum education and teaching with film, with an emphasis on the Holocaust. Alan is a faculty fellow for the Holocaust Institute for Teacher Educators at the United States Holocaust Memorial Museum and coauthor of *Teaching History with Film: Strategies for Secondary Social Studies* (2018) and coeditor of *Teaching Difficult History through Film* (2017). His current research is evaluating the potential and limitations of virtual interactive Holocaust survivor testimony.

GEOFFREY P. MEGARGEE is the Senior Applied Research Scholar at the United States Holocaust Memorial Museum's Mandel Center for Advanced Holocaust Studies, where he has been the project director and editor in chief for the museum's seven-volume *Encyclopedia of Camps and Ghettos, 1933–1945* since 2000. The first three volumes of the *Encyclopedia* were published in 2009, 2012, and 2018. The first volume won a National Jewish Book Award and the Association of Jewish Libraries' Judaica Reference Award, among other distinctions. He is also the author of *Inside Hitler's High Command* (2000) and *War of Annihilation: Combat and Genocide on the Eastern Front, 1941* (2006).

ILANA F. OFFENBERGER is a scholar of history and author of the publication *The Jews of Nazi-Vienna, 1938–1945: Rescue and Destruction* (2017), published by Palgrave Macmillan as part of a larger series in the history of genocide. Offenberger received a PhD in history from Clark University in 2010. Since 2012, she has been teaching in the Department of History at the University of Massachusetts–Dartmouth. She offers courses on the history of the Holocaust and other topics in European history. Offenberger is president of the American Friends of the Documentation Center of Austrian Resistance.

AVINOAM PATT is the Doris and Simon Konover Chair of Judaic Studies and director of the Center for Judaic Studies and Contemporary Jewish Life at the University of Connecticut. He is the author of *Finding Home and Homeland: Jewish Youth and Zionism in the Aftermath of the Holocaust* (2009); coeditor (with Michael Berkowitz) of a collected volume on Jewish Displaced Persons, *We Are Here: New Approaches to the Study of Jewish Displaced Persons in Postwar Germany* (2010); and is a contributor to several projects at the USHMM, including *Jewish Responses to Persecution, 1938–1940* (2011). Most recently, he is coeditor of a new volume on *The Joint Distribution Committee at 100: A Century of Humanitarianism* (2019) and is currently writing a book on the early postwar memory of the Warsaw Ghetto Uprising.

STEVEN P. REMY is a professor of history at the City University of New York, Brooklyn College and the Graduate Center, where he teaches courses on modern German and European history. He is the author of *The Malmedy Massacre: The War Crimes Trial Controversy* (2017) and *The Heidelberg Myth: The Nazification and Denazification of a German University* (2003).

AMY SIMON holds the William and Audrey Farber Family Chair in Holocaust Studies and European Jewish History at Michigan State University. She teaches in James Madison College, the Department of History, and the Michael and Elaine Serling Institute for Jewish Studies and Modern Israel. She previously worked as a researcher at the United States Holocaust Memorial Museum in Washington, DC, and regularly participates in workshops and conferences in the United States and Israel. Her work on Holocaust fiction, memoir, and diaries has appeared in *Holocaust Studies: A*

Journal of Culture and History, Jewish Historical Studies, Journal of Jewish Identities, and several edited volumes.

MARK E. SPICKA is a professor of history at Shippensburg University. He earned his PhD from The Ohio State University in 2000 in modern European and German history. He is the author of *Selling the Economic Miracle: Economic Reconstruction and Politics in West Germany, 1949–1957* (2007). He has published articles in *German History, German Studies Review, German Politics and Society, Journal of Contemporary History,* and *Immigrants and Minorities* and is currently researching guest workers and city policy in West Germany in the 1960s and 1970s.

Index

Index

The Harvey Goldberg Series
for Understanding and Teaching History

Understanding and Teaching the Holocaust
Edited by Laura J. Hilton and Avinoam Patt

Understanding and Teaching American Slavery
Edited by Bethany Jay and Cynthia Lynn Lyerly

Understanding and Teaching the Civil Rights Movement
Edited by Hasan Kwame Jeffries

Understanding and Teaching the Age of Revolutions
Edited by Ben Marsh and Mike Rapport

Understanding and Teaching the Cold War
Edited by Matthew Masur

*Understanding and Teaching U.S. Lesbian, Gay, Bisexual,
and Transgender History*, second edition
Edited by Leila J. Rupp and Susan K. Freeman

Understanding and Teaching the Vietnam War
Edited by John Day Tully, Matthew Masur, and Brad Austin